# Presidents,
## *the* Presidency,
### *and the* Political
# Environment

Also by John H. Kessel

*The Goldwater Coalition: Republican Strategies in 1964*

*Micropolitics: Individual and Group Level Concepts* (coedited with George F. Cole and Robert G. Seddig)

*The Domestic Presidency: Decision Making in the White House*

*Presidential Campaign Politics: Coalition Strategies and Citizen Response*

*Presidential Parties*

*Theory Building and Data Analysis in the Social Sciences* (coedited with Herbert B. Asher, Herbert F. Weisberg, and W. Phillips Shively)

*Researching the Presidency: Vital Questions, New Approaches* (coedited with George C. Edwards III and Bert A. Rockman)

# Presidents, *the* Presidency, *and the* Political Environment

## John H. Kessel
*Ohio State University*

## CQ PRESS

A Division of Congressional Quarterly Inc.
Washington, D.C.

CQ Press
A Division of Congressional Quarterly Inc.
1414 22nd Street, N.W.
Washington, D.C. 20037

(202) 822-1475; (800) 638-1710

www.cqpress.com

Printed and bound in the United States of America
05 04 03 02 01   5 4 3 2 1

Typeset and designed by Karen W. Doody
Cover by Ed Atkeson

♾ The paper used in this publication meets the minimum requirements of the American National Standard for Information Sciences—Permanence of Paper for Printed Library Materials, ANSI Z39.48-1992.


Library of Congress Cataloging-in-Publication Data

Kessel, John H. (John Howard)
    Presidents, the presidency, and the political environment / John H. Kessel.
        p.  cm.
    Includes bibliographical references and index.
    ISBN 0-87187-794-5
    1. Presidents--United States. 2. Presidents--United States--Staff.
  3. Presidents--United States--Evaluation.  I. Title.
JK516.K396 2001
973.92–dc21

                                                                00-012501

*To Sarah, Ellen, and Jonathan*

# Contents

# Preface

This book addresses two great questions: What is the nature of the American presidency? How should American presidents be evaluated? Such questions are too broad to permit simple responses. Therefore I shall consider several aspects of them, each of which casts some light on the central topic.

Five components of the presidency will be analyzed: the units working with Congress and with the media, as well as those concerned with foreign policy, economic policy, and domestic policy. I begin each assessment by introducing the principal actors, both individuals and organizational units. While discussing the units, I describe how they came into being and how they have been modified in subsequent years. I then explore their behavior, distinguishing between common activities and task-specific activities. The common activities in which all units engage are coordination, information gathering, decision making, and exerting influence. The task-specific activities are characteristic of individual units—for example, aid to members' campaigns extended by the congressional liaison staff, negotiations engaged in by the National Security Council staff, and departmental monitoring undertaken by the domestic policy staff. My goal is to give enough detail so that readers can grasp what is taking place without being drowned in excessive information.

Throughout, I place the organizational units between the president they serve and institutions located outside the White House. My general argument is that these units must adapt to both the work style of the incumbent and the habits of the clientele groups (journalists, diplomats, legislators, and so forth). By serving the needs of both the president and the external institutions, they stabilize the White House within the political environment and ensure their own survival from one administration to the next.

I argue that presidents have been evaluated too negatively in recent decades. Every time a president fails at a single task—getting a bill through Congress, reducing unemployment, gaining reelection, or whatever—analysts leap to the barricades to trumpet the latest evidence of general presidential failure. I believe that overall accomplishment should be the basis for presidential evaluation. More specifically, given the modern presidency and the political environment in which it is situated, analysts should ask what a president can realistically be expected to accomplish. I begin this analysis by inspecting selected results in each administration from Eisenhower through Clinton. These samples show that every administration has successes, failures, and mixed outcomes. Why should this be so? I explain the behavior of individual presidents by using an elementary theory that rests on expertise and attitude strength. I then turn to a more general argument that a president begins with a set of policy skills, takes the power he has (or lacks) to build support with the electorate and Congress, considers what he regards as good public policy, and arrays his resources against the challenges he faces in each policy arena. By interpreting this process probabilistically, I argue that the chances of total success or total failure are exceedingly small and that success is more common than failure.

This is a general book on the presidency, not a comprehensive treatment and certainly not a presidential encyclopedia. Working within a limited compass, I had to be selective, and therefore I chose topics that best illuminate the institutional presidency and the behavior of presidents.

From time to time, the reader will encounter quotes without citations. Almost all of these quotations are from interviews I have conducted myself. A very few are drawn from public sources. I also employ an unusual convention in the mini–case studies in Chapter 7. Since I am drawing on several sources that cover the same general topics, I have listed them together in a footnote at the beginning of each case study.

I had the privilege of learning about the presidency through interviews with White House staff members. I should like to thank David L. Aaron, Martin C. Anderson, James A. Baker III, Aram Bakshain Jr., Douglas L. Bandow, Richard S. Beal, Danny J. Boggs, Zbigniew Brzezinski, William H. Cable, Robert B. Carleson, Bert Carp, Richard B. Cheney, David Chew, Kenneth W. Clarkson, Kenneth R. Cole, Lloyd N. Cutler, W. Bowman Cutter, Lynn M. Daft, Michael K. Deaver, Kenneth M. Duberstein, Eugene Eidenberg, Stuart E. Eizenstat, Shannon Fairbanks, James Fallows, Fred F. Fielding, Ronald B. Frankum, Max L. Friedersdorf, Craig L. Fuller, Robert L. Garrick, David R. Gergen, Rex L. Granum, Edwin J. Gray, Edwin L. Harper, Stephen Hess, Kevin Hopkins, Robert Hunter, Richard G. Hutcheson III, Carrell Ray Jenkins, Dennis M. Kass, Alfred H. Kingon, Lawrence

Kudlow, Simon Lazarus III, Alonzo L. McDonald, James T. McIntyre Jr., Edwin
Meese III, Robert E. Merriam, James C. Miller III, Powell A. Moore, Donald W.
Moran, Lyn Nofziger, M. B. Oglesby, Gilbert S. Omenn, Roger B. Porter, Jody Powell, John F. W. Rogers, David Rubenstein, Katherine P. Shirmer, Charles L.
Schultze, Evelyn Small, Karna Small, Larry M. Speakes, Al Stern, Dan C. Tate,
James A. Thomson, Robert N. Thomson, Claudia M. Townsend, Pamela J. Turner,
Michael Uhlmann, Wayne H. Valis, Erica A. Ward, Jack H. Watson Jr., Murray L.
Weidenbaum, Anne Wexler, Richard S. Williamson, and Joseph R. Wright Jr. I
should also like to extend silent thanks to eighteen members of the Nixon Domestic Council staff and to five members of the Reagan National Security Council
staff to whom I promised anonymity. While I have drawn on a great many other
sources in writing this book, the interviews were individually informative and collectively very important in shaping my own view about how the White House
works.

I have been fortunate in past years to be a guest scholar at the Brookings Institution and a visiting scholar at the American Enterprise Institute for Public Policy Research. I should like to thank both institutions for their hospitality and for
providing bases from which research could be conducted in Washington. It is also
a pleasure to acknowledge the aid of the National Science Foundation, which supported my research through grants GS-2660, GS-35084, and SES-80-24079.

Many kind persons provided helpful criticism. Ryan J. Barilleaux, Roger H.
Davidson, David M. Olson, and James P. Pfiffner read the entire manuscript. Fred
I. Greenstein read several chapters, and Marie Hojnacki, Martha Kumar, James
M. Lindsay, Samuel C. Patterson, M. Stephen Weatherford, and Robert C. Wood
read individual chapters. I should also like to acknowledge the comments of
anonymous readers. My conversations with Richard F. Fenno Jr. when the book
was first taking shape were very helpful, and Jon A. Krosnick guided my thinking on expertise and attitude strength. I appreciate the willingness of George C.
Edwards III to share his data on presidential support and that of Ole R. Holsti and
James N. Rosenau to share their data on militant and cooperative internationalism. Finally, I am very grateful to Joanne D. Daniels, Shana Wagger, Brenda W.
Carter, and Gwenda Larsen for their good counsel (and their patience!) while I
was working on the book, and I should like to thank Nola Healy Lynch for substantial improvements in the readability of my prose.

# 1. The Contemporary White House

## *The President and the Presidency*

For more than a century after George Washington's inauguration, the presidency as an institution was nearly synonymous with the president himself.[1] By the twentieth century, however, Americans no longer relied solely on the personal capacities of the nation's presidents. As the chief executive's responsibilities have multiplied, presidents have been given much more institutional support. The change was gradual at first, but it accelerated and culminated during the third quarter of the twentieth century. Since then, the White House has been fundamentally different from that in which Franklin D. Roosevelt and his predecessors had served. Although Americans still seek presidents of extraordinary ability, many of the executive functions once carried out by the president are now part of the work of the institutional presidency.

An institutional presidency needs a president to lead it. The president must energize his presidency. He must set the goals for his administration, articulate them, and build political support for them. He must distinguish between the significant and the ephemeral in the flood of information that comes to the Oval Office. The president must select associates who have the necessary skills for their

---

[1] Undoubtedly, a woman will become president of the United States someday, and the probability increases as the number of politically active women grows. My use of the masculine gender to refer to presidents is not a comment about the absence of a female so far or about the likelihood that there will be one someday. I just prefer the simpler prose style.

1

jobs, and he must develop relationships of mutual trust with them (compare Greenstein 2000). Absent these, the presidency can carry out many tasks, but it cannot provide the executive leadership essential in modern U.S. government.

What is the institutional presidency? Broadly speaking, the institution is made up of the presidential staff and the political appointees in the executive departments. These individuals assist the president with his day-to-day job activities by, for example, arranging press conferences, gathering information on tax issues, and so on. They make a great many decisions themselves, acting in the name of the president. In fact, the majority of White House decisions—all but the most crucial—are made by presidential assistants. More important, though, the actors of the institutional presidency provide connections between the president and the political environment.

When Howard Baker became chief of staff for Ronald Reagan, he spoke with as many of his predecessors as possible. Baker said he learned little of value because everyone told him that he would have to find out how *his* president liked to work. Each president has his own working style, and the members of his staff must discover his style and adapt to it. But that is only part of the story. Each element of the presidency also works with actors in some particular segment of the political environment: legislators, journalists, ambassadors, financiers, leaders of political movements, and so forth. All these persons have their preferred ways of doing business, and the staff members who are going to work with them have to discover how to relate most effectively to them. It is the discovery of the preferred working styles of everyone involved that gives the presidency an ability to maintain stable relationships between the White House and the surrounding political environment. Consequently, what distinguishes the presidency is *dual adaptation*, adapting to the president's work style within the White House while simultaneously adapting to the work styles of relevant clienteles outside the White House.

We need to give serious attention to *both* the president and the institutional presidency. Think of books that focus on just one or the other. A book that concentrates on the president alone will tell us about his personality, his political career, and his policy preferences. We will learn to assess how the president will react in specific situations. A book devoted exclusively to the institutional presidency will tell us how the president is linked to the surrounding political environment, what information is communicated to the president, and what choices are presented to him. We may come to understand the larger context in which he serves. Both books have shown us important ways to approach and analyze their topics, but neither can give us a full understanding of both the president and the institutional presidency.

## Major Components of the Political Environment

Take any normal day. It is easy to imagine what White House aides might be doing. A member of the congressional liaison staff is conferring with a senator who is leaning toward voting with the administration on an upcoming bill. A deputy press secretary is searching for some fact requested by a *Baltimore Sun* reporter. A National Security Council (NSC) staff member is writing out talking points for an upcoming meeting with the Australian foreign minister. An examiner in the Office of Management and Budget (OMB) is going over the Energy Department's budget requests. An economist on the staff of the Council of Economic Advisers (CEA) is analyzing data that have just arrived from the Commerce Department. An analyst on the Domestic Policy Council is meeting with a representative of a hospital association. The list goes on and on. These individuals work in their own offices, most of which are scattered through the Old Executive Office Building just west of the White House. Their personal work routines are dictated by their own responsibilities: attending to developments in their spheres, gathering information, and explaining administration policy. But all are acting in the name of the president, and all are involved in well-defined regions of the political environment.

The congressional liaison and the deputy press secretary are working with the most important political audiences in Washington. Members of the congressional liaison staff work to advance the president's legislative program on Capitol Hill. To that end, they must know the voting proclivities of the members and be able to sense what arguments will increase the chances the legislator will vote with the president. The press office provides information for reporters from the various media, hoping to convince them that certain stories are worth reporting and attempting to ensure a spin favorable to the president. Press office staffers must know about reporters' work routines and understand the differing priorities of the various media.

The other aides in our examples are working in policy environments. National Security Council aides provide advice to the president on how foreign governments might be persuaded to follow desired policies. To give such counsel requires expertise about the foreign countries in question. OMB examiners look at the proposed policies of executive departments and the effects their intended outlays are likely to have on total federal spending. The Council of Economic Advisers analyzes the reams of data generated by government agencies to find hints about economic performance. To accomplish this, the OMB and CEA personnel must not only know economics, they must also have some knowledge of the decision makers in the public and private sectors. Domestic aides are continually looking for segments of the society that might be responsive to government action. Whether aides are concerned with politics or policy, they need to know what's happening in their area of the political environment to be effective.

There are, of course, many other groups in the presidential environment: lawyers, judges, governors, mayors, and so forth. They are not inconsequential to the White House, but Congress, the media, and the policy communities are more consequential most of the time. For our purposes, therefore, we divide the political environment into five components: Congress, the media, and the institutions concerned with foreign policy, economic policy, and domestic policy.

## Activities of the Presidency

If there are different actors in each area of the environment, does it follow that each unit in the presidency has a different activity pattern? Not quite. There are *common activities* in which all units of the presidency engage. These are

> coordination;
> information gathering;
> decision making;
> exerting influence.

Why these? Take coordination first. "Any decision worth getting the president involved in," said Carter's chief domestic aide, Stuart Eizenstat, "almost inevitably involves two or more departments. It just wouldn't get to his level if it was such a finite decision that only one agency was involved." Eizenstat is by no means alone in making such a statement. And since multiple agencies are involved—the Department of State and the Department of Defense, or the Department of Agriculture and the Department of Interior, or any number of other combinations—there must be some means of making sure everyone is on the same page. The same point can be made about units within the president's staff, for example, making sure the Domestic Policy Council and the Office of Management and Budget are marching in the same direction. Hence a need for coordination is endemic in government.

The other common tasks are derived from the president's own needs. Richard Neustadt argued at mid-century that there were two tasks presidents cannot delegate to anyone else. The president's first responsibility is as *"maker of the residual choices no one else will make"* (1956, 616; emphasis in original). Dwight D. Eisenhower and John F. Kennedy discussed this. Kennedy said that when he met with Eisenhower prior to assuming office himself, Eisenhower told him he would have no easy choices to make. If there was an obvious choice, Eisenhower continued, someone would notice and want to take credit for making the right choice. Thorny problems, on the other hand, would get pushed upward and eventually land on the president's desk.

The president's second personal function is *"persuader of those otherwise indifferent or unmoved"* (Neustadt 1956, 617; emphasis in original). President Reagan provides good examples of this. In late April 1981, his budget was having difficulties on Capitol Hill. Reagan, convalescing from the March assassination attempt, went to Congress to give a prime time televised address. After thanking the American people for all their good wishes, he said he would like to discuss the health of the economy. It was one of his best performances, and in early May the House backed the Reagan program by a vote of 253 to 176. Just before another crucial vote at the end of June, Reagan was busy on the telephone calling House members who needed presidential shoring up. The vote was closer this time, 217 to 210, but it guaranteed passage of the budget the president wanted. Aides can do many things for presidents, but no aide can appeal to the American people through a televised address before Congress, and no aide can bring as much influence to bear on individual legislators.

Obviously, these personal activities tell us what the president spends his time doing. Less obviously, but equally important, the needs of the president establish fundamental processes of the presidency. Choice requires information. Persuasion requires influence. Therefore the institutional presidency is characterized by flows of information to the points of decision, decisions being made, and flows of influence outward in support of the decisions. Coordination, information gathering, decision making, and exerting influence are the fundamental activities, the heartbeats of the White House. They mold the daily life of the presidency, much as hearings, markup sessions, and roll call votes shape Congress, and certiorari, oral argument, and opinion writing distinguish the Supreme Court.

Whatever else White House officials are doing, they all take part in these activities. But while the names of the common activities are the same in all of the White House units, the activities themselves are not identical. To see why, let's look at congressional liaison and foreign policy activities.

When the president is working with Congress, the president and legislative leaders meet to coordinate their strategies. They need to know whether members intend to vote for or against proposed legislation. With that information in hand, the president and his legislative aides must decide whether they are going to try to get a certain bill passed if they are, say, eleven votes short of a majority, or whether they will postpone action if they lack thirty-five votes. If the administration decides to go ahead, its emissaries will try to exert influence on members who are undecided or perhaps leaning toward a negative vote.

What do the same processes mean in foreign policy? Coordination often involves getting the State Department, Defense Department, CIA, and other government agencies to follow the same policies. Assessing information means sorting through the incoming fragments of information from the country in question—legislative elections, an increase in the strength of the local currency, rumors of coups—to detect evidence of probable change. Decision making often concerns an adjustment in U.S. policy. Should troops be dispatched, a repayment schedule on a foreign loan be extended, a foreign development be welcomed or protested, or just what? Exercising influence is delicate because the United States is dealing with sovereign powers who are entirely free to pursue their own courses of action.

In addition to common activities, each staff unit has *task-specific activities,* for example, holding press briefings for journalists or doing macroeconomic analysis. These task-specific activities are more distinctive than the common activities. Those working with Congress obtain White House hearings for members' proposals, handle their projects and patronage, help members campaign, and maintain goodwill. Foreign policy activities include being custodians of the process, policy advocacy, planning, negotiation, symbol manipulation, defending the president, and handling foreign economic policy. Some of the task-specific activities of different offices may look similar. For example, both congressional emissaries and the State Department wish to maintain goodwill in anticipation of possible negotiation with members of Congress and foreign countries, respectively. But supporting a member's reelection campaign is very different from developing foreign economic policy.

In brief, there is a partial overlap in activities between congressional relations and foreign policy. The same thing could be said when comparing the activities of any other pair of White House units. Hence, we need to be alert to the similarities *and* the differences in understanding presidential units. They are different in many ways, but they are engaged in parallel activities that serve the president.

## The Development of the Presidency

### A Sketch of Institutional Development

The institutional presidency is a twentieth-century development, accelerating and culminating in the period bracketed by the Eisenhower and Nixon administrations. As late as the 1940s, "presidential" programs were developed in the departments and agencies because there was no presidential staff (or, equivalently, White House staff) capable of handling such tasks. How did the institutional evolution come about? In Chapters 2 through 6, we examine the policy and liaison staffs in some detail. At this point, we need only consider an outline of this development.[2]

Box 1–1 gives a limited first look at the development of selected presidential staff units, specifically the dates of origin of the White House staff units we shall examine. In some respects dates are deceptive. For example, it may seem as if no development took place during the Kennedy and Johnson administrations. This is not true. Among other things, President Kennedy gave the Council of Economic Advisers a formal role to play in economic forecasting, and President Johnson assembled a staff of domestic advisers nearly as large as the Domestic Council staff that would later serve President Nixon. But the dates do provide hints about the relative importance of administrations in institutional development.

Franklin D. Roosevelt is often cited as the person who originated the modern presidency. Clearly, he was a modern president. He seized the initiative on policy

---

### Box 1–1  Years of Origin of Selected White House Staff Units

| President | Staff Unit | Year |
|---|---|---|
| Harding | Bureau of the Budget | 1921 |
| Hoover | Press Secretary | 1929 |
| Roosevelt | Bureau of the Budget (Moved to Executive Office of President from Treasury Department) | 1939 |
| Truman | Council of Economic Advisers | 1946 |
|  | National Security Council | 1947 |
| Eisenhower | Chief of Staff | 1953 |
|  | Office of Congressional Affairs | 1953 |
| Nixon | Office of Communications | 1969 |
|  | Domestic Council | 1970 |
|  | Office of Management and Budget (Reorganized Bureau of the Budget) | 1970 |

---

[2.] For a detailed account of organizational development from Hoover through Johnson, see Charles Walcott and Karen Hult's *Governing the White House* (1995). John Burke's *The Institutional Presidency* (1992) begins with Franklin Roosevelt, but has more information on the Carter, Reagan, and Bush presidencies. For an interpretation of this institutional development, see "The Institutionalization of the American Presidency, 1924–1992" by Lyn Ragsdale and John J. Theis III (1997).

matters, made the White House vastly more important in government, and became the prime focus of public attention (Greenstein 2000, chap. 2). Furthermore, there were institutional developments during his presidency: two administrative entities, the White House Office and a more inclusive Executive Office of the President, were created in 1939, and the Budget Bureau, which had originally been located in the Treasury Department, was moved to the new Executive Office of the President that same year. Even so, studying the Roosevelt administration does not tell us very much about the presidency as it exists today. The Roosevelt presidency was quite small, lines of authority were informal when they were anything more than whims of the president, and presidential aides tended to be generalists rather than specialists in any substantive area. All these things have changed.

The Truman administration would be a better place to begin. There was a small personal staff, a robust Bureau of the Budget standing firmly astride the central processes of budgeting and legislation, a small but well-established press secretary's office, and the newly formed National Security Council and Council of Economic Advisers. The outlines of the contemporary presidency were coming into focus. Still, "Truman's White House rather represented a senatorial establishment writ large: the staff informal, almost family-like, assignments shifting casually among jacks-of-all-trades, organization plastic, hierarchy slight, and anything liable to be mulled over with the president" (Neustadt 1956, 641). Further, half a century has passed since Truman was in the White House. The presidency of Bill Clinton stands to that of Harry Truman as Truman's presidency stood to that of William McKinley. You could tell *something* about Truman's presidency by studying McKinley's, and *something* about Clinton's presidency by studying Truman's, but in both instances enough change had taken place that the parallels are only approximate.

Dwight Eisenhower was the most important president in this organizational development. He came to office when institutional responsibilities were multiplying rapidly. He had a deep personal interest in organizational theory, and he came to the White House with more experience in large-scale organization than any other president (Greenstein 1988b; 2000, 55). As Eisenhower wrote in his memoirs:

> Organization cannot make a genius out of an incompetent; even less can it, of itself, make the decisions which are required to trigger necessary action. . . . Organization makes more efficient the gathering and analysis of facts, and the arranging of the findings of experts in logical fashion. Therefore organization helps the responsible individual make the necessary decision, and helps assure that it is satisfactorily carried out (1963, 153–154).

If anything, Box 1–1 underestimates Eisenhower's role. Not only he was the first to work with a chief of staff and install a congressional liaison operation in the White House, but he also directed significant reorganizations of the relatively new National Security Council and Council of Economic Advisers and gave both units much greater responsibility. Eisenhower was not the only person who could have taken such steps. These organizational modifications were, after all, long-term responses to increased responsibilities. As such, they would have occurred sooner or later anyway. The real impact of Eisenhower's interest in administration was to accelerate this institutional development and to give it a rather orderly cast.

The rest of these new units originated during the Nixon administration. His interest in administration was different from Eisenhower's. Nixon "wanted methodical organization," his Chief of Staff H. R. Haldeman once explained, "but he didn't want to create it himself." At the beginning of the administration, an Office of Communications was set up to coordinate communications strategy. A year later, the Domestic Council was created to provide a channel through which domestic plans would flow to the president. At the same time, the Nixon administration changed the Budget Bureau's name to the Office of Management and Budget as a sign that OMB should become the president's principal management agency as well as his budget staff. With these changes, organizational links to Congress and the media as well as units to handle foreign, economic, and domestic policy were all in place. Even though there have been further modifications, rearrangements of responsibilities, and fairly frequent name changes, these units (or their functional equivalents) have continued to do business in all succeeding administrations.

## General Patterns

Several common threads are woven through this story of institutional development. To begin with, the activities were not new when the political and policy units were established. For instance, close to the end of World War II President Truman organized the State, War, Navy Coordinating Committee. This committee continued consultations that the secretaries of the three departments had been engaged in for some time; it played some of the integrating role later assumed by the National Security Council (Hobbs 1954, 126–127). As another example, two men in the Eisenhower White House and three or four in the Kennedy administration handled domestic policy before Johnson and Nixon established much larger domestic staffs. In general, when an informal adaptation is a response to a real institutional need, a more formal organization is likely to follow.

The more important question is how the new staff unit survives. Part of the answer is that it must adapt to the needs of the president and to the institutions outside the White House with which it is in contact. For example, the legislative liaison office created by Dwight Eisenhower was a low-key, largely behind-the-scenes operation. Under John Kennedy, however, the office had a much higher profile, and its staff attracted public attention on their own. These changes were consistent with Eisenhower's and Kennedy's own work styles. In fact, Eisenhower and Kennedy ensured that legislative liaison teams would adapt to their own styles by appointing heads with whom they had worked for some time. Members of Congress, too, discovered the legislative liaison staffs could help them. The staff members certainly kept senators and representatives aware of White House wishes about the legislative agenda, but they also acquired information about the legislators' needs, and in many cases were able to arrange political favors for them. Once they began performing valuable services for both the president and the legislators, they had the two crucial sources of support.

Dual adaptation to the needs of the president and of external clients is one requirement for survival. The other is to serve a continuing institutional need as opposed to the interests of a single president. The legislative liaison office manifestly met a continuing need: Congress and the president simply had to coordinate their actions. What happens if a president tries to eliminate a unit that serves a continuing institutional need and has successfully developed ties with a supporting constituency? Postwar presidents have always had sources of science advice: Eisenhower had his President's Science Advisory Committee, and Kennedy transmuted this into the Office of Science and Technology. Richard Nixon's elimination of this office in 1973 led many scientists to protest that the president needed solid advice on scientific issues. Gerald Ford moved quickly to reestablish an appropriate office, submitting legislation to that end in the spring of 1975. It took a while for the House and Senate to work out their differences, but by May 1976, the new Office of Science and Technology Policy was created (Stever 1980). On the other hand, a staff unit that reflects the wishes of a single president, or a passing need, is likely to be short-lived. George Bush's Points of Light Foundation is an example of this.

Notice, too, that these adaptations have taken place in Republican and Democratic administrations, in liberal and conservative presidencies, and under the aegis of active and passive presidents. Presidents who were especially interested in organization made more modifications, but that's about the only difference. These developments are not the product of a given political party, ideology, or personality type. The emergence of such units, and more their survival, is due to the larger institutional needs of the presidency in responding to the environment in which it is situated.

The survival of so many staff units marks a transformation of the presidency. Richard Neustadt (1954, 1955) rightly thought that President Eisenhower's preparation of a presidential program using the same process as President Truman was an important institutional development. But the press secretary's office has now survived *eleven* transitions, and without counting its previous incarnation in the Treasury Department, the Bureau of the Budget/Office of Management and Budget has survived *ten*. The shortest-lived agency we have discussed, the Domestic Council, has made it across *five* transitions. This does not mean that each unit will continue indefinitely. Three important units (including the Domestic Council) came under challenge during the Reagan administration. These staff units will thrive only so long as presidents feel that it is in their interests to have their functions performed.

This is the key. What Richard Neustadt wrote at mid-century, "There are no laws requiring a president to build or use the staff facilities as actually evolved, or any other, for that matter; the growth that has occurred and now survives has been organic, not a graft" (1955, 1018), remains true at the beginning of a new century. These units have adapted themselves to work with very different presidents and to accommodate the needs of external institutions. Moreover, no modern president has been free to ignore Congress or the media or foreign policy or economic policy or domestic policy. Therefore, as staffs have developed to deal with each of these areas of the political environment, they have all been kept in place.

What does this analysis imply about the time period we should cover? Whatever the arguments for viewing Franklin Roosevelt as a modern president, there was little of the institutional presidency in the Roosevelt White House. It would not occur to legislative scholars to analyze modern congressional behavior by studying the maneuvers of William B. Bankhead and Joseph T. Robinson, the Speaker and Senate majority leader during the 1930s. Presidential scholars should not go back that far either. The same argument applies to the Truman administration, though with less force. More elements of the modern presidency were beginning to emerge in the Truman administration. We do, however, need to include the period from Eisenhower to Nixon because significant institutional developments took place during that time. The period from Ford to Clinton includes more recent variations and allows us to understand the contemporary presidency.

## *Organizational Structure*

The organization of the modern presidency is much more complex than we have thus far suggested. Aside from the principal liaison offices and policy-making units, which are the focus of our analysis, there are a great many other units; these either have specialized liaison or policy-making responsibilities or serve the president in other ways. A brief look at all these other presidential staff units is in order. These units are organized into the White House Office and the Executive Office of the President.

## White House Office

The White House Office was created in 1939, and the new organization added six administrative assistants to the existing presidential secretaries. These persons were to serve as the president's personal staff. Along with the rest of the institutional presidency, the White House Office has grown many times in the ensuing decades.

The units that comprised the White House Office in 2000 are listed in Box 1–2. Here they are grouped in five categories according to the functions they perform. In an important sense, these categories are more important than the names of the units. Virtually every new administration makes some alterations in organization, dropping a few units, adding others, changing the persons to whom some units report, and frequently changing the names of existing units. Within the White House, names change but essential activities continue. If you were to memorize the names of the units that existed in 2000 and then examine the units that exist in, say, 2013, chances are you would find that some units had "disappeared." But if you kept track of the essential activities, it is likely you would find one or more units charged with those responsibilities.

Let's begin with the administrative staffs. (We shall skip the major units in this discussion, as they will be amply described in subsequent chapters.) The *staff secretary* is quite important for internal coordination. Most of the documents going to the president for approval or disapproval are routed through this office. If the staff secretary thinks that material the president would need is missing, the document is sent back for further work before being submitted. Once the president has made his decision, the materials are again sent through this office for distribution to other staff members. The *cabinet secretary* has been a key player, especially in the Reagan administration, when cabinet councils were often foci for decisions. More generally, the Office of Cabinet Affairs has a secretariat that keeps cabinet records and prepares for meetings. The *Office of Presidential Personnel* is especially important at the beginning of an administration, when personnel with requisite skills have to be assembled for every position from secretary of state down to special assistants to deputy assistants of minor bureaus, but there is enough turnover throughout an administration

---

**Box 1–2　Units Within the White House Office as of 2000**

---

*Administrative Units*
**Office of the Chief of Staff**
Office of the Staff Secretary
Office of Cabinet Affairs
Office of Presidential Personnel
Office of Management and Administration

*Liaison Units*
**Office of Legislative Affairs**
**Office of the Press Secretary**
Office of Public Liaison
Office of Intergovernmental Affairs
Office of Political Affairs

*Logistical Units*
Office of Scheduling
Office of Advance

*Policy-Making Units*
**Office of National Security Affairs**
White House Counsel's Office

*Specialized Units*
Office of the First Lady
President's Foreign Intelligence Advisory Board
President's Initiative for One America
Office of National AIDS Policy

---

Source: *Federal Yellow Book Spring 2000.* Washington, D.C.: Washington Monitor.
Note: Boldface units are discussed at some length later in the book.

---

that this office is kept busy. The *Office of Management and Administration* handles routine business; given the size of the presidential staff, this is a considerable responsibility.

There are three liaison units in addition to the Press Office and Congressional Liaison Office. The *Office of Public Liaison* handles contact with interest groups. It augments the work of the Congressional Liaison Office by integrating interest groups into congressional strategy. The *Office of Intergovernmental Affairs* stays in touch with state and local governments. Governors, mayors, county officials, state legislators, and state and local judges all have interests that are affected by federal policy one way or another, and this office coordinates White House agendas with theirs. The *Office of Political Affairs* provides a similar welcome to party officials and the president's political supporters. In an institution that must constantly balance substantive and political interests, the staff members of political affairs remind their colleagues what the political interests are.

The scheduling and advance offices provide different kinds of logistical support. The *Scheduling Office* copes with all the demands on the president's time, and for this reason is headed by (or reports to) one of the president's most trusted confidants. Whenever the president is making a trip, the *Advance Office* will send someone out beforehand to time the distance to the destination from the airport, make sure the facilities are to the president's liking, arrange for overnight accommodations if needed, and so forth. Though it is rarely mentioned, the advance personnel often work closely with the secret service. The secret service is charged with protecting the president, of course, but protection and advance work involve many of the same considerations.

In the absence of any other domestic staff, the *Counsel's Office* handled domestic policy in the Roosevelt administration, the Truman administration, and the Kennedy administration. Beginning in the Eisenhower years, though, it evolved into a source of independent legal advice for the president. The Counsel's Office usually handles contact with the Justice Department on such matters as judicial nominations, and the office defends the president against legal actions. Some counsels, such as Bush's Boyden Gray, have intervened in certain policy matters, but most deal with policy only when a particular substantive issue raises some legal question.

The *Office of the First Lady* is a support staff that handles the first lady's travel schedule, requests for appearances, social responsibilities, and correspondence.[3] The *President's Foreign Intelligence Advisory Board* is a bipartisan group that provides the president with an independent source of advice on the quality of intelligence collection and analyses. The other two specialized units, the *President's Initiative for One America* and the *Office of National AIDS Policy,* are typical of narrowly focused units that serve the particular interests of one president.

---

[3.] First ladies have often had some policy interests of their own, for example, beautification with Lady Bird Johnson, mental health with Rosalynn Carter, and literacy with Barbara Bush. The scope of Hillary Clinton's policy interests was unusually wide; in many cases she was helped by persons on other substantive staffs. Ira Magaziner, who worked with her on health care, was assigned to the Domestic Policy Council.

## Executive Office of the President

The Executive Office of the President is an umbrella organization that includes all of the elements of the presidential staff. In fact, the White House Office is an organizational unit *within* the Executive Office of the President. The first two elements listed in Box 1–3 are the president's staff (that is, the White House Office) and the *Office of the Vice President.*

The vice president has a personal office in the White House, but the much larger Office of the Vice President is located in the Old Executive Office Building next door. The vice president has a small staff of his own; Vice President Bush, for example, had a staff of seventy. The key elements of a president's staff—a chief of staff, congressional relations, press, national security, domestic policy (but not economic policy), legal counsel, scheduling, advance, and administration—are all represented.

---

**Box 1–3  Units of the Executive Office of the President as of 2000**

*President's and Vice President's Staffs*
White House Office
Office of the Vice President

*Policy-Making Units*
**National Security Council**
**Office of Management and Budget**
**Council of Economic Advisers**
**Office of Policy Development**
   **Economic Policy Council**
   **Domestic Policy Council**
Office of the U.S. Trade Representative
Office of Science and Technology Policy
Council on Environmental Quality
Office of National Drug Control Quality

*Administrative Unit*
Office of Administration

Source: *The United States Government Manual, 1999/2000.* Washington, D.C.: Office of the Federal Register, National Archives, and Records Service, General Services Administration.

Note: Boldface units are discussed at some length later in the book.

---

Most of the units within the Executive Office of the President are policy-making units. Here are to be found the National Security Council staff, the Office of Management and Budget, the Council of Economic Advisers, the Domestic Policy Council, and the Economic Policy Council, all of which will be dealt with further in the book.

The four other policy-making offices are all consequential but have somewhat narrower mandates than the major units. The U.S. trade representative is the president's principal adviser on international trade and represents the United States in major bilateral and multilateral negotiations. The trade representative does not have free rein in international economics; Treasury is concerned about international finance, and Treasury, CEA, OMB, and the Federal Reserve are all concerned with fiscal and monetary policy. But as long as trade becomes more global and less national, the *Office of the U.S. Trade Representative* will play an increasingly important role because of its activity in trade negotiations.

One would think that the growing importance of science would increase the prominence of the *Office of Science and Technology Policy.* The office's staff members are charged with advising the president on science and with coordinating the substantial federal investment in science. But their voices are muted because so few occupants of the West Wing have enough scientific background to grasp what is, and is not, significant. The *Council on Environmental Quality* has a broad mandate to give advice on environmental questions, but it has a very small staff. The Environmental Protection Agency (an independent agency) is more prominent in developing and implementing environmental policy. The *Office of National Drug Control Policy* coordinates such aspects of drug policy as demand reduction, intelligence, and supply reduction.

Finally, there is the *Office of Administration.* It handles personnel, financial matters, data processing, libraries, records, and general office procedures for the Executive Office of the President.

## Comparing the Organizational Entities

What are the differences between the White House Office and the Executive Office of the President? Obviously, the Executive Office of the President is the more inclusive organization. Besides the White House Office, there are a number of large independent units under the aegis of the Executive Office of the President. The National Security Council staff and the Office of Management and Budget are examples. But more important, different types of offices are located in the White House Office and the Executive Office of the President.

The White House Office has administrative units, liaison units, logistical units, and a few specialized units. The administrative units, especially the Offices of the Chief of Staff and the Staff Secretary, supply high-level coordination as well as internal administration. The liaison units provide outreach between the president and various political institutions. The logistical units are also personal to the president, planning the use of his time and attending to travel details. The only units that can be classified as policy making are the Office of National Security Affairs, essentially a White House Office beachhead for the large NSC staff located in the Executive Office of the President, and the Counsel's Office. At one time, the Counsel's Office was the home of domestic policy making, but now it deals largely with legal affairs.

In addition to a single administrative unit, the Executive Office of the President contains the president's and vice president's staffs and all of the policy-making units. These policy-making staffs must be large enough to have specialists in all of the areas with which the units deal. They provide contact with the relevant policy communities, submit the options from which the president and his senior aides will make their basic policy decisions, and then work out the details for full-fledged policy proposals.

## The Presidential Staff

The barriers between the White House Office and the Executive Office of the President are very slight indeed. The de facto integration is signaled by the framed presidential commissions that hang on the office walls of all presidential assistants or deputy assistants, regardless of whether the tenant works in the White House Office or some other unit of the Executive Office of the President. Signed by the president, they read, "Reposing special trust and confidence in your integrity, prudence, and ability, I do appoint you . . . ." The staff member's title as assistant to the president (most senior), deputy assistant to the president, or special assistant to the president (most junior, not formally commissioned) indicates his or her rank. The rest of the titles suggest what the staff members' responsibilities might be. Thus, the principal domestic aide is "Assistant to the President for Domestic Policy and Director of the Domestic Policy Council," the person in charge of House liaison is "Deputy Assistant to the President for Legislative Affairs/House Liaison," and a speechwriter is "Special Assistant to the President and Senior Speechwriter." If you understand that the first part gives the person's rank and the second part (no matter how grand the language) alludes to the person's responsibilities, these titles tell a great deal about the staff member's relation to the president; it is more useful to know a person's title than to know whether he or she works in the White House Office or elsewhere in the Executive Office of the President.

As we have already seen, the presidential staff has been growing for years. In the Eisenhower White House, the only person bearing the title of assistant to the president was Sherman Adams, the chief of staff. All the other staff members were special assistants. The Nixon administration instituted the use of three ranks: assistant, deputy assistant, and special assistant. At the end of the Clinton administration, there were twenty-three assistants to the president, forty-seven deputy assistants, and forty-nine special assistants (or their equivalent).[4] In addition, there were the fourteen department heads who serve as members of the cabinet by long custom, and eleven more who had been given cabinet rank by the president. Of the eleven, two were senior members of the White House Office, four more were heads of units in the Executive Office of the President, and four were heads of independent agencies; the final cabinet member was the U.S. ambassador to the United Nations.

Obviously, a group of ninety-three persons—the total number holding presidential commissions or cabinet rank—is not a decision-making body. This raises the question of whom the president consults when he is making up his mind. In fact, there is a good deal of variation from president to president, and from subject to subject within an administration. Consequently, we look for general guidelines rather than hard-and-fast rules. One indicator that a person may be consulted is that the individual will have to carry out the policy being decided upon. A closely related consideration is whether a person has expertise on the subject, whether the president has discovered that this person can bring facts to his attention that are useful in making a decision. A third clue is propinquity, whether the person has a White House office so that the president has had frequent contact with him or her. The final guide is trust, whether the president has come to depend on this individual's candor and counsel.

Let's say that a president must decide on the budget for intelligence. It would be easy to imagine that the president might meet with the secretary of state, secretary of defense, director of central intelligence, chief of staff, national security assistant, budget director, associate budget director for national security and international affairs, and deputy associate budget director for the national security division. This assemblage would include two cabinet members, one head of an independent agency, two members of the White House Office, and three per-

---

[4.] There are a few titles that differ from the general pattern. In the Clinton Counsel's Office, for example, there was one counsel to the president, one assistant to the president and deputy counsel, and one deputy assistant to the president and deputy counsel. Almost all the other lawyers were termed "associate counsels."

sons from OMB, a unit in the Executive Office of the President. None of these persons would be there solely because of his or her institutional affiliation. All of them would be there because their responsibilities and their knowledge give them standing to advise the president on the topic in question. To confer on other topics, different people would be invited because of their experience and expertise relevant to those issues.

Since the cast changes depending on the topic before the president, scholars often refer to the importance of meetings with trusted advisers without saying that one assistant is always present or that another is always absent. Thomas Cronin, for example, speaks of an *inner cabinet* consisting of the secretary of state, secretary of defense, secretary of the treasury, and attorney general, and increasingly, some ranking members of the White House staff (1980, 276–278). By naming the four cabinet members, Cronin recognizes the importance of their domains for the presidential agenda, and by not specifying the staff members, he allows for variation depending on expertise and trust. Similarly, Fred Greenstein speaks of a president's *principal associates.* Greenstein's phrase also emphasizes each president's reliance on a small set of confidants while permitting appropriate modification in the membership of this inner circle.

In this book, I shall refer to the presidential staff as including the major liaison and policy-making units: those working with Congress, working with the media, and developing and implementing foreign policy, economic policy, and domestic policy.[5] Obviously, this excludes a number of White House and Executive Office units. They are not being excluded because they are unimportant; all the units are needed. It is simply that the major liaison and policy-making units are more significant for our purposes. Put another way, I am focusing on the most important activities rather than trying to describe everything done in the name of the president.

## *The Rest of the Book*

### The Institutional Presidency

The next five chapters will be an extended discussion of the institutional presidency. Chapters 2 and 3 will examine the working relationships between the White House and two major political institutions, Congress and the media.

---

[5.] At the beginning of this chapter, the institutional presidency was defined as the presidential staff plus the political appointees in the executive branch. I also mentioned earlier that I am using "presidential staff" and "White House staff" interchangeably.

Chapters 4, 5, and 6 will address policy: foreign policy, economic policy, and domestic policy, in that order.

Each of these chapters will follow a common outline. First, the organizational actors—usually units of the White House staff, but sometimes cabinet departments or agencies—will be introduced. Next we shall ask how their activities are coordinated. Coordination is a common activity, but the methods that have been developed vary a bit from one area to the next. Once we know who our actors are, we shall turn to their task-specific activities: negotiation in foreign policy, coping with business cycles in economics, handling projects and patronage in congressional liaison, and all the rest. Finally, we shall look at the common activities—information gathering, decision making, and exerting influence—to see how they are affected by the area of the political environment being discussed.

## Presidential Accomplishment

In the concluding section of the book, we shall ask what American presidents have been able to accomplish. Our general argument is that an individual president begins with a set of policy skills, takes the power he has (or lacks) as a result of his election and support in other political institutions, considers what he regards as good public policy, and then arrays his resources against the challenges he faces in each policy arena. In Chapter 7, we shall look at one instance of success, one instance of failure, and one instance that led to diverse results for each president in the second half of the twentieth century. These samples of what the presidents have accomplished, or failed to accomplish, illustrate the mixed records that are the lot of all presidents. No president is successful in everything he undertakes; no president fails in everything he undertakes.

Chapter 8 focuses on patterns of presidential accomplishment. It begins with a discussion of a presidential agenda composed of topics that most presidents must address. Next comes an argument that two individual attributes—expertise and attitude strength—forecast the behavior each president is likely to exhibit in the various policy areas. Finally, we return to the question of success and failure addressed in Chapter 7. But now we assess the presidents' records in a larger number of their endeavors, large enough to speak of patterns. With a larger number of cases to analyze, we see again that presidents experience both successes and failures, but we add to this that successes are more common than failures.

# 2. Working with Congress

## *The Legislative Terrain*

The U.S. Constitution created, in Richard Neustadt's famous phrase, "separated institutions *sharing* powers" (1960, 33; emphasis in original). The president has an opportunity to shape the legislative agenda in the State of the Union Message and to participate in the legislative process by signing or vetoing bills. Congress, however, decides how much of the agenda will be enacted into law and how much money will be appropriated to carry on the business of government. With powers thus mixed, no president is assured safe passage across the legislative terrain. A fortunate few will find an easy journey; most must surmount trying obstacles; some will be confronted by jagged peaks that cannot be scaled.

Charles O. Jones has frequently analyzed the circumstances that lead to presidential success or failure in dealing with Congress (1968, 1970, 1981, 1983, 1988a, 1988c, 1994). The classic bargain is "designed to convince the members of Congress that cooperation is in their own best interest or [is] based on an interpretation of what is good for the nation at a particular time" (1983, 97). When such a bargain is struck, presidents are able to obtain most of what they want. More commonly, the difficulty of the legislative terrain is determined by political circumstances. Broadly speaking, these include the president's level of public support, whether the president's party enjoys a majority in the House and Senate, the congruence between the president's policy agenda and congressional preferences, and the skills of the legislative leadership. Many legislative scholars—Jones, Edwards (1980, 1989), Bond and Fleisher (1990), Ripley (1972, 1988) Peterson

(1990) and others—have shown links between these circumstances and a president's fortunes.

## Public Support for the President

Public support is most visibly demonstrated when a president is elected. If post-election headlines proclaim that the president has been swept into office by a decisive majority, he will be in a strong position vis-à-vis Congress. But if the victor barely defeats his opponent, skeptical observers will doubt his political strength.

Table 2–1 presents the percentages of the popular vote garnered by the winning candidates. It is ordered from Lyndon Johnson in 1964 and Richard Nixon in 1972, whom everyone regarded as landslide winners, to John Kennedy in 1960, Richard Nixon in 1968, and Bill Clinton in 1992. Kennedy adorned his slim vote with graceful words— "The margin may be narrow, but the responsibility is clear"; Lyndon Johnson was in a much stronger position four years later.

**Table 2–1    Results of Presidential Elections**

| Winner and Year | Popular Vote for Winner | Congressional Seats Gained by Winner's Party | |
| --- | --- | --- | --- |
| | | House | Senate |
| Johnson, 1964 | 61.1% | 37 | 1 |
| Nixon, 1972 | 60.7 | 12 | −2 |
| Reagan, 1984 | 58.8 | 14 | −2 |
| Eisenhower, 1956 | 57.4 | −2 | −1 |
| Eisenhower, 1952 | 55.1 | 22 | 1 |
| Bush, 1988 | 53.9 | −2 | 0 |
| Reagan, 1980 | 50.8 | 34 | 12 |
| Clinton, 1996 | 50.1 | 9 | −2 |
| Carter, 1976 | 50.1 | 1 | 0 |
| Kennedy, 1960 | 49.7 | −22 | −2 |
| Nixon, 1968 | 43.4 | 5 | 6 |
| Clinton, 1992 | 43.3 | −10 | 0 |

Sources: Adapted from Gary King and Lyn Ragsdale, *The Elusive Executive: Discovering Statistical Patterns in the Presidency* (Washington, D.C.: CQ Press, 1988), Table 7–24; Norman J. Ornstein, Thomas E. Mann, and Michael J. Malbin, *Vital Statistics on Congress, 1995–1996* (Washington, D.C.: Congressional Quarterly, 1996, Table 2–3); Gerald M. Pomper, "The Presidential Election," in *The Election of 1996*, ed. Gerald M. Pomper (Chatham, N.J.: Chatham House, 1997), 178; and Marjorie Randon Hershey, "The Congressional Election," in ibid., 224.

There are a few things that should be noted in these victory figures. First, the four largest votes all went to candidates for reelection, that is, incumbents. Most of those with lower popular votes were running for office for the first time. Second, the winner's percentage reflects the strength or weakness of his opposition. Presidents Johnson and Nixon had the good fortune to run against Barry Goldwater and George McGovern, respectively, both of whom spoke for unpopular causes. Jimmy Carter, John F. Kennedy, and former vice president Richard M. Nixon (in 1968), on the other hand, were opposed by much stronger rivals. The vote proportions for Ronald Reagan in 1980, Nixon in 1968, and Bill Clinton in 1992 were reduced by the third-party candidacies of John Anderson, George Wallace, and Ross Perot, respectively.

In any case, the size of a president's victory, taken alone, is a poor forecaster of congressional success. It is at least as important to know whether the president's party in Congress is gaining or losing seats while he is winning the White House. If a president's victory increases his party's standing on Capitol Hill, legislators are more likely to follow his lead than if the presidential contest does not affect the partisan balance in Congress or if the president's party actually loses seats.

These data are presented in the other two columns of Table 2–1. On average, a president's party can expect to gain eight seats in the House and a single seat in the Senate. These mean figures suggest little relationship between presidential votes and swings in congressional seats. There were, however, four elections in which a party made real gains in Congress when it won the White House. These partywide victories came with the election of Ronald Reagan in 1980, when the Republicans captured the Senate for the first time in twenty-six years and picked up thirty-four House seats; with Lyndon Johnson's 1964 victory, when the Democrats gained thirty-seven House seats; with Dwight Eisenhower's 1952 election, which produced a Republican House and Senate; and to a lesser degree with Richard Nixon's 1968 success, when the GOP picked up half a dozen Senate seats. All four of these victories occurred when presidential candidates were making their first runs for the White House.

When Richard Nixon and Ronald Reagan were reelected in 1972 and 1984, the Republicans did just slightly better than normal in the House and lost two Senate seats. The same thing happened to the Democrats when Bill Clinton was reelected in 1996. Dwight Eisenhower's 1956 reelection was accompanied by small Republican losses in both chambers. Hence all these reelections were interpreted as personal victories rather than party triumphs. When John Kennedy recaptured the White House for the Democrats in 1960, the Democrats lost twenty-two House seats and a pair of Senate seats, and Bill Clinton's 1992 victory was accompanied by a loss of ten House seats. These results, in combination with their own narrow margins, left Presidents Kennedy and Clinton in weak bargaining positions with Congress.

A president's public popularity can also be demonstrated by his approval rating. When public approval drops off, lawmakers are more likely to oppose the president. The chief evidence for this comes from sharp declines, as with Nixon's Watergate-caused 30-point drop from December 1972 to December 1973 (Edwards 1989, 114–116). A high approval rating, however, usually helps the president only if it is combined with other favorable circumstances. Reluctant legislators will not go along with presidential proposals just because a chief executive has high approval ratings. For example, George Bush had considerable difficulty in arriving at a budget agreement in the late summer of 1990 even though he was enjoying a 75 percent approval rating at the time.

### Party Support in the House and Senate

The second circumstance affecting the president's chances of legislative success is the support available from the congressional parties. Tables 2–2 and 2–3 present the relevant data. Table 2–2 indicates the size of the congressional majority or minority with which the president must work, and Table 2–3 reveals how many of these votes are likely to be cast for the president's programs. The most striking fact in Table 2–2 is how frequently Congress has been controlled by the opposition. Of the twenty-four Congresses since 1952, thirteen have been in the hands of the opposition. Three more were split, and only eight were controlled by the president's own party. There was a clear partisan difference here. Among the Republicans, only Eisenhower ever had a Republican Congress (though Reagan had three Republican Senates), and among the Democrats, only Clinton had to work with a GOP Congress. Otherwise, all the Democrats were benefited by Congresses controlled by their parties, and all the Republicans had to contend with Congresses led by their opponents. Johnson was in the strongest position with the Great Society Congress (1965–1967), while Ford was in the weakest position in the House, and Eisenhower was in the weakest position in the Senate from 1959 to 1961.

Table 2–3 presents data on the extent of support presidents have received from their own parties, and from the opposing parties, on key votes.[1] These differences

---

[1.] Key votes are selected by Congressional Quarterly. One key vote, which in the judgment of Congressional Quarterly is the most important in determining the outcome, is selected on each major controversy facing Congress in each session. See Edwards 1989, 20–31, chap. 3.

**Table 2–2 Congressional Majority (Maj.) or Minority (Min.)**

| President | Congress (Years) | House | Senate |
|---|---|---|---|
| Eisenhower | 83rd (1953–1955) | 10 vote maj. | 1 vote maj. |
| | 84th (1955–1957) | 29 vote min. | 1 vote min. |
| | 85th (1957–1959) | 33 vote min. | 2 vote min. |
| | 86th (1959–1961) | 130 vote min. | 30 vote min. |
| Kennedy | 87th (1961–1963) | 89 vote maj. | 30 vote maj. |
| Kennedy/Johnson | 88th (1963–1965) | 81 vote maj. | 34 vote maj. |
| Johnson | 89th (1965–1967) | 155 vote maj. | 36 vote maj. |
| | 90th (1967–1969) | 59 vote maj. | 28 vote maj. |
| Nixon | 91st (1969–1971) | 56 vote min. | 14 vote min. |
| | 92nd (1971–1973) | 74 vote min. | 10 vote min. |
| Nixon/Ford | 93rd (1973–1975) | 47 vote min. | 14 vote min. |
| Ford | 94th (1975–1977) | 147 vote min. | 23 vote min. |
| Carter | 95th (1977–1979) | 149 vote maj. | 24 vote maj. |
| | 96th (1979–1981) | 119 vote maj. | 18 vote maj. |
| Reagan | 97th (1981–1983) | 51 vote min. | 6 vote maj. |
| | 98th (1983–1985) | 104 vote min. | 8 vote maj. |
| | 99th (1985–1987) | 70 vote min. | 6 vote maj. |
| | 100th (1987–1989) | 83 vote min. | 10 vote min. |
| Bush | 101st (1989–1991) | 85 vote min. | 10 vote min. |
| | 102nd (1991–1993) | 100 vote min. | 12 vote min. |
| Clinton | 103rd (1993–1995) | 88 vote maj. | 12 vote maj. |
| | 104th (1995–1997) | 27 vote min. | 4 vote min. |
| | 105th (1997–1999) | 19 vote min. | 10 vote min. |
| | 106th (1999–2001) | 11 vote min. | 10 vote min. |

Source: Adapted from Lyn Ragsdale, *Vital Statistics on the Presidency: Washington to Clinton* (Washington, D.C.: CQ Press, 1996), Table 8–1.

between administrations are worth noting, especially at the extremes. Some presidents were better at cultivating opponents than others. Dwight Eisenhower was able to enlist 42 percent support from House Democrats while John Kennedy only got 17 percent support from House Republicans. Lyndon Johnson, working with Republican Minority Leader Everett Dirksen, was able to get 49 percent support from Senate Republicans, whereas neither Ronald Reagan nor George Bush could obtain more than 28 percent help from Senate Democrats. Even more important, some presidents have been better at eliciting support from fellow partisans. John Kennedy got 74 percent support from House Democrats—a far higher level than the 59 percent support elicited by Jimmy Carter. George Bush enjoyed 79 percent support from Republicans in the Senate, while Gerald Ford was able to coax only

57 percent support from Republican senators. In fact, Reagan, Bush, and Clinton have *all* had greater support from fellow partisans in both the House and the Senate than almost all their predecessors.[2] There have been occasions when this increased partisan support was critical. For example, it enabled President Clinton to pass his first budget without a single Republican vote.

While the differences between administrations are not trivial, the most important message in Table 2–3 is that most presidents get *approximately* the same degree of backing from their own party. On average, presidents could expect the votes of 66 percent of their fellow partisans in the House and the Senate from 1953 through 1980 and 75 percent from 1981 through 1996. Consequently, presidents usually do better by increasing the size of their party than by trying to woo the opposition. Much was made of Lyndon Johnson's prowess in moving Great

**Table 2–3   Presidential Support on Key Votes by Party**

| | House | | Senate | |
|---|---|---|---|---|
| *President* | *Fellow Partisans* | *Opponents* | *Fellow Partisans* | *Opponents* |
| Eisenhower | 65% | 42% | 71% | 37% |
| Kennedy | 74 | 17 | 65 | 32 |
| Johnson | 68 | 29 | 65 | 49 |
| Nixon | 65 | 35 | 67 | 38 |
| Ford | 68 | 34 | 57 | 29 |
| Carter | 59 | 29 | 64 | 33 |
| Reagan | 72 | 28 | 74 | 28 |
| Bush | 73 | 33 | 79 | 28 |
| Clinton* | 76 | 29 | 75 | 37 |

Source: Adapted from George C. Edwards III, *At the Margins: Presidential Leadership of Congress* (New Haven: Yale University Press, 1989), Table 3–4. Professor Edwards kindly supplied data for 1987 through 1994. The support figures for Nixon and Ford in 1994 and those for Clinton in 1995 and 1996 were calculated directly from Congressional Quarterly support scores using a method that produces close approximations to those of Professor Edwards.

*Clinton support scores are for 1993 to 1996.

---

[2] Some of this increased backing is likely related to the greater polarization in Congress and increased party homogeneity in recent years. But that leaves a puzzle: Why is the jump in own-party support not matched by an equal drop in support across the aisle? Further, an increase in support by the president's fellow partisans has taken place with Republican and Democratic presidents, and when the congressional parties have had majority and minority status, so this seems to be a consequential result.

Society legislation through the 89th Congress, and properly so. He understood the importance of taking advantage of the large Democratic majority in that Congress. But as we can see in Table 2–3, John Kennedy was actually supported by a larger proportion of the Democrats in the House of Representatives. Lyndon Johnson just had a larger Democratic Party in the House, and that made all the difference.

A party's composition may be as important as its size in determining the extent of support its members will provide. Congressional parties are in fact coalitions of issue groups. There is agreement within issue groups but not across issue groups. For instance, Aage Clausen found that Southern Democrats in the 85th and 86th Congresses (1957–1961) consisted of three issue groups. One, the Dixie populists, was conservative on social welfare and international involvement but liberal on economics and agriculture. Another, the Dixie liberals, was conservative on civil liberties but liberal on social welfare, international involvement, economics, and agriculture (1973, 110–112). Furthermore, although some issue groups might have consistent preferences for liberal (or moderate or conservative) policies in every issue area, it is common to find issue groups whose preferences vary across policy areas. In the 95th Congress (1977–1979), for example, there were eight issue groups among House Democrats, five among House Republicans, four among Senate Democrats, and five among Senate Republicans. Of these twenty-two issue groups, only one had consistent policy preferences across the eight policy areas examined (Kessel 1984b, chap. 7).

## Congruence of the Presidential Agenda

A third factor shaping the legislative terrain is what the president wants. It follows from what we have just seen that presidential persuasiveness depends on the congruence between his policy preferences and those of the issue groups on Capitol Hill. If his party has a decided majority, then the preference structure within that party will be the most important consideration. If his party has only a narrow majority, and certainly if his party is in the minority, the president must pay some attention to the issue groups in the opposition party.

What would this lead us to expect about Jimmy Carter's experience with the 95th Congress? Let's assume that President Carter had made a moderate request in economic management. No Democratic issue groups had moderate preferences on economic management in either the House or the Senate. Only one Republican issue group had such preferences; it was in the Senate. The dominant Democratic issue coalition in both chambers was liberal; the dominant Republican issue coalition in the House was moderate conservative, and the dominant

Republican issue coalition in the Senate was conservative. Consequently, a moderate economic program would have been criticized by Democrats as insufficiently liberal and by Republicans as insufficiently conservative. As we can see in Table 2–2, President Carter's difficulty was not a lack of Democrats on Capitol Hill. Rather, there was little congruence between Carter's agenda and the issue preferences of the congressional parties.

The scope and novelty of each president's agenda are also important in his efforts to gain legislative acceptance. John Campbell suggested using these properties in a study of Japanese policy regarding aging (1979). His classification has been applied to presidential politics by Paul Light (1999, 119–126, 289–298) and Mark Peterson (1990, 151–159, 196–202). The scope of a proposal can be classified as large or small. President Johnson's creation of Medicare would be a large program; President Reagan's suggestion of urban enterprise zones would be regarded as small. Novelty refers to whether a proposal is new or old. President Carter's proposal for a separate Department of Education was new; extension of the public housing program during the Ford administration was old.

These categories can be combined to create a taxonomy of large new, large old, small new, and small old programs. Given the resources involved, it requires the greatest legislative effort to pass a large new program, the least to renew a small old program, with small new programs and large old programs ranking somewhere in between. Inspection of programs submitted by the presidents from Kennedy through Clinton confirms this. Lyndon Johnson, who after 1964 had the most political capital to expend, was likeliest to submit large new programs. John Kennedy and Lyndon Johnson prior to 1964, working with smaller Democratic majorities, had the greatest propensity to ask for large old programs. Richard Nixon, who was anxious to demonstrate Republican initiatives but faced a Democratic Congress, was the most likely to submit small new proposals. Gerald Ford, who was in the weakest position, relied on small old programs; Bill Clinton relied even more on small old programs after 1994; and George Bush, who combined a weak position with a propensity for very modest initiatives, relied on small old programs most of all (Light 1999, Table 34).

Clearly, the size of the president's legislative agenda is not fixed across presidents. If the legislative terrain is favorable, then the scope and novelty of the incumbent's program can increase. In less auspicious circumstances, the president's legislative requests are likely to be more modest. It fact, it has been shown that these circumstances are better predictors of the scope and novelty of presidential proposals than the likelihood of obtaining congressional approval (Peterson 1990, Table 6–2).

## The Legislative Leaders

Presidents and their legislative aides work through the leaders of the House and Senate parties. Sometimes presidents wish that they could work with someone else, but they have no real choice. The House and Senate leaders have power bases independent of the president; the leaders have been elected by their own peers. Therefore the president must deal with them. Further, the power of the president and the legislative leaders is enhanced when they work closely together. The president ought to give the legislative leaders advance notice of his plans so they can reinforce his message when it arrives on Capitol Hill. Senate and House leaders ought to give the president accurate vote counts so he can make his plans accordingly. If there is any lack of communication, to say nothing of an open struggle, leaders at both ends of Pennsylvania Avenue are likely to be embarrassed.

All those elected to leadership positions have been competent legislators, but over time there have been varying degrees of leadership skill. Sam Rayburn was the longest-serving and most powerful Speaker of the House in the twentieth century. Thomas P. (Tip) O'Neill presided over a House with much greater diffusion of power, but he worked with considerable skill to assemble Democratic majorities in behalf of Jimmy Carter and in opposition to Ronald Reagan. Reagan owed much of his success in the early 1980s to the Republican leaders. Speaking of the House, Reagan aide M. B. Oglesby said: "The story that really wasn't widely reported was [Minority Leader] Bob Michel's unbelievable ability to hold Republicans together as a voting bloc on the issues. He and [Minority Whip] Trent Lott have become a very effective team. . . . They're our lead people, and whether we agree, or don't agree, they're the ones we always go to."[3] Referring to Senate Majority Leader Howard Baker, Reagan's chief legislative assistant Max Friedersdorf said simply, "They're blessed with good leadership up there."

Conversely, two House leaders, Republican Joseph W. Martin Jr. and Democrat John W. McCormack, became less effective toward the ends of their careers because of advancing age. Republican Senate Leader William Knowland was determined, but he lacked subtlety and adaptability. And Democrat Mike Mansfield, the longest-serving Senate majority leader, was unwilling to line up votes. Lyndon Johnson therefore turned to Majority Whip Hubert Humphrey and often worked closely with Minority Leader Everett Dirksen. If the president's party has

---

[3.] As I mentioned in the preface, almost all of the uncited quotations in the book are drawn from interviews I have conducted myself. This is true of M. B. Oglesby's statement and of all but three of the uncited quotations in this chapter.

sufficient majorities in both chambers, then leadership skills in the majority party are going to be more important. But since presidents have often faced opposition Congresses, leaders in the minority party frequently have vital roles to play.

In view of all these circumstances, the constitutionally mixed powers do not guarantee that presidential leadership will lead to success or end in failure. If a president is fortunate enough to have a favorable legislative terrain—if the president's electoral majority was large, his approval ratings are high, his party has a majority in both the House and the Senate, congressional preferences correspond with his own, and his legislative partisans are ably led—then Congress is likely to follow the president's lead. If a president lacks some of these advantages, presidential leadership is possible, but only if the president and his legislative aides have the requisite skill to maneuver on more difficult terrain. And if a president should have the ill fortune to face totally adverse circumstances—having barely crawled into office, earning a low approval rating, facing opposition majorities in both chambers, and being saddled with less qualified leaders in his own party—then even the most skillful efforts in dealing with Congress are likely to be unavailing.

## *The Shepherds of Presidential Proposals*

### The President's Own Liaison Staff

The Office of Legislative Affairs was created by Dwight Eisenhower to follow the legislation with which the president was most concerned.[4] Eisenhower was well aware of the highly effective Pentagon liaison with Congress, and he thought a similar operation was urgently needed in the White House.[5] To be head of this legislative liaison staff, he selected Wilton B. (Jerry) Persons, a retired major general who had dealt with Congress on behalf of the army since World War II. A soft-spoken southerner, Persons was "probably personally acquainted with more congressional members than any other individual in the city" (Eisenhower 1963, 156). Joining Persons were such experienced men as Bryce Harlow, a former staff director of the House Armed Services Committee, who eventually succeeded him.

---

[4.] As is true of other White House units, this office has had several names. The most common has been the Office of Legislative Affairs under Presidents Eisenhower, Nixon, Ford, Reagan, Bush, and Clinton. It was the Office of Congressional Relations during the Kennedy and Johnson administration, and the Office of Congressional Liaison in the Carter White House. The most common informal name is the congressional liaison office.

[5.] The Truman administration had two messengers on Capitol Hill—Charles Maylon on the House side and Joseph Feeney on the Senate side—but that was all (Heller 1980, 229).

Already very well acquainted with many legislators, they took a low-key approach. They sought to explain the legislation that was being offered, and they tried to deal with problems as they were encountered. This soft-sell technique was appropriate both for the not very tractable old guard Republicans and for the Democrats whose votes were needed for bipartisan majorities.

President Kennedy maintained the legislative liaison office, appointing Lawrence O'Brien, who had been organization director of his 1960 presidential campaign, as head. The office's responsibilities were similar to those of Eisenhower's liaison office. Working on the Hill with O'Brien were five staff members who handled House liaison and one who worked on the Senate side. Kennedy's staffers were, however, more visible, and they followed a much more partisan approach. (Box 2–1 lists the heads of the congressional liaison office.)

The staffing pattern established in the Eisenhower and Kennedy administrations has persisted over time. Although there has been a fair amount of turnover within administrations, the general pattern has been for a larger group to work with the more numerous House members, a smaller group to handle Senate liaison, and a small unit to remain in the White House to coordinate communications with the staff members who are usually up on Capitol Hill. Both Carter's and Reagan's staffs had five people dealing with the House. The Reagan staff increased the number of people working with the Senate to four, and subsequent administrations have had roughly equal numbers assigned to the House and the Senate. In the spring of 1997, the Clinton staff had fourteen members, with four specifically assigned to the Senate and five specifically assigned to the House.

## Departmental Relations with Congress

With so few people, the White House congressional liaison operation cannot begin to keep tabs on all the administration's bills on Capitol Hill. Staff members' attention is restricted to the legislation the president regards as most important. But almost all of the departments maintain liaison offices of their own. They look out for bills that are consequential primarily to the departments they represent. Many of these departmental liaison offices antedated the White House liaison office. Several originated in the departments' solicitor's or counsel's office. In time, most departments appointed assistant secretaries to handle their legislative affairs (Holtzman 1970, 10–11). By the time of the Bush administration, every department except Interior and Transportation had an assistant secretary in charge of legislative liaison.

The assistant secretary has the same relation to the secretary as the head of the White House liaison office does to the president, essentially one of advising the

## Box 2–1  Legislative Liaison Heads

| President | Liaison Head | Years |
|---|---|---|
| Eisenhower | Wilton B. Persons | 1953–1958 |
| | Bryce N. Harlow | 1958–1961 |
| Kennedy | Lawrence F. O'Brien | 1961–1963 |
| Johnson | Lawrence F. O'Brien * | 1963–1967 |
| | Harold Barefoot Sanders Jr. | 1967–1979 |
| Nixon | Bryce N. Harlow | 1969–1970 |
| | William E. Timmons | 1970–1974 |
| Ford | John O. Marsh * | 1974–1977 |
| | William E. Timmons | 1974 |
| | Max L. Friedersdorf | 1975–1977 |
| Carter | Frank Moore | 1977–1981 |
| Reagan | Max L. Friedersdorf * | 1981 |
| | Kenneth M. Duberstein | 1981–1983 |
| | M. B. Oglesby | 1983–1986 |
| | William A. Ball | 1986–1988 |
| | Alan Kranowitz | 1988–1989 |
| Bush | Frederick D. McClure | 1989–1992 |
| | Nicholas E. Calio | 1992–1993 |
| Clinton | Howard G. Paster | 1993 |
| | Patrick J. Griffin | 1994–1996 |
| | John L. Hilley | 1996–1998 |
| | Lawrence Stein | 1998–2000 |
| | Charles Brain | 2000– |

*O'Brien was also a member of the Johnson cabinet as postmaster general from 1965 to 1968; Marsh served as counselor to the president and had overall charge of legislative relations; Friedersdorf returned to the White House for a brief period in 1985 to chart legislative strategy.

secretary, coordinating legislative affairs, and expediting congressional requests within the department. As Arthur Goldberg, labor secretary in the Kennedy administration, explained:

> The Hill is a special institution, and a secretary is too busy with other tasks, many unrelated to Congress. Even if he is competent and aggressive himself regarding Congress, he does not have the time or complete specialization

himself to do the day-to-day job. . . . I needed a specialist to give me the feel of what was going on and the problems we would encounter and were meeting (Holtzman 1970, 21).

Coming to the White House after a long congressional career, Lyndon Johnson took congressional relations quite seriously. At the beginning of the 89th Congress in 1965, he gave instructions to his cabinet members: "I want you to get the best legislative liaison you can; I want you to devote overtime to the new members and your new committees; and I want your people to work closely with each other through Larry O'Brien" (Bowles 1987, 46). A first-term Democratic member described the results: "I had heard a lot about lobbyists before I came to Washington, and I expected to be besieged when I arrived. I was. To my amazement, the first ten lobbyists who came to see me were from the ten executive departments, offering assistance, literature, and advice on their legislative programs." The pattern of departmental lobbying was set, and it continued to develop. By the time of the Carter administration, the Defense Department (which had the largest legislative operation) employed an estimated 1,500 persons—nearly three for every single member of Congress. Individual departmental lobbyists exhibited skills of their own. For example, by working with committee staffs early in the process, they could often get agreement on critical details before partisan posturing took over in floor debates (Collier 1997, 254).

## Legislative Clearance

The process of legislative clearance (which gives concerned parties a chance to express their views on proposed legislation) was established by Franklin Roosevelt. In 1935 he said he thought of legislation as falling into three categories: first, "the type of legislation that, administratively, I could not give approval to . . ." second, "the type of legislation which we are perfectly willing to have the department or agency press for . . . [but which] is all your trouble, not mine, . . . [and third,] major administration bills" of personal concern to the president (Neustadt 1954, 650). The Budget Bureau, which had already established procedures for financial clearance, began to move toward legislative clearance. This did not happen at once, but by 1939 a small staff of civil servants, which in time became known as the Office of Legislative Reference, was following fixed clearance routines.

The first routine was to review a bill before it was sent to the Hill. Whenever any agency conceived legislation, it would first be sent to the Office of Legislative Reference. The proposed legislation would then be sent to any other departments and agencies that might be affected, together with a request for their views of it. The office already knew the president's views; it maintained a collection of campaign speeches and party platforms as well as the president's speeches and messages to Congress. After the statements of approval or disapproval came in from the agencies, agency views were compared with the president's own statements, and the proposed bill was designated as being not in accord, no objection, or in accord (which eventually came to be abbreviated i/a) with the president's program. This trichotomy roughly corresponded to FDR's three categories.[6] The classification helped legislators know where the administration stood, and in 1947 congressional committees began sending Hill-drafted legislation down to the Office of Legislative Reference for similar screening (Wayne 1978, 74).

The information gathered by the Office of Legislative Reference was helpful in the second routine: recommending whether the president should sign or veto an enrolled bill.[7] When Congress sent a bill to the White House for signature or veto, the Office of Legislative Reference (which had been following the bill since its initial clearance) gathered agency views once again, compiled them, and forwarded the agency views together with its own recommendation about a signature or veto, as well as a statement the president could release on signing the bill and a veto message that could be sent to Congress if the president chose that course. By 1939, there was a recognized White House staff member who received these recommendations from the Budget Bureau and forwarded them to the president (Neustadt 1954, 656).[8]

The Office of Legislative Reference did not give up these functions when President Eisenhower created the legislative liaison office. It continued to monitor virtually all legislation moving to and from the Hill, while the liaison staff was active on major bills. The legislative reference office remained influential because of its head, Roger W. Jones. Jones, a career civil servant, was highly respected for his knowledge and professionalism and was among those President Eisenhower chose

---

[6] A much larger number of bills are now designated "in accord" (which facilitates their sponsoring agencies' tasks in seeking support for them) than can possibly be of prime concern to the president. "Things get on that [in accord] list for a lot of different reasons," an OMB official explained.

[7] An enrolled bill has been passed by the House and the Senate but not yet signed into law by the president.

[8] In time the information accumulated by these clearance procedures gave the Budget Bureau an invaluable historical perspective. If someone in an administration made a proposal in, say, 1969, the bureau could tell the president and his immediate advisers that something similar had been proposed in 1941; that there had been another variation on this idea in 1947; that in 1962 still another approach had been tried, and so on.

to consult. "For reasons best known to himself," Jones later recalled, "Ike would sometimes stop and talk to me when he saw me around the White House. Several times he took me out in the backyard when he was getting ready to hit golf balls" (Wayne 1978, 77).

The legislative liaison office and the Office of Legislative Reference work closely together, but they do different jobs. The White House legislative liaison team lobbies in behalf of legislation of greatest interest to the president, while the Office of Legislative Reference conducts its clearance procedures for all legislation.

In recent decades, the task of clearance on enrolled bills has been split between the Office of Legislative Reference and the Domestic Policy Staff. The Office of Legislative Reference continues to act as the link between the president and the executive agencies. Once the agency opinions are in hand, they are forwarded to the OMB director's office. A memorandum summarizing agency views, as well as stating OMB views, is then sent to the president over the signature of the OMB director. The domestic staff does essentially the same job within the White House. Staff members canvass the views of the legislative liaison office, the counsel's office, and other relevant White House personnel. The domestic staff memo goes to the president over the signature of his assistant for domestic policy. Like the OMB memo, it summarizes the views of other participants and gives the personal view of the head of the domestic staff about whether the enrolled bill should be signed or vetoed.

## Coordination

*Coordination at the Top.* When Franklin Roosevelt was president, Rep. Sam Rayburn sent word that it would be useful if the congressional leadership could meet with the president from time to time. Thus began a series of regular White House meetings between the president and congressional leaders to coordinate White House and congressional strategy at the very top. As is the case with other useful innovations, these meetings have continued in succeeding administrations.

These meetings have been particularly useful when the president is personally interested in the progress of legislation on the Hill and when there is unified party control so there can be an open discussion of strategy. This was the case in the Kennedy and Johnson administrations. The agenda for the meeting was a large chart giving the status of each major bill. Discussion proceeded from item to item, with the president expressing his wishes and the legislative leaders giving their estimates of the likelihood of passage. Strategy agreements tended to be rather general, with details left in the hands of the congressional leaders (Johnson 1971, 456; Edwards 1980, 122–123).

Leadership meetings have been part of every administration's calendar. "The Big Ritual in every White House has been the formal meetings with the legislative leaders" (Patterson 1988, 152). Yet the frequency of such meetings declined sharply during the Clinton administration. During the second year of the Bush administration, thirty-six gatherings were held: twenty-three with congressional leaders, eleven with Republican leaders, and two with Democratic leaders. (Nine more meetings were held with various members of Congress, sometimes including leaders.) In contrast, only seven meetings with legislative leaders occurred during the entire second year of the Clinton administration. President Clinton spent little time coordinating strategy with legislative leaders.

*Coordinating Liaison Units.* Staff-level coordination began after the creation of the White House Legislative Liaison Office in the Eisenhower administration. The departmental liaison heads, acting independently, soon realized they "were killing each other" and began meeting in the White House (Holtzman 1970, 259). They met on Saturday morning in anticipation of a Tuesday meeting between the president and the congressional leadership, and their conversation shaped the agenda for the Tuesday meeting (Lacy 1967, 25). The links between the White House and departmental liaison operations were tightened during the Kennedy administration. "I called in the directors of these agency congressional relations offices," Larry O'Brien recollected, "and reminded them that there must be one administration legislative program, not dozens of competing agency programs" (O'Brien 1974, 110). O'Brien adapted the Eisenhower system by instructing the departmental liaison directors to submit a report by noon every Monday, and these were used to prepare for the Tuesday morning meeting with the legislative leadership. The weekly reports have become routine, arriving regularly at the White House over the years. But while all White Houses are able to coordinate lobbying on matters of personal interest to the president, administrations have varied in their ability to keep all the departmental liaison personnel reading on the same page (Collier 1997, 244–246).

## Congressional Liaison Activities

### Obtaining a Hearing for Members' Proposals

Kenneth Duberstein, speaking when he was Reagan's principal assistant for legislative affairs, said he and his staff went out of their way to be accessible to members, and they picked up a lot of ideas in which members were interested. When members were asked if the administration would consider an idea, liaison personnel would put it into White House policy channels and track it. At a minimum, Duberstein explained, they would see to it that the idea "gets a fair hearing and make sure that one way or another they get a good response and sometimes [liaison personnel would] weigh in on their behalf." Dan Tate, Senate liaison for the Carter administration, made a similar point about helping particularly important senators:

> Let's say it's the chairman of the Finance Committee, and he wants a tax credit for something. Well, even though we may be opposed to tax credits generally, we have to take into account that it is the chairman of the Finance Committee, the tax-writing committee, that wants this tax credit. So I will call Stuart Eizenstat, Jim McIntyre, and the secretary of the Treasury, and try to find out if there is any way that we can accommodate him. Maybe not support what he wants completely, but give him, say, a modified version.

It is worth emphasizing the portion of Ken Duberstein's comment where he says that the liaison personnel want to make sure that the member's idea "gets a fair hearing . . . and a good response." This doesn't mean agreement. What the liaison staff wants to do is to ensure that the proposal is considered, avoid trouble, and make sure the member gets a candid answer. Carter House liaison Bill Cable reinforced the view that members preferred getting accurate information about their legislative proposals, even if the news was negative:

> Even if the answer is that it is the worst goddamned project that has ever been sent to the Department of X, that it has no merit, and that it will never be funded even if you try for the next 500 years, a guy is much happier with an accurate answer than he is with being jerked around for six or eight months, and then getting an answer that says all this time has been wasted anyway.

## Handling Projects and Patronage

Projects, particularly those that involve spending large amounts of money and hiring numerous employees, are important to members who want to help their districts. Many of these come from the Departments of Defense and Housing and Urban Development. The Kennedy administration worked out a manner of handling defense projects that spread the political credit. To protect merit, Defense Department contract specialists would first decide to whom the project should be awarded; to gain favor on Capitol Hill, the White House would notify members that the project was going to be awarded to their district or state; to gain credit with the voters, the member would make the public announcement. Defense Secretary Robert McNamara eventually objected to this after Sen. Margaret

Chase Smith, the ranking minority member of the Armed Services Committee, complained that Sen. Edmund Muskie was getting to make all the announcements about projects benefiting their home state of Maine. President Johnson raised the subject with Larry O'Brien, who said that "those announcements were our life's blood, our chief means of supporting those members of Congress who supported us" (O'Brien 1974, 183). The president sided with O'Brien on this, and the system remained in place.

Both the White House and the members spend a great deal of time on congressionally inspired projects. One estimate is that White House staffers made some 12,800 telephone calls in 1965 to pass along good news to the members (Bowles 1987, 78). When working in behalf of a 1963 public works bill, the Kennedy administration compiled a list of some 250 members whose districts would be nurtured by passing the legislation (Ripley 1972, 18). On the congressional side, in the spring of 1963 Carl Perkins sent the White House staff eighteen separate requests for projects for his Kentucky district. All these were approved, and Perkins asked for still more (Bowles 1987, 82). And House liaison Henry Hall Wilson sent a note to a Johnson administration defense official:

> Would you get with Rep. Gonzales (D-TX), and tell him I sent you . . . and ask him if there are any problems in the Defense area you can help him with. You'll get plenty. His district has always been represented by a member of the Armed Services Committee. Through the years they have totally loaded it up with installations, and he thus is compelled to fight a constant rearguard action to hold what he has. But he's totally our guy and we need to help him heavily at least to hold the status quo (Bowles 1987, 89).

Part of Jimmy Carter's early difficulties with Congress resulted from his distaste for such pork barrel politics. He considered most water projects to be a waste of public money. Determined to confront the practice head on, Carter's initial budget deleted nineteen water projects in seventeen states. President Carter may have been right in his judgment of the merit of many of the projects, but his decision came without notice and affected many Senate and House committee chairs. This was one of several moves that Carter thought were good policy but that undermined the trust needed to sustain good relationships between the White House and Congress (Jones 1988a, 143–149).

Patronage presents closely related problems. Administrative positions are highly prized by senators and representatives, not only because such positions give them an opportunity to reward loyal supporters but also because they give them a pipeline into the agencies concerned. Yet patronage is a less useful device for cultivating Congress than it once was. The number of positions is quite limited in comparison to the demand for jobs. (In the first three weeks after the 1980 election, according to one estimate, the incoming Reagan administration received 8,000 resumes.) This means, of course, that more people must be turned down than can be placed in jobs, and the rejection displeases their congressional sponsors. Many jobs require skills that can command greater salaries in the private sector. This isn't to argue that legislators have given up trying to place protégés, or that administrations don't try to accommodate them, only that are too few appointments for patronage to be used routinely as a way to keep legislators happy.

## Helping Members Campaign

"He's coming." Thus began a conversation between a presidential staffer and an aide to a senator who was in a difficult race for reelection. The senator was anxious for the president to make an appearance on his behalf; when that was established, the aides could turn to such specifics as the date and time of the chief executive's arrival. Even if a president cannot transfer his personal popularity to a congressional candidate, he can attract crowds and media attention to the legislator's campaign.

Every modern president does this, even those reputed to be unconcerned about politics. Dwight Eisenhower, for example, was cautioned against campaigning for a candidate in New Jersey on the grounds that the candidate's probable defeat could be attributed to Eisenhower, thus lowering the president's prestige. Eisenhower replied that he didn't care. "He's our man, and I want to help him." John Kennedy campaigned for Democrats in congressional races in 1962 until he was forced to return to Washington by the Cuban Missile Crisis. Richard Nixon sought an "ideological majority" in 1970. Gerald Ford strove to limit Watergate damage to Republican incumbents in 1974. Ronald Reagan and George Bush crisscrossed the country in behalf of legislative candidates while they were in the White House. And all presidents sent their vice presidents and other administration spokespersons into the fray on behalf of their party's candidates.

Fellow partisans are invited to the White House for a picture-taking session with the president. This is a mass affair. Each candidate has only a moment to shake the presidential hand, smile into the camera, and perhaps say a word or two. But the photo can be featured on television and in newspaper ads as evidence that the president hopes the candidate will be elected. Similar use can be made of letters sent to representatives or senators thanking them for their help in passing particular pieces of legislation.[9]

---

[9.] For that reason, John Kennedy would send thank you notes to Democrats but telephone Republicans who had been particularly helpful.

Perhaps most important is the president's fund-raising capacity. From the spring of 1985 through late October 1986, Ronald Reagan made thirty-one appearances on behalf of Republican Senate candidates. The smallest amount of money he raised on these occasions was $72,000 in North Carolina, but he had already picked up $620,000 in that state on a previous visit. And George Bush had raised an estimated $80 million by late October 1990. Campaigning is becoming ever more expensive, but when presidents can attract this amount of money, they can help legislators who help them.

## Maintaining Goodwill

Among the many recommendations forwarded to President Ford by his legislative liaison staff was a request that he meet with the nephew of a representative. No business was involved. The nephew and his wife were going to be in Washington and simply wanted to meet the president. The representative was not particularly influential; he was not a committee chair and certainly not a party leader. Was this meeting worth the time of the president of the United States? The legislative liaison staff thought so, and Gerald Ford, who had spent a quarter-century on Capitol Hill, agreed. So he took a few minutes to greet the couple, asking them to please give his respects to their uncle. This was not a matter of state but a personal favor to the member. A great deal of attention is given to such small kindnesses.

Presidents keep a supply of small gifts—tie clips, cufflinks, pens, bracelets, and so forth—close at hand so these tokens can be given to congressional guests. Each has the presidential seal (or some other reminder of the president) affixed. In some respects, they are similar to the campaign gimmicks, such as combs, emery boards, and football schedules, the members themselves pass out to constituents while campaigning. Why should they be moved when a president does essentially the same thing? Part of the answer is the importance of the president. Each token is a tangible reminder of their personal tie to this most influential leader.

Personal visits to the White House are also meaningful. Legislative leaders, of course, see the president regularly. When Hubert Humphrey, close to the end of his career, was unable to gain election as majority leader, Democratic senators created the post of deputy president pro tempore for him. "When the leaders go down to the White House to meet with the president, I'll be going with them," Humphrey commented. "That's what's important." Rank-and-file members are included in larger gatherings. During the Kennedy administration all Democrats in the House and Senate were invited for receptions in groups of fifty, and coffee hours and bill-signing ceremonies brought 500 members of the two houses into contact with the president. The legislative liaison office kept careful records of the number of contacts between President Kennedy and legislators. There were some 2,500 in the first year alone (O'Brien 1974, 111; Ripley 1972, 18).

Cruises on the presidential yacht and trips on the presidential aircraft provide still more opportunities for personal contact. Legislative liaison personnel are more likely to ride on the yacht than the president himself, but an invitation to go down river to Mount Vernon and back is attractive. The evening cruises are primarily social, but they do afford time for substantive conversation. Larry O'Brien claimed the *Sequoia* was "the most effective lobbying device I ever found" (1974, 149). Jimmy Carter, anxious to show he was not wasting money on an opulent lifestyle, sold the yacht, and, as Nigel Bowles has pointed out "saved a little money at the price of sorely needed influence" (1987, 97).[10] Trips aboard *Air Force One* are a little different because of the president's presence. Members have contact with the president, and they gain the public recognition of stepping off the aircraft with the president when he arrives in the member's home state. If there is a public ceremony, TV cameras show the legislator along with the president. President Ford paid close attention to invitations to members to ride on Air Force One.

The importance of purely social contacts should not be overlooked. If a representative can arrange for a constituent to meet briefly with the president, it is a demonstration that the representative is a person of consequence. When a senator is able to say, "When I was talking with the president last Thursday . . . ," it is a reminder that the legislator is part of a vital decision network. And perhaps most important of all, attention to the personal needs of legislators is within the capacity of the president and his staff to bestow. When legislators ask for help with a project requiring substantial funds, the White House must consider its cost and may have to say no. Further, the president almost always has to oppose some members on particular pieces of legislation. But the president can always smile and shake hands. Subject only to the limits of time, presidential and staff attention to the members' personal needs is one of the most expendable resources the White House has.

## Information Gathering in Congressional Relations

Everyone needs information on whether legislators intend to vote for or against a bill. Assembling head counts is vital business. In February 1961, Larry O'Brien, still unacquainted with many House members, met with veteran Democratic

---

[10.] Another presidential yacht was purchased with private funds when Ronald Reagan entered office.

representatives Frank Thompson (N.J.), Richard Bolling (Mo.), and Carl Elliott (Ala.). The members "went through the entire list of the House membership, recalling invaluable details about each member's friends, interests, and voting record, while [aides] Henry Wilson, Dick Donahue, and I scribbled furiously" (O'Brien 1974, 110). The analysis showed that the Kennedy administration was twenty votes short of what it needed to pass liberal legislation, and dictated attention to Southern Democrats who might provide the missing votes. By the time of the Johnson administration, head counts on individual bills contained detailed information on individual members' positions. On the surtax to help cover expenses of the Vietnam War, for example, liaison staff members reported:

Harley Staggers: I'll do whatever the president wants. Just tell me.

Mo Udall: I can go either way. The $6 billion [spending cut that was to accompany the tax cut] is too high, but I'll support it if the president wants it.

John Brademas: What really bothers [me] is that the surtax package . . . does not contain anything that is calculated to make it politically attractive to the voters of [my] district (Bowles 1987, 124; Sullivan 1990, 1175).

In order to estimate the likelihood the House would pass President Carter's 1977 energy bill, the legislative liaison staff worked with a brief questionnaire distributed to their colleagues by Democratic representatives Bob Eckhardt (Texas) and Andrew Maguire (N.J.). Eckhardt and Maguire had asked the members' views on a few energy-related issues. As House liaison Bill Cable explained, the results were entered into a computer file, and staff members added votes members had cast on energy-related issues in preceding years. This combination of attitudes and votes allowed them to predict probable votes on several important roll calls. On the Senate side, Dan Tate did not share his head counts with anyone. He placed senators into five categories: committed for the president, leaning for, undecided or unknown, leaning against the president, and committed against. Tate would concentrate his efforts on those who were leaning toward the president's position or were undecided, but wouldn't neglect the senators who were leaning against.

Just before the crucial June 1981 procedural vote that allowed final passage of the Reagan budget, the president was given a list of members whom he phoned from the West Coast. Max Friedersdorf, Reagan's chief congressional liaison, said that it was relatively easy to put together the list of persons to be contacted:

We've had enough votes now that the patterns are established. We know who on the Republican side and who on the Democratic side are vulnerable to switching for or against us. Our House staff of five members constantly monitors those House members to know if there's any slippage. The essential thing is that we had the correct intelligence on who was being ripped away by the Democrats, and who needed presidential shoring up.

The techniques of head counting have varied slightly from one person to another, but the need to obtain this information has remained constant.

Although information about support and opposition to bills is the crucial component of legislative intelligence, liaison personnel pick up other news as well. Legislative anger is reported as well as legislative pleasure. For example, Sen. Mike Mansfield received a notice from the Veterans' Administration that it intended to close a VA hospital in Montana. This was important to Mansfield; it would require his constituents to drive great distances to reach another VA hospital. "Lawrence," the soft-spoken senator said after a brief discussion with O'Brien, "I have a message for you to give the President. You tell him that I object strenuously to this action and I don't intend to accept it." Lyndon Johnson felt strongly that the hospital should be closed to save money, but it stayed open. Even Lyndon Johnson couldn't resist the wishes of the Senate majority leader on an issue such as this (O'Brien 1974, 171).

The importance of information from Capitol Hill depends on the president's view of Congress. Lyndon Johnson and Gerald Ford, both former legislative party leaders, had considerable respect for Congress. Ford stressed not only that it was important to listen to legislators, but that they should be consulted before decisions were made about the content of the legislative program:

> I think a president has to give the leaders in the Congress and influential members of both parties an open door to come and take part in policy decisions. He doesn't have to guarantee he will do what they say, but at least they have to have the feeling that their views are considered before the fact, not after. . . . Even if he does not agree with [their advice], he can then go back [to them] and ask for their help, and he would be in a much better position to get results (Jones 1988a, 71).

Closely related to the president's view of Congress is the question of whether a congressional liaison chief has immediate access to the president. Lyndon Johnson gave standing orders to the White House switchboard to put Larry O'Brien through to him at any hour of the day or night (O'Brien 1974, 170). Similarly, aides spoke of the unlimited access President Carter granted his chief congressional liaison, Frank Moore: "There was no shop in the White House, thanks to Frank, who had better communication and more instant communication with Jimmy Carter on [legislative] issues and on tactics and strategy than we did" (Jones 1988a, 110). Richard Nixon, however, had less interest in congressional liaison, and especially in the latter days of his administration, it was difficult to get through to him.

## Decision Making in Congressional Relations

Many decisions about legislation have to be made on the spot, and therefore are made by legislative aides rather than the president. Larry O'Brien recalled an incident concerning a bill to raise the minimum wage. O'Brien was meeting with Speaker Sam Rayburn and other Democrats concerned with this bill. At one point, he said, "Everyone in the room turned to me and said, 'well what's [President Kennedy's] view?' Well, I wasn't going to pick up the phone and ask the president, when I was in a better position at the moment perhaps than he was. It was up to me to do it and I made the judgment" (Wayne 1978, 148). Carter's Senate aide, Dan Tate, discussed the staff's role a little more generally:

> A senator or his staff person will say, "We don't think we are going to be able to help you on this particular issue because you haven't been helpful to us on a matter that we've been working on. Well, I have to make the decision. Can I commit to him to try to help him with the issue he's been working on? Sometimes I don't have much time to decide. Almost invariably, I'll know either that we're interested in it, but we just haven't been able to devote much manpower to it, and I'll say sure, we'll be happy to, or I'll know that the issue is not an administration priority, or we may even be opposed to it, and I'll tell him no. In that respect, I'm announcing a policy decision based on what I believe our administration policy would be if we sat down and had a meeting over it.

Presidents are not disturbed about senior liaison personnel exercising this kind of discretion. In fact, Lyndon Johnson gave his congressional liaison staff blanket authority to make trades involving an exchange of favors, contracts, and the like. The members of the staff, following Congress more closely than other White House staffers, were more likely to be conservative in their use of presidential bargaining chips (Bowles 1987, 85).

Presidents vary in the ways they make their decisions and the strategies they use to implement them. Lyndon Johnson tended to focus on persons he called the Whales, members held in high regard by their colleagues, whether they held formal leadership positions or not. For example, when Earl Warren tendered his resignation as chief justice in 1968, Johnson decided to elevate two close associates: Associate Justice Abe Fortas to become chief justice, and Homer Thornberry to be promoted from the Federal Court of Appeals to Fortas's seat on the Supreme Court. In this instance, Johnson followed a strategy he often used in the Senate, working through Sen. Richard Russell of Georgia to obtain the support of southern Democrats and relying on Minority Leader Everett Dirksen to bring along fellow Republicans. In this case, though, the strategy was ill-fated. Russell withdrew his support because he thought the nominations were related to a patronage matter in Georgia; Dirksen underestimated his fellow Republicans' determination to oppose any Johnson nominee and ultimately joined the opposition himself (Bowles 1987, chap. 7; Clifford 1991, 554–559; MacNeil 1970, 332–335).

As Charles O. Jones has pointed out, each of Johnson's successors had a distinctive decision-making style. In Richard Nixon's case, timing had a lot to do with it. If the decision came close to the beginning of the Nixon administration, or if a bill was on Capitol Hill and needed congressional support for the president's position, legislative views were likely to be taken into consideration. But if it was a matter of general administration priorities, or came later when Nixon increasingly saw himself surrounded by enemies, he didn't care as much about Congress. Gerald Ford was much more sympathetic to congressional views. He was hampered, though, by a lack of public support after the Nixon pardon and by an oversize Democratic majority after the 1974 election. Aides saw Jimmy Carter as "a common cause monarch" who wanted to speak on behalf of the people. Especially at the beginning of his administration, Carter felt decisions should be made on the basis of what was right and that legislators should recognize the intrinsic merit of administration bills (Jones 1981, 229–231; Jones 1988a, 79–83).

The Reagan administration had several venues for making decisions, of which the most important was the legislative strategy group (LSG). This group was chaired by Chief of Staff James Baker and met in Baker's office. Its regular members were Ed Meese and Mike Deaver (who, along with Baker, were the senior troika during Reagan's first term), Craig Fuller (the cabinet secretary), Richard Darman (Baker's principal assistant, who drafted the group's agenda), and Ken Duberstein (Reagan's principal legislative aide). Cabinet members were asked to meet with LSG when their departments had business to be discussed. This practice both supplied departmental expertise and, since the cabinet members were there by invitation, made it clear that the senior White House staff had the upper hand in decisions. Sometimes LSG would discuss as many as eight agenda items, in which case the meetings might last as long as two-and-a-half hours. More commonly, however, the meetings dealt with only one or two items and were concluded in fifteen or twenty minutes. The LSG was clearly action oriented, and was arguably the most important decision-making group in the Reagan White House.

Since chiefs of staff are so important, and there is not a chapter devoted to them, a sketch of their responsibilities is presented in the accompanying (Box 2–2). A list of those who have served as chief of staff appears in (Box 2–3).

**Box 2–2   The Chief of Staff**

The chief of staff's position originated at the beginning of the Eisenhower administration with the appointment of New Hampshire governor Sherman Adams (see Box 2–3). For some time, there was argument over whether a chief of staff was needed, but by the late twentieth century the position was a fixture. His responsibilities may be summarized as presenting information to the president, communicating the president's wishes to others, often making decisions himself in order to free the president for more consequential choices, and increasingly, taking the lead in specific activities in which he has an interest.

Donald Rumsfeld, Ford's first chief of staff, states that it's rare for an issue worthy of presidential attention to involve only one cabinet member or one element of the White House staff (Kernell and Popkin 1986, 112). Consequently, one responsibility of the chief of staff is to see to it that all information bearing on choices the president must make is presented to the president. As Andrew Goodpaster, Eisenhower's staff secretary, put it, "When an issue [that cuts across several agencies] comes up, it is the duty of the staff, first of all, to call on people to get their facts in hand and prepare themselves, and if it's an important issue, to bring in the people who have the responsibility so they can sit in front of the president so the thing can be shredded out" (Kernell and Popkin 1986, 114).

Sometimes special action is needed to make sure a president hears arguments from all his advisers, and not just from those with whom he is likely to agree. Richard Nixon, for example, was much taken with Treasury Secretary John Connally. Hence one of Chief of Staff H. R. Haldeman's obligations was to figure out ways to ensure that his other economic advisers—Paul McCracken, Herbert Stein, George Shultz, and Arthur Burns—got a chance to explain their views to the president as well (Kernell and Popkin 1986, 171).

When a chief of staff is speaking to other White House aides or members of the administration, it must be clear when he is speaking for the president and when he is expressing his own views. Arthur Flemming, Eisenhower's secretary of health, education and welfare, once told about an experience with Sherman Adams. He had brought a series of proposals to the White House; Adams, a taciturn New Englander, was going down the list, "yes, no, no, no, yes," telling Flemming what the decisions would be. Then he came to one item, looked up, and commented, "I don't know what he thinks about this." So saying, Adams got up, and he and Flemming walked into the Oval Office to ask Eisenhower's view about this one item. That done, the two returned to Adams's office, and he resumed conveying the rest of Eisenhower's decisions to Flemming.

*(continued)*

An important part of the chief of staff's coordinating responsibilities is dealing with officials who are upset over a decision that has been made or who are angry with some other member of the administration. When there is a collision between strong egos, someone has to mollify the combatants. As Dick Cheney recalled:

> I can't count the number of times I would get a phone call, probably about once a month, and it would be a situation in which Pat Moynihan was calling or Henry Kissinger was threatening to resign because they didn't like each other. I remember . . . [one] very hot day in July in Williamsburg, Virginia. . . . I was in a closet upstairs on the White House telephone with Pat Moynihan trying one more time to keep Pat from resigning because Henry had said something about him that had been printed in [the *New York Times*] (Kernell and Popkin 1986, 149–150).

There is a limit to this kind of stroking. Hence, a chief of staff always has to weigh the time it takes to calm someone down against the cost of recruiting a suitable replacement if the appointee does resign.

Many interpersonal conflicts involve policy choices. The chief of staff, Jack Watson explained,

> is a problem solver, someone to whom problems are brought that people don't necessarily want to take to the president, or [even more important for the chief of staff's own problem-solving responsibilities] some cases that they would like to take to the president, but which ought not to be taken to the president. It's the responsibility of the chief of staff in that role to get the necessary people together to reconcile differences.

In addition to directing staff activity, some chiefs of staff take an active role in specific substantive areas. All recent chiefs of staff have been involved with Congress. In the first Reagan term, James Baker was *the* key player as head of the Legislative Strategy Group. Second-term chiefs of staff Howard Baker and Ken Duberstein had been Senate majority leader and Reagan's principal legislative liaison, respectively. Bush Chief of Staff John Sununu kept much decision-making authority for himself, leaving the principal legislative liaison, Frederick McClure, out of the loop and without enough standing on Capitol Hill (Collier 1997, 234). Leon Panetta, erstwhile chair of the House Budget Committee, had a better feel for Congress than President Clinton, and Erskine Bowles was effective in maintaining ties to his fellow southerners who were leading the congressional Republican Party.

Box 2–3    **White House Chiefs of Staff**

| President | Chief of Staff | Years |
|---|---|---|
| Eisenhower | Sherman Adams | 1953–1958 |
| | Wilton B. Persons Jr. | 1958–1961 |
| Nixon | H. R. Haldeman | 1969–1973 |
| | Alexander Haig | 1973–1974 |
| Ford | Donald Rumsfeld | 1974–1975 |
| | Dick Cheney | 1975–1977 |
| Carter | Hamilton Jordan | 1979–1980 |
| | Jack H. Watson Jr. | 1980–1981 |
| Reagan | James A. Baker III | 1981–1985 |
| | Donald T. Regan | 1985–1987 |
| | Howard H. Baker Jr. | 1987–1988 |
| | Kenneth Duberstein | 1988–1989 |
| Bush | John H. Sununu | 1989–1991 |
| | Samuel K. Skinner | 1992 |
| | James A. Baker III | 1992–1993 |
| Clinton | Thomas F. (Mack) McLarty III | 1993–1994 |
| | Leon E. Panetta | 1994–1996 |
| | Erskine B. Bowles | 1997–1998 |
| | John Podesta | 1998– |

## Exercising Influence in Congressional Relations

Obtaining congressional support for presidential initiatives is the principal concern of all White House–Capitol Hill contacts. Appeals to members can be made directly, or the White House can work through someone else. A solicitation from the president himself is the most difficult for a representative or senator to resist, but since it is the ultimate appeal, it is not invoked too often. If members feel they can talk directly with the president, they may not be willing to speak frankly with his emissaries, and of course the White House wants members to feel that conversations with the president are something special.

Virtually all presidents make direct appeals.[11] In one instance, the Senate had

---

[11.] Richard Nixon was an exception. He did not have much contact with members, and when there was personal contact he did not want to ask members for their votes (Jones 1983, 114).

reacted sharply to President Carter's approval of India's 1980 request for nuclear fuel for its Terapur power plant. There were strong arguments on both sides. Opponents, led by Sen. John Glenn (D-Ohio), maintained that since India had used U.S. and Canadian fuel to build an atom bomb in 1974, the issue was a test of U.S. determination to follow its announced nuclear nonproliferation policy. President Carter's supporters felt the United States had an overriding concern with preserving close ties to India, particularly in view of the Soviet invasion of Afghanistan in late 1979. The secretaries of state or defense were asked to make initial appeals to wavering senators. Once their reports were in, Senate liaison Dan Tate went from senator to senator to ascertain their intent. Then the administration started all over again, with the secretary of defense lobbying those who had been contacted by the secretary of state, and vice versa. Finally, President Carter made calls to appeal to undecided and uncommitted senators. The administration ultimately won an extremely close vote.

Lyndon Johnson was quite willing to put pressure on, as in this televised encounter with Virginia's reactionary Sen. Harry Byrd:

Johnson: I know that you will take an interest in the orderly scheduling of this matter and giving it a thorough hearing. (Byrd said nothing.) Would you care to make an observation?

Byrd: There is no observation I can make now, because the bill hasn't come before the Senate. Naturally, I'm not familiar with it.

Johnson: And you have nothing that you know of that would prevent hearings coming about in reasonable time, nothing ahead of it in the Committee?

Byrd: Nothing in the Committee now.

Johnson: So when the House acts and it is referred to the Senate Finance Committee you will arrange for prompt hearings and thorough hearings?

Byrd: Yes.

Johnson: Good!

President Clinton was also willing to make very direct appeals. One member recalled his saying: "Pat, without your vote the bill is dead. My presidency is on the line. I need you, pal!"

Liaison staff members customarily begin their work on Capitol Hill by checking in with the leaders of the president's party. When working on behalf of Reagan, Ken Duberstein began by talking with Senate Majority Leader Howard Baker, and with Bob Michel and Trent Lott, the Republican leader and whip, on the House side. From there, he would fan out, with the identity of his contacts varying depending on the issue. Pam Turner, the Reagan administration Senate liaison, told how she would first go to Howard Baker to "explain the administration position to him, the reasons for taking that position, and ask him for his guidance. Often [Baker] will hear things from other Republican members and will tip us off as to where our problems might be or who might be helpful." From that point, she would expand her contacts with the relevant committee chairs, committee members, and so forth. Party leaders are also very helpful in bringing along recalcitrant members in the later stages of majority building.

At times, presidents work with their partisan opponents, especially when the president's party has a small majority and needs opposition votes to compensate for defections or when his party is in the minority and must augment its numbers. And, of course, appeals to partisan opponents are more likely on issues on which agreement is possible. The small majority in the Kennedy administration was in need of votes, but the administration tended to seek Republican aid only on foreign policy and civil rights, issue areas where GOP members were most likely to agree with Kennedy. For example, Dwight Eisenhower and Richard Nixon both endorsed Kennedy's limited test ban treaty in 1963, and Minority Leader Dirksen worked for its ratification. Lucius Clay, a retired general who was close to Eisenhower, sent a letter to selected Republicans urging them to support foreign aid that same year (Ripley 1972, 17). The Reagan administration had the advantage of a Republican Senate for six years but faced a Democratic majority in the House. The administration worked very closely with Phil Gramm of Texas, who was then a Democratic member of the House Budget Committee. With Gramm's help, especially his willingness to provide confidential Democratic plans to the Republicans, the Reagan administration was able to pick up enough votes from conservative Southern Democrats to prevail on the 1982 budget. When Bill Clinton was facing a Republican Congress, his aide John Hilley was willing to give Speaker Newt Gingrich some concessions to reduce animosity when the president's agenda was being considered (Simendinger 1997, 2254).

Still another route goes through interest groups. The most comprehensive effort was led by Anne Wexler when she headed Carter's Office of Public Liaison. Interest groups' goals were taken into account as the administration's program was being assembled. Every fall Wexler and her aides met with various groups to make sure they understood what the interest groups' priorities were, and to make sure that the groups were aware of administration plans and what the White House expected of them. Once the legislation was drafted, the public liaison staff continued to work to be sure that "people who work at the subcommittee level have an opportunity to lobby with us, but also to testify on our behalf." The number of meetings with interest groups increased as the congressional session moved forward. Sometimes, Wexler continued, by the end of a legislative session, we're having biweekly or even daily meetings "with ten different coalitions because we've got ten different priorities all working on the Hill at the same time. It gets very crazy at the end."

The most effective interest group network supporting the Reagan administration was the business community's effort to support reductions in federal spending. The structure of the Budget Control Working Group, as it was known, had an executive committee, a steering committee, and roughly five hundred companies and trade associations as members. Another six hundred or so companies and trade associations were associated with it at the peak of its activities. Wayne Valis, the Office of Public Liaison staff member who maintained contact with the business community, recalled:

> I would go to the steering committee meeting of typically eighty people and give them information about where we were having difficulties on the Hill, where we were going to need help, what our legislative timetable was, and what our strategy was. They would give me information on what they were picking up on the Hill, intelligence, what members were saying what, who needed work, what they were objecting to in private, information that we could tailor so that the president or other [White House] staff could then go back to those members and try to dispose of their objections.

A single trade association generated 15,000 telegrams to different members of Congress, so it is no exaggeration to say that this business network triggered millions of communications to representatives and senators about the need to reduce federal spending.

Finally, a president can appeal to citizens in the hope that they will let members know that the president's proposals have public support. John Kennedy did not make many public appeals in 1961 because his initial agenda consisted of programs already familiar to Democrats on the Hill. In 1962 and 1963, however, he began to speak out to build support for more novel bills. Kennedy addressed both the National Association of Manufacturers and the AFL-CIO (the largest organization of labor unions) in behalf of a 1962 trade-expansion bill, spoke at a pro-Medicare rally in Madison Square Garden in May 1962, and laid out details of a forthcoming tax-revision proposal late that same year (Ripley 1972, 15–16).

One of the most convincing speeches in behalf of a single bill was given by Dwight Eisenhower in August 1959. Revelations of union scandals, especially in the Teamsters, led to calls for anticorruption legislation, and the administration had made proposals. The Democratic-led Senate, however, passed a bill introduced by Sen. John F. Kennedy that was closer to what organized labor wanted. The House was to consider three bills: a Shelley bill endorsed by the AFL-CIO, an Elliott bill that was similar to the Kennedy bill passed by the Senate, and a Landrum-Griffin bill that contained many provisions of the Kennedy bill but also administration pro-posals excluded in both the Shelley and the Elliott bills. In his speech, Eisenhower outlined the three bills and then said of Landrum-Griffin: "I want that bill." He spoke with such force that the resulting mail convinced a third of the Democrats to vote for Landrum-Griffin. One presidential speech prevailed in the face of a 283 to 154 Democratic majority and determined labor union opposition.

## Summary

*Actors.* Staff members of the White House legislative liaison office are the agents who speak most directly for the president and who are most concerned with high-priority legislation. The departmental legislative units cooperate with the White House staff on administration legislative initiatives but are specifically responsi-ble for legislation originating in their home department. The Office of Legislative Reference judges all legislation to determine whether or not it is in accord with the president's overall program, and tracks it thereafter. Coordination between the president and legislative leaders is handled in meetings between these parties, while the president's chief legislative assistant coordinates efforts between his or her staff and departmental legislative units.

*Congressional Liaison Activities.* Those working with the members make sure the administration is aware of the legislators' proposals, channel their requests for projects and patronage to administration decision makers, help members obtain campaign help, and go out of their way to maintain members' goodwill. These activities help smooth the way for legislation, but the chances of success are deter-mined more by whether the president was elected by a large majority, whether his party was able to gain seats in the same election, whether he has a high approval rating, whether his party has majorities in both chambers, whether the issue groups have preferences that correspond to the president's, and whether the leg-islative leaders and the president himself are endowed with leadership skills.

*Common Activities in a Congressional Environment.* In a congressional environment, information about whether legislators intend to support or oppose bills is the most vital. Head counts allow the president, his legislative aides, and the congressional leaders to decide whether to try to pass a bill or to hold it for a more propitious time. Further decisions are then made about whether a trade will lead a member to sup-port a bill, and about whom to contact to build legislative support. Members are sometimes approached quite directly with requests to vote for administration bills and sometimes indirectly through interest groups or the general public.

# 3. Working with the Media

## Voices of the Presidency

"I think," Pierre Salinger reflected, "that a press secretary is not in charge of handling the image of the president. The president does his own image. And John Kennedy [whom Salinger served] was a man who had a method of communication with the public which was dynamic, and was understood by people in the United States" (KPBS 1990, 2). True enough. The president's own voice is more likely to be heard by the American people than any other. But a president cannot always speak for himself, so the White House needs to call on other voices to maintain communication with the many presidential audiences.

## The Press Secretary

*Origins of the Office.* Contact between the press and the presidency has existed for a very long time. When Civil War information was lacking at the War Department, reporters went to the White House. "I know what you have come for," said Abraham Lincoln. "You want to hear more about the good news [of a Union victory]." "You have hit the matter precisely, Mr. President," one replied, "that's exactly what we want—the news" (Kumar 1995, 17). As the press grew in the late 1800s, contacts became regularized. Presidents then had only a single secretary to assist them, but Cleveland, Harrison, and McKinley all appointed men with newspaper experience. By the turn of the century, reporters had work space in the White House, received news regularly, could obtain corroboration of news they had developed themselves, and had a series of tacit understandings about the use of the news. Once publicity channels were in place, it would take only a president with the imagination to develop an activist program to transform the nature of the presidency. Theodore Roosevelt was that president (Kumar 1997b).

By the time of the Hoover administration, the presidential staff had grown to three secretaries and an administrative assistant. Hoover hired George Akerson, a former Washington correspondent, as one of the secretaries, and Akerson was referred to as the press secretary. (All of the presidential press secretaries are listed in Box 3–1.) Thus, by 1929 dealing with the press was recognized as a full-time job. Stephen Early, a newsman Franklin Roosevelt had known since 1913, was the first person to be formally appointed as press secretary when a new president took office. His office was the center of press activity; in 1935 the State Department assigned Early an assistant. The Pulitzer Prize–winning journalist Charles Ross, who had been a high school classmate of Harry Truman's, worked with one assistant when he served as Truman's first press secretary, and his successor had two assistants (Grossman and Kumar 1981, 20–26; Hult and Walcott, 1989; Kumar 1997a, 105).

When James C. Hagerty became Dwight Eisenhower's press secretary in 1953, the responsibilities of the office were well defined. Press secretaries issued press releases, held daily press briefings, alerted the president himself to probable questions before news conferences, dealt with crises, and handled logistics for reporters traveling with the president. Hagerty was assisted by a staff about as large as his immediate predecessors': an assistant press secretary, his personal secretary, and five stenographers.

Hagerty had two attributes essential to success in the office: long prior experience and the absolute confidence of his president. The son of a respected *New York Times* political correspondent, James A. Hagerty, he worked for the same paper himself until he became New York governor Thomas E. Dewey's press secretary. Hagerty spent nine years (including two presidential campaigns) working for Dewey before he became General Eisenhower's press secretary in the 1952 campaign. Hagerty was fully aware of the needs of reporters and of officeholders when he came to the White House, and in turn, reporters and officials respected him.

Two stories illustrate Eisenhower's confidence in him. When the president suffered a heart attack in Denver in 1954, Eisenhower's physician told him that Hagerty was flying out from Washington. The president said simply, "Tell Jim to take over and make the decisions—and handle the story." On another occasion, Hagerty was asked about informal influence he might have. He answered that Eisenhower had talked about his own difficulty as a member of General MacArthur's

**Box 3–1  Presidential Press Secretaries**

| President | Press Secretary | Years |
|---|---|---|
| Hoover | George Akerson | 1929–1931 |
|  | Theodore Joslin | 1931–1933 |
| Roosevelt | Stephen T. Early | 1933–1944 |
|  | Jonathan Daniels | 1944–1945 |
| Truman | Charles G. Ross | 1945–1950 |
|  | Joseph Short | 1950–1952 |
|  | Roger Tubby | 1952–1953 |
| Eisenhower | James C. Hagerty | 1953–1961 |
| Kennedy | Pierre E. Salinger | 1961–1963 |
| Johnson | Pierre E. Salinger | 1963–1964 |
|  | George Reedy | 1964–1965 |
|  | Bill Moyers | 1965–1967 |
|  | George Christian | 1967–1969 |
| Nixon | Ronald Ziegler | 1969–1974 |
| Ford | Jerald F. terHorst | 1974 |
|  | Ronald H. Nessen | 1974–1977 |
| Carter | Jody Powell | 1977–1981 |
| Reagan | James Brady | 1981 |
|  | Larry Speakes | 1981–1987 |
|  | Marlin Fitzwater | 1987–1989 |
| Bush | Marlin Fitzwater | 1989–1993 |
| Clinton | Dee Dee Myers | 1993–1994 |
|  | Michael McCurry | 1995–1998 |
|  | Joseph Lockhart | 1998–2000 |
|  | Richard J. (Jake) Siewart | 2000– |

Sources: Karen M. Hult and Charles Walcott, "To Meet the Press: Tracing the Evolution of White House Press Operations" (paper presented at the annual meeting of the Midwest Political Science Association, Chicago, April 15–17, 1989); Martha Joynt Kumar, "The President and the News Media," in *The President, the Public, and the Parties*, 2d ed. (Washington, D.C.: CQ Press, 1997).

staff in the Philippines. MacArthur never wanted to hear bad news. When Hagerty had unpleasant information to bring to Eisenhower's attention, he would go into the Oval Office and say, "Mr. President, do you remember that young major in the Philippines?" Eisenhower would respond, "All right, what's the problem now?" and the two would get down to business. Their close relationship helped.

"There wasn't any answer that I made when I *thought* I was reflecting the President's viewpoint [when speaking to the press]. The only answers I made were when I *knew* I was reflecting the President's viewpoint" (Grossman and Kumar 1981, 150).

Pierre Salinger's relationship with John Kennedy was not as close as Hagerty's with Eisenhower, nor were his responsibilities as broad. Still, some essentials of the job were the same. Salinger's initial staff was about the same size, and the relations between the press and the presidency remained respectful. Salinger reports there were "even reporters who would at my press conferences call me 'Mr. Secretary'" (KPBS 1990, 9). Two post-Salinger developments, however, changed the press office and the relationship between the press and the presidency in succeeding years: the collapse of credibility brought on by Vietnam and Watergate, and the increasing size of the press corps.

*Vietnam and Watergate.* The relations between the White House and the media have always been symbiotic and adversarial. Both need each other. The White House needs the media to communicate with the public; the media needs White House access to secure information. But the interests of the two institutions are not identical. The president needs public support to achieve political goals, and so he wants a series of favorable stories. Further, the White House wants to release stories after developing policies and building support for them within the policy community. The press, on the other hand, wants all the information, not just favorable information; furthermore, being first with the news brings the reporters and their employers valuable attention, and each paper and television outlet scrambles to publish information on the president's plans. Maintaining a balance between the mutual needs and rival goals is difficult, and is easiest to do when both sides understand the ground rules and respect one another. Unfortunately, when White House–media relations soured between 1965 and 1975, mutual respect was the casualty. The relationship became precarious on both sides.

The serious deterioration began with the Vietnam War. When President Johnson decided in July 1965 to authorize the use of 200,000 troops, he only announced an increase from 75,000 to 125,000, and just hinted that he had made an open-ended commitment (Burke and Greenstein 1989, 230). Not wanting to threaten his domestic goals, and still hoping that the war would be short, Johnson continued to make optimistic statements about the war. When the publication of the *Pentagon Papers* showed real disparity between the actual decisions and the information given to the public, reporters concluded that they had been fed a series of official lies.

Watergate had even more adverse consequences. At first the 1972 break-in at Democratic national campaign headquarters was dismissed as a "third-rate burglary" with no connection to the Nixon administration; but more serious and damning information came out over the next two years. Events led to the indict-ment of senior administration figures, passage of articles of impeachment by the House Judiciary Committee, and ultimately President Nixon's resignation. As incriminating information emerged, the attitudes in the press room turned nasty. In a private conversation during the closing months of the Nixon administration, a senior White House aide and a veteran newsman agreed that the atmosphere in the briefing room had become quite treacherous.

Members of the press had their own conflicts. Older journalists were accus-tomed to the norm of mutual respect between reporters and government. Younger journalists, more aggressive and less trusting, asked why their seniors were so deferential. With the Watergate revelations, senior reporters were left without any answer. Moreover, the most important reporting of Watergate was done by two members of the *Washington Post* metropolitan (that is, local Wash-ington area) staff, Robert Woodward and Carl Bernstein. How, the White House reporters were asked by their colleagues, could you be that close to the Oval Office and miss a story this big? So the White House press corps became much less trust-ing. And, in *Washington Post* reporter David S. Broder's words, the reporters' "pro-fessional fury carried over to the presidencies of Gerald R. Ford, Jimmy Carter, and Ronald Reagan. The style of questioning at the official White House briefings became, after Watergate, almost more prosecutorial than inquisitive" (1987, 167). Reagan's press secretary Larry Speakes concurred. "By the time I had gotten there, and I think my predecessors experienced it, it was—you would walk out there with an announcement and there was an automatic presumption in the press corps that you were lying, and so you were faced with 'Prove you're not lying'" (KPBS 1990, 11). When Marlin Fitzwater was introduced as Speakes's successor, the very first question asked was, "Will you ever lie to us?" (Fitzwater 1995, 200).

*Growth of the Press Corps.* "Once you pass a certain number of people in the press corps, all the ground rules are different, and all the relationships are different." So spoke *New York Times* correspondent James Reston after covering Washington for nearly half a century (Hess 1984, 112). The White House press corps has grown, with much of the increase taking place in recent decades. Counting the reporters who covered the White House full time and attended the press secretary's daily briefings (the "regulars"), there were fifteen to twenty during the Roosevelt administration and not many more than twenty-two decades later. By the time of the Ford administration, sixty reporters attended Ron Nessen's briefings, and roughly a hundred regulars covered the Carter White House (Mackaye 1960, 54; Grossman and Kumar 1981, 135).

About 1,700 persons hold White House press credentials today, but the number of regulars determines the size of the press staff and the facilities the White House must have to accommodate their needs. Fifty to sixty people can squeeze into the present-day press secretary's office, and under exceptional circumstances a hundred can be accommodated. The briefing room on the ground floor of the White House can hold perhaps 150. A larger briefing room in the Executive Office Building can seat roughly 250, and the room can accommodate 300 if some are willing to stand. Back when there were only twenty regulars, they could all come into the press secretary's office and have a relatively informal exchange. With the size of the present-day White House press corps, a more formal briefing is necessary.

The White House press corps has been expanding for several reasons. One is the rise of television. With the development of half-hour evening newscasts and, later, cable news services came additional reporters and their crews (plus space-hogging equipment). Another reason is the increasing importance of the federal government. Because so many presidential decisions affect individual lives, local media in many cities want their own correspondents at the White House to pursue local angles. Foreign media are equally interested in having U.S. news reported in ways their audiences can understand. Consequently, there is now a sizable international press detachment, especially from Europe and Japan. Finally, many individual correspondents are anxious to be given the White House beat. This assignment has often been a stepping stone to desirable positions in journalism (KPBS 1990, 31–34).

In part as a consequence of the increasing number of correspondents, and in part because of additional activities the press office has assumed, the White House press staff has grown. In contrast to the total staff of eight during the Eisenhower administration, there were forty-two during the Carter administration. The number dropped to seventeen in the Reagan administration, but there were thirty more in a separate communications office. Units shifted from one administration to another, but however they were organized, it still took between forty and fifty people in the principal media liaison units to deal with the needs of the press.

*The Modern Press Office.* In the contemporary White House there are several units within the press secretary's office. First, there is the *upper press office* on the first floor of the West Wing, where the press secretary and two deputy press secretaries are located. The press secretary has contact with the president, attends senior staff meetings, and communicates the wishes of the president and his key advisers to the rest of the press staff. The deputy press secretaries are the principal assistants; they handle whatever duties are assigned to them. For example, in the Carter White House, where Jody Powell was one of the president's principal advisers in addition to being press secretary, the deputy press secretaries felt a responsibility to ease Powell's workload as much as possible.

The *lower press office* is adjacent to the area where the White House–based reporters have their desks and cubicles. Claudia Townsend, an associate press secretary who headed this office in the Carter administration, explained her responsibilities this way:

> There is a large amount of routine. When you get an answer to a given question, the chances are good that particular question is going to be asked a hundred times that day. It's not necessary for Jody [Powell] to answer it a hundred times; it's not necessary for me to do so; but it's necessary for somebody to make that information available, to talk about the president's schedule [and similar matters].

By the time of the Clinton administration, two deputy press secretaries, two assistant press secretaries, and an office manager were all located in the lower press office.

The *news summary* originated in the Nixon administration. It was prepared overnight by a staff of about five and was placed on the president's desk by eight o'clock each morning. About fifty pages in length, it contained summaries of the major television newscasts, the wire service stories, and samples of stories that ran in various papers across the country. President Nixon used the summary as an administrative tool. He marked up his own copy with reactions ("This is fine." "I thought we were going to do something about this. What happened?"), and circulated it to senior aides who carried out his instructions. The news summary was used by succeeding administrations, but in the Clinton administration it was little more than a collection of clippings.

Another half-dozen persons work in the *press advance* office. Their functions are primarily logistical. They make transportation arrangements, secure hotel accommodations, and so forth, for media personnel traveling with the president. Finally, there is a *photo office* that supplies photographers to record White House events, both for internal purposes (such as giving autographed photos to guests as souvenirs of their visit with the president) and for distribution to the media.

Although the modern press secretary supervises a large staff, the press corps' judgment still rests on the criteria that Hagerty satisfied so well: having the full confidence of the president, being well informed about events throughout the White House, and knowing enough about reporters to attend to their needs in a timely fashion. Among recent press secretaries, reporters gave high marks to Jody Powell, Marlin Fitzwater, and Michael McCurry. Many complained, however, that Ron Ziegler, Ron Nessen, Larry Speakes, and Dee Dee Myers had been too often "out of the loop," and hence were less reliable sources of information (Kumar 1997a, 107).

## The Office of Communications

At the outset of the Nixon administration, the Office of Communications was created. Nixon's long-time press secretary, Herbert Klein, was appointed as communications director, while Ron Ziegler, a protégée of Nixon's Chief of Staff H. R. Haldeman became press secretary. Several considerations led to the establishment of the new office. One was simple power: Haldeman wanted his people to be in key positions throughout the White House, and Ziegler was his man. Another was the growing importance of television, with the concomitant need to monitor television coverage. Still another was Richard Nixon's desire to go around what he regarded as a hostile White House press corps and deal more directly with the general public (Maltese 1992, chap. 1). Beyond all this, though, creation of the new office came as the White House press staff was taking on more responsibilities. The press secretary's responsibilities had a core: briefing the White House correspondents and dealing with their day-to-day needs. But someone else was needed to coordinate the newer activities—hence, a communications director. (All of the communications directors are listed in Box 3–2.)

In practice, the responsibilities of individual communications directors have been remarkably plastic. The tasks of the office depend on a particular director's skills and the power structure elsewhere in the White House, especially the influence of the chief of staff and the press secretary. Herbert Klein did his best to keep lines of communication into the Nixon White House open and to provide pro-Nixon information to media throughout the country. During the early Carter administration the office did not exist, but it was resurrected when Gerald Rafshoon, who had handled Carter's campaign advertising, was brought into the White House to improve the president's public image. During Reagan's first term, David Gergen, working under chief of staff James A. Baker, conceived a media strategy and worked to put it into effect. Patrick Buchanan, Reagan's second-term communications director under chief of staff Donald Regan, gave the office a hard partisan edge. Some chiefs of staff have simply installed persons with whom they had close working relationships. Thus, when Howard Baker became Reagan's chief of staff after the Iran-contra scandal, he appointed Thomas Griscom, and when James A. Baker came back to the White House at the end of the Bush administration, he designated long-time aide Margaret Tutwiler.[1]

---

[1.] Within this individual variation, some patterns are evident. Administration and planning are continuing responsibilities. Communications directors try to present their presidents in a positive light, particularly when they are running for reelection or are about to leave office. Some provide context to explain their presidents, and one was an unabashed partisan (Kumar and Sullivan 1996).

Box 3–2  Communications Directors

| President | Communications Directors | Years |
|---|---|---|
| Nixon | Herbert G. Klein | 1969–1973 |
| | Ken W. Clawson | 1974 |
| Ford | Paul Miltich and James Holland | 1974 |
| | Gerald L. Warren | 1974–1975 |
| | Margita White | 1975–1976 |
| | David R. Gergen | 1976–1977 |
| Carter | Gerald Rafshoon | 1978–1979 |
| Reagan | Frank A. Ursomarso | 1981 |
| | David R. Gergen | 1981–1984 |
| | Michael A. McManus Jr. | 1984–1985 |
| | Patrick J. Buchanan | 1985–1987 |
| | Thomas C. Griscom | 1987–1988 |
| | Mari Maseng | 1988–1989 |
| Bush | David F. Demerest | 1989–1992 |
| | Marlin Fitzwater | 1992 |
| | Margaret Tutwiler | 1992–1993 |
| Clinton | George Stephanopoulos | 1993 |
| | Mark D. Gearan | 1993–1995 |
| | Donald Baer | 1995–1997 |
| | Ann Lewis | 1997–1999 |
| | Loretta Ucelli | 1999– |

Sources: John Anthony Maltese, *Spin Control: The White House Office of Communications and the Management of Presidential News,* 2d ed., rev. (Chapel Hill: University of North Carolina Press, 1994); Martha Joynt Kumar, "The President and the News Media," in *The President, the Public, and the Parties,* 2d ed. (Washington, D.C.: CQ Press, 1997).

One communications unit, the *Office of Media Relations,* deals with the out-of-town press. Many presidents like to go around the Washington press corps and place their stories directly in non-Washington outlets. There are two basic ways of doing this. One is to hold news conferences for local press when the president is on the road: Nixon in Louisville, Ford in San Diego, and so on. The other is to invite out-of-town press to the White House for a session created especially for them. All of the editorial writers from New England, for example, or all of the news directors of major television stations from the Midwest, are invited for a morning of briefings by major administration leaders. The climax is often a luncheon for all of them with the president. After lunch, they have an opportunity to ask questions (duly recorded for television), and then everyone leaves by 1:30 so they will have time to write their stories.

While there have been television advisers since the advent of that medium, the *television office* was first formally created in 1971. President Nixon wanted professional aid on such matters as the number and location of cameras, appropriate backdrops, makeup and wardrobe, and the like. Further, he wanted this advice to be available full time so that he would be in a position to go on television on very short notice.[2] In practice, the television office was reinvented by successive administrations when someone decided that the president's television appearances could be improved. This happened when Gerald Ford was preparing for his 1976 reelection campaign and in 1978 when Gerald Rafshoon joined the Carter staff to try to improve the president's image (Maltese 1992, 59–60, 140, 161). And, of course, excellent television advice can be provided by various staff members. Mike Deaver, whose formal title was assistant to the chief of staff, contributed to Reagan's television appearances by having the Oval Office windows backlighted, having backdrops painted a particular shade of blue that would portray Mr. Reagan's skin color to advantage, and paying particular attention to the camera angles from the Normandy cliffs when President Reagan broadcast from France on the fortieth anniversary of the invasion of Europe.

*Speechwriters,* part of the White House staff since Judson Welliver in the Harding administration, have often been lodged in the Office of Communications. Typically, there have been only a few wordsmiths, with one person sometimes designated as chief. Richard Nixon, for example, worked with three principal writers. For his more formal addresses, he used Raymond Price, who had edited the editorial page of the *New York Herald-Tribune.* When he wanted an uncompromising partisan tone, he called on Pat Buchanan, a staunch conservative who later became a frequent guest on talk shows and even a third-party presidential candidate. And for general purpose writing he could call on William Safire, subsequently the author of several books as well as a language column in the *New York Times.* Nixon's speechwriters were hardly the only ones of such notability. A number of other presidents also employed writers who became well known in their postgovernment careers.

---

[2.] There had been good advice available to earlier presidents, for example, that given to Dwight Eisenhower by actor Robert Montgomery. These advisers, however, were called in only when the president had a major address to deliver.

# Coordination

*Degrees of Control.* In the 1950s, coordination of press relations was carried out largely by James C. Hagerty himself. In addition to the normal press secretary's activities—briefing the press, making press conference preparations, suggesting stories that might be developed—Hagerty cleared any reporter wishing to speak to any staff member; if a reporter called a staff member without being cleared, the call was often routed to Hagerty's office. This system facilitated coordination, but it also meant that other presidential assistants were not well known to the general public.

Pierre Salinger did things differently. He felt that "all of JFK's staff had his full confidence, and . . . had an expertise in their specialties which [Salinger] could not hope to match" (1966, 127). Further, neither Kennedy nor his senior aides were willing to be "managed" by a press secretary. So Salinger let it be known that the White House would be an open beat where staffers could be contacted directly. There were a few problems with this: some reporters attributed a staffer's views to Kennedy, and stories about staff conflict appeared when two aides expressed different opinions.

Succeeding administrations leaned one way or the other, depending on the attitudes of the presidents. Both Lyndon Johnson and Richard Nixon exerted greater control. President Johnson required all staff members to submit a list of all press contacts to Bill Moyers (and thence to him) by five o'clock each afternoon. President Nixon wanted all requests for interviews reported to Ron Ziegler. It often took a couple of days to get permission, so whenever John Ehrlichman really wanted to see a reporter, he just "forgot" to ask Ziegler (Patterson 1988, 179). Ronald Reagan was content to leave these choices in the hands of his chief aides. The result was that during the first term James Baker and Michael Deaver made a real effort to let reporters know what was happening within the executive mansion, whereas Donald Regan leaned toward a closed system in the second term.

*Line of the Day.* Meanwhile, a new coordination mechanism had been developed in the Nixon administration, the "line of the day." The idea was to control the news agenda by giving the media a single theme to write about. By 1972, the line of the day was decided upon in a senior staff meeting run by Chief of Staff H. R. Haldeman. Once it was decided upon, the line of the day was disseminated to White House staffers, cabinet members, and executive branch personnel. Whomever reporters interviewed tried to echo the line of the day, and the White House kept careful track of the frequency of its use on the evening television news

(Maltese 1994, 1–3, 94). This technique was not used in the Carter and Bush administrations (Maltese 1994, 150; Kumar and Sullivan 1996, 9), but was employed in the Ford, Reagan, and Clinton White Houses.

*Meetings and the Chief of Staff.* Important as it was as a coordination vehicle, the development of the line of the day signaled two other consequential shifts. One was a spreading concern with public relations, sometimes at the expense of well thought out policy. The other was the emergence of the chief of staff as a player in communications strategy. His skills, of course, affected media relations. When the astute James A. Baker held the post under Reagan, things went smoothly, but when the domineering John Sununu was Bush's chief of staff, his personal feuds impeded good relations (Fitzwater 1995, 179–180).

When overall decisions are made at the chief of staff's level, their implementation is handled by the press secretary and/or the communications director. For example, when Marlin Fitzwater was Reagan's press secretary, he first attended a private staff meeting in Chief of Staff Howard Baker's office at 7:30 each morning. This was followed by the general senior staff meeting at 8:00 and then by Fitzwater's meeting with his own staff at 8:30. This last meeting was devoted to identifying what half-dozen stories would be important that day, what questions were likely to be asked, and what facts would be needed to respond to reporter's questions (Fitzwater 1995, 90–94).

By the 1990s, further complications were added by a twenty-four-hour news cycle. Gone was the stately pace built around morning and afternoon papers, or even morning papers and evening television news. Dozens of cable channels, including continuous all-news channels, had been added to the mix. White House press aides were continually being asked to respond to just-breaking news (Kumar 1997a, 124–125). Nonetheless, the Clinton administration used a series of morning meetings to coordinate public relations with the policy agenda. When Erskine Bowles was chief of staff, he began with a private meeting at 7:30 and followed with a senior staff meeting at 7:45. The major communications meeting at 8:15 was chaired by Deputy Chief of Staff John Podesta, to whom Bowles had delegated public relations. Political advisers, economic and domestic policy aides, and representatives of Vice President Al Gore's office were present, in addition to all the senior press and communications personnel. Decisions were made here as to who would speak on a topic, whether remarks would be on the record, what news organizations and media would be kept informed, and most important, how the message was to be integrated with the desired policy focus. Finally, at 8:45, Podesta chaired a briefer meeting dealing with presidential scandals (Kumar 1994, 26–29).

## Media Liaison Activities

### Press Briefings

The daily press briefings are the principal continuing means of disseminating information to the media. From the Kennedy administration through the Reagan administration, the press secretary met the White House press corps nearly twenty-eight times a month. In a single four-year term, a press secretary will brief the press more than 1,000 times. Larry Speakes, who served as Ronald Reagan's press secretary from April 1981 through January 1987, briefed the press on more than 2,000 occasions (Patterson 1988, 170).

The times of the press briefings have varied considerably from one administration to another. James Hagerty for the Eisenhower administration and Pierre Salinger for the Kennedy administration met the White House journalists twice a day in their own offices (remember, there were fewer in those days). Hagerty's briefings were scheduled at 10:30 A.M. and 4:00 P.M., and Salinger's were held at 11:00 A.M. and 4:00 P.M. The morning briefing provided news for the afternoon newspapers (which were much more important at the time), and the afternoon briefing provided stories to be published the following morning.

This general pattern continued through the Johnson administration. But some consequential changes came at the beginning of the Nixon years. A single midday briefing was substituted for the twice-a-day pattern. There were two reasons for this. President Nixon attempted to control the news, and the single briefing reduced reporters' opportunities to ask questions. Also, with the growing importance of television, a midday briefing gave the electronic journalists time to get their pictures and stories ready for the evening newscasts. At about the same time, a new briefing room was added to the ground floor of the West Wing. (This room is often seen on television as the site of announcements and press conferences.) The larger space gave the White House room to handle the larger number of reporters, and the setting for the briefing became more formal (Grossman and Kumar 1981, 138).

The midday briefing took place at 11:30 A.M. during the Ford and Carter administrations and at 1:00 P.M. during the first Reagan administration. Then in 1985, Larry Speakes moved the briefing ahead to 9:15 in the morning, a time at which he had been meeting about twenty reporters in his own office (Patterson 1988, 169; Hess 1984, 73). The earlier hour gave Speakes a better chance to set the tone of the day's news from Washington. Marlin Fitzwater, press secretary from 1987 through 1993, faced the press corps each morning about 11:00, an hour that gave him time to gather the information he needed. Clinton's Michael McCurry went back to a twice-a-day schedule, meeting roughly two dozen White House regulars about 9:00 A.M. in a session commonly called the "gaggle," and then holding a larger, formal session in the downstairs briefing room in the afternoon (Kurtz 1998, 2–12).

The press briefing itself begins with statements the press secretary wishes to make. These include an outline of the president's schedule, as well any announcements the White House is ready to make. By beginning the briefing with these statements, the official gains some control of the agenda. The appointment of a new ambassador to Bulgaria will not divert the press from questions about a scandal in the Treasury Department, but an announcement of a Supreme Court resignation can elicit questions about a possible successor. After the announcements, members of the press have their opportunity to ask about topics they regard as important. The reporters' own questions fill most of the briefing, and the grilling can be quite pointed.

While briefings can be serious and straightforward, the tone is often raucous. "White House briefings, Stephen Hess tells us, resemble a fraternity party. Reporters mostly shout, laugh, and interrupt."[3] For example, Larry Speakes once said that he had never gotten to finish answering a question at the previous day's briefing.

Q. What was your answer?

A. I don't know. I forgot . . . Okay, you've got the fat bill with a billion dollars that is coming down here today, which I would anticipate the president will veto. Then you have the so-called skinny bill which is also the short bill.

Q. Short and skinny?

A. Yes, short and skinny bill. It . . .

Q. Is it . . .

A. Now, see, I didn't get through it. I didn't get through it. Do you really want to know? Do you really want to know or would you rather not? (Hess 1984, 67).

In spite of the bantering tone, a good deal of information is being exchanged. The briefer has facts to convey and must be prepared to answer reporters' questions as well (Grossman and Kumar 1981, 139–140; Patterson 1988, 167–168).

Jody Powell raised questions about the extent of the briefer's preparation. "About the only function that is always identified with the press secretary is the daily briefing, which is unfortunate. That responsibility, important as it may be,

---

[3.] Hess contrasts White House briefings with those at the State Department, where emphasis is on "nuance journalism" (concern with slight shadings of words), and the Defense Department, where their briefers emphasize facts and reporters are very direct in challenging them.

is too time-consuming for the senior person in charge of press relations to discharge" (Powell 1984, 303). Powell's point is that the time and concentration required to prepare for the briefing prevent planning of a broader communications strategy for the president. Marlin Fitzwater, who briefly held both positions in 1992, reached the same conclusion: "Dealing with the press is a short-term function, while communications—mostly planning and scheduling—is long term. There wasn't enough time in the day to do both jobs" (1995, 325). The difficulty with this one-job-or-the-other approach is that linkage to the press and communications planning are both vital, and the person most trusted by the president is in the best position to do both.

## Press Conferences

Presidential press conferences began during the Wilson administration, but from the Harding administration to the beginning of the Eisenhower administration, presidential statements were customarily published in the third person ("The president believes . . ." rather than direct quotations), and both newsreel and television cameras were banned. James Hagerty took steps that modified the press conferences in important ways. He first brought a stenotypist to press conferences so there would be an accurate record of what the president had said. Soon the *New York Times* started printing transcripts of news conferences. Reporters then asked Hagerty to permit them to use direct quotations, since the president's exact words were in the *Times* anyway. Hagerty agreed. The admission of cameras was made possible by a technical development. Eastman developed a new film that did not require intensely bright lights, and television cameras began filming the reporters' questions and the president's answers. Thus by 1955, print stories generated by press conferences were supplemented by television pieces on the evening news.

The next step was live television coverage. This came when John F. Kennedy entered the White House in 1961. In making their decision, President Kennedy and Pierre Salinger considered the arguments pro and con. The strongest positive argument was that Kennedy could speak directly to the American people; the press could not screen his words. The most serious argument against was that a president addresses multiple audiences: voters, partisan supporters, partisan opponents, executive branch employees, allies and enemies abroad, and so on. Each audience could interpret the same words differently, and a presidential misstatement could trigger a crisis. John Kennedy was confident of his ability to avoid errors. He instructed Pierre Salinger to find out if the TV networks were interested. The networks responded quite positively. Live television worked out well for Kennedy. The State Department auditorium was filled for the first such press conference, and the television ratings revealed an audience of 60 million. President Kennedy continued with live press conferences every other week. Each of them drew at least 400 correspondents (Salinger 1966, 55–58, 140).

None of Kennedy's successors followed this pattern. Lyndon Johnson tried a variety of settings—coffee and conversation in the Oval Office, televised conferences in a different State Department auditorium, answering questions during a walk around the South Oval—but never seemed to find a setting in which he felt secure. He did not come across as well on television as his predecessor had, and he was extremely sensitive about comparisons with Kennedy. Richard Nixon simply did not trust the press. He relied on speeches and held as few press conferences as possible. Gerald Ford was not particularly telegenic, but he restored amicable relations with the press corps. Jimmy Carter alternated televised news conferences with nontelevised conferences with out-of-town reporters. Veteran White House correspondents ranked Carter's press conferences as the equal of Eisenhower's— and second only to Kennedy's—in candor and informativeness (Broder 1987, 172).

Reagan's press conferences provided an unusual combination of presidential advantages and disadvantages. On the plus side were counted Reagan's professional skill, his infectious optimism, and stunning visual settings. As R. W. Apple put it: "To most television viewers who saw him emerge from behind a closed door, stride purposefully down a long, imperially furnished, red-carpeted corridor, then fairly bound onto a platform framed in the doorway to the East Room, much of the message—vigor, authority, relaxation—had been communicated before he spoke" (1986). But when he did speak his statements were so studded with errors that his considerable ignorance about public policy was revealed. President Bush was most likely to be successful when he spoke from a visually imposing setting—in front of the Iwo Jima memorial, for example, or from the Rose Garden—or when he had an announcement of real import (Cook 1992). Yet all three networks rejected his request to televise a news conference in the summer of 1992 because they thought it would be merely a campaign event. Their refusal to carry a presidential news conference showed how much had changed since 1961, when the networks leapt at the chance to cover John Kennedy's press conferences.

Extensive preparation for press conferences originated with World War II army chief of staff George C. Marshall. Roger Tubby learned to assemble ample briefing books when working for Marshall in the postwar State Department and continued the practice when he moved to the Truman White House as assistant press secretary (Patterson 1988, 172). In the Eisenhower White House, various departments were asked the day before press conferences to provide background on likely topics; at times, reporters would tell James Hagerty about questions they intended to ask (Grossman and Kumar 1981, 140). Hagerty would go over this with the full White House staff (then about 40 persons) from 7:00 A.M. to 8:30 A.M., then continue over breakfast with a smaller group. At 9:45, this group, often joined by the secretary of state, would brief the president, concluding perhaps ten minutes before his 10:30 press conference (Mackaye 1960, 54). Similar preparation has continued to this day, with changes dictated by the work habits and needs of individual presidents.

John Kennedy was more involved personally, reflecting the greater importance of press conferences in his presidency. Pierre Salinger met with the press officers of the major agencies the day before, then put together a list of likely questions. That evening Salinger would give the president the questions, a proposed answer to each, and briefing material where necessary, and Kennedy would study this material before going to bed. A practice session took place at breakfast the next morning, with Vice President Johnson, Secretaries Dean Rusk and Robert McNamara, and senior White House staff present. Salinger asked the questions, the president would give his answer, and usually, there would be some discussion. Where necessary, Salinger would dig up further information prior to the press conference (Salinger 1966, 137–138).

In the Nixon era, press conference preparation took at least forty-eight hours. Speechwriter Pat Buchanan would query agencies with questions he had made up, and they would propose answers. Buchanan assembled these into briefing books for President Nixon. But instead of a briefing or rehearsal, Nixon would go into his study for about eight hours, pore over the briefing books, and decide for himself how he wanted to respond to the likely questions (Patterson 1988, 173).

Ronald Reagan required the most extensive preparation. Roughly five days before the press conference, agencies would send David Gergen extensive compilations of expected questions together with proposed answers. Gergen boiled this material down to a twenty-five- to thirty-page notebook that he sent to the president three to four days in advance of the press conference. The day before, a dress rehearsal took place. Senior aides would ask questions, first on domestic policy, then on foreign policy. After Mr. Reagan's answers, there would be a general discussion of themes that should be emphasized, items that should be announced at the beginning of the conference, and items that should be mentioned only in response to a question (Gelb 1982). After Gergen left the staff, Larry Speakes followed the same general pattern (Speakes 1988, 237–238). With all this preparation, it is fair to ask why President Reagan still made so many misstatements. One Reagan aide surmised that it was not that Reagan was unable to master new information, but instead that he had too firm a grip on old stories (such as the frequently referred to "welfare queens") that were incorrect. Reagan's answers were a mix of new information (often with details mixed up) and old beliefs that had been his stock-in-trade for years.

Dwight Eisenhower, John Kennedy, and Lyndon Johnson averaged two news conferences a month.[4] From 1969 on, however, the overall frequency of press conferences dropped to only one a month, a statistic that would be even lower without George Bush's presidency. There was also a good deal of variation among the recent presidents. Richard Nixon, Ronald Reagan, and Bill Clinton were least willing to meet the press, while George Bush held more press conferences than any other modern president. (The number and frequency of presidential news conferences are presented in Table 3–1.)

The reasons for the extremes were unique to each man. Nixon was contemptuous of the press. Denying reporters the opportunity to question him was one way to stay on the message he had chosen. Ronald Reagan was rumored to dislike the effort of preparing for news conferences, and his aides were worried about the

**Table 3–1   Presidential News Conferences, 1953–1996**

| *President, Term* | *Total Conferences* | *Monthly Average* |
|---|---|---|
| Eisenhower, I | 99 | 2.1 |
| Eisenhower, II | 94 | 2.0 |
| Kennedy | 65 | 1.9 |
| Johnson* | 132 | 2.1 |
| Nixon, I | 30 | 0.6 |
| Nixon, II | 9 | 0.5 |
| Ford | 41 | 1.4 |
| Carter | 59 | 1.2 |
| Reagan, I | 23 | 0.5 |
| Reagan, II | 21 | 0.4 |
| Bush | 140 | 2.9 |
| Clinton, I | 40 | 0.8 |

Sources: 1953–1984, Gary King and Lyn Ragsdale, *The Elusive Executive: Discovering Statistical Patterns in the Presidency* (Washington, D.C.: CQ Press, 1988), Table 5–4; 1985–1996, extracted from various editions of the *Public Papers of the Presidents of the United States* (Washington, D.C.: Federal Register Division, National Archives and Records Service, General Services Administration).

*November 1963 through January 1969.

---

4. This was a decline from the pace set by their predecessors. Coolidge averaged 6.8 a month; Hoover, 5.6; Roosevelt 6.0; and Truman 3.2 (Ragsdale 1996, Table 4–4).

need to correct his numerous mistakes. Bill Clinton was encouraged to hold more press conferences by Chief of Staff Leon Panetta and Press Secretary Michael McCurry, but he was urged not to do so by political advisers and legal counsel, who felt they could defend him better if he avoided making public statements (Kurtz 1998, 112, 135). Clinton, who had long blamed the press for his difficulties, chose to hold fewer press conferences.[5] George Bush, on the other hand, chose to hold frequent press conferences. These gave reporters an opportunity to ask and follow up on their questions, and with the president and the reporters doing their jobs, the exchanges were quite civil (Broder 1990b).

The declining frequency of press conferences is discouraging. It is often asserted that presidents limit the number of their press conferences because it takes too much time to get ready. The consequences of a presidential blunder are so adverse, the argument goes, that extensive preparation is necessary, distracting the president from other essential tasks. There is something to this argument, but it ignores the value to the president of the process. The questions and answers submitted by the agencies as preparation also alert a president to developments within his administration. The questions asked by reporters serve as an additional check on what he has learned in the preconference briefings. By the time a president finishes, he is more knowledgeable about a range of things, and what he learns can improve his performance across the board. It may not be accidental that Watergate, Iran-contra, and the Lewinsky scandal occurred in the administrations of the presidents who took these voyages of discovery least often (Broder 1987, 200).

## Speeches

When should a president give a major speech? The dilemma is obvious. If a president speaks too frequently, the public becomes habituated to his appearance. He invites a reaction of "There he is again" when he appears on television. But if a president rarely speaks, he surrenders opportunities to shape opinion about public events. Therefore, presidents seek a golden mean that allows them to address important topics without their appearances becoming too commonplace.

Each decision depends on whether a particular topic is sufficiently important. In such cases as the 1962 Cuban Missile Crisis, the 1971 wage-price freeze, the 1978

[5] The Clinton figures in Table 3–1 refer to full-scale press conferences at which reporters could question him on topics of their choosing. In addition to the full-scale press conferences, Clinton expanded on a Bush innovation by holding a number of joint press conferences with foreign leaders. Reporters frequently asked questions there which they would have pursued in a "normal" press conference (Kumar 1997a, 118).

Camp David agreement, and the end of operation Desert Storm in 1991, the answer has been yes. Further, a general pattern can be discerned. An analysis of discretionary[6] speeches shows that presidents from Eisenhower through Clinton have an average interval of 3.3 months between addresses. Presidents tend to speak when their approval rating has changed (moving either up *or* down) or when military threats are receding. Presidents tend not to give addresses when either the unemployment rate or the inflation rate is going up (Ragsdale 1984, 1996). Presidents do not shrink from responsibility when the American people must be told of a crisis, but otherwise they prefer not to be identified with bad news.

There are, of course, all kinds of speeches: major policy addresses, words of welcome to groups visiting the White House, brief Saturday morning radio speeches, and so on. Major policy speeches evolve through a series of steps. Information about likely content is either gathered by, or forwarded to, the speechwriters. The person working on the speech will shape the material into an initial draft, which is circulated to relevant senior staff. Their comments are incorporated into the draft, at which point it may be recirculated. Eventually the draft speech is sent to the president. As he indicates his personal preferences, the speech begins to take on a fixed character.

Presidents have varied in the extent of their personal participation. Kennedy, Nixon, and Reagan were active collaborators in drafting their important speeches. The Kennedy speechwriting process would begin with a meeting of senior advisers to discuss content. The president would indicate what he intended to say, and others would add their views. Ted Sorensen participated both as the principal speechwriter and as the senior domestic adviser. His presence enabled Sorensen "to spell out the reasons and sometimes the very words [President Kennedy] had used in those meetings. Groups of advisers could suggest outlines and alterations, and they could review drafts, but group authorship could not produce the continuity and precision of style he desired, or the unity of thought and argument he needed" (Sorensen 1966, 370). After circulation of the drafts had yielded agreement on content and emphasis, Kennedy would add his own changes and it became his speech (Salinger 1966, 66).

Richard Nixon also made his main contributions at the beginning and the end. For his August 1971 speech announcing wage-price controls, for example, he wrote six pages of notes for speechwriter William Safire (ending "I don't want this to be brittle and beautiful, but brutal and effective") and dictated an entire first draft (Safire 1975, 519–521). Raymond Price has written of meeting

---

[6.] In contrast to State of the Union Messages that are required by the Constitution, a discretionary speech is one that is not specifically mandated.

with President Nixon in the presidential lodge at Camp David just hours before an important speech because the president wanted to go over last-minute changes (1977, 100).

Reagan speechwriter Aram Bakshian said that Ronald Reagan "was much more involved in the process and had a better ear for phraseology" than other presidents for whom Bakshian had written. Having written a newspaper column and radio broadcasts in his prepresidential days, Reagan had more background than most politicians. Reagan often just sat down and wrote one of his five-minute Saturday radio speeches. In the drafting process on major speeches, Bakshian said, the president would sometimes take out old pages and replace them with five to ten handwritten pages of his own. If presidents have the gift of language, they can significantly shape the speeches they will ultimately deliver.

Less fortunate presidents find themselves refereeing conflicts between rival drafts. Gerald Ford, for instance, had scheduled a televised speech on Monday evening before the 1975 State of the Union Message. The draft prepared by Robert Hartmann was, according to Ron Nessen, "awful—ten minutes too long, full of clichés, flowery, with the major points blurred." Chief of Staff Donald Rumsfeld asked Nessen, and Alan Greenspan and Robert Goldwin, to prepare alternatives, which were combined into a single draft. Ford ultimately chose some paragraphs from the Hartmann draft and others from the Rumsfeld-Greenspan-Goldwin-Nessen draft. These were combined into the speech he gave (Nessen 1978, 80–82). Carter speechwriter James Fallows recounted a 1978 conflict between Secretary of State Cyrus Vance's "emphasis on a SALT treaty and [National Security Assistant] Zbigniew Brzezinski's habitual pugnaciousness in the face of the Soviet Union." Vance sought a speech to clarify U.S. policy. Carter agreed, but "then assembled the speech essentially by stapling Vance's memo to Brzezinski's without examining the tensions between them" (Fallows 1979, 43).

This last example points to another basic question: Has the fundamental policy decision been made? If so, then it's simply a matter of drafting a speech, circulating it for comments, incorporating them, and sending it in to the president for his input. If the basic contours of policy are still undetermined, then interested parties will angle for a speech that conforms to their preferences, sending in draft passages, arguing that one phrasing is much to be preferred to another, and so forth.

Another consideration is the complexity of the speech. A State of the Union Message is the classic complex speech because it touches every aspect of government. Bryce Harlow, writing for Eisenhower, remembered that he once "had a cabinet officer with me and another four waiting to see me, each of them insistent that the area involving their activities be expanded. . . . I had to respond that the president says he wants [it] kept shorter than a two-hour speech" (Patterson 1988, 195). The demand for more coverage for each agency always competes with the constraints of length and coherence. The president's role is important here, too. Ray Price said that a typical Nixon State of the Union Message would pass through ten to fourteen drafts. Rather late in that process, President Nixon would pick out some theme and begin to weave the rest of the materials around that motif so it became increasingly his own speech rather than a mere assemblage.

With a very simple speech, the appropriate agency will do most of the work. If, for example, a toast is needed for a dinner honoring a visiting dignitary, the State Department will send over a draft. The speechwriters may edit it a bit, but most of what the president says comes from the State Department draft.

Finally, there is the never-ending contest between memorable imagery and political prudence. The John Kennedy–Ted Sorensen team produced "vivid, energetic, and memorable" cadences that rank high in presidential oratory. Yet Kennedy, without consulting any foreign policy aides, added provocative language about Soviet intentions to his first State of the Union Message. This may well have escalated tensions between the United States and the Soviet Union (Bose 1998a, 27, 33). Peggy Noonan, who wrote for both Reagan and Bush, contributed "Read My Lips: No New Taxes" to George Bush's 1988 acceptance speech. Bush's economic advisers, concerned that new taxes might prove necessary, kept deleting the passage. Noonan "kept putting it back in. Why? Because it's definite. It's not subject to misinterpretation. It means, I mean this" (Noonan 1990, 319). She was quite right about the passage's clarity, but it proved to be a source of great embarrassment when a tax increase became necessary in 1990. Harry Thomason, a television director and close friend of Bill Clinton, taught him how to deny a liaison with Monica Lewinsky in a way that would capture the public's attention. He had Clinton lean across a lectern, shake his finger, and say, "I want you to listen to me. . . . I did not have sexual relations with that woman, Miss Lewinsky" (Toobin 1998, 29). That, too, became a source of great embarrassment when details of the affair came out. In all three cases, gifted wordsmiths elevated phrases far above the vast sea of forgettable prose. But when words provoke foreign adversaries, or stake out positions from which later retreat is impossible, presidents would be better served by more commonplace language. Poetry is not always feasible. The most realistic aspiration is for graceful phrases that will not collide with political needs.

## Coping with Crises

A news crisis develops when an unexpected event is important enough to become a major news story. Because such an event is unexpected, both the press secretary and the press corps lack information about it. Because it is important, the press wants facts immediately and will persist in its search for material for as long as the story lasts.

Eisenhower press secretary Hagerty was taking a Saturday afternoon nap when he was awakened by an urgent call from Assistant Press Secretary Murray Snyder, who was in Colorado. "Jim, Dr. [Howard] Snyder [no relation] has just called me and told me that the president has suffered a heart attack and that they are taking him to Fitzsimons Army Hospital. I am going to tell the press that the president has had a mild coronary thrombosis and, of course, I wanted to let you know first" (Ferrell 1983, 233). Hagerty agreed with Snyder that the news should be released immediately; he caught a plane and was in Denver by 11:30 that evening. Dr. Paul Dudley White, an eminent cardiologist, arrived midday Sunday to act as a consultant, and both of them briefed the press Monday morning. In Hagerty's opinion, "Dr. White did a marvelous job at his press conference, one of the best I have ever attended, and it did much to clear the air on the president's illness" (Ferrell 1983, 237). The frankness with which Murray Snyder and James Hagerty dealt with the press, and the clarity of Dr. White's explanations of the medical facts, led many to point to Eisenhower's heart attack as an example of how a news crisis ought to be handled.

Hagerty and his colleagues deserved the praise they received, but certain elements of the story should be emphasized. First was Hagerty's own standing in the Eisenhower circle. He made some phone calls as soon as he received the news. One was to Wilton B. Persons, then the legislative liaison head: "It's up to you," Hagerty said, "to take over on the staff in the absence of [Chief of Staff] Sherman Adams." With others looking to him for their instructions, Hagerty had no problem ascertaining whatever he wanted to know. Second, the physicians knew what Eisenhower's problem was. Dr. Snyder believed that his patient was suffering a heart attack, and waited only until his diagnosis had been confirmed and Eisenhower had been taken to the hospital before letting press aides know. Finally, there was no need to keep some facts secret. Eisenhower's heart attack precipitated a sharp drop on the stock market and led to speculation about who might run in 1956, but there was no military information that must be hidden from an enemy (Ferrell 1983, 233–237; Donovan 1956, 362–370). Each of these elements—the press secretary's access to the decision makers, whether the relevant facts are known, and the need for secrecy—affects the ease with which press crises can be handled.

Larry Speakes was not told of the pending invasion of Grenada in 1983. In fact, he had been approached by CBS's Bill Plante, who had information that the United States was going to invade. When Speakes approached National Security Council aide John Poindexter through Poindexter's own press aide (note that

Speakes was operating at two removes from the decision makers here), the word had come back: "Preposterous! Knock it down hard." At 5:45 A.M. the next morning James Baker gave Speakes background material and told him to announce the invasion at 7:00. Speakes later recalled:

> Not only was I furious about having been deceived, but I had been given just an hour or so to go through dozens of pages of material and prepare myself to present it to the press and the world in some coherent fashion. . . . I had never been so mad in my life, but I knew there was nothing I could do except to choke it down and head out there in front of the press and try to do my job (1988, 153–154).

Pierre Salinger had more notice at the time of the Cuban Missile Crisis. Salinger knew something was about to happen because so many reporters were asking questions. On Saturday night, he called President Kennedy to relay another question. "Pierre," Kennedy asked, "how much longer do you think this thing can hold?" "Whatever the story is," Salinger replied, "too many good reporters are chasing it for it to hold much longer. I would say through tonight and maybe tomorrow." "All right, Pierre, I'll have Bundy fill you in on the whole thing in the morning" (Salinger 1966, 253). Consequently, Salinger had thirty-four hours to aid in the preparations for Kennedy's Monday night address and to get ready for his own press briefings.

Sometimes the facts are not known. At the time of the 1975 attempted assassination of President Ford in San Francisco, the presidential motorcade hurriedly left the hotel to go to the airport. Ron Nessen had jumped into the car carrying wire service reporters. Veteran UPI correspondent Helen Thomas contacted her office over the car phone. "Was it a shotgun?" she asked others. Perhaps the driver nodded; anyway, Thomas told UPI it had been a shotgun. Nessen then told her what he had seen, and Thomas added that to her story. But neither Nessen nor anyone else in the car knew whether or not President Ford had been hit (Nessen 1978, 185–186). At the time of the attempt on President Reagan's life in 1981, Mike Deaver's initial message to the White House was that the president was all right, and secret service agents reported that James Brady had been killed. It was some time before the White House staff learned how serious the president's wound was, and ABC repeated the false report that Brady had died (Speakes 1988, 5–8). The early inaccuracies were not the reporters' fault. No one knew what the true situation was.

Marlin Fitzwater was in rural Virginia on Saturday afternoon May 4, 1991, when an emergency message call came to his assistant, John Herrick. When he located a pay phone, he learned that President Bush had collapsed. He dictated a short statement:

> At approximately _____ P.M. while jogging at Camp David, President Bush suffered a shortness of breath. He was taken to the Camp David medical facility and was examined by Dr. Michael Nash, one of the president's physicians, and was determined to have _____. Dr. Nash says the president is in stable condition but will require further examination at Bethesda Naval Hospital. The president departed Camp David for Bethesda Naval Hospital aboard *Marine One* at _____. The president is in a stable and safe condition.

Dr. Nash was to supply the crucial information about Bush's precise medical condition, and Herrick was to release the statement to the wire services as President Bush was moved to Bethesda Naval Hospital and to tell reporters that any further information would come from the White House. This done, Fitzwater headed for the White House, where he held an 8 P.M. briefing. It was two-and-a-half days before doctors learned that Bush's atrial fibrillation (an irregular heartbeat) had been caused by a thyroid problem, and two more days before they determined it was caused by Graves' disease, but Fitzwater released the information that was available, assured the public that Bush was safe and receiving good medical care, and set up procedures to provide further facts as they became known (Fitzwater 1995, 274–292).

When the crisis involves enemies or terrorists, certain information must be kept secret. Extreme measures were taken to prevent the Soviet Union from knowing that their missiles in Cuba had been discovered, let alone getting an inkling of what the U.S. response would be. As the time neared for the American response, President Kennedy himself asked both the *New York Times* and the *Washington Post* to hold the story on the grounds of national security. Another problem is classified information that has been released by another source. The first Soviet ship to be halted by U.S. warships was not carrying any contraband, and it was permitted to proceed. News of this, however, came not from the administration but from a Republican member of Congress who had been briefed and then convened his own news conference. The aerial photographs of the missile sites were first published in Britain in response to the U.S. ambassador's plea that he needed some evidence to convince the British public. Only then were the photographs permitted to appear in the American press. Neither of these events affected the resolution of this crisis, but both point to obstacles in handling news crises (Salinger 1966, 261, 292–294).

## Information Gathering in Media Relations

As we have seen, information gathering is crucial in White House–media relations. Whether they depend upon the continual trolling for facts that precedes
every briefing, or the frantic search for accurate information that marks a crisis,
those who speak for the president must exactly know what they are talking about.

Gathering intelligence before the daily press briefing is no less intensive
because it is routine. No single press secretary's search is completely representative, but take that of Pierre Salinger. When he was picked up at home in the morning, the car contained six major newspapers, which Salinger scanned on the ride
to the White House. Once there, he would learn more from phone calls and by
looking at the wire service teletype copy. About 9:30, he would meet with President Kennedy to discuss the content of his 11:00 A.M. briefing. After he left the
president, he would contact White House staff members and the most important
executive departments (Salinger 1966, 121).

The ways in which others vary from the Salinger pattern depend on access to
the president, the number and time of the briefings, and institutional developments since the Kennedy administration. If a press secretary has the access to the
president that Salinger did, he can get his instructions from that most important
of all sources. If not, he must deal through an intermediary or rely on staff meetings. When the White House pattern is to hold a single briefing after midday, there
is more time to gather information than if an early morning press briefing is followed by another in the afternoon. Recent press secretaries have had the advantage of a larger staff to help them gather needed facts from the now more complex White House, but whatever the pattern, briefers must be knowledgeable
about developments in the White House and must anticipate probable questions
before they face the reporters.

Even if a press secretary unintentionally provides misinformation, reporters
will hold him or her responsible. Clinton's press secretary Michael McCurry told
reporters that the White House had no knowledge that Webster Hubbell, a former deputy attorney general sentenced to prison for fraud, had been hired by
Clinton friends after leaving the Justice Department. But Bruce Lindsey did know,
and it was eventually discovered that two chiefs of staff, Mack McLarty and Erskine Bowles, had made phone calls to help Hubbell line up jobs. Neither Lindsey
nor McLarty nor Bowles had mentioned their activity to McCurry, but it was
McCurry who was blamed by major newspapers for giving out false information.
In this instance, McCurry was saved from further damage because most White
House reporters felt he was an honest man who would not intentionally mislead
them (Kurtz 1998, 118–121, 179–180).

Presidents themselves may call stories to their press secretaries' attention. John Kennedy's newspaper reading did not stop with the *New York Times* and *Washington Post*, but included three other New York papers, two more Washington papers, two Chicago papers, as well as the *Baltimore Sun, Atlanta Constitution, St. Louis Post-Dispatch,* and *Wall Street Journal.* In addition to these thirteen newspapers, President Kennedy read two Sunday newspapers published in England and ten magazines (Salinger 1966, 117). He would frequently ask his press secretary where a story had been published, or he would request that someone check into the facts of another. President Eisenhower was less well known for his reading, but as James Hagerty once said, "I wish those people who say he doesn't read were with me in the morning when I have to answer all his questions about things that have appeared in the press."

The spokesperson's personal standing among staff members is critical for gathering information within the White House. Jody Powell, whose personal relation with Jimmy Carter went back to Carter's gubernatorial days, was able to attend almost any meeting he wished during the Carter administration:

> It was much easier for me to drop in because if the Joint Chiefs were sitting there they didn't bat an eyelash if I walked in and plopped down. . . . I think you shouldn't underestimate the import of setting up a good system to gather information, but . . . you have go beyond [the system], and be there in a way that allows you to sort of grab the cabinet secretary on the way out the door and say, "Listen, you said so and so, and I'm not sure I understood you, but if that's what you said, I wondered about so and so." That's something that I think got very well developed over time as I got to know people and I think they generally developed some respect for my judgment and discretion.

Powell was respected, but he was careful to use his standing principally in behalf of his press secretary's job. In Powell's opinion, you must

> stay clear of policy fights [because] they can be enormously destructive of the sort of internal relationships that a press secretary needs to do his job. . . . Getting information [on what actually has happened] can be more difficult than it is ordinarily if the press secretary and the person he is calling for help have been on opposite sides of the bloody fight involving the matter under discussion (1984, 302).

Having standing within the administration is particularly important when secret matters are being discussed. The argument for including the press spokesperson in confidential meetings is that the secretary is going to have to explain the policy sooner or later, and he or she will then be better able to defend the administration's policy from a stronger position. The argument against is that if the spokesperson doesn't know the administration is contemplating some particular action, he or she cannot inadvertently reveal something that would benefit an enemy. This latter argument carries greater weight with the most important, and most secret, plans. Consequently, a less influential press secretary is likely to be excluded on the most vital matters.

Larry Speakes's troubles illuminate the difficulties of exclusion. When terrorists hijacked TWA flight 847 during June 1985, Speakes was the Reagan administration briefer. Much of the communication between the terrorists and the administration was taking place via the media, but Speakes was not part of the crisis management group. After CBS correspondent Dan Rather told Speakes that the leader of the hostage takers had asked him, "What did Speakes say today?" Speakes told Chief of Staff Donald Regan he couldn't brief anymore because "Every word I say is heard instantly in Beirut. . . . Anything I say could cost the hostages their lives, and I'm not going to brief anymore." Regan agreed that Speakes should be in on the crisis meetings, but Secretary of State George Shultz would not agree. A compromise was worked out in which NSC head Bud McFarlane would tell Speakes what had happened after each meeting of the crisis management group. This provided information but still left Speakes at one remove from the decision makers themselves (Speakes 1988, 168–169). He still had to go to the president on occasion and plead, "Look, I'm not the [Associated Press]. You can tell me" (KPBS 1990, 17).

When Marlin Fitzwater was appointed press secretary, he asked President Reagan for assurance of access, and he repeated that request when President-elect Bush asked him to stay on. Fitzwater decided that he would attend any meeting on the president's schedule if he needed to be there, without waiting for an invitation. Having established this right, he was never asked to leave a meeting (Fitzwater 1995, 79, 144, 173). Michael McCurry continued the practice of having access to all meetings in the Clinton administration (Thurman 1998). Having access to key White House meetings doesn't guarantee that a press secretary will have full information, but listening to discussions between the president and his principal aides does convey a good sense of the nuances and limits of decisions that have been made.

## Decision Making in Media Relations

In dealing with the media, every administration must decide what information to release. "The press," Pierre Salinger wrote, "insists on its right to know and print what is happening in government. The president insists on his right to conceal or withhold information whose publication might threaten national security. Generally, each respects the other's right. . . . But the question is: *who shall draw the line?*" (1966, 149; emphasis in original). The right of each party to define what should be released and what should be withheld is a matter of constant struggle. It is crucial to the ability of the president to build public support, and crucial to the media's ability to keep the public informed. But an equally important question is, *Where shall the line be drawn?* Salinger's claim that the president has the right to withhold information threatening national security seems simple enough, but what information genuinely threatens national security? And what other information is an administration entitled to withhold to protect itself or the rights of individuals?

The clearest case for secrecy is in wartime (or under warlike conditions) when lives would be put at risk by revealing information. When Soviet missiles were discovered in Cuba, Salinger wrote, "The stakes were the highest possible, the lives of hundreds of millions of persons, and the president was resolved that no news leak was going to impede the possibility of the United States making its decision and implementing it without the knowledge of the Soviet Union and Cuba" (1966, 286). The secret was kept, and U.S. Navy ships were in position to implement the blockade when President Kennedy made his speech.

Another life-threatening situation was the spring 1980 attempt to rescue American diplomats being held hostage in Tehran. Jody Powell had been present at two planning sessions in the preceding weeks. President Carter had offered him the opportunity to avoid the second, but Powell felt he might need to lie to protect the military operation and that he could do so most effectively if he were fully informed. Powell's moment of truth came when *Los Angeles Times* bureau chief Jack Nelson asked directly about a military rescue operation. "You people really aren't thinking about doing anything drastic like launching a rescue operation, are you?" "If and when we are forced to move militarily," the press secretary replied, "I suspect it will be something like a blockade, but that decision is a step or two down the road." As soon as the rescue mission became public knowledge Powell apologized to Nelson, but he made it clear he would do the same thing again to protect lives (Powell 1984, 229–232).

A second circumstance involves confidential negotiations with a foreign power. Jody Powell once had to cope with a rapid change in negotiations. President Carter had gone to the Middle East in March 1979 to attempt to revive active negotiations between Israel and Egypt. On his last full day in Jerusalem, there was every indication the Israelis were going to break off negotiations. Just before he briefed the press that evening, Powell learned that a last-minute meeting was taking place between Secretary of State Vance and Israel's Foreign Minister Moshe

Dayan, but Powell had no idea what it was about. Feeling that he must rely on the last reliable communication from the Israelis, he warned the correspondents that the outlook was bleak, and a number of stories were filed saying that. When the American party reached Cairo the following morning, however, President Carter announced that agreement had been reached. Dayan had urged that Carter make one final attempt that morning, and the president had won Prime Minister Menachem Begin's assent (Powell 1984, 93–99). What should Powell have said? What were his responsibilities to President Carter, to the Israeli government, and to the Egyptian government? Further, what could he have said without endangering the chances of success in the negotiations?

What can be revealed without compromising the privacy of an individual? Let's say that a lawyer is under consideration for a cabinet appointment, that the decision has not yet been made, and that the lawyer does not know whether he would accept the job if it were offered. The press secretary is asked at a briefing if the person is being considered. If he answers yes, he limits the president's freedom to choose whomever he wishes, not to mention the lawyer's relation with the clients who are depending on him for advice and representation. If the press secretary denies that the lawyer is being considered, he will have compromised his standing with the press if the president later chooses to nominate him. Now let's say that a background check has turned up an allegation that the lawyer mishandled one of his client's funds and that the president had already decided on *other* grounds to appoint a business executive to the cabinet post. A reporter who has heard about the charge against the lawyer asks the press secretary about it. Should the press secretary (who has no way of knowing if the allegation is true) say anything at all about it? Is it more important to avoid harm to the lawyer's professional reputation or to protect the president's political reputation by indicating that the president would not want such a person in his cabinet?

The president's health leads to difficult decisions. As we have already seen, news of Eisenhower's heart attack was released as soon as the press secretaries knew what had taken place. But this has not always been true. Take the case of Reagan's cancer. In July 1985 physicians discovered that President Reagan had colon cancer and operated immediately. All this was made known to the press; but in an interview with reporter Lou Cannon afterward, Reagan said, "I didn't have cancer. I had something inside me that had cancer in it and it was removed." This statement worried Larry Speakes, but one of the doctors told him, "Ignore it. It's simply the president's way of dealing with cancer." Shortly afterward, the president's physician noticed a scab on the side of his nose and had that biopsied. It, too, turned out to be cancerous. This time Mrs. Reagan refused to allow any public acknowledgment. In spite of Larry Speakes's advice that "our credibility is on the line and we should do everything we can to preserve it," she insisted that the public statement omit the word *cancer*. When President Reagan later acknowledged that the scab had been cancerous, Press Secretary Speakes came under attack from White House correspondents for misleading them (Speakes 1988, 188–199). He was caught in the middle, but the questions remain. To what degree should the president and his family be allowed privacy in a time of medical danger, and to what degree does the public deserve to be told of a medical situation that might limit a president's ability to carry out his duties?

What about policy? Whenever a policy is decided upon, other options are considered and rejected. Should a president's spokesperson reveal these alternatives? Or is it enough just to make a case for the administration's preferred policy? If other possibilities are presented to the press, the complexities of decision making are more realistically portrayed. But in a political world where opponents are surely going to attack any plan as ill-considered, a fully argued brief for the president's policy may be the only way to get it adopted. Another question is whether a press secretary should reveal the president's own doubts. Speaking of Lyndon Johnson's concern about Vietnam, Bill Moyers recalled, "You'd go back to when you see the furrows on the brow and you'd feel the great, deep fear in his own heart that it wasn't going to work out." But feeling that an admission of doubts would doom the policy, "you'd have to go out there and put the best face on . . . [the policy knowing that in view of the] facts and realities that hope didn't seem justified" (KPBS 1990, 16). Jerald terHorst, who resigned as President Ford's press secretary because he disagreed with the Nixon pardon, replied that when "you have some inner doubts . . . you . . . sometimes mirror that to the press . . . [and thereby] create some of the credibility problems" (KPBS 1990, 16).

How much should a press secretary say about a policy that has been *almost* decided upon? We are not discussing "trial balloons" in which information is deliberately given out in order to test political reaction. What is at issue here is how much to say about recommendations that are before the president, that he is likely to confirm, and that will be announced shortly. If it is, say, a matter of international trade policy being discussed by the Departments of State, Commerce, and Labor, the president's foreign trade representative, and several foreign embassies, it is hardly a secret. Any enterprising reporter who asks the right questions at two or three of the agencies involved can put most of the story together, then may come to the White House for confirmation. Bill Moyers explained:

When a president decides that he's going to do something, a vast array of forces contrary to his purpose begins to organize to thwart him: lobbyists, foreign governments, agencies of his own government, members of Congress, the House, the Senate, members of the newspaper business. The moment he wants to do something, he's got to start persuading a coalition of people to support him, . . . [since] there's [already likely to be] a coalition forming against him (KPBS 1990, 27).

Presidents need time to get their allies lined up to support the policies they have decided upon. The president's spokespersons can hardly deny that a policy is under consideration, but they can buy some time by saying that final decisions have not yet been made.

Finally, to whom should information be released? As an example, take information about donors to the 1996 Clinton campaign, some of whom later received invitations to stay overnight in the Lincoln bedroom or to ride on *Air Force One*. The dissemination of such information was not going to create favorable publicity, and there were two views about how it should be handled. Press Secretary Michael McCurry and Lanny Davis, a lawyer advising on this matter, wanted "document dumps" in which as much information as possible would be given at one time to reporters asking for it. Lawyers from the White House Counsel's Office, on the other hand, were trying to cooperate with House and Senate Committees investigating this topic, and they wanted the information to be sent to Capitol Hill (Kurtz 1988, 167–168). Should the information be given to reporters to maintain credibility with the press or to the investigating committees to live up to promises of cooperation? There is no easy answer.

The decisions just discussed—what to say when lives are at stake, when negotiations are under way with foreign governments, when allegations might defame an innocent person, when medical information is involved, when presidents and their associates have doubts about policies, when a policy is not yet ready to be announced, or when there are several claimants to the information—are among the most difficult choices a press secretary faces. Many announcements—for example, that a diplomat is being appointed ambassador to Uruguay—require little reflection. But when making the difficult decisions, the press secretary is poised on a tightrope. If he leans too far in one direction, he reveals information that can be damaging to the president. If he leans too far to the other, he sacrifices the credibility that is essential if reporters are to trust him.

## Exercising Influence in Media Relations

What posture should the White House take vis-à-vis the media? To begin with, neither the president nor those who work in his behalf exercise control over the press. The White House has resources, and presidential press aides are skilled in using them. Consequently, they have some ability to persuade reporters. But they cannot command journalists to tell a story a particular way, any more than White House colleagues can command foreign countries to support an American foreign policy initiative or Congress to pass a bill just the way the president wants it.

In the words of Bill Moyers, "We build bridges between the president and the press, and a lot of traffic goes across that bridge for which we are not responsible." The press secretary is the key person, the most visible contact between the president and the press, but by no means the only link between the media and the chief executive. The network of relationships is much more complex than that. After all, Moyers continued, "It's a porous White House and a porous government and the links to the White House are legion and reporters have their own sources and presidents have other links to the press than through the press secretary" (KPBS 1990, 4). There are multiple channels. The press secretary may be the person in the best position (after the president, of course) to affect the content of the news, but he is not the only one.

It is also important to understand that the White House and the media control different resources. The White House not only decides what information it is going to release, but who shall announce it, when and in what setting it shall be made public, and how much fanfare will accompany the announcement. The White House also controls the ease with which reporters can contact other members of the presidential staff. Those who make the media decisions, for their part, decide the relative importance of the story in comparison with other stories being released that day, as well as how many reporters they are going to assign to it and therefore how much related information they can gather to provide context.

The relationship resulting from this combination of multiple channels and dissimilar resources is captured in Timothy Cook's phrase "the negotiation of newsworthiness." Neither the press office nor the reporters dominate. Rather, the White House has more control over the visual content for television because staffers choose the setting and staging, and the reporters have more control over the verbal content because they decide how much critical comment to add to the announcement. The ultimate story is "determined by the resources the president brings to bear in each case, by the ability of the reporters to elicit critical statements from other authoritative sources besides the president, and by the journalistic quality of the presidential media event (including production values and importance considerations) in comparison to the other news of the day" (Cook 1992, 6).

Stephen Hess did not find evidence of manipulation in his study of the government-press connection. Neither press aides nor journalists saw themselves as the initiators in this relationship. Instead, both believed that they were reacting.

Without any prompting from Hess, "White House Press Secretary Larry Speakes and White House correspondent Andrea Mitchell on the same day complained in the same words, 'They [reporters/officials] push the stories they want'" (Hess 1984, 109). Both have their own agendas, but since each needs the help of the other to reach their goals, both have to work with their opposite numbers.

There are limits to the White House's ability to influence the media. Yet some spokespersons feel that they must have some control if they are to serve their president effectively. For example, Richard Cheney, reflecting on his experience as chief of staff to Gerald Ford, argued: "You've got to control what you put out. You don't let the press set the agenda. The press is going to object to that. They like to set the agenda. They like to decide what's important and what isn't important. But if you let them do that, they're going to trash your presidency" (Maltese 1992, 130).

In the contest between the press corps and the White House the latter enjoys one tremendous advantage: the president himself. Most reporters do not cover the White House; they cover the president.[7] Anything the president says is news. So, the first question for the White House is whether something is important enough for the president to announce. If so, the press office turns its attention to subsidiary questions. As David Gergen explained it, "We first of all figure out what forum [he should use] and on what basis he should speak, whether it should be something in the Rose Garden, a speech out on the road, a television address at night, whatever it may be, that is the initial issue. [Next,] how are you going to frame the issue, how would he frame the issue?" And, of course, how do you persuade the media to focus on the central theme of the presidential message, rather than discussing some side issue? Still, *if* the issue is sufficiently important for the president to address it himself, it will be reported.

How a presidential statement is received depends on the president's own reputation for honesty. "A president perceived as honest," Marlin Fitzwater has written, "can get away with a multitude of errors, but a president perceived as dishonest will have every mistake magnified." The White House press corps makes a collective decision about each president, and their view determines how they treat presidential explanations. Ford, Carter, Reagan, and Bush were regarded by reporters as generally honest, Fitzwater believed, whereas Johnson, Nixon, and Clinton were not (Fitzwater 1995, 198). Statements by any of the first group were certainly examined, but statements by Johnson, Nixon, and Clinton were treated more suspiciously.

---

[7.] Think about the number of times you have seen stories about the president returning to the White House from a trip or accepting a Thanksgiving turkey, and how infrequently you have seen anything on a meeting of, say, the Council of Economic Advisers.

What alternatives are available if the topic isn't important enough for the president to make a statement? A cabinet member or top White House aide can make the announcement. Reporters can be invited for a background session. Someone may have lunch with a columnist. A friendly person outside the administration itself, a senator or conceivably an ex-president, may call the matter to public attention. The White House works very closely with the morning, evening, and Sunday talk shows in lining up their guests, so administration spokespersons can be placed on talk shows where they can publicize a chosen topic. The list isn't endless, but it's long enough that the White House has a reasonable chance to get stories out.

Substantive policy proposals present special problems. Not only are the stories relatively complex, but White House reporters—principally political writers or generalists—are unlikely to have the background to understand them fully. Moreover, journalistic production values—a preference for simple, dramatic, and easily described stories with clear winners and losers—do not correspond to the intricacies of policy development. Consequently, stories are often balanced halfway "between the complexity of policies and the simplicity of news and between the news media's desire for clarity and closure and the president's need to keep options open as long as possible" (Cook and Ragsdale 1998, 349–350).

There are a couple of ways to handle complex stories. When an administration is launching some initiative, or if there are complex circumstances, officials may lead reporters through the subject and clarify matters they find confusing. For example, when the Clinton administration was requesting fast-track authority for international trade agreements, Treasury Secretary Robert Rubin, Commerce Secretary William Daley, Trade Representative Charlene Barshefsky, and economic aides Gene Sperling and Dan Tarullo jointly briefed the press. When President Clinton was in Beijing, Professors Paul Gerwirtz and Alan Turley (one temporarily with the State Department and one with the U.S. embassy in Beijing), Peace Corps Director Mark Gearan, and Assistant Energy Secretary Robert Gee explained various aspects of Sino-American negotiations then under way. In such circumstances, reporters are also likely to be supplied a fact sheet written by those who worked on the subject.

One interesting alternative was suggested by Carter press aide Claudia Townsend. When you have a complicated story to tell, it is best to rely on experts in the area concerned. "You will call in five or six folks who cover the [relevant beat] . . . the environmental writers, or the womens' writers . . . and sit down." This provides enough time to go over the details with writers who are already knowledgeable. The specialists write their stories. After these stories appear, others will ask about the subject. Then a background briefing can draw on the already written pieces to spread the story to a wider audience.

Returning now to general strategies for getting stories out, the White House often works through the press corps' own influence structure. Certain news organizations are vastly more important than others. The *Washington Post,* the *New York Times,* and the *Wall Street Journal* are important because they are so widely read in Washington. The news magazines—*Time, Newsweek,* and *U.S. News and World Report*—the wire services, and the television networks are important because of their large national audiences. Therefore press aides pay particular attention to their needs. Larry Speakes writes that he "was accused from time to time . . . of catering to the big newspapers. I would never have admitted it publicly, but obviously we did because the *Post* and the *Times* had the most influence with opinion makers. . . . The lead story in the morning [*Times*] would very likely be the lead story that night on the television news" (1988, 229, 228). Stephen Hess found that 89 percent of Washington reporters said they read the *Washington Post* regularly and 73 percent said the *New York Times* was regular reading. So if press aides can get a story into the *Washington Post* or the *New York Times,* they are likely to get wider follow-up coverage (1981, 25).

The White House can influence television stories by providing pictures. For example, when President and Mrs. Reagan made a trip to the Far East in 1983, they brought back two Korean children who needed heart surgery. Mrs. Reagan posed with the children on *Air Force One.* The resulting tape was taken off the plane at a stop in Alaska and offered to the networks for their morning news shows. All three used the pictures of Mrs. Reagan cuddling the children (Broder 1987, 202). When President Clinton nominated Ruth Bader Ginsburg for the Supreme Court, the colonnade was hung with U.S. flags that framed Mr. Clinton and Mrs. Ginsburg as they entered the Rose Garden. These appealing pictures made it more likely that positive stories would be carried on television.

Finally, how can the press staff prevent the publication of unfavorable stories? Often they can't, but there are some means at their disposal. One is release of information when there is not likely to be a lot of coverage. Late Friday is a favored time. An adverse story is put out too late for use on Friday evening television shows, with the expectation that since Saturday papers are slimmer than the weekday papers, the bad story might get less coverage. Round-the-clock news coverage has reduced the White House's ability to hide a story, but release time still has some effect. Also, if the president or senior aides are candid with the media about developments, reporters are more likely to kill a misleading story. John Kennedy had a number of backgrounders in his office, and Pierre Salinger believes that reporters' resulting knowledge of Kennedy's thinking prevented many inaccurate stories (1966, 129).

The White House can appeal to reporters in the name of national interest. For example, a Russian submarine was sunk near Hawaii with its code books and other secret material intact. The CIA wanted to use a specially equipped ship to recover it, and thought they could do so if the Russians weren't embarrassed by having the recovery become public knowledge. CIA director William Colby drove from news office to news office explaining the situation, and every major news organization agreed not to publish (KPBS 1990, 24–25).

Sometimes the media may be offered a story that diverts their attention from something the White House wants to downplay. In June 1982, Britain's Prime Minister Margaret Thatcher visited President Reagan. The White House was not anxious to call attention to the visit because the Falklands fighting had just ended, and Latin American countries were upset because the United States had sided with Great Britain. So on the day of the visit reporters were taken out to CIA headquarters in Virginia, where President Reagan signed a bill and made a speech about what a fine job the CIA was doing. The Reagan-Thatcher meeting concluded late in the afternoon, making it difficult for television networks to get pictures ready for the evening newscasts. No matter. The White House made an effort to delay the story, but all three networks used much more footage from the Reagan-Thatcher meeting than from the CIA ceremony (Hess 1984, 50–51). Judgments about newsworthiness trumped White House efforts to divert attention from awkward developments.

## Summary

**Actors.** The press secretary has the core responsibility of briefing the press. He or she is assisted by deputy and assistant press secretaries (and their staffs) in the upper level press office and the lower level press office, and by still others who work in the photo office and handle press advance. The responsibilities of the communications director are more plastic, but they include long-term planning and focusing on relatively specialized communication channels. All try to present their president in a positive light, but the means of doing so vary from one communications director to the next. Speechwriters have their organizational home somewhere in this communications complex, but the location varies from administration to administration. Coordination is carried out through senior staff meetings, and in many administrations encompasses a "line of the day." The chief of staff is now heavily involved in coordination, and often personally plays a major communications role.

**Media Liaison Activities.** The media relations activities include daily press briefings, presidential press conferences, and preparing speeches for the president. Each of these activities involves an enormous amount of work. The day-to-day activities are punctuated by press crises triggered by unexpected events that have major news consequences.

*Common Activities in a Media Environment.* Information gathering requires reading as widely as possible, listening to questions raised by the president, senior aides, and the journalists themselves, sitting in on morning staff meetings, and attending as many other White House meetings as time permits. High standing with the president and other senior aides eases the press secretary's information-gathering tasks considerably. Decision making revolves around what information to release, when, and under what circumstances. Such decisions are difficult to make when lives are at stake, when delicate negotiations are under way, when medical information is involved, and when presidential policies are still being shaped. Since the government and the media control different resources, exercising influence is not a matter of persuasion per se but instead of what Timothy Cook has called "the negotiation of newsworthiness." Those briefing the press want to use governmental resources to focus on stories important to the White House while maintaining their own reputations for integrity.

# 4. Foreign Policy

Foreign policy is almost always on the president's mind. Having emerged from World War II and the cold war as the strongest country in the world, the United States is inescapably involved in international affairs. The U.S. government is constantly being asked to give aid, lend encouragement, take sides in international disputes, send troops to strengthen an ally, supply expertise and money in disaster relief, and so on. Even inaction on the part of the United States has consequences. Presidents hear constantly from ambassadors, foreign ministers, and heads of state. U.S. involvement in the affairs of the world generates an unending stream of Oval Office visitors and a constant flow of paper across the president's desk.

Gerald Ford and Bill Clinton provide nice illustrations of the inevitability of international involvement. When Ford was a congressional leader he had been primarily concerned with domestic affairs. But as president he was immediately pushed into the international arena. Shortly before he assumed the presidency, the military junta then running Greece instigated a coup on Cyprus. Turkey (many of whose nationals lived on the island) sent troops and soon occupied a large part of Cyprus. This "foreign" crisis had domestic political impact because several important members of Congress (John Brademas, Paul Sarbanes) had Greek forebears. Greek colonels may have precipitated this crisis, but the congressional reaction was anti-Turk. Bill Clinton, as governor of Arkansas, had even less international experience and little interest in foreign affairs. "The reason I was elected," he maintained, "was to focus on domestic problems." But on the Sunday evening prior to his inauguration, Gen. Colin Powell, chairman of the Joint Chiefs of Staff, met with him at Blair House. Powell needed instructions from the president-elect about his intentions in Somalia and Bosnia. Even new presidents as innocent of prior international concern as Ford and Clinton find foreign policy demands their attention from their first moments in office.

Further, the primacy of this policy area builds as the presidential term goes forward. Presidents tend to give more attention to international events in their second year than in their first, and still more in their third. They do shift back to domestic questions when running for reelection in the fourth year; but if they win reelection, international events are more important in their second term than in their first. Along with economics, foreign affairs is a policy area that the presidency must tackle. The language presidents use ("we must," "we cannot avoid") tells us this policy area is compelling. The United States cannot avoid international responsibilities, and neither can the nation's presidents (Kessel 1974; compare Quandt 1986, 14–27).

## Guardians of American Interests

The boundary between foreign policy and domestic policy is quite porous. Just as the actions of the State and Defense Departments have many domestic implications, a great many "domestic" agencies have real impact on foreign policy. As we will see, the Treasury Department is centrally concerned with international trade and monetary policy. The Agriculture Department has its own foreign service. The Commerce Department is concerned with business opportunities overseas. The Energy Department is involved with nuclear proliferation. And so on. In this section, we shall examine those agencies whose prime responsibilities relate to foreign policy, but we must remember that many other agencies deal with some aspects of foreign policy.

### The National Security Council

The international support staff most closely associated with the president himself is the National Security Council (NSC). In I. M. Destler's view, the council has had three major effects: it has been a committee of senior officials who meet to review foreign policy issues for the president; it has provided a focus for formal planning and decision-making processes; and it has provided the institutional base for the emergence of a presidential foreign policy staff. "The first of these," Destler tells us, "was how its founders mainly saw it; the last is what it has most importantly become" (1975, 6).

It is easy to confuse the National Security Council, the national security assistant, and the National Security Council staff because of the similarity in their names, but there are important distinctions between them. The National Security Council is a very senior group of officials chaired by the president himself. The national security assistant is the president's principal security adviser on the White House staff. The NSC staff is composed of foreign policy experts who work under the direction of the national security assistant. (Postwar national security assistants are listed in Box 4–1.)

To understand how the national security assistant[1] emerged as a major player in U.S. foreign policy, and how the NSC staff developed as a presidential foreign

---

### Box 4–1 National Security Assistants

| President | National Security Assistants | Years |
| --- | --- | --- |
| Eisenhower | Robert Cutler | 1953–1955 |
| | Dillon Anderson | 1955–1956 |
| | William Jackson | 1956 |
| | Robert Cutler | 1957–1958 |
| | Gordon Gray | 1958–1961 |
| Kennedy | McGeorge Bundy | 1961–1963 |
| Johnson | McGeorge Bundy | 1963–1966 |
| | Walt W. Rostow | 1966–1969 |
| Nixon | Henry A. Kissinger | 1969–1974 |
| Ford | Henry A. Kissinger | 1974–1975 |
| | Brent Scowcroft | 1975–1977 |
| Carter | Zbigniew Brzezinski | 1977–1981 |
| Reagan | Richard V. Allen | 1981 |
| | William P. Clark | 1982–1983 |
| | Robert P. McFarlane | 1983–1985 |
| | John M. Poindexter | 1985–1986 |
| | Frank C. Carlucci | 1987 |
| | Colin L. Powell | 1987–1989 |
| Bush | Brent Scowcroft | 1989–1993 |
| Clinton | Anthony Lake | 1993–1997 |
| | Samuel R. Berger | 1997– |

---

[1] Early on, the principal national security aide was a special assistant to the president. In Eisenhower's day, only Chief of Staff Sherman Adams had the title of assistant; everybody else was a special assistant. With the growth of the staff, symbols of rank emerged. The principal aides (such as national security aide Henry Kissinger) were now styled assistants; the second tier was made up of deputy assistants; all the rest were special assistants.

policy staff, one needs to know a bit about the history of the National Security Council. The National Security Act of 1947 created three important entities: the Department of Defense, the Central Intelligence Agency, and the National Security Council. The NSC has four statutory members—the president (as chair), vice president, secretary of state, and secretary of defense—and two statutory advisers—the director of central intelligence and the chairman of the joint chiefs of staff.[2] The intent of Congress was that the president would consult with this body when making major national security decisions.

President Truman did not view the National Security Council as a major deliberative body (Staats 1980, 171; Heller 1980, 139), but President Eisenhower did. Eisenhower made the National Security Council the central organ of his conduct of foreign affairs. Formally, he presided over 92 percent of the frequently held council meetings himself; informally, he employed other channels of information and made sure that everyone understood the basis for his decisions (Greenstein 1982, 124–138). Another distinctive aspect of Eisenhower's style is that he had one person (Robert Cutler most of the time) manage the NSC process and another (Col. Andrew Goodpaster, later commander of NATO forces as a four-star general) manage security matters. Both briefed Eisenhower, so he was not dependent on one channel of communication.

When John Kennedy appointed McGeorge Bundy, a Harvard dean, as his national security assistant, several changes took place. Bundy took over the responsibilities of both Cutler and Goodpaster, and given Kennedy's lack of interest in meetings and process, put more emphasis on day-to-day decisions. Bundy also installed teletype machines to get an early look at cables addressed to the State and Defense Departments, and recruited a small staff to provide independent evaluation of policy alternatives for the president (Destler 1981). Lyndon Johnson was more willing to attend meetings than Kennedy, but he didn't use the council as a decision-making body either. His fundamental forum was the Tuesday Lunch, a private meeting with the secretary of state, secretary of defense, and national security assistant in the president's own dining room on the second floor of the White House (Graff 1970). Under Johnson, Walt W. Rostow, who succeeded Bundy as national security assistant, transmitted all messages to and from the departments regarding any foreign events besides Vietnam, thus further strengthening the role of the national security assistant.

Richard Nixon was deeply interested in foreign policy and determined to run

---

[2.] There are also invited members, such as the secretary of the treasury and the chief of staff, who serve at the invitation of the president. The list of invitees varies from one administration to the next.

it from the White House. This, together with the appointment of Henry Kissinger as assistant to the president for national security affairs, led to the apotheosis of the NSC staff as the dominant force in foreign policy. Kissinger assembled a staff of fifty professionals (a mix of academics, military men, and foreign service personnel) and eighty support employees. This staff was organized around eight committees or groups, seven of which were chaired by Kissinger and all of which reported through him. Nixon met with the council more frequently than Kennedy or Johnson had, but the real decision-making system was closed at the top. Kissinger would make up his own mind and then make recommendations directly to Nixon (Destler 1975, 26). In addition, Nixon used Kissinger as an emissary, sending him to Beijing to negotiate for the resumption of diplomatic relations and to France for negotiations to end the war in Vietnam. Kissinger also emerged as the administration's principal foreign policy spokesman. Eventually, Kissinger became secretary of state as well as the national security assistant. President Ford retained Kissinger as secretary of state but appointed Brent Scowcroft as national security assistant. Breaking with the pattern of an increasingly powerful national security assistant, Ford told Scowcroft he did not want him to be a public advocate.

President Carter returned to a combination of few council meetings and a strong NSC staff headed by a very visible Zbigniew Brzezinski. Carter held regular Friday morning breakfasts with Secretary of State Cyrus Vance, Secretary of Defense Harold Brown, and Security Assistant Brzezinski, and these senior aides themselves met for private luncheons. By the end of the administration, Brzezinski headed a staff of some forty professionals. He had been sent on important diplomatic missions (to China, for example), had appeared frequently on television, and was prepared to argue for positions in which he believed.

The Reagan administration came to office knowing the national security assistant had become a rival to the secretary of state, and therefore deemphasized the national security position. This decision, however, led to a different set of problems. None of the administration's first four national security assistants had any real knowledge of foreign policy, the trust of the president, and the standing to referee disputes between the State and Defense Departments.[3] Their poor judgment about activities in which the NSC staff should engage eventually led to the Iran-contra disaster. In the aftermath of Iran-contra, stronger NSC leaders (Frank Carlucci and Colin Powell) were found and the staff took on a more professional tone, but six years had already been lost.

George Bush brought back Brent Scowcroft, Ford's NSC head. Scowcroft, a member of the Tower Commission, which had investigated Iran-contra, was

---

[3.] Some had one of these qualifications, but no one came close to having all three.

appalled by the buccaneering of Oliver North and was resolved to prevent any similar activities.[4] Scowcroft became a personal counselor to President Bush and left much of the day-to-day work in the hands of the Deputies Committee (Hoffman, 1989c). Anthony Lake, Clinton's first national security assistant, also opted for a low-key operation. Both Scowcroft and Lake were dispatched on diplomatic missions, and both were men of standing in the administrations they served, but neither exhibited the flamboyance of Kissinger or Brzezinski. Samuel Berger, Clinton's second national security assistant, was a lawyer and Democratic activist. He appeared more frequently than Lake as an administration spokesman.

What does this developmental sequence mean? Consider the precedents now available as models for the NSC staff: planning papers developed by the NSC staff (rather than coming from line departments and being reviewed by that staff); a substantial portion of the president's information coming through this single channel; and (though only in the Reagan administration) foreign operations conducted directly by the NSC staff. As for the precedents available to the national security assistant: he recruits and directs this staff; he is sent on important diplomatic missions; and he is a leading public spokesman on foreign policy. These precedents could be combined to justify a very strong NSC staff led by a dominant national security assistant.

To understand the various patterns that have actually occurred, we must remember that changes in the NSC have not followed a straight path. The highly visible Kissinger-led NSC in the Nixon administration was followed by a low-key Scowcroft NSC in the Ford administration, and the undisciplined NSC staff of the Iran-contra years was succeeded by more professional NSC staffs led by Carlucci, Powell, Scowcroft, and Lake. The elements that have been common to most administrations are an NSC that meets as often as the president wishes; a national security assistant with knowledge and standing;[5] and an expert staff made up largely of State Department detailees, Defense Department detailees,[6] and academic experts. Beyond this, the NSC is quite malleable. If one president wishes to

---

[4.] North was a Marine lieutenant colonel on the Reagan NSC staff who decided to overcharge Iranians for arms, then use the profits to support contras, who were fighting against the Nicaraguan government.

[5.] There have been a few exceptions.

[6.] Detailees are persons who are sent to the White House staff for a period of time by government agencies for which they work. Their salaries continue to be paid by their original agencies, and if they work at the White House for less than six months they are not considered White House staff, thus reducing the *apparent* cost and size of the White House. In this case, they bring expertise that the NSC staff needs to do its job.

rely on a strong staff and a dominant national security assistant, that is possible, and if another president wishes to draw his advice from the council members and assign the NSC staff to a supporting role, that is equally possible.[7]

## The Department of State

The Department of State differs from the National Security Council staff in some fundamental ways, many of which are typical of the differences between *any* cabinet department and *any* White House staff unit. Broadly speaking, "bureaucracies for the most part provide ballast. They represent continuity and constancy. While the president [and any presidential staff unit] generalizes, the bureaucracy in its various parts specializes" (Rockman 1997, 21). There are also several specific distinctions. First, State is much larger. State employs about 5,000 professional diplomats (known as foreign service officers or FSOs) among its 20,000 to 30,000 employees. In contrast, there are only 40 to 50 professionals on the NSC staff. Second, the State Department is responsible for the implementation of policy while NSC is charged with policy coordination at a very abstract level. In part because of these differences in responsibilities, and in part because of differences in experience, State and NSC have distinctive ways of thinking. Diplomats adapt to their clienteles in foreign countries just as others respond to the environments in which they are placed. Therefore foreign service officers gain detailed, particularistic perspectives in the countries where they are stationed. These FSOs know just how local cultures and politics are interwoven, and therefore they see more possibilities in incremental change. The NSC staffers, however, sum up presidential foreign policy goals in broad themes and hope they may lead to dramatic shifts. Third, FSOs are far removed from the president, not only in physical distance from the White House but in the number of layers of bureaucracy between them. The NSC staff is much closer in both senses. Fourth, since being a foreign service officer is a career, the FSO is more likely to have a long-term perspective, whereas the NSC staffer serving at the pleasure of a particular president is more attuned to the electoral cycle. Greater proximity to the president and sharing a similar time perspective leads to a fifth distinction. The NSC staff is much more likely to frame proposals that will elicit domestic support, and hence be attractive to the president. Conversely, the State Department is more sensitive to the costs of implementing a policy in Italy or

---

[7.] For more complete discussions of the National Security Council, see Clark and Legere 1969; Destler 1974, 1975, and 1981; George 1980; Nelson 1981; Destler, Gelb, and Lake, 1984; Inderfurth and Johnson 1988; Prados 1991; and Auger 1997.

Thailand or Nigeria than to think of political costs to the president. Given this contrast, it is not surprising that NSC policy proposals are often more attractive to White House politicians than State Department recommendations are (Gelb 1980; Rockman 1981).

As noted, all the foregoing characteristics—greater size, responsibility for implementation, detailed knowledge of particular situations, a long-term perspective, and less acquaintance with the thoughts and priorities of the president— typify distinctions between any department and any White House staff unit. There are other features, though, that apply primarily to the State Department. The foreign service officers who make up the core of the State Department carry out instructions from their superiors much as military officers execute orders that are given them. Thus, the president need not worry about whether his foreign policy will be implemented. The culture of the foreign service, however, tends to emphasize traditional political tasks—negotiation, representation, and reporting—rather than modern activities—international trade, foreign aid (both military and developmental), public information, scientific exchanges, and so forth—that have been important elements of foreign policy for half a century. Since FSOs primarily interpret political trends, "the modal technology of the State Department is soft and impressionistic, and thus endlessly vulnerable" (Rockman 1981, 915). White House staff members believe they also know how to interpret political trends, and as long as their views are regarded as plausible on Pennsylvania Avenue and are consistent with the president's policies, they often carry the day.

If foreign service officers make up the core of the State Department, the organizational heart is directed by the under secretary for political affairs. Here are found the regional bureaus (Bureau of East Asian and Pacific Affairs, Bureau of European and Canadian Affairs, and so on), and within the regional bureaus are found the country "desks," actually offices (such as the Office of German Affairs) that send instructions to diplomats abroad, receive their reports, and monitor bilateral relations. There are other units within State dealing with such matters as economic relations, international security, human rights, science, and so on. For decades, there has been discussion of how the practitioners of the "new diplomacy" could be better integrated with political affairs—whether, for example, it would make more sense to have a separate bureau dealing with, say cultural and exchange issues, or whether it would be better to add appropriate expertise to the regional bureaus. For practical purposes, personnel are integrated quite well overseas, especially in smaller embassies where foreign service officers lunch regularly with members of the agricultural foreign service and foreign service information officers.

Too much should not be made of the differences between State (and other agencies) and the NSC staff. There is considerable horizontal mobility between the two organizations. For example, Bush's Secretary of State James Baker had served as an invited member of the National Security Council during the Reagan administration. Clinton's National Security Assistant Tony Lake had been head of State's Policy Planning Staff in the Carter administration. And detailees from the State and Defense Departments make up a substantial portion of the NSC staff. Still, there are tendencies, and the cognitive habits of those in particular offices have consequences in policy making: "Despite the well-deserved reputation of Foreign Service officers as people of exceptional ability, few have the ability or are trained to formulate policy.... The ethos of maintaining flexibility [to take advantage of future diplomatic opportunities] is exceptionally strong in the diplomatic profession, and the more flexibility one seeks, the more vacuous the policy" (Gelb 1980, 35).

Presidents, of course, do not deal with the entire Department of State or the entire NSC staff. They meet with the secretary of state (Box 4–2), with the national security assistant, or with their top aides. But to the degree that the Department of State gains a reputation for vacuous policy recommendations, it poses a dilemma for the secretary of state. Should the secretary be associated with departmental recommendations and thereby risk being viewed as ineffectual? Or

---

**Box 4–2  Secretaries of State**

| President | Secretaries of State | Years |
| --- | --- | --- |
| Eisenhower | John Foster Dulles | 1953–1959 |
| | Christian A. Herter | 1959–1961 |
| Kennedy | Dean Rusk | 1961–1963 |
| Johnson | Dean Rusk | 1963–1969 |
| Nixon | William P. Rogers | 1969–1973 |
| | Henry A. Kissinger | 1973–1974 |
| Ford | Henry A. Kissinger | 1974–1977 |
| Carter | Cyrus R. Vance | 1977–1980 |
| | Edmund S. Muskie | 1980–1981 |
| Reagan | Alexander Haig | 1981–1982 |
| | George P. Shultz | 1982–1989 |
| Bush | James A. Baker III | 1989–1992 |
| | Lawrence S. Eagleburger | 1992–1993 |
| Clinton | Warren M. Christopher | 1993–1997 |
| | Madeleine K. Albright | 1997– |

should he or she abandon the knowledge and analysis of department professionals and rely instead on his or her personal reputation and standing with the president? For various reasons, Secretaries Dulles, Rusk, Kissinger, Vance, Baker, and Christopher all chose to act more or less independently of the department. Only George Shultz made a serious attempt to work with both the foreign service professionals and the president.

## The Department of Defense

The Department of Defense was created by the National Security Act of 1947. It provided a degree of unification of the armed services, stopping well short of complete unification but instituting more centralization than proponents of separate services would have liked. Up to that time, there had been a separate Department of War and Department of the Navy. Within the new Defense Department, there was now a Department of the Army, a Department of the Air Force (a branch that had been the Army Air Corps), and a Department of the Navy (which retained its own air squadrons and the Marine Corps). Each had its own service secretaries and military commands. Over all of this were a secretary of defense and associated administrative offices, and alongside it were the Joint Chiefs of Staff. Important as this administrative reorganization was, new American global responsibilities brought about an even more fundamental change in the role of the armed forces. Throughout U.S. history, there had been a very small standing army and navy. Additional personnel were recruited as needed for relatively brief periods of war. In the last half-century, there has been a vast military establishment whose influence has been felt throughout the government. Secretaries of defense for presidents since Eisenhower are listed in (Box 4–3.)

The Defense Department differs from the NSC staff in the same ways as the State Department does, but it differs from State in ways that give it more independence. Whereas State's characteristic skill lies in the interpretation of political trends, the Defense Department spends billions of dollars a year on personnel, maintenance, and the acquisition of new weapons. In order to intervene meaningfully in these defense processes, one must first master complex budgetary details, and then learn enough science and technology to be prepared to argue, for example, that a new missile will or will not work for given reasons. These formidable tasks do not invite a lot of competition. Further, if a critic is wrong, the risks are quite substantial. If a secretary of state tells a congressional committee that a certain action will anger, say, the Swedish government, the reaction may be "too bad." But if a secretary of defense claims that a budget cut will weaken the country, leading to battle deaths and perhaps to military defeat, the reaction tends

**Box 4–3 Secretaries of Defense**

| President | Secretaries of Defense | Years |
|---|---|---|
| Eisenhower | Charles E. Wilson | 1953–1957 |
| | Neil H. McElroy | 1957–1959 |
| | Thomas S. Gates Jr. | 1959–1961 |
| Kennedy | Robert S. McNamara | 1961–1963 |
| Johnson | Robert S. McNamara | 1963–1968 |
| | Clark M. Clifford | 1968–1969 |
| Nixon | Melvin R. Laird | 1969–1973 |
| | Elliot L. Richardson | 1973 |
| | James R. Schlesinger | 1973–1974 |
| Ford | James R. Schlesinger | 1974–1975 |
| | Donald H. Rumsfeld | 1975–1977 |
| Carter | Harold Brown | 1977–1981 |
| Reagan | Caspar P. Weinberger | 1981–1987 |
| | Frank C. Carlucci | 1987–1989 |
| Bush | Richard B. Cheney | 1989–1993 |
| Clinton | Les Aspin | 1993–1994 |
| | William Perry | 1994–1997 |
| | William Cohen | 1997– |

to be more cautious. Finally, for a very long time, all of the military services have successfully cultivated close relations with individual members of Congress. The military bases and industrial suppliers spread across the country and in almost every congressional district constitute the military-industrial complex against which President Eisenhower warned in his farewell address. Weapons acquisition affects not only military security but job opportunities.

The chair of the Joint Chiefs of Staff became a more important player within the defense constellation with the passage of the Goldwater-Nichols Act in 1986. Prior to that time, the chair could take only positions on which all of the chiefs were agreed, leading to lowest-common-denominator statements that encouraged each service to go its own way. Goldwater-Nichols made the chairman, as an individual, the principal military adviser to the defense secretary and the president, gave the Joint Staff (formed by officers from all four services) to the chair as personal staff and increased its attractiveness, allowed the chair to review individual service budgets, and made the chair responsible for unified theater commands. This considerably increased the status of the chair. The first two chairs to have these powers used them to adapt very rapidly to the end of the cold war. Adm. William Crowe began a series of cooperative ventures with the Soviet military (Zisk 1997), and Gen. Colin Powell put together a Base Force program that called for a 25 percent reduction in military expenditures (Stockton 1997). No one knows how chairs will behave in the future, but the new powers cast the person who holds that position as a very strong ally or formidable opponent among foreign policy decision makers.

## Central Intelligence

The National Security Act of 1947 created the Central Intelligence Agency and made the director of central intelligence (DCI) responsible for coordinating U.S. intelligence activities. (Directors of central intelligence since 1953 are listed in Box 4–4.) Half a century later the CIA is still evolving; although the DCI remains a

**Box 4–4   Directors of Central Intelligence**

| President | Directors of Central Intelligence | Years |
|-----------|-----------------------------------|-------|
| Eisenhower | Allen W. Dulles | 1953–1961 |
| Kennedy | Allen W. Dulles | 1961 |
| | John A. McCone | 1961–1963 |
| Johnson | John A. McCone | 1963–1965 |
| | William F. Raborn | 1965–1966 |
| | Richard M. Helms | 1966–1969 |
| Nixon | Richard M. Helms | 1969–1973 |
| | James R. Schlesinger | 1973 |
| | William R. Colby | 1973–1974 |
| Ford | William R. Colby | 1974–1976 |
| | George Bush | 1976–1977 |
| Carter | Stansfield Turner | 1977–1981 |
| Reagan | William J. Casey | 1981–1987 |
| | William H. Webster | 1987–1989 |
| Bush | William H. Webster | 1989–1991 |
| | Robert M. Gates | 1991–1993 |
| Clinton | R. James Woolsey | 1993–1994 |
| | John Deutch | 1995–1996 |
| | George J. Tenet | 1997– |

statutory adviser to the National Security Council, this position has not achieved a status equal to that of the chairman of the Joint Chiefs of Staff. There are several reasons for these developments: technology, the extent of intelligence activities outside the CIA, conflicting goals within the CIA, and changes on the international scene.

Although many spy novels feature lonely operatives in enemy countries, much more information is now gathered technologically. Aerial observation became a mainstay of intelligence with the development of U-2 aircraft in the 1950s, and satellites have expanded that activity in recent decades. The National Reconnaissance Office (NRO), which runs the satellite program, now spends more than any other intelligence agency. The National Security Agency (NSA) employs the most personnel and is the second most expensive. NSA is in charge of electronic eavesdropping and cryptography. Both NRO and NSA are part of the Defense Department, not the CIA, and together with the Defense Intelligence Agency and military intelligence services, spend an estimated 80 percent of the total intelligence budget of $26.7 billion (Smith and Pincus 1995; Weiner 1998b).[8] The CIA itself spends only about $3 billion. Hence, the director of central intelligence can coordinate intelligence activity only with the cooperation of the secretary of defense.

The CIA itself was originally given responsibility for collection, evaluation, and dissemination of information about foreign affairs. Collection employs both human sources and technical sources. Evaluation means explaining the pieces of information by putting them in a larger context, and dissemination means a constant flow of information, especially to senior decision makers. The CIA quickly acquired two more missions, counterintelligence against foreign intelligence operations and covert operations to influence events overseas (Johnson 1997, 136–137).

Within the CIA the two most important units were the Intelligence Directorate, responsible for analysis, and the Operations Directorate, responsible for the case officers overseas. Long kept completely isolated from each other, intelligence personnel saw the operations case officers as reckless cowboys, and operations personnel regarded the intelligence analysts as timid scholars (Johnson 1997, 142). This isolation accentuated rivalries between bureaucratic subcultures. The extent to which these organizational rivalries affected the quality of intelligence is hard to say. But the intelligence the CIA has disseminated to policy makers has ranged from very good (such as the U-2 photographs that alerted

---

[8.] George Tenet was the first DCI to disclose the amount of intelligence spending. By way of comparison, the fiscal 1998 budget of $26.7 billion is about 10 percent of all defense spending and a little less than the budgets of the Departments of Education or Housing and Urban Development.

President Kennedy to Soviet missiles in Cuba) to pathetic (as when the CIA's leaders, with 65 percent of their resources devoted to the Soviet Union, brushed aside predictions from the agency's Soviet experts that Gorbachev's leadership would lead to major changes in Russia) (Johnson 1996; 1997, 152; Zisk 1997).

The effort devoted to one activity or another has been a function of foreign developments, the predilection of the director of central intelligence, and his standing in the government. Recently the focus of intelligence has been shifted from Russia to potential terrorist states, and DCIs have tried to get the best efforts from both operations and intelligence personnel.

## Coordination

*National Security Council Meetings.* From our review we can see that these entities all have important, and differing, responsibilities. Moreover, the leadership positions—especially the secretaries of state and defense—are often filled by strong-minded, experienced persons whose views on policy may not coincide. There have been three general responses to the thorny problem of coordinating the activities of these agencies. The first possibility is that the National Security Council itself provides coordination. The best example of this comes from the Eisenhower administration, when Robert Cutler was the national security assistant.[9] The frequent council meetings were marked by "spirited, no-holds-barred debate" between the principals. Eisenhower wanted "the members of the [National Security Council to] become familiar, *not only with each other, but with the basic factors of problems,* that might, on some future date, face the president" (Burke and Greenstein 1989, 54, 278; emphasis in original). Having participated in open discussion of policy alternatives with the president, his principal assistants were in a much better position to coordinate the policy that was put into effect.

Eisenhower did not rely on the council alone for coordination; he supplemented it with other means. One such unit was the Operations Coordinating Board. Like the NSC, this board was chaired by the national security assistant; members included senior officials from State, Defense, CIA, the United States Information Agency, the Agency for International Cooperation (which handled foreign aid), and others, depending on the subject matter. Once the National Security Council made a decision, the OCB was charged with implementation

---

[9.] Cutler actively resisted the creation of a separate national security staff, and Eisenhower's other national security assistants, Dillon Anderson and Gordon Gray, agreed with Cutler on the proper role of the national security assistant (Nelson 1981, 250). Thus the Eisenhower administration's emphasis was still firmly on the council, not the NSC staff.

and coordination. If action was wanting on the part of relevant agencies, the OCB could expedite affairs. In addition, President Eisenhower engaged in an endless series of private meetings that modified and illuminated the formal decisions. His staff secretary, Colonel Goodpaster, coordinated day-to-day national security operations. By the second term, Goodpaster was accepted as a major player able to argue with Eisenhower himself (Destler, Gelb, and Lake 1984, 177).[10]

*Coordination Through Committees.* A second approach has been to create other organizations that substitute (at least in part) for the National Security Council in providing coordination. This was done more frequently as the NSC staff grew, gaining power at the expense of the council. Committee names changed rapidly from one administration to the next. One of the first was the Senior Interdepartmental Group (SIG, a venerable bureaucratic title), created by Lyndon Johnson in 1965 under the chairmanship of the under secretary of state, to keep routine decisions off the president's desk. Henry Kissinger devised several committees during the Nixon administration, including the Washington Special Action Group, which dealt with crises; the Verification Panel, through which Kissinger controlled arms control; and the Intelligence Committee, which set general policy for U.S. intelligence activities. All these committees were chaired by Henry Kissinger. At Jimmy Carter's direction, Zbigniew Brzezinski reduced the number to two committees. The Policy Review Committee was usually chaired by the secretary of state, and the Special Coordination Committee, chaired by Brzezinski, dealt with crises, arms control, and intelligence. A blizzard of committees blew through the turmoil of Reagan's national security apparatus (Prados 1991).

The Bush administration simplified the committee structure. The Principals Committee (chaired by the national security assistant, with the secretaries of state and defense, UN ambassador, chairman of the joint chiefs, and director of central intelligence as members) was the most prominent. The Deputies Committee, created in October 1989 after communications failures prevented information about a Panamanian coup from reaching the top level of the Bush White House (Fitzwater 1995, 201–211), did much of the work. The Clinton administration retained these two committees (Auger 1997).

---

[10.] Goodpaster relates that Eisenhower said to him, "I've said that I want to start reducing our forces in Europe. You know that's our policy, and I want action to be initiated on that." Goodpaster replied, "Well, Mr. President, it isn't quite our policy. That's the goal that's stated—to work down to the long-term strength—but it's conditioned on the ability of the Europeans to fill the gap that's there, the gap we created." Goodpaster was supported on this by Secretary of State Dulles, and he prevailed (Kernell and Popkin 1986, 23–24).

*Avoiding the National Security Council.* A third approach, often combined with the second, is to keep foreign policy business *away* from the National Security Council. President Kennedy liked to appoint select individuals to ad hoc task groups.[11] President Johnson had lunch on Tuesday with his closest foreign policy advisers in the family quarters of the White House. President Nixon preferred to rely on Henry Kissinger rather than Secretary of State William Rogers or Secretary of Defense Melvin Laird, and did this by routing business through one or another of Kissinger's committees. President Carter had Friday breakfasts with his national security assistant, secretary of state, and secretary of defense (much like Johnson's Tuesday lunches); his three principals' aides lunched together weekly; meetings of the National Security Council itself were relatively rare.

The principal decision-making vehicle in the Bush White House was a "core group" consisting of the president, vice president, secretary and deputy secretary of state, secretary of defense, national security assistant and deputy assistant, and chief of staff, which met informally (Bush and Scowcroft 1998, 41–42). President Clinton and Vice President Gore rarely attended Principals Committee meetings. In their absence, half-measures were more likely to be adopted than clear strategies (Holbrooke 1998b, 81). Presidential motivation to keep business away from the National Security Council varies. A president may wish to exclude a National Security Council member (for example, Vice President Humphrey, who had reservations about the war in Vietnam, was not invited to Johnson's Tuesday lunches); another president may wish to use a smaller group to reduce leaks; still another may not be interested in foreign policy. The quality of coordination, of course, depends on the leadership provided by the president.

## Foreign Policy Activities

### Custodian

Because of his roles in planning and more general coordination, the national security assistant occupies a position of considerable potential influence. The question is how the assistant should exercise that influence.[12] One notable answer from

---

[11.] The famous Ex Comm that met with Kennedy during the Cuban Missile Crisis began this way.

[12.] Here as elsewhere, it is convenient to focus on the special assistant for national security affairs rather than the NSC staff. Nonetheless, we must remember that "the national security assistant and the NSC staff are *not* the same actors, nor necessarily of common mind" (Rockman 1981, 912).

Alexander George is that the national security assistant should be a *custodian* who should *"scrupulously refrain from becoming an advocate himself"* (1972, 781; emphasis in original) and instead act as a neutral guardian of the decision-making process. The custodian should balance actor resources, strengthen weaker advocates, bring in new advisers to argue for unpopular options, set up new channels of information so the president will not be dependent on a single channel, arrange for independent evaluation of options when necessary, and otherwise protect the quality of information reaching the president. This argument has been criticized on two grounds. First, much of the national security assistant's strength "stems from his predominance as an operational coordinator . . . in virtually all phases of the policy-making process." Without this substantive involvement, where would he get the leverage to carry out his responsibilities (Destler 1972, 787)? Second, confining him to the custodian's role asks him to deny his own potential. If he has command of foreign policy issues and the political skills for a senior White House position, why shouldn't he use these capacities in behalf of policies he favors? (For a discussion of similar questions concerning the chief of staff, see Box 4–5.)

Nonetheless, having a custodian helps to implement a system of multiple advocacy in which the president is given several well-supported options from which to choose. Eisenhower's Robert Cutler acted as a custodian most of the time. He intervened only to keep the process on track. For example, when discussion at an NSC meeting began to address the question of providing arms to U.S. troops if they went to Vietnam, Cutler broke in to say that there was nothing whatever in the planning document "which authorized the introduction of U.S. combat forces into Indochina at this time" (Burke and Greenstein 1989, 55).

## Policy Advocacy

A custodian, Alexander George argues, should renounce policy advocacy. Nonetheless, there are reasons why the national security assistant should advance ideas of his own. The recommendations coming from State, Defense, and other sources may be unwise. The national security assistant, familiar with the president's thinking because of his proximity, and familiar with department positions because of his responsibilities for coordination, may be in the best position to suggest alternatives. Whatever the arguments, many post-Eisenhower national security assistants have considered policy advocacy to be part of their job. McGeorge Bundy, who served Kennedy and Johnson, saw the NSC staff as an independent source of policy advice for the president, and he argued for specific courses of action. In February 1965 he wrote the president: "We believe that the best available way of increasing our chance of success in Vietnam is the development and execution of

**Box 4–5    Questions About the Chief of Staff**

Similar questions to those about the custodian's role for the national security assistant pertain to the role of the chief of staff. One concerns the chief of staff's relation to the president, and the other asks the extent to which a chief of staff should intervene in tasks assigned to other staff members.

On the first question, there is a contrast between the way Richard Cheney served Ford and Ken Duberstein served Reagan, and the way Donald Regan served Reagan. In the Cheney-Duberstein mode,

> White House staffers with key roles perform their roles, often with their own direct access to the president. The focus is on maximizing the president's strengths, with the staff acting to inform him of options, to give him a range of views, to provide a pragmatic understanding of the political terrain for him to balance with his own strong views. This does not mean a weak chief of staff . . . but the system is designed to serve the president, not the ego or the power lust of the chief of staff (Ornstein 1988).

In the Regan mode, "Access to the president, including phone calls, were tightly controlled and dominated by the chief. Other White House employees worked for him—not the president. Regan eagerly accepted any and all credit for Reagan successes, and found excuses for any failures" (Ornstein 1988). The Regan mode certainly generates more publicity for the chief of staff, but the Cheney-Duberstein mode gives the president a better chance to exercise his broad political judgment on important questions (Neustadt 1987).

The second question involves the increasing tendency of chiefs of staff to take control of crucial decisions regarding congressional relations, the press, or the three policy areas. The extreme case here is the Sununu mode, since he dealt himself in on all five major tasks in the Bush White House. There are reasons for chiefs of staff to become involved in certain areas. A chief of staff may know more about some particular area than his president. Howard Baker certainly knew more about the Senate than President Reagan, and Leon Panetta had a much better sense of the House than President Clinton. But if the chief of staff is a political generalist, and if the heads of specific staff units have expertise in their own fields, the chief of staff risks overriding staff recommendations that have been very carefully developed in areas about which he knows relatively little. And coordination is a huge task by itself. If the chief of staff dips into Middle Eastern policy, health care, Senate quorum calls, and all the other issues swirling about the White House, he will be spread too thin to do his primary job adequately.

*(continued)*

It is clear, however, that chiefs of staff are using their influence to intervene in specific areas. We have already reviewed their involvement in congressional and media relations. Most recent chiefs of staff have been invited members of the National Security Council or participants in informal foreign policy decision-making groups, and have been involved in decision making on economics and domestic policy. But the question of balance remains. Chiefs of staff must reserve enough time to be effective in their primary responsibilities. They must also discover ways to serve their president *and* make full use of the talents of their colleagues.

a policy of *sustained reprisal* against North Vietnam—a policy in which air and naval action against the North is justified and related to the whole Viet Cong campaign of violence and terror in the South" (*Pentagon Papers* 1971, 423).

Zbigniew Brzezinski, for example, gave his view of the tasks of the NSC staff as "coordinating and integrating the work of the State Department, Defense, and Central Intelligence and also giving the president an independent policy perspective, thereby influencing the policy choices he would make." There was noticeable conflict between Brzezinski and Secretary of State Vance, first over Soviet activity in the Horn of Africa (that is, Ethiopia and Somalia), where Brzezinski advocated a more vigorous U.S. response. Then as the African troubles were joined by the Iranian revolution and the Soviet invasion of Afghanistan, Brzezinski saw a need for American reactions in the larger "arc of crisis" (Hargrove 1988b, 149–156; Prados 1991, 432–433).

In September 1995, when Croatian and Bosnian offensives were retaking land held by the Bosnian Serbs, Anthony Lake argued that the United States should urge the Croatians and Bosnians to exercise restraint. Richard Holbrooke, supported by Secretary of State Christopher, believed the recapture of territory held by the Serbs would facilitate forthcoming peace negotiations between the warring parties (Holbrooke 1998b, 159, 172).

## Planning

Dwight Eisenhower came to office accustomed to thorough preparation. He wanted a comprehensive planning capacity in the White House, but he also understood full well that planners could not anticipate every future development. "Rely on planning, but never trust plans" was a phrase he often used (Greenstein 1982, 133). Before a topic ever reached the Eisenhower's National

Security Council, its substance had been thrashed out by his Policy Planning Board "over weeks, sometimes even months, of preparation" (Cutler 1956, 57). On important matters, Eisenhower was not satisfied to have a single plan. When the National Security Council began discussing the military situation in Vietnam in January 1954, they had a Planning Board paper (NSC 177) before them that reviewed various military options. This included a "policy split" (a disagreement among Planning Board members) over predictions of the consequences of a French defeat. [13] By the end of March, there were three separate analyses of Southeast Asia on the table (Burke and Greenstein 1989, chap. 2). Eisenhower's elaborate planning machinery did not survive his own administration,[14] but the need for planning did.

A second example of planning is provided by Nixon's and Kissinger's assessment of Vietnam early in 1969. Both had ideas before the inauguration; with the aid of the RAND Corporation, Kissinger had prepared a series of questions (what were the possibilities of negotiation, how effective was the South Vietnamese army, what was the impact of pacification, and so on) to be sent out immediately to the agencies as NSSM-1.[15] A series of memoranda flowed back and forth between NSC and the agencies during Nixon's first three months, and by April Nixon had decided to place more of the burden of the war on South Vietnam. This policy was consistent with American interests, but it meant that Washington would have to bring pressure on Saigon if a negotiated settlement was to be reached (Prados 1991, 268–272).

George Bush's first extended meeting with Mikhail Gorbachev was planned for Malta in December 1989. A series of intensive briefings preceded this conference. "Brent [Scowcroft] offered me about twenty topics to choose from," Bush wrote. "I took them all. I wanted to be prepared for everything" (Bush and Scowcroft 1998, 153–154).

---

[13.] Whenever a policy split occurred, the arguments on both sides were set forth in parallel columns. This format increased the likelihood that the divisive issues would be debated by the full council.

[14.] President Kennedy eliminated much of Eisenhower's planning and coordination structure, but soon found it necessary to replicate some of Eisenhower's processes (Patterson 1988, 52).

[15.] Each administration had its own acronyms for memoranda. The Nixon administration used NSSM for National Security Study Memorandum and NSDM for National Security Decision Memorandum. Thus NSSM-1 stood for the first memorandum directing that a study be made.

## Negotiation

For some time, presidents have sent national security assistants on negotiating missions. Early in 1965, Maxwell Taylor, speaking both from his military background and as ambassador to South Vietnam, raised questions about the problems the United States would have fighting a difficult war on the Asian mainland. He suggested that McGeorge Bundy be sent to South Vietnam. Bundy's cables to Taylor (prior to the trip) indicated that he would speak not only for himself but also for the president (Patterson 1988, 196; Burke and Greenstein 1989, chap. 6). Later that spring, Bundy led a negotiating team to the Caribbean at the time of a crisis in the Dominican Republic (Prados 1991, 146–147).

Negotiation became even more prominent under Henry Kissinger. By January 1970 Kissinger was shuttling back and forth to Paris, where he was conducting secret negotiations with Le Duc Tho over ending the Vietnamese War. Then, one spring evening in 1971, a message arrived in Washington from Beijing stating that the Chinese were ready (after two years of diplomatic overtures) to receive a high-level envoy. President Nixon decided to send Kissinger. In three days of secret negotiation with Premier Chou En-lai, arrangements were made for Nixon to visit China the following year, thus resuming direct diplomatic contacts between China and the United States (Kalb and Kalb 1974, 272–287).

Although Kissinger's successors have not been as prominently involved in foreign affairs, virtually all have engaged in diplomatic missions. Zbigniew Brzezinski visited Beijing in May 1978 and went to Pakistan shortly after Russia invaded Afghanistan in December 1979. Robert McFarlane made numerous trips to the Middle East during the Reagan administration. Brent Scowcroft made a secret trip to Beijing immediately after the Tiananmen Square massacre in 1989 to explain the American view of that incident. In August 1995 Anthony Lake led a negotiating team to Europe to brief allies on U.S. plans to bring peace to Bosnia. And in the wake of Taiwanese elections in March 2000, Samuel Berger was dispatched to Beijing.

Whether national security assistants should be engaged in diplomatic negotiations is an open question. If the national security assistant is a person of standing within the administration (as is usually the case), he can speak more authoritatively than someone who can report to the secretary of state and president only through channels. But if the national security assistant travels freely in the name of the president, his availability can sometimes undercut the capacity of foreign service officers on the scene to get governmental leaders to speak frankly to them. Nonetheless, presidents have used national security assistants (and not infrequently *their* assistants) for diplomatic chores and are likely to continue to do so.

## Symbol Manipulation

Much of foreign policy involves symbols and subtlety. For example, when over-tures were being made to Beijing early in the Nixon administration, it was announced that the United States and China would resume bilateral talks "at the Chinese Communist Embassy" in Warsaw. Shortly thereafter, a correction was put out saying that the talks would be resumed "at the Embassy of the People's Repub-lic of China," the style preferred by the Chinese and which by 1970 the United States was willing to use. When using particular words is so important, the White House press office is reluctant to speak because of the chance of inadvertent error. NSC staffers who have been involved in the formulation of the policy are more likely to know just what words are appropriate.

How much time a national security assistant devotes to publicity depends on his own desires and the instructions received from his president. There is considerable variation to this, especially at the extremes. The mean number of annual references to the assistant in the *New York Times Index* is a convenient guide to each one's vis-ibility. These are listed in Table 4–1. The press lavished attention on Kissinger and

**Table 4–1 Press Attention to National Security Assistants**

| President | National Security Assistants | Mean Annual References |
|---|---|---|
| Kennedy, Johnson | McGeorge Bundy | 40 |
| Johnson | Walt W. Rostow | 38 |
| Nixon, Ford | Henry A. Kissinger | 295 |
| Ford | Brent Scowcroft | 16 |
| Carter | Zbigniew Brzezinski | 130 |
| Reagan | Richard V. Allen | 70 |
|  | William P. Clark | 61 |
|  | Robert P. McFarlane | 49 |
|  | John M. Poindexter | 17 |
|  | Frank C. Carlucci | 31 |
|  | Colin L. Powell | 20 |
| Bush | Brent Scowcroft | 17 |
| Clinton | Anthony Lake | 12 |
|  | Samuel R. Berger * | 21 |

Sources: 1961–1980, I. M. Destler, "National Security II: The Rise of the Assistant (1961–1981)," in *The Illusion of Presidential Government,* ed. Hugh Heclo and Lester M. Salamon (Boulder, Colo.: Westview, 1981), 275; 1981–1998, extracted from various edi-tions of the *New York Times Index* (New York: *New York Times*).

*Data for Samuel Berger are for 1997 and 1998.

Brzezinski, while Scowcroft, Poindexter, Powell, and Lake got little coverage. The others were somewhere in between. Kissinger and Brzezinski courted the press, whereas Scowcroft, Poindexter, Powell, and Lake probably tried to avoid attention. In fact, Eisenhower told his national security assistant, Robert Cutler, not to give any speeches, make any public appearances, or have any contact with reporters. Gerald Ford also instructed Brent Scowcroft to minimize his press contacts.

Richard Nixon wanted to control foreign policy from the White House and therefore directed news coverage himself to the extent possible. He sent Henry Kissinger a constant stream of instructions on how specific matters should be handled (Prados 1991, 313–314). Kissinger was more than willing to orchestrate press coverage. He cultivated relationships with the media assiduously. While in Washington, he was constantly on the phone to reporters, and when he traveled, he was accompanied by reporters covering foreign affairs. In contrast to tongue-tied members of the Nixon administration, Kissinger was entirely at home in the world of words and ideas. And, of course, many of the dramatic events Kissinger was involved in were headline news. His first public briefing came on October 26, 1972, when he began, "Ladies and gentlemen, we have now heard from both Vietnams, and it is obvious that the war that has been raging for ten years is drawing to a conclusion."

No shrinking violet himself, Zbigniew Brzezinski was determined to be heard from as Carter's national security assistant. He immediately appointed his own press officer, began giving background briefings, and in less than three months, began his own on-the-record press conferences. At one point, he had to be reined in by President Carter himself with a reminder that he was speaking for the president and should not go too far (Prados 1991, 388, 393, 423). Secretary of State Alexander Haig, anxious to avoid competition for publicity, proposed that "there must be no independent press contact with the office of [the president's] national security [assistant]" (Inderfurth and Johnson 1988, 139). William Clark swiftly revived the office of press spokesman once he became President Reagan's national security assistant.

## Defending the President

The fates of the national security assistant and the president are bound together. If the president is strong, the national security assistant has greater freedom to maneuver in foreign policy formulation. If the national security assistant has served him well, the president can take longer strides on the world scene. Earlier in this chapter, we saw that the national security assistant had the advantage of proximity to the president and knowledge of his political concerns. He can maximize these strengths by defending the president.

To a considerable extent, this argument applies to *any* staff member, whether an economist, a health specialist, or a media spokesperson, and whether the individual is a ranking staffer or at the outer fringes of the White House. Defending the president is an important element in anyone's portfolio. However, the lack of consensus on U.S. foreign policy makes this task particularly important in international affairs.

During the Eisenhower years, there was an internationalist consensus that centered on the idea of containment of the Soviet Union. With the coming of the Vietnam War, though, this consensus collapsed (Holsti and Rosenau, 1984; Wittkopf 1986). There was continued support for an international leadership role for the United States. Most political leaders—and all presidents—favored this. But underneath this internationalist umbrella, there was disputation "on the goals, strategies, and tactics that should be employed in implementing that role" (Holsti 1997). One major cleavage in public opinion, and elite opinion, has been whether greater emphasis should be given to *militant internationalism* (using military power to resist aggression, a willingness to employ covert methods, and so forth) or *cooperative internationalism* (working through the United Nations to settle disputes, helping to improve the standard of living in poor countries, and so on). These two dimensions, studied by Ole Holsti and James Rosenau ever since 1976, imply three different kinds of internationalists: *militant internationalists* who prefer to rely on force, *cooperative internationalists* who are more disposed to work with other nations, and *full internationalists* who are willing to use force, cooperation, or some combination of the two depending on the circumstances (Holsti and Rosenau 1988, 1993; Holsti 1997).[16]

None of these three approaches has had enough continued support to be dominant. Among the foreign policy elite, cooperative internationalists have been most common, full internationalists next most frequent, and militant internationalists least common. In 1984, 1988, and 1992, cooperative internationalists were a bare majority but in no position to overpower their rivals, and the rest of the time none of the three groups have been a majority (Holsti and Rosenau 1993, Table 4; 1997). Here we see the importance of this typology to presidents: in the absence of a foreign policy consensus, *every* president will be politically vulner-

---

[16.] In order to stress their common internationalism, I have changed the names given to these groups by Holsti and Rosenau. Militant internationalists are what they call hardliners; cooperative internationalists are what they call accommodationists; what I call full internationalists because of their willingness to use either approach, Holsti and Rosenau call internationalists. I do not discuss a fourth group, isolationists, who reject both militant and cooperative internationalism.

able. *Whatever* position a president attempts to develop will be open to attack. A full internationalist policy, for example, can be attacked from one direction by cooperative internationalists and from the opposite direction by militant internationalists. In this situation, presidents covet political champions who will defend their policies. Small wonder that Jimmy Carter, being urged to instruct Zbigniew Brzezinski to take a lower profile, responded, "I need Zbig to speak out publicly. He can go after my enemies. He can protect my flanks" (Gelb 1980, 26).

## Foreign Economic Policy

Virtually the entire Thanksgiving Day 1997, and again throughout a December "vacation," Treasury Secretary Robert Rubin was on the phone with his aides and other economic officials. Something had to be done about the rapidly deteriorating South Korean economy. South Korea had the world's eleventh largest economy. If it collapsed, other economies might also be endangered. Eventually it was decided to ask American, British, German, Japanese, and French bankers to spread out their Korean loans and to speed up loans from the International Monetary Fund (IMF). The South Korean economy was stabilized (Weisberg 1998). This activity was not unusual. Since 1995, Treasury officials have intervened in Mexico, Thailand, Indonesia, Russia, and Brazil. In each case, instability in one country threatened other economies.

Concern with international economics—monetary policy, international trade, aid to developing countries, and so on—is hardly new. Beginning with the creation of the International Monetary Fund, the World Bank, and the General Agreement on Trade and Tariffs (GATT), America has been the leading player in international finance. I. M. Destler suggests that economic foreign policy in recent decades can be divided into three periods. During the Eisenhower, Kennedy, and Johnson administrations economic policy was directed by an under secretary of state or a ranking NSC staff member. In the 1970s and 1980s, however, as the NSC staffs became preoccupied with security matters, a separate economic cluster appeared.[17] The treasury secretary, the U.S. trade representative, and related actors played a larger role in economic decisions. By the 1990s, with the end of the cold war and the increasing volume of foreign trade,[18] economic decisions and security decisions were seen as equally important (Destler 1994).

---

[17.] As we shall see in Chapter 5, specialists in international economics were included in the coordinating units dealing with economic policy.

[18.] Exports rose from just over 4 percent of GDP in 1970 to more than 10 percent in 1990.

Public opinion about foreign trade and related affairs was distributed differently than attitudes about other foreign policy matters. Regardless of where they fell on the cooperative–militant dimension, businesses wanted to trade overseas, and farmers and agribusiness saw foreign countries as a vital part of their markets. On questions such as pressure on Japan and Europe to open their markets, support for American firms doing business in China, NAFTA, GATT, and the World Trade Organization, backing for the president (whether Bush or Clinton) tended to come from the middle of the ideological spectrum, while opposition came from liberals with close ties to labor unions and from the Christian right (Holsti 1997, 15).

## Information Gathering in Foreign Policy

In June 1959 Dwight Eisenhower wrote a memorandum to the secretary of defense about the possibility of stationing intermediate-range ballistic missiles (IRBMs) in Greece. He had eight questions he wanted answered:

1. Do we in fact have a firm plan for stationing IRBMs in Greece?
2. Did the Greek government initiate a firm request for these weapons?
3. Assuming the answer is "yes," did the appropriate NATO authority concur?
4. What additional numbers of uniformed services would be stationed in Greece?
5. What would be the total number of such American strength in that country?
6. What particular advantage do you expect to gain from putting these weapons in Greece in view of the fact that country is both small and exposed?
7. Does the State Department see any great advantage in stationing these weapons in that particular country?
8. Finally, what additional sums for defense support and economic assistance would be requested of the Congress as a result of such action?

I do not want this memorandum widely circulated or worked on by junior staffs . . . these matters involve high policy and so I should like this paper handled by the fewest possible people (Greenstein 1982, 135).

Here we have a president notable for seeking information. He was in the seventh year of his presidency and operating in the area of his greatest personal expertise. Consequently, we can conclude this episode is representative of superior presidential performance.

Normally, information in international affairs does not arrive in a neat and systematic fashion. In Destler's wording, "Issues generally arise not all at once or once and for all, but bit by bit" (1974, 59). Larger questions are thereby obscured. On a given day, for instance, news items may include a collapse of the Italian government, a change in the exchange rate between the dollar and the Japanese yen, and a demonstration in northern England over unemployment. The State Department will no doubt analyze the positions likely to be taken by the incoming Italian government; the Treasury Department will be concerned about the strength of the dollar; the situation in England may be seen as a domestic question in the United Kingdom. There is nothing in this collection of information that would suggest a reformulation of American foreign policy—even though such elements as these can lead to political change.

Alexander George has shown that international decisions are often characterized by *value complexity* and *uncertainty* (George 1980, chap. 2; compare Steinbruner 1974, chap. 4).[19] Value complexity "refers to the presence of multiple, competing values that are embedded in a single issue" (George 1980, 26). Does the United States restrict the importation of foreign cars to protect the jobs of American auto workers? Or does the government decide to admit as many as the foreigners can manufacture, because Americans believe in a free market and want to be able to buy less expensive automobiles? When Americans were outraged by the slaughter of Chinese students in Tiananmen Square, should the United States have adopted harsh sanctions, or should the government have reacted with restraint to protect potential commercial opportunities in the Chinese market? Such competing values are to be found in a great many foreign policy decisions.

Uncertainty is a constant handmaiden of foreign policy choices. For example, the Bush administration was surprised by a coup mounted by Soviet hardliners against Mikhail Gorbachev in August 1991. President Bush's immediate reaction was to phone foreign leaders, including Britain's John Major, France's François Mitterrand, Germany's Helmut Kohl, Japan's Toshiki Kaifu, Canada's Brian Mulroney, Spain's Felipe Gonzáles, Czechoslovakia's Václav Havel, and Poland's Lech Walesa. No one knew very much; the best-informed was Boris Yeltsin, president of the Russian Republic, who was actively opposing the coup. Bush wrote in his diary: "My problem is that, during Iraq a year ago, we knew what had to happen. What had to happen is Iraq had to get out of Kuwait. Here, I'm not sure what *has* to happen." In his calls, Bush encouraged foreign leaders not to accept the coup, and in public statements he called the coup "disturbing" and added that "coups can fail." As it turned out, his course was the proper one. The coup collapsed two days later, and Bush was able to congratulate Gorbachev

---

[19.] While George's concern is with foreign policy, value complexity and uncertainty apply to many economic and domestic decisions as well.

and Yeltsin on their success. Still, the key point is that neither President Bush nor anyone else could act with certainty because information was lacking (Bush and Scowcroft 1998, 519–533).

With modern technology, information can come in too fast, in too fragmentary a form. Just this happened in May 1975, when Cambodian forces captured the American merchant ship *Mayaguez,* took the ship to nearby Koh Tang Island, and held the crew there. President Ford convened a meeting of the National Security Council to consider what action to take. While the President and other NSC members were sitting in the Cabinet Room, radio reports were coming in from a pilot who was flying over a smaller boat that was taking members of the *Mayaguez* crew to shore. The information was quite fragmentary, statements like "I see people there. They look like Caucasians, and they are half-way to the shore." Here information moved directly from the pilot to the president of the United States with no evaluation whatsoever. In this instance, Gerald Ford decided to let the boat proceed. As Ford's Chief of Staff Dick Cheney said later, it "turned out to be the right decision, but it was basically just dumb luck" (Kernell and Popkin 1986, 54–58).

There are some occasions when "new" information turns out not to be so new after all, and is therefore quite deceptive. In the summer of 1979, there were rumors of Soviet troops in Cuba. The intelligence agencies were asked to find out more, and in mid-August National Security Assistant Brzezinski reported to President Carter that there was a Soviet brigade in Cuba. When this story became public, many called for stern action to be taken. Ultimately, it turned out that the Soviet brigade wasn't new at all. As Secretary of State Cyrus Vance later wrote, "Appallingly, awareness of the Soviet ground force units had faded from the institutional memories of the intelligence agencies. . . . By late September it was evident that the unit in question had almost certainly been in Cuba continuously since 1962" (1983, 362, cited in Neustadt and May 1986, 93–95).

What can an administration do when working with information of this character? Most administrations begin with comprehensive reviews of existing foreign policy. The National Security Council sends directives to the agencies asking for studies about topics of concern. Just as Henry Kissinger sent out many study memoranda at the beginning of the Nixon administration, the Carter administration began with a broad-ranging assessment of military policy. Agency responses were the basis for an extensive monograph prepared by senior NSC staffers. The incoming Bush administration took some months to review the Reagan administration's policies regarding the Soviet Union. Taking time for these studies serves two important functions. The early reviews acquaint policy makers with many important details and give them an understanding of the agencies' capacities and the biases they are likely to bring to policy questions.

In another early step national security assistants discover how particular presidents like to work. McGeorge Bundy had a comfortable relationship with John Kennedy, but he had to establish new ties when President Johnson was thrust into the Oval Office. When he had bad news, he found it advisable to talk rapidly, not giving the president a chance to interrupt, and then exit quickly to escape the presidential temper (Prados 1991, 137). With the advantage of long acquaintance, William Clark knew Ronald Reagan had little foreign policy background. He therefore began to give him decisions to make, reasoning that Reagan could learn about foreign policy by playing a more active role. And Brent Scowcroft accommodated George Bush's desire for a personal counselor by spending many hours at his side (Hoffman 1989c, 6). Such adaptations have little to do with content but contribute much to the assistant's ability to bring information to the president's attention.

Finally, professionals on the national security staff and those in State, Defense, and other agencies can often supply context that gives meaning to the fragments of information. Perhaps the word that best describes foreign policy staff work is one they sometimes use themselves: *sherpa,* as in "I was the president's sherpa at the recent economic summit." The original sherpas, of course, are the skilled Tibetan mountain climbers who draw on their detailed knowledge of the topography to guide more famous mountaineers up the slope. Similarly, foreign policy experts lend the president their detailed knowledge of international affairs. In the fall of 1995, for example, President Clinton asked if NATO bombing of Bosnian Serbs had reached a point of diminishing returns. "No, Mr. President," Ambassador Holbrooke replied. "There may come a time when continued bombing would hurt the peace efforts, but we're not there yet. . . . It is hurting the Bosnian Serbs, and helping us." Secretary of State Christopher added, "It would be a mistake to back off now." With this information in hand, President Clinton assented to a continuation of the bombing (Holbrooke 1998b, 145).

## Decision Making in Foreign Policy

In the international arena, the awesome presidential responsibility for nuclear weapons looms over all. It does not overdramatize the decision to use such weapons to say it could lead to the destruction of civilization. No president since World War II has made that decision, but all have known that they might have to. Indeed, the dread of having to face this choice has introduced caution into many foreign policy decisions.

Neither should we forget the costs of conventional warfare. Over 50,000 died in Vietnam before American participation in that civil war finally ended. But whether the losses are 50,000 in Vietnam, 19 servicemen killed in a Saudi Arabian bombing, or a single soldier assassinated on an outpost somewhere, the consequences are grave. Decisions about using the armed forces are never made lightly.

International decisions are frequently crisis decisions. A crisis is defined as involving a severe threat to important values and having a limited time for response. Some authorities include an element of surprise in their definition (Hermann 1969; Holsti 1988). The outbreak of war is obviously a crisis. An attack on the United States certainly threatens American values, and orders to the armed forces must be issued swiftly. An attack elsewhere may also be a crisis. When Israel attacked southern Lebanon in the spring of 1982, U.S. policy makers were in Paris. Yet they still had to determine a response in a very short time. Crises need not involve any armed forces. When the Mexican peso collapsed in December 1994, Treasury Secretary Rubin and Deputy Secretary Lawrence Summers recognized the possibility of a run on markets in other developing nations. At their urging, President Clinton quickly agreed to a $12.5 billion loan to stabilize the Mexican economy. Crises are not limited to foreign policy—a railroad or airline strike, for instance, would threaten the domestic economy and require quick action—but a greater proportion of foreign policy decisions must be made in these stressful circumstances.

Policy frequently has a shifting character. We sometimes think of all decisions as being fixed. But as Harold Saunders points out, policy is subject to continuous change:

> When I went to work on the National Security Council Staff in the White House in 1961, a senior colleague told me: "Remember policy is not made on paper. It is a continuously changing mix of people and ideas." . . . A decision is no sooner made than a new development changes the situation before it can be fully implemented. . . . [A classic] concept of international relations [is] as a strategic chess game of discrete power moves between adversary national leaderships. . . The picture I carried in my mind when I left government was of a never-ending squash or racquet-ball tournament with players on a five-sided court with six balls in motion at the same time (1988, 10, 58, 59).

Policy is continuously modified because many positions are taken vis-à-vis another nation. If the initial U.S. position is accepted by this second nation, fine; but often the second nation will respond that the particular American policy is not acceptable to them, though in somewhat altered form it might be. Or other countries friendly to the second nation may urge the United States to alter its original policy. U.S. policy makers must then decide if they wish to modify the American position. This process implies more or less continuous policy adjustment.

Foreign policy is also contingent. After the collapse of communist power in eastern Europe in 1989, there were two fundamental goals in American policy. NATO should continue to exist because it was the vehicle that allowed U.S. forces to be kept in Europe, and a reunited Germany should be a full member of NATO because most U.S. troops were stationed on German bases (Bush and Scowcroft 1998, 231). Yet whether circumstances would permit achievement of these goals could not be foreseen. What would the attitudes of other NATO members be? Britain's Margaret Thatcher thought a decision on German reunification should be deferred pending a larger strategic discussion. Canada's Brian Mulroney was concerned about the economic imbalance between West Germany and East Germany. What would be the result of East German elections? If the Social Democrats won, they might not want to unite with the rival Christian Democratic government in West Germany. And what would be the attitude of the Soviet Union be? Memories of the 1941 German invasion were very clear. Would the Soviets be willing to see their World War II enemy reunited, to say nothing of allowing it to join the alliance of their cold war rival? By September 1990—in an astonishingly short time—all these matters had been settled and a reunited Germany was in NATO. Had any of these contingencies developed differently, the outcome might have been different (Bush and Scowcroft 1998, chaps. 10–12).

The level on which decisions are made depends on how important they are and on how clearly administration policy has been stated. Zbigniew Brzezinski explained, for example, that "most of the decisions in terms of communications to foreign leaders, or regarding the movement of forces, or choices in our SALT negotiations were made by me on behalf of President [Carter], though reported to the President. And of course the more basic decisions such as MX basing, China normalization, strategic modernization, and so forth were made by the President." A member of the NSC staff used arms sales as an example of decisions he might make:

> Let's say someone called and said we want to sell Jeeps to the United Kingdom. I would say yes. But if someone called and said we want to sell the B-1 to Bolivia, I would say that's just not going to happen. Now, if someone called and said that they wanted to sell F-16s to some third-world country, I would say put together a paper giving the pros and cons, and we'll send it up and see what happens. Once a policy has been set, you know pretty well how particular decisions are going to be made.

A lower-ranking NSC staffer may be the effective decision maker on the strength of doing the initial analysis. The key steps at the working level involve what one NSC staff member called the concurrence-getting process:

This means touching base with the people who would also be concerned with the issue. If I'm writing the talking points for the president for a meeting with the bipartisan legislative leadership and one of the issues has to do with the War Powers Resolution, if I haven't talked with the lawyers on the NSC staff and gotten their concurrence, the weight of what I say is lessened. So what you want to do is to get your concurrences before something goes over to the West Wing of the White House. If you do this, 90 percent of the time, the recommendations will flow upward through the staff and get to the president. Mainly without revision.

This does not mean that NSC staff members are making the final decisions themselves. Rather, staff members can shape the decision. If they work carefully and understand their superiors' policy preferences, there is a strong probability that their work will be ratified by the ultimate decision maker.

### Exerting Influence in Foreign Policy

External influence cannot begin until there is an administration decision, until, that is, all the necessary agencies have reviewed the proposed decision and the president (or someone empowered to speak for him) has made his choice. The very next step is to make sure that all units within the executive branch will actively support the decision. For example, the Bosnian peace accord reached at Dayton in November 1995 called for sending 20,000 U.S. troops. At a White House meeting immediately afterward, Vice President Gore spoke to Defense Department leaders: "I've had lots of conversations with the Congress. They have told me that our military representatives on the Hill usually leave their audience more uncomfortable than when they arrived. I'm not saying they're trying to undercut our policy, but they're losing us votes up there." President Clinton then looked directly at Joint Chiefs Chairman General Shalikashvili: "We can't close the deal without the Pentagon's support. I know there has been some ambivalence among some of your people—not you, Shali, but some of your people, about Bosnia, but that is all in the past. I want everyone here to get behind the agreement." Clinton and Gore had coordinated their statements in order to nail down Pentagon support for the agreement (Holbrooke 1998b, 316).

It is, of course, more difficult to exercise influence overseas. For a brief period at mid-century, American influence was artificially high. The United States emerged from World War II as the strongest country in the world, in part because the war had destroyed the economies of so many other nations. For a decade or so, it seemed that the United States could accomplish a great deal and that the country's *relative* power could make this possible. This imbalance could not last. As other countries rebuilt their economic strength, the relative power of the United States declined. First Western Europe and then Japan regained a measure of economic power, and as they did so, they were less disposed to follow an American lead. And even though the United States was far wealthier than any developing countries, many political leaders abroad found domestic political capital in resisting Yankee wishes. Therefore, while the United States remains strong in an absolute sense, its relative influence has declined.

If a subject is worth the president's personal attention, he can phone or meet with foreign leaders. For instance, between late March and the end of May 1990, George Bush held extended talks with Poland's Tadeusz Mazowiecki, Britain's Margaret Thatcher, France's François Mitterrand, and Germany's Helmut Kohl on the general topic of German reunification. In each case, the talks dealt with the subject of greatest interest to the particular foreign leader. With Mazowiecki, Bush discussed the German-Polish frontier; with Thatcher, he explored the future of NATO and the need for a German commitment to keep nuclear weapons on their soil; with Mitterrand, he discussed the relative roles of NATO, the European Community (an economic bloc), and the Conference on Security and Cooperation in Europe (a larger but somewhat nebulous political organization); with Kohl, the focus was on internal politics in Germany and relations between West Germany and East Germany. By the time Mikhail Gorbachev arrived at Camp David on May 31, George Bush knew just what would be acceptable to all of these leaders, and Bush and Gorbachev agreed to German reunification with the question of NATO membership to be left to the united Germany (Bush and Scowcroft 1998, 260–286). Note that all this consultation was carried out before any public announcements were made. Further, since policy was still in a fluid state, it could be modified if the president encountered any serious objections.

If the subject is being handled below the presidential level, or if details need to be worked out, emissaries may be dispatched. When a post–cold war vision of NATO was being previewed in 1989, and again in 1990, when a negotiating position on conventional forces in Europe was being developed, Deputy National Security Assistant Robert Gates and Deputy Secretary of State Lawrence Eagleburger were sent to major European capitals (Bush and Scowcroft 1998, 80, 213–214). (In an interesting demonstration of the "special" relationship between the United States and the United Kingdom, Prime Minister Thatcher made clear her personal wariness about the NATO plans, but then added, "If the president wants it, of course we will do it.") When the Bosnian Serb mortar attack on

Sarajevo in August 1995 made NATO bombing likely, the news was conveyed by ambassadors already in place. Ambassador to the Court of St. James (and former admiral) William Crowe explained the U.S. position to his British counterparts. NATO ambassador Robert Hunter and NATO commander George Joulwan gained the assent of other NATO allies (Holbrooke 1998b, 99).

Still, barriers of sovereignty can limit American influence. Foreign governments are perfectly free to do whatever they wish within their own domains. All the U.S. government can do is ask for their cooperation in an enterprise. When dealing with a foreign power, a compelling case must be made that the proposed policy is in *their* interest as well as the American interest. If the foreign government thinks otherwise, it goes its own way. In the early 1980s, Russia was building a natural gas pipeline to Western Europe. When martial law was declared in Poland in November 1981, the Reagan administration forbade export of technical equipment needed for the pipeline. European nations objected because the pipeline would provide an energy source and jobs. Secretary of State Shultz spent months working out an agreement under which the ineffectual sanctions would be lifted. When President Reagan was about to announce it, French President Mitterrand refused to take Reagan's phone call, and the French government announced it was not a party to the agreement (Barrett 1983, 300–302). The limits to American influence overseas are substantial.

## Summary

**Actors.** While many agencies play some role in foreign policy, the principal agencies include some of Washington's most experienced and strong-willed actors. The list begins with the national security assistant, supported by the national security staff. It continues with the State Department, the Defense Department, the Joint Chiefs of Staff, and central intelligence. Given his personal responsibilities in this policy area, the president, and/or his national security assistant, oversees much of the coordination. Other foreign policy coordination is conducted through the National Security Council or other presidentially devised groups. The latter often have the effect of keeping foreign policy away from the National Security Council.

**Foreign Policy Activities.** One notable proposal is that the national security assistant should act as a custodian, giving full attention to maintaining the policy process. However, many assistants have become policy advocates and planners in their own right, as well as defenders of the president and his foreign policies. They have also taken part in the traditional diplomatic activities of negotiation and symbol manipulation. Foreign economic policy, increasingly important at the turn of the century, is usually handled by a different set of actors.

*Common Activities in an International Environment.* Information about international affairs is likely to be fragmentary, to present value conflicts, and to be shadowed by uncertainty. Consequently, a great deal of effort is devoted to extrapolating larger patterns from the bits of data that arrive from all over the world. Standing decisions about foreign policy are sometimes made, often at the beginning of an administration. More frequently, though, international decision making must be adapted, either in response to crises or because of changes in the international environment. The long-used metaphor of a static diplomatic chessboard is out of date. Perhaps the greatest difficulty with foreign affairs comes in persuading people to support a given policy. The domestic constituency is divided into militant internationalists, cooperative internationalists, and full internationalists. And these domestic problems are minor compared with the difficulties in eliciting cooperation overseas. Foreign governments are guided by their own interests, which are often quite different from American interests. Presidents, advisers, and diplomats all try to convince other governments that it is in their interest to cooperate with U.S. policy, but if they don't agree, nothing can be done.

# 5. Economic Policy

## *The Major Players*

Just to the east of the White House stands the Treasury Building. Immediately to the west is the Old Executive Office Building, where the Office of Management and Budget (OMB) and the Council of Economic Advisers (CEA) are located. Thus the White House is bracketed by the Treasury, OMB, and CEA, the principal sources of its economic advice. Several blocks to the southwest is the Federal Reserve Building. The Federal Reserve is independent, protected from presidential control by status as well as distance; but as the central bank it also has a critical position on the economic scene.

These four agencies do not exhaust the economic roster by any means. As Murray Weidenbaum (the first chair of Reagan's Council of Economic Advisers) explained, "The economic policy of any administration is a summation of decisions on taxes, budgets, monetary matters, labor, agriculture [and so forth], not all of which are made in the context of general economic policy, but which may have a strong impact on that policy." So the sources of economic policy are also to be found in the Commerce Department, the Labor Department, the Agriculture Department, the independent regulatory agencies—indeed, all over town. But the Employment Act of 1946 declared it to be national policy "to use all practicable means . . . to promote maximum employment, production and purchasing power." The efforts of the Treasury, the OMB, the CEA, and the Federal Reserve have the greatest impact on an administration's ability to achieve these broad goals.

## The Treasury Department

The secretary of the treasury was part of the original cabinet, and in protocol, ranks right after the secretary of state. From Alexander Hamilton's time on, the treasury secretary has exercised very real power. Although the treasury secretary is no longer the president's only economic adviser, he or she can be *primus inter pares,* the first among equals. When explaining his right to criticize the budget just released by President Eisenhower, George Humphrey said, "I am speaking for the Treasury Department largely. We are responsible for the federal finances . . ." (Fenno 1959, 140). On another occasion, Humphrey told Eisenhower that if anyone mentioned money, "Just ask them if they've talked to George." And as if influence over federal finances and money weren't enough, the treasury secretary is often a forceful person who is trusted by the president. This was certainly true of George Humphrey, Robert Anderson, John Connally, George Shultz, Donald Regan, James Baker, Lloyd Bentsen, and Robert Rubin. All were dominant figures in their administrations (Box 5–1).

The Treasury Department is a formidable establishment with an annual budget of $300 billion (second only to HHS among the cabinet departments) and 160,000 employees (ranking third behind the Defense and Veterans Affairs Departments). It has the general characteristics of cabinet departments discussed in the previous chapter: it is large, it has responsibility for implementation, its staff members have detailed knowledge of particular situations, and its people have a long-term perspective. Treasury has enough professionals to produce detailed analyses of economic policy. As Alfred Kingon (an assistant secretary for policy planning who moved to the Reagan White House as cabinet secretary) put it, "I had more analysts over there than the entire staff over here."

What tendencies do Treasury officials bring to policy discussions? One important clue to the answer is the department's operating responsibilities, which center on tax and financial policies. Among other things, Treasury is concerned with tax collection and the disbursement of funds for the federal government, debt management (borrowing money to pay the interest on the national debt), financial institutions and markets, and international trade. Not surprisingly, those in the department prefer policies that make it easier to carry out their responsibilities. Other things being equal, the Treasury Department would prefer a tax that is acceptable to the business community and therefore perhaps easier to collect. Its officials would choose a policy that fosters a low inflation rate, thereby reducing the amount of money they need to borrow to fund the national debt. And they do not like actions that disturb international monetary transactions.

**Box 5–1  Secretaries of the Treasury**

| President | Secretaries of the Treasury | Years |
|---|---|---|
| Eisenhower | George M. Humphrey | 1953–1957 |
|  | Robert B. Anderson | 1957–1961 |
| Kennedy | Douglas Dillon | 1961–1963 |
| Johnson | Douglas Dillon | 1963–1965 |
|  | Henry H. Fowler | 1965–1968 |
|  | Joseph W. Barr | 1968–1969 |
| Nixon | David M. Kennedy | 1969–1971 |
|  | John B. Connally | 1971–1972 |
|  | George P. Shultz | 1972–1974 |
|  | William E. Simon | 1974 |
| Ford | William E. Simon | 1974–1977 |
| Carter | W. Michael Blumenthal | 1977–1979 |
|  | G. William Miller | 1979–1981 |
| Reagan | Donald T. Regan | 1981–1984 |
|  | James A. Baker III | 1985–1988 |
|  | Nicholas F. Brady | 1988–1989 |
| Bush | Nicholas F. Brady | 1989–1993 |
| Clinton | Lloyd Bentsen | 1993–1994 |
|  | Robert E. Rubin | 1995–1999 |
|  | Lawrence H. Summers | 1999– |

Presidents tend to pick secretaries of the treasury who come from corporate or financial backgrounds. Eisenhower's George M. Humphrey, president of Hanna Steel; Kennedy's Douglas Dillon of Dillon, Read; Reagan's Donald Regan, president of Merrill Lynch; Bush's Nicholas Brady, also of Dillon, Read; and Clinton's Robert Rubin, co-chairman of Goldman, Sachs are typical.[1] Reasons for this tendency are not hard to find. Treasury, after all, needs to be in touch with the financial markets if it is to carry out its responsibilities, so it is advantageous for the president to pick a secretary from this network. Secretaries of the treasury, in turn, often select subcabinet officers from similar backgrounds. Hence, Treasury tends to have businessmen at the top and a huge career cadre underneath.

---

[1] Nixon's George Shultz and Clinton's Lawrence Summers, who had served in other capacities before being promoted to secretary of the treasury, were exceptions to this tendency. Both came from academic life.

Among the president's economic counselors, Treasury officials are most likely to speak for the financial community.[2]

## Office of Management and Budget

The Budget and Accounting Act of 1921, which mandated an executive budget and created the Bureau of the Budget to assemble it, is a landmark in U.S. administrative history.[3] The new bureau was placed in the Treasury Department. Its initial masters—Presidents Warren G. Harding and Calvin Coolidge and Directors Charles G. Dawes and Lord—emphasized economy and efficiency and had a rather narrow conception of economy. There were semiannual meetings during which the president exhorted department heads to reduce spending, and Director Lord reportedly pursued economy by searching desk drawers to make sure bureau staffers weren't using too many paper clips or pencils (Neustadt 1954, 645). Soon, however, the bureau developed important routines. Staffers learned how to turn agency requests into an annual budget, and by the 1930s bureau employees were beginning to review legislative requests to determine whether they were consistent with the president's priorities. (The process is known as clearance.) By 1939 it had become evident that the Budget Bureau could be a tool for executive management, and it was moved from Treasury into the new Executive Office of the President.

The Bureau of the Budget was at the height of its influence during the presidencies of Roosevelt, Truman, Eisenhower, and perhaps Kennedy. It was *the* general purpose presidential staff agency, the principal point of contact between the president and the executive branch. The bureau's power was based in three functions. First, its central responsibility was, and has remained, the development of the budget the president submits at the beginning of each year. Since this budget by and large controls federal spending, it has a major impact on fiscal policy. Second, the Budget Bureau was in charge of legislative clearance, and before Eisenhower's presidency no other executive unit was charged with congressional

---

[2.] Throughout this section, there are a number of statements saying that Treasury is most likely to, or OMB is most likely to, or CEA is most likely to do such-and-such or represent so-and-so. While these represent intrinsic tendencies, the statements are best understood comparatively. In this case, Treasury is more likely than OMB or CEA to speak for the business community.

[3.] As usual, there were precursors. For some time, various groups called for a coordinated national budget, and President Taft had submitted two president's budgets in 1912 and 1913.

relations. Third, as long as the White House staff remained small, the Budget Bureau had no institutional rivals dealing with economic and domestic policy. Further, all three mid-century presidents—Roosevelt, Truman, and Eisenhower—had a high regard for the bureau. Budget directors since Eisenhower's time are listed in (Box 5–2.)

By the time of the Johnson administration, the Budget Bureau was facing difficulties. Rival staffs began to appear elsewhere, and these often disagreed with Budget Bureau positions. The Johnson administration began to move more policy decisions into the White House. "They didn't use the Budget Bureau

### Box 5–2   Directors of the Budget Bureau/Office of Management and Budget

| President | Budget/OMB Directors | Years |
|-----------|---------------------|-------|
| Eisenhower | Joseph M. Dodge | 1953–1954 |
| | Rowland R. Hughes | 1954–1956 |
| | Percival F. Brundage | 1956–1958 |
| | Maurice Stans | 1958–1961 |
| Kennedy | David E. Bell | 1961–1962 |
| | Kermit Gordon | 1962–1963 |
| Johnson | Kermit Gordon | 1963–1965 |
| | Charles E. Schultze | 1965–1968 |
| | Charles J. Zwick | 1968–1969 |
| Nixon | Robert P. Mayo | 1969–1970 |
| | George P. Shultz | 1971–1972 |
| | Casper Weinberger | 1972–1973 |
| | Roy L. Ash | 1973–1974 |
| Ford | Roy L. Ash | 1974–1975 |
| | James P. Lynn | 1975–1976 |
| Carter | Bert Lance | 1977 |
| | James T. McIntyre | 1978–1981 |
| Reagan | David Stockman | 1981–1986 |
| | James C. Miller III | 1986–1988 |
| Bush | Richard G. Darman | 1989–1993 |
| Clinton | Leon E. Panetta | 1993–1994 |
| | Alice Rivlin | 1994–1996 |
| | Franklin D. Raines | 1996–1998 |
| | Jacob J. Lew | 1998– |

as an institution," claimed one observer. "They used individual Budget Bureau staff as legmen to do pick and shovel work" (Berman 1979, 80). And ever since the Eisenhower administration, there had been continuing pressure on the bureau to take on more managerial responsibilities for the president. Two external studies and two self-studies had all said that the Budget Bureau should do this, but the bureau had resisted. It was so good at budgeting that new, relatively difficult, managerial responsibilities were an unwanted distraction. But early in the Nixon administration, the Ash Commission made the same recommendation, and in 1970 the erstwhile Bureau of the Budget was transmuted into the Office of Management and Budget (Berman 1977).

The hope was that having Management as its middle name would lead OMB to provide management skills for the presidency. Managerial oversight of the huge federal bureaucracy is a real need; of the many presidential tasks, oversight has the least institutional support and is done least well (Cronin 1980, 155). OMB has given management constant attention but has had only intermittent success. It has oscillated between two approaches: separating the "M" (for Management) and "B" (for Budget) sides or adding management specialists to the budget offices.[4] OMB started with separate "M" and "B" sides in 1970, switched to four integrated offices under Roy Ash and Frederick Malek in 1973, switched back to the first pattern during the Carter administration, and switched once again to an integrated structure in 1994 (Benda and Levine 1986). OMB now has five Resource Management Offices—Natural Resources, Energy & Science; National Security & International Affairs; Health and Personnel; Human Resources; and General Government—each of which reviews budget requests and oversees agencies within its substantive area (Office of Management and Budget 1994).

Budget directors have always spoken for their presidents, whether the directors were politicians (as Bert Lance, David Stockman, and Leon Panetta) or came from a budgeting or economics background (as James McIntyre, James C. Miller, and Alice Rivlin). In the OMB incarnation, the agency's balance between neutral competence and supporting a particular president's agenda has tipped a bit toward more political support. This greater advocacy has had some costs in lower

---

4. The argument for a separate "M" side is that OMB must produce the annual budget, and having a separate management cadre assures that management gets some attention. The arguments for combining management and budget personnel are that good management is an integral part of good budgeting and vice versa, and that working with budget analysts would allow managers to take advantage of the budgeteers' knowledge of the agencies' substantive problems.

credibility and morale (Haas 1988, 2187). But the director of OMB has always been a political appointee. And in contrast to treasury secretaries and CEA chairs, who often speak for constituencies (the financial community and professional economists, respectively), budget directors have a constituency of one. They reflect the views of the president.

## Council of Economic Advisers

The Council of Economic Advisers was created by Congress as part of the Employment Act of 1946, which provided a congressional mandate for government leadership of the economy. Congress stipulated that there should be three economists, not connected with any other agency, who would provide advice to the president. The council had a mixed record in the Truman administration. President Eisenhower, uncertain whether he wanted to continue the council, asked Arthur Burns to study the situation. Burns concluded that the president needed professional economic advice, and that a three-member deliberative body would serve this need, but that a single chair should hire the staff and report to the president. Eisenhower accepted the recommendations and appointed Burns chairman (Hargrove and Morley 1984, 95–97). The CEA has kept this organization ever since.

The Council of Economic Advisers is by far the smallest of the four economic units. In contrast to the five hundred to six hundred OMB staffers, CEA has less than forty, including about a dozen economists, the three council members, and some younger economists who make up the staff. Although the staff is small, it has included some of the best minds in economics. The Kennedy CEA included one council member, James Tobin, and two staff members, Kenneth Arrow and Robert Solow, who were future Nobel Prize winners. The Eisenhower CEA staff included Charles Schultze, who became CEA chairman himself in the Carter administration, and Joseph Pechman, who was to head the economics staff at the Brookings Institution. By appointing persons who are willing to take a couple of years' leave from their universities, CEA gains some formidable talent.[5]

The CEA chairs come from three sources. At the beginning of an administration, the incoming president usually taps a sympathetic economist from a major university. For example, Eisenhower's Arthur Burns came from Colum-

---

[5.] Alan Greenspan, Ford's CEA chair who came from his own consulting firm rather than a university, pointed out that academics often lacked experience in working for clients, and they too often mistook their econometric models for reality (Hargrove and Morley 1984, 426–427).

bia, Kennedy's Walter Heller from the University of Minnesota, Nixon's Paul McCracken from the University of Michigan, Bush's Michael Boskin from Stanford, and Clinton's Laura Tyson from the University of California at Berkeley. This is often the case with midterm appointments as well. But when a chair leaves to return to academia, a CEA member is sometimes promoted to chair. On three occasions, Republican presidents have appointed economists from the business world: Herbert Stein, Alan Greenspan, and Beryl Sprinkel. Chairs since Eisenhower's presidency are listed in (Box 5–3.)

In contrast to the other economic units, the CEA has few defined responsibilities. Its members write the annual *Economic Report of the President,* and as Paul McCracken points out, "articulation makes policy" (Hargrove and Morley 1984, 339–340). The CEA transmits a lot of economic data (originated elsewhere in the government) to the president and does microanalyses of the economic effects of various policy proposals. But the Council of Economic Advisers lacks

---

**Box 5–3  Chairs of the Council of Economic Advisers**

| *President* | *CEA Chairs* | *Years* |
|---|---|---|
| Eisenhower | Arthur F. Burns | 1953–1956 |
| | Raymond T. Saulnier | 1956–1961 |
| Kennedy | Walter W. Heller | 1961–1963 |
| Johnson | Walter W. Heller | 1963–1964 |
| | Gardner H. Ackley | 1964–1968 |
| | Arthur M. Okun | 1968–1969 |
| Nixon | Paul W. McCracken | 1969–1971 |
| | Herbert Stein | 1972–1974 |
| Ford | Herbert Stein | 1974 |
| | Alan Greenspan | 1974–1977 |
| Carter | Charles L. Schultze | 1977–1981 |
| Reagan | Murray L. Weidenbaum | 1981–1982 |
| | Martin Feldstein | 1982–1984 |
| | Beryl Sprinkel | 1986–1988 |
| Bush | Michael J. Boskin | 1989–1993 |
| Clinton | Laura D. Tyson | 1993–1994 |
| | Joseph E. Stiglitz | 1995–1997 |
| | Janet L. Yellen | 1997–1999 |
| | Martin Baily | 1999– |

institutional responsibilities of its own. Instead, the group has a client to advise. If a particular president is intellectually curious, or interested in economics, or simply comes to trust the CEA, the council can be very influential. If a president is bored by "the dismal science," or feels more comfortable with other advisers, the council is impotent and there's nothing it can do about it. In practice, most presidents fall in between these extremes, but the potential difference is captured in two examples. President Eisenhower was so taken by his first briefing by Arthur Burns that he called in his appointments secretary. "I have just had a fascinating talk with this fellow Burns," Eisenhower said. "Now you put him down for an appointment with me each week for one full hour, from now on, without fail" (Hargrove and Morley 1984, 98). In contrast, Michael Boskin tried for weeks in the fall of 1991 to see George Bush to warn him that the recession was lingering; he had to threaten to resign before Chief of Staff John Sununu allowed him to see the president (Woodward 1992). The consequences were that Eisenhower had Burns at his elbow to guide him through the 1954 recession, and Bush was defeated in 1992 largely because of the weak economy to which Boskin was trying to direct his attention.

While there are many accomplished economists in the Treasury, OMB, the Federal Reserve Board, and elsewhere in Washington, the Council of Economic Advisers is the governmental beachhead of academic economists. They share the orientation of their professional colleagues. Whereas the Treasury Department and the Federal Reserve Board have institutional responsibilities that orient them to free markets, stable relationships, and low inflation, council members are more likely to think in terms of cost-benefit analysis, and they tend to favor economic policies that will reduce unemployment and stimulate growth.[6]

## The Federal Reserve Board

The Federal Reserve System was created by Congress in 1913 to regulate the supply of money and credit. For much of the nineteenth century there had been impassioned debate over the money supply: should it be controlled by an elite (private bankers) or the masses (a governmental entity subject to political forces)? Congress compromised by creating a joint public-private system consisting of a policy-making board of governors, twelve regional Federal Reserve banks that carry on most of the system's routine business, and private member banks

---

[6.] There is, of course, a lively debate among economists over what policies will lead to economic growth. See King 1993.

throughout the country. The Federal Reserve Board was insulated from direct political intervention in three ways:

1. The governors' terms do not coincide with the president's. The chairman is appointed for a four-year term, and all seven governors of the Federal Reserve (including the chairman) hold fourteen year terms;
2. Fed policies must be approved by a majority of the governors, and some must be approved by the Federal Open Market Committee, which also includes the heads of five regional Federal Reserve banks;
3. The Fed is self-financing, so it does not have to please any other governmental entity to obtain funding (Kettl 1986, 1–5).

Over time, the Federal Reserve Board has assumed control over U.S. monetary policy, but since the system was created as a central bank, its origins affect the way the Fed does business.

The chairman of the Federal Reserve Board is the governor most likely to be known to the general public. His is the voice of the Fed; he articulates Federal Reserve policies in speeches, in congressional testimony, and at international conferences. While in theory the chairman could be outvoted, in practice he is usually the dominant figure. His crucial skill is the ability to assess both economic circumstances and current political forces. He must devise appropriate monetary policy, maintain enough support from other political figures, and construct a strategy that will integrate these economic and political decisions (Kettl 1986). Further, the chairman is supported by more than 200 economists on the Fed staff. He makes the key hiring decisions, including three staff directors (the so-called Barons) who handle critical international contacts and supervise preparation of analyses of the U.S. economy and financial markets (Uchitelle 1989; Berry 1996). In order to retain the confidence of the Fed's core constituencies, chairmen are usually selected from those known to be well respected by the national and international financial communities. As a consequence of all this, the ideal Fed chairman is a skilled economist with high-level governmental experience who is esteemed on Wall Street. Recent chairmen have basically fit this profile. Chairmen since the Truman administration are listed in (Box 5–4.)

The Federal Reserve controls the money supply in three ways: it buys and sells government securities through the open market desk at the New York Federal Reserve Bank; it sets the discount rate, the interest it charges banks to which it makes loans, which in turn affects the interest the individual banks charge customers; and it stipulates the amount of money banks must hold as reserves. The

Box 5–4    **Chairman of the Federal Reserve Board**

| President | Federal Reserve Chairman | Years |
|---|---|---|
| Truman | William McC. Martin | 1951–1970 |
| Eisenhower | | |
| Kennedy | | |
| Johnson | | |
| Nixon | | |
| Nixon | Arthur F. Burns | 1970–1978 |
| Ford | | |
| Carter | | |
| Carter | G. William Miller | 1978–1979 |
| Carter | Paul A. Volcker | 1979–1987 |
| Reagan | | |
| Reagan | Alan Greenspan | 1987– |
| Bush | | |
| Clinton | | |

Fed uses the thorough studies of staff economists (as well as other sources of information) to guide these decisions. All have the effect of expanding or contracting the money supply and are therefore matters of intense concern to Americans. The higher the rate of real interest (the difference between the rate of inflation and the nominal interest rate), the costlier it is for a business to build a new plant or for the average person to buy a home or a car. The lower the rate of real interest, the easier it is to complete these transactions. Therefore tightening or loosening the money supply is often an important means of managing the economy. For instance, by increasing the cost of borrowing late in the Carter administration, the Federal Reserve Board did much to bring down inflation early in the Reagan administration.

As with all other economic units, the Federal Reserve has been enjoined to increase production, boost employment, stabilize prices, and maintain moderate long-term interest rates. But given the tools at their command and the backgrounds of the governors, they are more likely to be concerned about stable prices and interest rates. The Fed focuses on inflation because it has been historically important and because it is the economic problem most easily dealt with by adjusting the money supply.

## Coordination

*Tensions and Amelioration.* Each of these four institutions has a charter to handle some aspect of economic policy, but none has a controlling voice over economic policy in general. As is usually the case when authority is dispersed, rivalries and alliances occur between the units, with the probability of either depending on similarity of outlook and on whether related responsibilities lead to a struggle for control or a need to cooperate.

Disputes are most likely to occur between the secretaries of the treasury and the CEA chairs. Treasury secretaries are usually chosen from the business or finance community and tend to favor low taxes and low interest rates. To them, CEA members are ivory-tower types without experience in the real world. Further, Treasury heads are likely to think they "have the real operating responsibility. The CEA can go mouth off about these things anywhere they want to, but we've got the responsibility" (Hargrove and Morley 1984, 336). CEA members, on the other hand, normally hold Ph.D.s in economics, and they tend to prefer economic growth and low unemployment rates. From their perspective, treasury secretaries are untrained in the discipline of economics, people who have spent their lives in boardrooms, where the focus is always on the bottom line rather than policy issues.

Sometimes the tension is recognized from the outset. When President Kennedy asked Walter Heller to chair his Council of Economic Advisers, he said: "I have Doug Dillon in the other room. I want him to be my secretary of the treasury and my right bower, and I want you to be my chairman of the council and my left bower" (Hargrove and Morley 1984, 188–189). Sparks flew in the relationship between these officials. Nixon CEA head Paul McCracken reacted to a comment by Treasury Secretary John Connally as follows:

> In [his] book Governor Connally is reported to have told the President that my advice was a disaster. Now upon reflection I found that comment downright reassuring because advice that qualified as a disaster could hardly be called trivial or meaningless. Fortunately, as we all know, the free-market economy was saved from disaster through wage-and-price controls and the Lockheed loan [both of which had been advocated by Secretary Connally].

Reagan's Treasury Secretary Donald Regan and CEA Chair Martin Feldstein had many run-ins. After Feldstein departed, no successor was appointed for some months. When Regan was asked when a new CEA chair was to be appointed, he replied, "I guess [the president] likes the advice he's getting now."

OMB tends to be neutral in controversies between the two other economic units. Unless the president has a position, in which case OMB normally sides with him, OMB usually does not have an institutional stake. This isn't to say that OMB is always neutral. Members of this office are interested in administrative reorganization, and OMB forms alliances with other economic units to oppose or reduce new spending. As an assistant director in the Carter administration explained:

> We usually have the Council of Economic Advisers and Treasury on our side. Stu Eizenstat, Anne Wexler, the vice president, and congressional liaison are on the other side. We have an institutional responsibility to raise questions, and we feel that programs ought to go in [the budget] at their true cost. The political leaders hope that things will turn out a little better than that.

The Federal Reserve's relationships with the other economic offices are a little different because the Fed is capable of independent action. The last major confrontation between the Fed and a president came in December 1965, when the Johnson administration was spending to build up the U.S. military forces in Vietnam without taking any preventive action to keep the economy from overheating. Fed Chairman William Martin thought action was necessary; the CEA wanted a joint decision on the *kind* of action to be taken; President Johnson had not yet decided whether to take any action on this matter. On December 3, believing that Vietnam expenditures were going to be much greater than announced, and that restraint by the administration was unlikely, the Federal Reserve Board voted 4 to 3 to increase the discount rate from 4 percent to 4.5 percent. It took a war that was to unleash a long period of inflation for the Federal Reserve Board to muster a single-vote majority for a relatively modest action contrary to the wishes of a president (Anderson and Hazleton 1986, 121–133; Kettl 1986, 103–105, 198; Hargrove and Morley 1984, 248–252).

Cooperation between the administration and the Federal Reserve is the more common pattern. Both the president and the Fed routinely assert that the Federal Reserve is an independent agency, thereby gaining maneuvering room for their own actions. The core of the relationship, though, lies in their mutual interest in cooperation, not in their legal independence from each other. For an administration's economic policies to succeed, the Fed should pursue a parallel monetary policy, and for the Fed's monetary policy to succeed, the administration should lend verbal support and adopt parallel economic policies. This isn't to argue that there aren't *any* disagreements between the administration and the Fed. Differences in policy goals may lead either the White House or the Federal Reserve to act independently from time to time, but their mutual dependence always looms in the background.

The Treasury Department and the Federal Reserve have closely related responsibilities and mutual concerns. The cost of borrowing, set by the Federal Reserve, has very real implications for the Treasury, which finances the federal debt. Both the Fed and the Treasury are in constant negotiations to coordinate their policies on international finance. And both the Fed and the Treasury are in touch with the markets, so they tend to have a common outlook.

The CEA tends to react to the Fed's policies as it does to Treasury's. The council assigns a higher priority to economic growth. In memos to four presidents, the CEA was slightly more likely to say that Fed monetary policy was too tight than it was to conclude that restraint was at the right level; the council *never* said that the Fed's monetary policy was too easy (Kettl 1986, 138).

Obviously, these general tendencies differ from administration to administration. Sometimes working relationships among the heads of the economic policy groups are quite close; at other times they are distant. Furthermore, there is enough lateral movement between the major economic posts to mitigate differences in outlook. Both Arthur Burns and Alan Greenspan were CEA chairmen who later headed the Federal Reserve. William Miller moved from the Federal Reserve to Treasury in the Carter administration. Charles Schultze was Lyndon Johnson's budget director and later headed Carter's CEA. George Shultz moved directly from the OMB post to the Treasury secretaryship in the Nixon administration. Both Paul Volcker and Murray Weidenbaum held subcabinet Treasury positions in the Nixon administration; Volcker was appointed chairman of the Federal Reserve by Jimmy Carter; Weidenbaum was Ronald Reagan's first CEA chair. Since actual behavior is determined by both personality and institutional tendencies, we need to keep both in mind when we examine particular situations.

*The Troika.* The basic coordinating group is the *troika*.[7] It is made up of the president's three principal economic counselors: the secretary of the treasury, the OMB director, and the CEA chairman. There were meetings of these three officials in the Eisenhower administration, but the group was organized more formally in the Kennedy administration. Responsibility for end-of-the-year data gathering was divided among the units these officials headed. The idea was that the Treasury would know the most about financial and tax questions and should provide revenue estimates, OMB would be most familiar with the budget and should provide

---

[7.] This word is Russian and refers to a three-horse team. It was used by Soviet spokesmen to indicate their desire for three co-equal secretaries general at the United Nations after Dag Hammarskjold's death in 1961. Since that time, it has been applied to several three-person groups.

estimates of expenditures, and CEA would have the best information about the U.S. economy and should provide economic forecasts.

Organizing the economic units was consequential for several reasons. First, it gave CEA an operating task beyond writing the annual economic report and providing advice to presidents who choose to listen. Second, the end of the year is when administrations make the basic policy decisions to be embodied in the State of the Union Message, the Budget Message, and the *Economic Report*. Giving each unit a role incorporates them in these consequential policy discussions. Third, the troika process originated by Kennedy has proven so useful that it has continued ever since.

*Coordination with the Federal Reserve.* Some organizational adaptation is necessary to bring the chairman of the Federal Reserve Board into decision making. While making allowance for the independence of the Fed, cooperation between the Fed and other financial agencies is mandatory if economic policies are to succeed. One vehicle for such cooperation is the "quadriad," the troika plus the Fed chairman, which also originated in the Kennedy administration.[8] When President Kennedy wished to meet with the Fed chairman, he would call a meeting of the quadriad. The Ford administration maintained contact through a larger group called the Economic Policy Board. CEA Chairman Alan Greenspan kept Fed Chairman Arthur Burns advised about its agenda. As Greenspan recalled: "I would call him and say, 'Arthur, there's an important meeting tomorrow morning on such and such. I think you ought to be there.' And he would show up. Or he would call me and say, 'I understand there's a meeting on such and such. Should I go?' I would say, 'No. It's a waste of time.'" Burns was, however, at virtually every meeting the Economic Policy Board had when President Ford was present; Burns also had sixty-nine private meetings with Ford, the most extensive Fed chair–presidential contact in the last half-century (Hargrove and Morley 1984, 429, 432; Kettl 1986, 135).

The other normal contact is a regular series of breakfasts or lunches between Fed chairs and secretaries of the treasury and/or CEA chairs. In the aftermath of the December 1965 confrontation between the Fed and the Johnson administration, all three CEA members began lunching with the entire Federal Reserve Board. Fed Chairman Burns, Volcker, and Greenspan have been in constant contact with their opposite numbers in the Treasury Department and CEA. A low

---

[8.] Walter Heller tells us that they wanted a short name for "the Fiscal and Financial Group." He consulted an unabridged dictionary, and found "quadriad: a group of four, rare" (Hargrove and Morley 1984, 190).

point in this liaison came when Bush's Treasury Secretary Nicholas Brady, who seemed to think that social pressure would lead Federal Reserve Chairman Alan Greenspan to see things his way, cut off all contact with him. "Whoosh! Boom! Stop!" he reportedly said. As soon as the Clinton administration began, Treasury Secretary Lloyd Bentsen resumed normal contact; he was able to argue for a $140 billion deficit reduction, knowing this was Greenspan's own position (Woodward 1994, 65, 121).

*Troika Plus Groups.* The troika and quadriad were the principal bodies throughout the Kennedy, Johnson, and Nixon administrations. During Nixon's administration, there was a little further augmentation. The troika was joined on occasion by Peter Flanigan, who was the executive secretary of the Council on International Economic Policy, and by Donald Rumsfeld in his capacity as chair of the Cost of Living Council. In more recent administrations, though, there has been a growing tendency to use troika plus groupings. The Ford, Carter, Reagan, and Clinton administrations all used somewhat larger units that included other persons as well as the troika.

Since the organizational form has varied from one administration to the next (rather than developing systematically over time), we'll move from the simpler to the more complex. The simplest was the Economic Policy Group used by the Carter administration. This began as a large group of cabinet secretaries and assistants, but the group proved to be too large to be useful for policy formation. It was cut back to the troika plus domestic staff head Stuart Eizenstat. When international economic matters were being discussed, the four were often joined by the under secretary of state for economic affairs and by Henry Owen, an expert on international economic affairs. Others were invited to join the group as appropriate (for example, the secretary of energy when energy matters were under discussion). The agenda was quite flexible. Once agreement was reached, a decision memorandum was sent from the entire Economic Policy Group to President Carter. This avoided split policy recommendations.

The Reagan administration had a variety of decision groups. "What evolved in the first two years," Penner and Heclo explained, "was a working committee of the presidency, composed exclusively of senior staff, meeting on a continuous daily basis, and responsible for meshing day-to-day tactics with longer-term goals. To put it most baldly, their loyalty was to the idea of a successful Reagan presidency rather than to any particular economic theory or policy agenda, apart from a general commitment to governmental retrenchment" (1983, 40). The most frequent locus for first-term economic decision making was the Cabinet Council on Economic Affairs. It was by no means the only group, but Roger Porter said that it tended to be the most important "because it [was] the most regular continual forum that [attracted] most of the major players."

During Reagan's second term, there was a rather differently constituted Economic Policy Council. It tended to handle routine matters. The persons most involved in high-priority matters, such as the 1985 negotiations on international exchange rates and the 1986 tax reform bill, were Treasury Secretary James A. Baker (who played the most important role), his assistant Richard Darman, chief of staff Donald Regan (who had just been treasury secretary), his assistant Alfred Kingon, Secretary of State George Shultz (a former treasury secretary who had been professionally trained as an economist), and Federal Reserve Chairman Paul Volcker (Kilborn 1985). This cluster of heavyweights was unusual in that the OMB director and the CEA chair were not included, but David Stockman had recently departed from OMB, and the Council of Economic Advisers was lightly regarded throughout the Reagan administration.

*Councils.* The most complex arrangements were the Economic Policy Board (EPB) of the Ford administration and the National Economic Council (NEC) of the Clinton administration. The heart of the Ford EPB was the executive committee, and the core of this committee was the troika and L. William Seidman, a longtime Ford confidant who was trusted to present arguments to President Ford without slanting them one way or another. The executive committee met 351 times over the two-plus years of the administration. A typical day's agenda would include three items, two with background papers prepared in advance. After the meeting, an options paper would go to the president in which the competing arguments were carefully preserved. About once a week, President Ford himself would meet with the EPB, a sign of his personal interest in both economic policy and the board. The Economic Policy Board was not the only locus of economic decisions. It was, however, the most important continuing forum for domestic affairs in the Ford administration (Porter 1980).[9]

Robert Rubin, the first director of Clinton's National Economic Council, also chose to manage the process of economic decision making. He guaranteed other decision makers a place on the agenda; demonstrated that he could get options before the president (or wherever they needed to be); and like Seidman before him, played a role as a trusted broker rather than an advocate. Principals' meetings included the troika plus the secretaries of commerce and labor (or others depending on the agenda). The NEC handled a number of major issues—the

---

[9.] This isn't to argue that the EPB was always a smoothly running organization. It wasn't, but the Ford Domestic Council had worse problems.

1993 economic program, the North American Free Trade Agreement, the General Agreement on Trade and Tariffs (GATT), the development of the Asia Pacific Economic Cooperation forum, extension of China's Most Favored Nation status, and Japanese trade—but had little to do with health care or with long-term planning. After Robert Rubin became secretary of the treasury and Laura Tyson became NEC director in 1995, the NEC was not as prominent. This was only partly a result of the change from Rubin to Tyson; circumstances were changed in 1995–1996 within the White House and on Capitol Hill (Destler 1996).

For a relatively cumbersome unit such as EPB or NEC to work at all—and both were consequential in the Ford and Clinton administrations—the director had to be trusted by the president, so that he or she had easy access, and trusted by the other players to make a fair presentation of their views to the president. But if there were important issues handled by EPB and NEC, other issues were kept off their agendas. Ford's CEA Chair Alan Greenspan has said EPB "was a very efficient mechanism for resolving minor administrative economic questions. On major macro policy questions it was not an efficient mechanism, and therefore we really worked around it in the key decision making processes. At least I did" (Hargrove and Morley 1984, 430). Both Special Trade Representative Mickey Kantor and political adviser Dick Morris worked around Clinton's National Economic Council (Destler 1996, 51). As long as those who disagree with the unit's conclusions, or who simply want to keep *their* business off the agenda, are able to make end runs, it is difficult for any unit to act as a general coordinating mechanism.

## *Economic Activities*

### Fiscal Policy

Economists divide their world into *macroeconomics* and *microeconomics*. Macroeconomic policies, which are concerned with national aggregates such as employment, income, growth rates, and production, are emphasized in the White House. Microeconomic policies, which are concerned with the behavior of individuals, businesses, and segments of the economy, are of less concern at the presidential level. Macroeconomic policies are further subdivided into *fiscal policy,* which involves spending and revenues, and *monetary policy,* which deals with money and credit (Pechman 1975, 37–44). Our interest here is not with economics per se, but in the extent to which the president, with the assistance of his economic experts, can use fiscal policy and monetary policy to manage the U.S. economy. Since government spending is coordinated through budgeting and government revenues are collected through taxation, we shall review those activities first. Then we shall turn to monetary policy, principally the province of the Federal Reserve System, and ask if presidential cooperation with the Fed gives the chief executive any influence in this area.

*Budgeting.* Budgeting is the most institutionalized of all the economic routines. The temporal sequence in which the president's budget is put together is as predictable as the cherry blossoms in the Washington springtime. Compare these descriptions of its beginning from the Eisenhower administration and the Carter administration. "In May, 1953, the Bureau of the Budget sent to multilith machines—in preparation for June 30 distribution—its annual call for estimates from Federal agencies, in this case for fiscal 1955" (Neustadt 1954, 984). As Carter Budget Director James McIntyre outlined the process nearly three decades later, "In the spring, we are involved with the spring budget review process. We usually conclude that by early June. Letters are sent out to the agencies telling them what we want in preparation for the next fiscal year's budget."

The rest of the budget process follows a standard script. Each agency spends the summer preparing its own request following the general guidelines provided in the call for estimates. These reach OMB about Labor Day. During September and October, each agency's estimate is gone over by a budget examiner specializing in that sector of government. The examiners' recommendations are aggregated for a director's review in November. In December, the OMB director takes his or her recommendations over to the White House for a president's review. At each stage, each agency has an opportunity to defend its own budget requests, proceeding upward from the budget examiner to the assistant director to the director. The final appeal within the executive branch comes from cabinet members to the president.

While this process has remained unchanged (save for occasional slippage depending on the president's calendar), the congressional side of the budget process has changed a good deal. For the first half-century of presidential budgeting, the executive branch was the great reservoir of information about the budget. Congress reacted to the president's budget, revising it as it was enacted into a series of appropriations bills. In these circumstances, the vital decisions were made within the executive branch.[10] Then in 1974, responding to the Nixon administration's wholesale impoundments (a refusal to spend monies appropriated by Congress), and taking advantage of Richard Nixon's political weakness at

---

[10.] Congress was by no means a quiescent partner in the budget process. For a splendid analysis of congressional reaction to executive budgets during this earlier era, see Fenno 1966.

the time of the Watergate scandal, Congress instituted a congressional budget.[11] The Congressional Budget and Impoundment Control Act of 1974 created the Congressional Budget Office to provide congressionally based information, a new budget process in Congress, and new budget committees.

The 1974 act called for two resolutions: a springtime budget resolution was to set spending targets to guide committee action on appropriations and authorizations, and a fall budget resolution would be adopted containing final revenue and spending figures. As things worked out, the targets were not strong enough to contain the political forces on Capitol Hill. In 1980 reconciliation was used for the first time, but late in the year. In 1981, reconciliation emerged as an even stronger feature of congressional budgeting. In this process, reconciliation instructions were included in the budget resolution, directing committees to change *existing* legislation to conform to spending and revenue figures embodied in the budget resolution. What had been intended as a technical correction to bring various spending and revenue figures into line was used for the strategic purpose of giving the budget resolution priority over other legislation. This change made the first budget resolution much stronger, and after 1982 Congress no longer bothered with a second resolution.[12]

Not only do executive budgeters now have to take congressional actors into account, but budget making has been further constrained by the availability of resources. With increasing budget deficits, there was greater and greater financial stringency. For some time, OMB has added up the relatively uncontrollable federal outlays: Social Security, medical care, interest on the national debt, obligations already incurred, and so on. In 1965, the mandatory expenditures made up 36 percent of the budget. By 1995, they were 64 percent. The president's discretion in budgetary matters had never been high, and from 1965 to 1995, discretionary resources were reduced by just over half. Then as surpluses emerged in the late 1990s, the budgetary debate turned into a contest over how the surplus should be used—to reduce the debt, for tax cuts, for new programs, or in some other way.

---

[11.] Congress had tried this once before, during the 80th Congress. It was not continued in the 81st Congress, and it was a quarter century before Congress tried again.

[12.] Since the intent of these changes was to strengthen the role of Congress, it is interesting to note that in recent years Congress has been giving the president a higher proportion of the funds requested than under the old system. For fiscal 1985 through 1995, the average congressional appropriations were 99.0 percent of the president's budget request. From fiscal 1968 through 1974, the average congressional appropriations were 95.8 percent of the budget requests.

With multiple actors and limited room for maneuver, negotiation is in order. In fact, Aaron Wildavsky interpreted the changes that took place in the late 1970s as having begun an era of perennial budgeting (that is, continual adjustments rather than the old annual budgeting) and continual negotiations over spending (1988a, 166–179). The results of the negotiations vary. If both presidential and congressional politicians insist on their ideological positions, the result is gridlock: an exchange of invective and passage of a continuing resolution (which authorizes agencies to continue spending at the rate of the previous year) because the participants cannot agree on anything else. In the most extreme case, the Republican 104th Congress and President Clinton came to an impasse in late 1995, and nonessential employees were furloughed for 21 days. On the other hand, if presidential and congressional politicians decide to compromise, then the process works reasonably well. In 1988, all the appropriation bills were passed by the October 1 deadline (for the first time since 1976) because a spending compromise had been reached in late 1987 that included 1988 spending ceilings. In brief, the budget process is now more complex, but it can be made to work satisfactorily—*if* the political will to do so is present.

*Taxation.* Taxation differs from budgeting in two important respects. First, budgeting is an annual routine. Taxation is not. The average time between major tax bills has been four and a half years. Most administrations do not send more than one major piece of tax legislation to Capitol Hill. Since budgeting is continuous and taxation is episodic, budgets are at least recognizable from prior years, whereas tax proposals are often quite different from their predecessors. Second, budgeting is a relatively modern technique for coordination of the executive branch. In contrast, taxation is an ancient power that belongs to the legislature. Therefore, taxation is clearly an area where the president proposes and Congress disposes—often passing tax legislation quite different from that suggested by the administration.

The agency most concerned with taxation is the Office of Tax Policy, which is headed by an assistant secretary of the treasury.[13] The office is subdivided into two principal units. Some thirty economists and statisticians provide analysis of the impact of present and proposed taxes on various segments of society as well as estimates of what revenue might be expected. Twenty-plus lawyers concentrate on the tax code, drafting language to be used in major tax legislation as well as working to clarify various problems that have been identified by the Internal Revenue Service.

---

[13.] Given both the episodic nature of tax legislation and the active role played by Congress, this sketch of tax preparation is only approximate.

These Treasury economists and lawyers are constantly analyzing existing tax legislation, considering possible revisions. They work closely with other staffs concerned with taxation, such as the congressional Joint Committee on Taxation and the Internal Revenue Service. Thus they can begin concentrated work on major tax legislation at any time, and they typically work for months before sending their work to the secretary of the treasury. When the secretary is satisfied with the proposed legislation, he will take it to the White House, ideally in mid-December, for discussion with the president. When that happens, the proposed tax and expected revenues are considered in the light of the budget and economic forecast that are on the president's desk at the same time (Pechman 1987, 39–43).[14]

The principal variation in this process depends on whether the tax legislation has been worked out by the Office of Tax Policy in conjunction with other specialists or whether a political decision has been made at a higher level. In 1954, the most thorough revision of the tax code since 1913 was led by Assistant Secretary of the Treasury Daniel Throop Smith, with considerable aid from the staff director of the Joint Committee on Taxation, Colin Stam (Witte 1985, 147; 1988, 177). In 1981, on the other hand, the Reagan administration had its own plan for a massive tax cut. This left very little room for contributions by the tax specialists in the Treasury Department (Campbell 1986, 134).

The president provides ample detail about his tax proposals. The main points are likely to be included in his State of the Union Message. The revenue the tax is expected to generate will be incorporated in his Budget Message, and the economic justification for the tax will be a part the president's *Economic Report*. A special Tax Message is also customary when a major tax bill is being sent to Congress. What happens thereafter depends on Congress. Sometimes the president gets essentially the tax that he has asked for. This happened both in 1954 and in 1981. At other times, though, Congress works its own will, as happened with the tax reform that was submitted in 1985. President Reagan proclaimed victory when he signed the bill in 1986, but the legislation was very different from his original proposal.

In peacetime, it is much easier to cut taxes than to increase them. With the exception of the Vietnam-related tax surcharge of 1968, there were no major tax rate increases in the Eisenhower, Kennedy, Johnson, Nixon, Ford, or Carter administrations (Witte 1985, 264; Stein 1985, 102; Pechman 1987, 40). The deficits caused

---

[14.] There is also a constant flow of minor or clarifying legislation from the Treasury Department to Congress. It is difficult to draw precise boundaries between major and minor legislation because specialists disagree about this. By major tax legislation, I mean the most important and far reaching revisions of the tax code. I recognize that tax specialists often work for months on "minor" legislation.

by the 1981 Reagan tax cut changed the situation.[15] Three major tax increases were needed to begin to bring the deficit back under control: a congressionally sponsored 1982 tax bill, legislation resulting from the 1990 Bush-Congress budget summit, and the 1993 Clinton tax bill.[16] The leadership agreement from the 1990 budget summit was rejected by the House of Representatives, the 1993 Clinton bill passed the House by a single vote, and Vice President Gore's vote was needed to break a tie in the Senate. These tax increases were not easy to pass, but the urgent need for revenue made them necessary.

Caught between the need for revenue and a reluctance to increase taxes, policy makers have resorted to several techniques. One has been relying on less visible tax increases. OMB Director Richard Darman was pleased at the initial outcome of the 1990 budget summit because it relied on taxes on gasoline, cigarettes, alcohol, and luxuries, as well as user fees (including entrance fees to national parks and the like), thus avoiding an increase in income tax rates. Another is to call the devices something other than taxes. Referring to revenue-enhancing changes in President Clinton's 1998 budget, Treasury Secretary Rubin said, "I don't know if I would call them tax increases. What I would call them is an elimination of loopholes and unwarranted subsidies" (Bennet 1997).

***Limits on Fiscal Policy.*** In theory, fiscal policy—the adjustment of tax and spending levels to promote goals such as economic stability and employment—can be used to help manage the economy. But notice the institutional limits on the presidential use of fiscal policy. First, taxation and spending proposals pass through separate processes. Hence, it is very difficult to adjust them simultaneously. Second, Congress is the senior partner in determining the level of taxes, and that body adjusts the president's budget to match legislative priorities. Third, it usually takes a very long time to pass a tax bill. On the spending side, the annual appropriations process takes at least sixteen months. Consequently, fiscal policy cannot be adjusted rapidly enough to respond to sudden changes in the economy. Fourth, there is great resistance to raising taxes, and fifth, only a third of the budget is controllable. Taking all of these limits together, presidents cannot use fiscal policy very effectively. The Employment Act of 1946 stipulates certain economic goals as

[15.] Not only was the tax cut deep, but taxes were also indexed for inflation to prevent taxpayers from being moved into higher tax brackets when they received inflation-related increases in pay. The resulting loss of revenue, together with increased military spending, led to unprecedented deficits.

[16.] The 1986 tax bill was intended to reform taxes by closing loopholes. It was advertised as being revenue neutral.

national policy, and it is a political fact of life that voters hold presidents responsible for inflation, unemployment, and other economic maladies. However, presidential use of fiscal policy requires the cooperation of Congress, takes a long time to put into effect, and usually affects the economy only at the edges.

## Monetary Policy

As we have already noted, monetary policy is made by the Federal Reserve Board. The Fed uses a variety of techniques to control the money supply. It follows a looser policy (making it less expensive to borrow money by increasing the money supply and/or lowering interest rates) when the economy is slack, and a tighter policy (making it more expensive to borrow money by restricting the money supply and/or increasing interest rates) when the economy is in danger of overheating. Further, since both fiscal policy and monetary policy have a better chance of succeeding when they are coordinated, both the administration and the Federal Reserve have an interest in cooperation.

The Fed's decisions are not simple to make. They require accurate assessments of the state of the economy (a relatively easy task when all the indicators are in the same direction, but difficult when they conflict) and good judgment about the particular techniques that are appropriate to economic conditions. Moreover, the Fed's decisions about the economy have differential impacts on various segments of the economy. They set poor against rich. If interest rates are decreased, it is easier for those living from paycheck to paycheck to borrow money and pay back existing loans. If interest rates are increased, the earning capacity of those with money to invest is increased (Greider 1987). Interest rate decisions also affect businesses. Automobile sales, housing sales, and farmers are all helped by low interest rates. Bankers are benefited by high interest rates.

How is the Federal Reserve likely to respond to these dilemmas? The overall economy is the Fed governors' prime concern, and they do their best to make proper judgments. But remember that the Federal Reserve was created to serve the needs of the banking system. Furthermore, some of the governors are bankers themselves. The important decisions about expanding or contracting the money supply are made by the Federal Open Market Committee. This committee is composed of the seven governors plus five presidents of the member banks, all of whom are bankers.[17] Since many of the decision makers are bankers, and all have

---

[17.] There are twelve member banks. The privilege of voting rotates among them, except for the president of the New York Federal Reserve Bank. Because of the importance of the New York bank, its president always casts a vote.

contact with members of the investment community, there is at least a sensitivity to bankers' arguments and a tendency for the Fed to make decisions consistent with "sound finance."[18]

The responsibilities of the Fed and its tendencies to make "sound" decisions limits its cooperation with presidents, and there have been disagreements from time to time. Richard Nixon once told aides, "The Fed *must* loosen—it must risk inflation." Fed Chairman Arthur Burns resented Nixon's meddling and resisted his advice (Kettl 1986, 120–122). Early in the Bush administration, officials wanted Fed Chairman Alan Greenspan to loosen credit, but Greenspan held back, feeling that a more credible fiscal policy should come first (Shuman 1992, 195). In such circumstances, the independence of the Fed is important.

The independence of the Fed rests on more than the formal arrangements. For one thing, the Fed is usually supported by the majority of the banking and business community. To move against the Fed, therefore, means taking on their political allies as well. For another, there is often political pain in moving toward a desirable economic goal. Let us say that inflation has reached an unacceptable level. One means of dealing with this is to reduce the money supply, thus increasing the cost of borrowing money. The consequences of tightening the money supply are likely to include more bankruptcies and higher unemployment. If you are running for office, it is easier to have an independent Federal Reserve System to blame than to convince jobless constituents that unemployment is a good thing (Wooley 1986).[19]

## Economic Policies and Economic Goals

In recent decades, fiscal policy has become so cumbersome that it is less useful than monetary policy in economic management. Extensive uncontrollable expenses, resistance to taxes, and the length of time required to change budgets and taxes all lead policy makers to turn increasingly to monetary policy (Kettl 1986, 136; Frendreis and Tatalovich 1994, 99). Changes in monetary policy can

---

[18.] By "sound finance," John Wooley means adherence to such principles as protecting the value of the dollar, sustaining moderate, stable economic growth, and promoting the development of financial institutions (1986, 256).

[19.] The Federal Reserve must be careful that criticism does not reach an unacceptable level. Its independence has now been long established, but it is analogous to the independence of the Supreme Court. Presidents nominate justices who are confirmed by the Senate, and Congress can at any time reduce the Court's appellate jurisdiction. So, too, with the Fed. If it took actions that were regarded as intolerable, the president could appoint governors with different views, and Congress could reduce its independence.

be put into effect more quickly. All it takes is a vote of the Federal Reserve Board or the Federal Open Market Committee.

But do changes in monetary policy lead to the desired goals? There are at least two circumstances in which they may not. One is the absence of a congruent fiscal policy. It may be that elected politicians are unable to resist the desire to spend more on politically popular programs such as Social Security or Medicare. Or it may be that the administration recognizes the need for increased taxes but can't persuade Congress to pass them. In either case, too much pressure is put on monetary policy, and it can't do the job by itself. The other circumstance is a recession. If the economy is overheated, high interest rates and a restricted money supply can slow spending by making it too expensive. On the other hand, lowering interest rates and increasing the money supply are permissive rather than stimulative. That is, the Federal Reserve can make money available at low interest rates, but if bankers do not choose to make loans or if business owners feel that their entrepreneurship will not be rewarded, economic activity will not increase. A looser monetary policy makes expansion possible, but the private sector must respond before expansion takes place.

From the perspective of the Oval Office, neither fiscal policy nor monetary policy is an end in itself. The goal of the president and his economic advisers is not, for example, to have federal spending of $1.45 trillion rather than $1.57 trillion or to see a discount rate of 7.5 percent rather than 6.75 percent. Instead, policy makers want to use both fiscal policy and monetary policy to achieve specific economic goals, such as high employment, low inflation, steady economic growth, and so forth. The problem is whether any combination of fiscal and monetary policies will lead to sought-after goals. Many of these policies are very blunt instruments. How, for example, is an increase of $250 billion toward food stamps going to lead to increased farm prices in the Dakotas? Or how can an increase of 0.5 percent in the money supply lead to lower unemployment in Ohio or bring prosperity to Texas oil fields? In short, presidents are in the position of having only partial control (shared power in fiscal policy, only power to persuade in monetary policy) over blunt instruments that only sometimes lead to the desired economic results.

## Forecasting

The structure for economic forecasting was put into place during the Kennedy administration.[20] There had been some forecasts before this time, but better esti-

---

[20.] Eisenhower's CEA Chairman, Arthur Burns, had resisted using forecasts. Burns preferred to rely on economic indicators he had come to recognize as a long-time student of business cycles.

mates were needed, especially at the end of the year. The State of the Union Message, the Budget Message, the *Economic Report*, and (if a bill is to be submitted) tax legislation all converge on the president's desk in December. Foreknowledge of economic conditions is needed to deal with each of these. President Kennedy wanted to use econometric models to develop such information, and he organized his economic counselors to provide forecasts.

Economic forecasting is hard to do. It is difficult to get dependable estimates of anything. Furthermore, everything depends on everything else. That is, the amount of revenue determines what the government can spend; the level of government spending and taxation has an impact on the economy; the state of the economy determines the amount of tax revenue that can be expected. The Kennedy structure divided the responsibility for forecasting among the troika, making each agency responsible for one of these elements. The Treasury Department became responsible for providing revenue estimates, OMB for estimating expenditures, and the Council of Economic Advisers for making judgments about the economy, as well as coordinating the exercise.

For purposes of the forecasting exercise, the troika is further divided into three levels, known as T1, T2, and T3. T1 is made up of the principals: the treasury secretary, the OMB director, and the CEA chair. T2 consists of the next level down: the assistant secretary of the treasury for tax policy, an associate director of OMB, and a member of the CEA. T3 is composed of staff members from all three agencies. Information, here as elsewhere, flows in both directions. The economic assumptions to be used are stipulated by the political appointees. The staff members gather information from such sources as the Commerce Department and the Federal Reserve and shape a forecast within the economic assumptions they have been given. They pass the forecast back up the line to T2. Once the participants on this level are agreed, it goes to T1. Ultimately the information is presented to the president as a recommended forecast.

These forecasts are often on the rosy side. Compared with private forecasts made at the same time, they tend to be a little more optimistic with regard to economic growth, inflation, unemployment, and so on. This isn't to claim that the forecasters are ignoring reality. After all, differences between various private forecasts result from different assumptions, data availability, and so on. But an optimistic forecast can ease immediate political problems. For example, by June 1981, OMB and CEA (but not Treasury) were agreed that the 1981 forecast was much too optimistic and needed to be revised. When the matter was raised in a meeting on June 5, "the political advice overwhelmed the economic analysis. Baker, Meese, Gergen, Regan . . . all argued that any significant change in the forecast would jeopardize the [pending] tax bill" (Stockman 1987, 358). The danger with assumptions that are too hopeful, however, is that other players will catch on and discount the administration's economic forecasts. So in projecting uncertain economic futures, administrations must choose between those providing more political maneuvering room and those offering greater economic credibility.

## Having Clear Ideologies

When we say that an administration has a clear economic ideology, we are speaking in relative terms. The economic ideology of the Eisenhower administration, for example, was more consistent than that of the Nixon administration (Weatherford 1987). We do not mean that the actions of any administration are internally consistent, or that they could be said to be controlled by a well-developed economic philosophy. There are too many divergent goals, and economic advice is too divided, for any administration to be governed by a single economic standard.

Three administrations were relatively clear about their economics: Eisenhower's, Kennedy's, and Reagan's. Eisenhower had an orthodox belief in capitalism, balanced budgets, and restraint in government spending. His advisers generally accepted the idea of governmental responsibility for economic stability and high employment, and they believed that the budget should produce a slight surplus in times of full employment (Stein 1985, chap. 3). The Kennedy administration was influenced by a modified Keynesian view (which advocated using fiscal and monetary policies to stimulate economic activity), recommending a tax cut in 1964 that "came straight out of the country's economic textbooks" (Heller 1967, 72).[21] Ronald Reagan came to the White House determined to reduce the role of government, to cut taxes and the level of domestic spending, and to give greater scope to market forces.

The more pragmatic presidencies have greater openness and greater adaptability in meeting a variety of economic challenges. They need not respond to every economic circumstance by cutting taxes or following some economic creed. This can be an advantage. A dogmatic answer is often the wrong answer. But if an administration is guided by a clear ideology, it can serve as "counterpoise to more myopic demands. With a relatively weak commitment to long-range goals, the president is open to all manner of diffuse, short-run economic and non-economic incentives; the electoral demands of his party colleagues and his own ambition are only two of

---

[21.] A person's view, of course, depends on his economic perspective. Kennedy CEA head Walter Heller began his *New Dimensions of Political Economy* with the confident sentence, "Economics has come of age in the 1960s." Nixon CEA head Herbert Stein entitled his chapter on the same period in *Presidential Economics*, "Activism Exhausted."

the more pressing among these" (Weatherford 1987, 927). Presidential assistants are almost always willing to follow the president's lead. When his goals are clear, they don't have to wonder what he wants them to do.

## Coping with Business Cycles

*The Problem of Business Cycles.* Viewed in historic perspective, macroeconomics has made considerable progress (Pechman 1975, 50). Whatever problems modern presidents face in coping with business cycles, their record has been much better than that of their predecessors. Consider the contractions (economic downturns) and expansions (economic growth) before and after 1945. From 1854 through 1945, there were 454 months of contraction compared with 636 months of expansion. From 1946 through 1992, there were only 97 months of contraction compared with 470 months of expansion (Frendreis and Tatalovich 1994, 170). And in the last half-century, we have not experienced anything close to the depression of the 1930s.

How did this improvement come about? For one thing, data were collected that made it possible to measure the properties of business cycles. As theories were developed, economists began to fathom countercyclical strategies. These strategies for restraining an overheated economy or stimulating a depressed economy did not always work, but they often did. Also, automatic stabilizers have moderated the business cycle without requiring any governmental action. Chief among them were the income tax, which takes excess money out of an economy that is growing too rapidly, and unemployment compensation, which sustains consumers' aggregate demand for goods during a downturn.

Even so, business cycles often present presidents with their principal economic problems. After interviewing ten CEA chairs, Erwin Hargrove and Samuel Morley concluded:

> It has often been said that the Democrats fight unemployment and Republicans fight inflation. . . . [But] the record really suggests that each administration fights the problem that it confronts. As it happened, the Nixon and Ford administrations confronted a serious inflation, while Kennedy and Johnson faced high rates of unemployment and low rates of inflation. It seems exceedingly likely that McCracken would have pushed for expansion had he been in Heller's place, and we know that Okun and Ackley pushed hard for contraction during the last three years of the Johnson administration (1984, 32–33).

George Bush and Bill Clinton also fought the battle forced on them rather than the one they would have chosen. In his 1988 campaign, Republican Bush said he would tell all comers, "Read My Lips. No New Taxes." In 1992, Democrat Clinton spoke of "growing the economy" and investing in human capital. Yet coming after Reagan, both had to deal with the deficit. Both opted, Bush in 1990 and Clinton in 1993, for deficit reduction. Party proclivities and ideology help determine *how* Republican and Democratic administrations address economic problems, but the economy itself presents the problems that will be their central concerns (Hargrove and Morley 1984, 33–34).

*Political Business Cycles.* Business cycles are of varying length, but presidents must run for reelection every four years. This fact suggests the concept of a political business cycle, which postulates that administrations try to manipulate the economy to produce favorable conditions at election time. Introduced by economist William Nordhaus (1975) and brought to the attention of political scientists by Edward Tufte (1978), the idea is that presidents will deflate the economy early in an administration and then inflate the economy just before a presidential election. By deflating the economy early in their term, they reduce the risk of inflation, and they accept the accompanying unemployment soon enough for other events to intervene before the election. By inflating the economy shortly before they run for reelection, they help ensure that voters will have increased income and decreased unemployment when making up their minds.

The idea that presidents try to arrange things to stay in office is familiar, but the notion that they can produce prosperity at just the right time requires some heroic assumptions. In terms of economic processes, it means that the administration's ideology will reflect reality, that the forecasts will be on target, that the correct levels of spending and taxation will be chosen, that an appropriate money supply will be available, that both Congress and the Federal Reserve will cooperate, that the policies chosen will be supple enough to have the desired effect, and that no untoward events will interfere. The likelihood that all these assumptions will be true is quite low.

Nevertheless, this idea has stimulated an enormous amount of research.[22] Basically, the research has shown that sometimes one can discern a political business cycle but often one cannot. In the late 1950s, the Eisenhower administration certainly did not follow a stimulative policy. Early in 1959, the administration abandoned some mildly stimulative measures (which had been in

---

[22.] For samples of this, see Beck (1982), Monroe (1984), and Weatherford (1986).

place because of the 1958 recession), giving priority instead to a balanced budget. This was done in the face of protests by 1960 candidate-to-be Richard Nixon, who had been warned by Arthur Burns of the probable consequences. The result was a mild recession in 1960, which Nixon felt contributed to his narrow election loss to John Kennedy. Nixon was determined not to repeat the mistake in 1972, and he provided Tufte's textbook example of a political business cycle (1978, 45–55). Wage and price controls were instituted in 1971 to hold down inflation. The administration encouraged the Federal Reserve to expand the money supply, and governmental transfer payments (such as Social Security) were speeded up. Economic analysts have questioned the efficacy of the administration's actions, but 1972 was a relatively prosperous year, and Richard Nixon was reelected.[23]

Since 1972, there has been little evidence of a political business cycle. Gerald Ford considered stimulating the economy in 1976 but decided against it. As William Seidman explained, "He believed that the country had been subjected to enough of that kind of manipulation and refused to go along with it one more time" (Reichley 1981, 401). The Carter administration certainly failed to produce favorable economic circumstances in 1980, and while the auspices could hardly have been better for Reagan in 1984, there is no evidence that the administration was working explicitly toward this end (Kiewiet and Rivers 1985, 83–87). In 1991–1992, George Bush decided against taking measures to stimulate the economy before the election (Hershey 1993). By 1996, the economy was in the midst of a long-term expansion, so Clinton had no need to take action.

## Information Gathering in Economic Policy

Economic information is gathered all over Washington: by the Bureau of Economic Analysis and the Census Bureau in the Department of Commerce, by the Bureau of Labor Statistics in the Labor Department, by the Joint Economic Committee, by the Federal Reserve, and by many other agencies. In economics, the problem is not so much to gather information as it is to characterize the state of

---

[23.] There is another problem with this example. As Stephen Weatherford points out, evidence based on aggregate economic data must be unpacked in two ways: elites must be shown to have intended the economic result, and individual voters must be shown to have taken the economic situation into consideration when making their decisions (1986, 38). Richard Nixon and his associates clearly wanted prosperity in 1972, but voters' comments about economic management that fall were more pro-Democratic than is usually the case (Kessel 1992, 270–271).

the economy based on the specific indicators, and then to translate that intelligence into a language that can be understood by key decision makers.

It is not difficult to understand the economic situation when its path is well established. If the economy is in the middle of, say, a seventy-month expansion and the leading economic indicators are all up, or in the middle of a ten-month contraction and the leading economic indicators are all down, then most economists will agree that the economy is healthy in the first instance and in a recession in the second. But what if the indicators are not stable, or experienced economists miss clues that something is about to happen, or the trends are so weak that economists are divided about their meaning? All three of these situations have occurred in recent decades.

When the major escalation of U.S. involvement in Vietnam took place, Lyndon Johnson's economic advisers began saying that taxes were needed to pay for the war and prevent inflation. All three members of the troika sent memos to that effect in spring 1966. But then in June and July, the economy showed some signs of slowing down. This development clearly implied less need for a tax increase to contain an overheated economy. Soon thereafter, the economy speeded up again, but in November the economy was slowing a bit, and by December several leading indicators were lower. Johnson had political reasons for resisting the advice to raise taxes, but the economy's rapid heating and cooling made the task of his pro-tax advisers more difficult.

When President Ford came into office, he had a meeting to discuss the economic outlook. Attending were Federal Reserve Chair Arthur Burns, Budget Director Roy Ash, Treasury Secretary William Simon, Ford confidant William Seidman, outgoing CEA head Herbert Stein, and incoming CEA head Alan Greenspan. Stein suggested that each should write a memo giving his personal views, and he would summarize them. "Nobody," Stein later revealed, "then foresaw the unemployment rate rising above 6 percent," even though the nation was on the eve of a sharp recession in which unemployment in fact rose to 9 percent (Hargrove and Morley 1984, 401–402). For all the confident references to leading economic indicators and models of the economy, accurate forecasting is a sometime thing.

Bush administration economists were divided in their interpretation of recovery from the 1990–1991 recession. There had been negative growth (hence "recession") in the last two quarters of 1990 and the first quarter of 1991. The recession ended with growth of 2 percent in the second quarter, but growth dropped to 1 percent in the third quarter and was almost invisible in the last quarter. The question was whether the economy would resume growing with enough vigor to reduce unemployment before the election the following

November. Treasury Secretary Brady argued that the economy would rebound; Budget Director Darman urged no action before the 1992 State of the Union Message; CEA Chair Boskin was worried that the administration was not providing enough fiscal stimulus and that economic growth would be too anemic (Hershey 1991, 1993; Woodward 1992). Economists are not prescient. When there is uncertainty shortly before an election, the choice often comes down to hope that the economy will right itself without administration action versus fear that immediate action is necessary if any impact is to be had before election day.

When we turn to the communication of information, the memoranda from the Council of Economic Advisers to Presidents Kennedy and Johnson are worth scrutiny. With President Kennedy, Walter Heller had learned that he could send ten-page memos to the Oval Office. Kennedy would read them, grasp their meaning, and discuss them later. The situation was different with Lyndon Johnson. Johnson aide Bill Moyers told Heller, "Walter, you can't just load everything into a wheelbarrow and bring it over here." Later, Johnson himself said: "Now I don't like long memos; those Treasury memos put me to sleep. I don't like these long, drawn-out affairs. I want them so there are generals and majors and sergeants and privates." Heller therefore developed a staccato form of presentation using indented bullets and dashes to aid comprehension. President Johnson was very pleased with this and commended it to others (Hargrove and Morley 1984, 177).

Gardner Ackley, Heller's successor, made more refinements in the memorandum style. He reasoned that the president was so busy that he deserved simple, clear memoranda. Vast amounts of time were therefore devoted to writing that was succinct and clear. As Ackley explained it:

> The single most important requirement for access to power is the ability to write clearly, simply, understandably, giving everything that's necessary but nothing that's extraneous, in sentences of no more than ten words, in words preferably of no more than two syllables, arranged on the page with a lot of space so you can see the organization of the argument by the arrangement of the space on the page, with dots and indentations and dashes and numbered points, and no solid paragraphs more than about three or four lines long. Then you don't have to read anything two or three times to figure out what it's saying.

Ackley knew this was important in access to Johnson because the president frequently sent someone else's memorandum to the CEA, asking council staff to rewrite it so he could understand it (Hargrove and Morley 1984, 227–228).

Clear, simple writing is always effective, but Ackley is saying more than this. First, the relationship is between a professional who is in a subordinate capacity and a layman (who happens to be president) with whom he is communicating. The professional's influence comes from his expertise, but if this expert knowledge is to shape the layman's thinking, it must be put into words a generalist can understand. Second, even the busy professional has more time than the president. The professional can afford to exchange time for influence. This trade-off justifies the time skilled professionals spend writing and rewriting and rewriting to say something more clearly. Third, when writing for presidents, the message is not that details should always be eliminated. Rather, an adviser must discover how the particular president's mind works, then include the amount and quality of information that the president needs to grasp the argument being presented.

## Decision Making in Economic Policy

"The most prominent tension in the economic advisory system of virtually every recent president," Weatherford and McDonnell tell us, "has been the one between economic and political advisors" (1995, 30). This isn't the only source of policy disagreement, but it certainly manifested itself in the Bush and Clinton administrations. The economic problem for George Bush was how to choose between the long-term danger of the enormous deficit and the short-term danger of a possible recession. Coping with the deficit meant cutting spending; coping with a recession meant increasing spending (Duffy and Goodgame 1992, 230). Bush's political problem was how to disengage himself from his "no new taxes" pledge. These problems were substantial, and Bush was trapped by both of them.

Once President Bush put taxes on the table in June 1990, real negotiations with the bipartisan congressional leadership became possible. Working in fits and starts until September 30, the negotiators arrived at a package of spending cuts, gasoline, cigarette and liquor taxes, and user fees adding up to $500 billion in savings over five years; they did not include the capital gains tax cut desired by many Republicans or the increase in tax rates on the very wealthy desired by many Democrats. Then things went badly wrong. Majorities of both parties voted against the package in the House; President Bush vacillated on what he would accept from Congress in the end (Dowd 1990); Democratic leaders concluded they would not get Republican votes and fashioned another package more acceptable to the majority Democrats. Congress passed that bill October 28. At this point, Bush's decision was whether to veto or to sign the less palatable budget agreement. Vice President Dan Quayle and political advisers Robert Teeter and Roger Ailes urged him to veto, while economic advisers Nicholas Brady and Richard Darman, joined by Chief of Staff John Sununu, argued that under the circumstances (the need to encourage the Fed to lower interest rates, an impend ing recession, and the distracting situation in the Persian Gulf), he should sign. Bush signed, even though he didn't particularly like the budget agreement (Weatherford and McDonnell 1996a, 25–35).

President Clinton made three crucial decisions in constructing his 1993 economic package. The first came in a January 7 meeting with his economic advisers in Little Rock.[24] After listening to Alan Blinder explain how deficit reduction could lead to lower long-term interest rates which, in turn, would benefit the economy, Clinton responded, "You mean to tell me that the success of the program and my reelection hinges on the Federal Reserve and a bunch of . . . bond traders?" (Woodward 1994, 84). Everybody nodded, and deficit reduction moved to center stage. The second choice was how much. Lloyd Bentsen, Robert Rubin, and Mack McLarty all advocated $140 billion. The arguments supporting this amount were set forth in memos that went to the president on February 5, and the amount was confirmed at a meeting on February 12. Since the deficit reduction plan included some new taxes, the third decision was to search for ways to cushion the blow on low-income groups. Increases in the earned income credit and food stamps were added for this purpose. There were other elements to the economic package President Clinton presented to Congress on February 17, specifically, the investments in infrastructure and human capital on which he had campaigned and a short-term economic stimulus, but deficit reduction dominated (Woodward 1994, chaps. 11–16; Ifill 1993b; Balz and Devroy 1993a).

Clinton's 1992 campaign managers did not like this economic policy emphasis. They felt Clinton had been elected because he connected with real people across the country, and the bloodless ideas of an economic elite were forcing middle-class concerns off the agenda (Woodward 1994, 94, 125–126). Clinton's response was that they could not ignore the deficit. But the dispute between politicians and economists was just as immediate as it had been in the Bush administration. The roots of the conflict are not hard to find. Some economic prescriptions—tax increases and spending cuts, for example—are bound to be unpopular, and politicians maintain support by doing popular things. But beyond this, politicians are concerned with maintaining their party's core support. Since

---

[24.] This meeting was organized by Robert Rubin to brief Clinton and to inaugurate his National Economic Council. Rubin presided, but he asked Lloyd Bentsen, Roger Altman, and Lawrence Summers of Treasury, Leon Panetta and Alice Rivlin of OMB, Laura Tyson and Alan Blinder of CEA, and Gene Sperling, Rubin's deputy at NEC, to speak about selected economic topics (Destler 1996, 14).

the parties' cores are polarized—labor and minorities in the Democratic Party, business and the more prosperous citizens in the Republican Party—programs designed for either party's core support seldom have enough scope to meet the needs of the national economy. Presidents, of course, need both the support of their electoral coalition and a prosperous economy. Consequently, they must listen to campaign managers and economists, then either weave their ideas together or choose between them.

Although presidents make the grand choices, a great many decisions are made well short of the Oval Office. The 1981 budget for the Department of Labor (the last submitted by the Carter administration) involved hundreds of small decisions, perhaps two dozen big decisions, and a few really consequential choices. All but four of these decisions were made by Gilbert S. Omenn, associate director of OMB for human resources, veterans, and labor. On those four decisions Omenn negotiated a figure, but he agreed that the political implications were substantial enough that the final decisions should be made by the president. President Carter upheld the negotiated figure in all four cases. An example of how a decision moved to a lower level comes from the Reagan administration. During the first year Budget Director David Stockman would decide whether or not supplemental budget requests should be submitted to Congress promptly or delayed due to legislative exigencies. By 1982, these same decisions were being made by OMB Executive Associate Director Donald Moran.

More often than not a president will follow the recommendations of his aides, but if he wishes, he can simply reject their advice. Given the fall off in revenues after the deep 1981 tax cut, Reagan's economic aides entered 1982 believing that a tax increase of some kind was desirable. As Murray Weidenbaum, Reagan's first CEA head, described it:

> In our group it was virtually unanimous. Everyone who spoke up felt, however reluctantly, that we were forced to recommend an increase in excise taxes. But the president said no. And that is the clearest indication, among many, that not only is the president formally the decision maker, but in practice as well. Normally, he concurs with our recommendations, but on occasion he will reach another decision.[25]

---

[25.] In May of that year, President Reagan finally acquiesced to a $95 billion tax increase package favored by most of his advisers and Republican members of the Senate Finance Committee. It was passed later in the summer with the active support of both President Reagan and the House Democratic leadership.

## Exerting Influence in Economic Policy

What happens once a decision is made, especially when it goes against economists' views? Support from economists is needed if the president's decision is to
be accepted by the business community as well as the economists' professional
peers. But as often as not political judgments have outweighed the economic
advice. What then? Alan Greenspan, who had greater influence with President
Ford than most CEA chairs have with their presidents, describes bargaining over
the nature of the decision:

> We had to fight very hard, and we had to give in certain areas because the
> president said, "We will go with this. I don't want you to come out with a fore-
> cast you cannot defend, but if the number were this instead of this, is that still
> a defensible number?" I said, "Less defensible but still defensible." . . . On sev-
> eral occasions, I went to him and said, "Mr. President, I cannot defend this
> position," and I explained to him why. He would reply, "Well, we better have
> another meeting." At the second meeting the whole thing resurfaced, and cer-
> tainly on one occasion, perhaps on two, the tentative decision was reversed
> (Hargrove and Morley 1984, 431).

Inclusion in the decision-making process is sufficient reason for most presidential aides to support the result, whether they initially supported it or not. Economists, however, are in a more difficult position than political aides because they
have to consider endorsing a decision that conflicts with their professional judgments. In most cases, they decide they can. Nixon CEA Chair Herbert Stein
pointed out that there is nothing inconsistent with giving the president objective economic advice in private and defending his policies in public.

> I suppose I felt, particularly in our case, that a very large proportion of the
> profession was hostile to us, and that the president deserved an exposition of
> his position from the standpoint of his economists. . . . I was a registered
> Democrat [when I was appointed] and so was Arthur Burns when he was
> appointed. But everyone in Congress knows when you come up there and tes-
> tify that you testify as the president's spokesman, and, of course, you give the
> economic rationale of the president's policy. If you can't find an economic
> rationale for the president's policy, you're a pretty poor economist (Hargrove
> and Morley 1984, 387).

Paul McCracken, Stein's predecessor as CEA chair, used a football metaphor to
distinguish between individual decisions and the whole thrust of policy. Even
though you don't think the quarterback has called the right play, he maintained,

you still run it. It is only when you feel that the whole game plan is wrong that you ought to consider getting off the team (Hargrove and Morley 1984, 326).

Furthermore, the U.S. economy is huge, and most economic decisions are made in the private sector. In 1996, the gross domestic product was just short of $7 trillion. The portion of this accounted for by government consumption and investment was only $1.3 trillion, and the majority of this was a result of the activity of state and local governments. The federal share was less than half a trillion, $473 billion, only 6.8 percent of the gross domestic product. While the federal government is the largest single actor in the U.S. economy, decisions affecting 93 percent of the economy are made by others. Decisions affecting 82 percent of the economy are made in the private sector.

What kind of influence can the president and other governmental officials bring to bear on private economic decisions? The most consistent effort was made in the 1960s, when Lyndon Johnson was unwilling to raise taxes but still wanted to restrain inflationary pressures resulting from Vietnam War spending. When Bethlehem Steel announced a price increase, the president sent them a confidential telegram saying: "The best economists of your government say that your announced price increase—particularly [when] your industry's after tax profits are 85 percent above 1963—is not in the interest of your country, nor in the long-run interest of your company. Your president . . . appeals to you to put the interests of your country first." President Johnson also invited some business executives to dinner at the White House, and he made many phone calls to others. He urged them to defer plans for expansion. The Council of Economic Advisers held more pointed conversations with business and labor, and Johnson had Secretary of Agriculture Orville Freeman deplore increases in farm prices. These efforts were sometimes successful, but as a White House aide put it in 1967, "What is going on increasingly amounts to government sermonizing on the need for restraint and business and labor responding in argumentative fashion" (Anderson and Hazleton 1986, 156, 159–60).

There were also steps that went well beyond exhortation. Strategic materials from government stockpiles could be sold, often depressing the price of the commodities involved. The government is a large purchaser, and could buy or withhold buying from certain suppliers. And there were legal powers as well, export and import controls, antitrust action, and regulatory policies (Anderson and Hazleton 1986, 162–166).

One of the most concerted attempts to influence a private economic decision came in the Kennedy administration, when, shortly after an administration-brokered labor agreement, U.S. Steel raised prices. Within the next seventy-two hours, President Kennedy denounced U.S. Steel at a press conference and hinted that there might be a restudy of a depreciation allowance of interest to steel; Estes Kefauver and Emanual Celler, chairs of judiciary investigation subcommittees in the Senate and House, respectively, called for hearings on the price increase and to study whether some revision of antitrust laws was in order; Solicitor General Archibald Cox began to draft revisions of the antitrust laws; other senators and representatives (including some Republicans) criticized U.S. Steel; the Federal Trade Commission announced an informal investigation of the price increase; the Department of Justice ordered a grand jury investigation of a price increase by Bethlehem Steel; and the Defense Department instructed contractors to purchase steel from companies that had not raised prices, and gave a $5 million contract to a steel company that had not done so.

As things turned out, the critical business decisions were made, not by U.S. Steel or other manufacturers who had followed its lead and increased prices, but by a small group of manufacturers who had not yet decided. Of these, Inland Steel announced it would not increase prices, and was rather quickly followed by Kaiser and Armco. Their actions led Bethlehem Steel to rescind its price increase, and U.S. Steel then gave in. Administration officials had been in touch with Inland Steel, but Inland's decision was based on business considerations. Orders were slack, and they thought the timing was wrong for a price increase. The others followed suit so as not to lose orders (McConnell 1963, chap. 5).

In an important way, exercising presidential influence in economics is similar to doing so in foreign policy. The president cannot command private sector actors (whether business, labor, or some other category) any more than he can command the leaders of foreign governments. All are free to make their own decisions. A president can argue that it is in the self-interest of an individual business, or a foreign county, to follow a policy he desires. He can also appeal to economic actors to think of the interests of the entire country, or ask foreign countries to follow the path of international cooperation. *If* the appeal to their own self-interest works, or *if* they are willing to cooperate to seek some larger goal, the president can prevail. Otherwise, there are real limits on presidential influence in these policy areas.

## Summary

*Actors.* The president relies on four principal institutions for economic advice. The Treasury Department has been the lead economic agency since the days of Alexander Hamilton. OMB originated in the twentieth century with the realization that budgeting was an important tool for executive coordination. The Council of Economic Advisers tends to reflect the views of academic economists. The

Federal Reserve System acts as the central bank. With all four units dealing with separate elements of economic policy, coordination is obviously needed. The means of coordination begin with the troika (Treasury, OMB, and CEA) and the quadriad (the troika plus the Federal Reserve) and proceed through increasingly complex arrangements culminating in the councils created in the Ford and Clinton administrations.

*Economic Activities.* All of these agencies participate in the economic activities, but their responsibilities mean that certain units play more prominent parts in certain activities. Given its budgeting responsibilities, OMB plays a key role in spending decisions, and because of its long-term concern with tax policy, Treasury is preeminent in gathering revenues. Monetary policy is the province of Federal Reserve. The Council of Economic Advisers does not dominate forecasting but has some responsibility for coordinating the exercise. All four units are concerned with devising means to achieve concrete economic goals, pursuing pragmatic or ideological policies depending on the administration, and coping with the challenges presented by the business cycle.

*Common Activities in an Economic Environment.* Information gathering in economics means selecting relevant data from the many governmental and private sources. Interpretation is easy if all the indicators point in one direction, but otherwise even skilled economists are sometimes uncertain. Since analyses are often quite technical, economists must pay special attention to explaining their meaning to the nonspecialists whom they serve. Decision making is more or less difficult depending on the murkiness or clarity of the economic environment at the time. And even if the economic argument is clear, the president must weigh it against compelling political considerations. Finally, the president's ability to influence others is limited. The president can usually deal with opposition within the executive branch if he is willing to devote the time and attention to doing so. But persuading Congress, or the Federal Reserve, or the private sector is another matter. In sum, presidents are held politically responsible for the health of the U.S. economy, but it is *very* difficult for them to guide the economy through their own actions.

# 6. Domestic Policy

## *The Sentinels of Domestic Policy*

### Coping with Complexity

The salient characteristic of domestic policy is its complexity. Domestic policy incorporates the resource concerns of the Agriculture, Interior, and Energy Departments; the business and industrial relations of the Commerce and Labor Departments; the human resource foci of the Departments of Health and Human Services (HHS), Education, Justice, and Veterans Affairs; and the community development emphases of the Housing and Urban Development (HUD) and Transportation Departments.[1] And there is much further division within these broad categories. The departments grouped together because they deal with human resources, for example, include activities as disparate as medical research, educational financing, protection of civil liberties, and care for aging veterans. These enterprises are very different from one another.

A complex system is never easily comprehended. With this array, the problem is compounded because mastery of each policy subdivision calls for a different expertise. The contrast with foreign policy and economic policy is striking. There is some core knowledge shared by all foreign policy experts, and by all economists, and they know what their professional disagreements are about. In domestic policy, however, many different professions are involved. For example,

---

[1.] Because of the sheer number of domestic cabinet departments, a discussion of each one is beyond the scope of this book.

agricultural marketing is different from the engineering problems of constructing a hydroelectric dam, and both differ from questions of nuclear safety. Having acquired such a range of responsibilities, the domestic side of the federal government requires many different kinds of expertise to deal with them.

The problems inherent in complexity—many foci and the need for many kinds of expertise—are exacerbated by two other attributes of domestic policy. The first is that domestic cabinet members have relatively little contact with the president. Thomas Cronin has distinguished between the *inner cabinet* (secretaries of state, defense, and the treasury; the attorney general; and senior White House staff members) and the *outer cabinet* (HHS, HUD, Labor, Commerce, Interior, Agriculture, Transportation, Energy, Education, and Veterans Affairs) (1980, 274–286).[2] The outer cabinet departments tend to be advocacy departments speaking for business, labor, and other constituencies. This advocacy for a single constituency can lead to conflicts with White House policy emphases. Moreover, even if a president is fascinated by the activities of some domestic departments, so much of his time is taken up by foreign policy and economic policy that comparatively little is left for outer cabinet concerns.

Another attribute of domestic policy is that so many components have the potential to blow up into a real political crisis without warning. An *Exxon Valdez* runs aground and spills oil all over Alaska's Prince William Sound. A new disease, such as Legionnaire's Disease or AIDS, emerges and there are impassioned demands for a cure even before the disease is understood. An unusually cold winter leads to a shortage of natural gas in the snow belt, or a shortage of grain produces an increase in prices for bread and beef. Revelations of fraud in awarding HUD grants lead to convictions of a number of high-ranking HUD officials. All of these—and more—have taken place in recent years. Any of them can move a department from the outer reaches to center stage very quickly, and when this happens presidential staffers undergo crash courses in the newly visible department's business.

The complexity of domestic policy presents several organizational dilemmas for the presidency. Should decisions be made in the White House or should they be left to the departments? What kind of expertise is required of those who formulate domestic policy? Can the presidential staff maintain any control over such a complex area as domestic policy?

---

[2.] The Justice Department has some characteristics of both inner cabinet and outer cabinet. Cronin is absolutely correct when he writes that the attorney general is one of the president's closest advisers. I include Justice as part of domestic policy in this book because it is not part of foreign policy or economics, and much of its routine business touches the lives of average citizens.

*The Locus of Decision Making.*  Not too long ago, there wasn't any question about decision making within the White House. In the absence of a consequential White House staff, policy was perforce made by the Commerce Department, the Agriculture Department, and their counterparts elsewhere. Although the White House now has policy-making capacity, there is still an argument that departments are better suited to handle domestic matters.

"The longer one examines the awesome burdens and the limited resources of those who help the president from within his immediate circle," observed Robert C. Wood, HUD secretary in the Johnson administration, "the more skeptical one becomes of a strategy of 'running' government by overseeing it from 1600 Pennsylvania Avenue" (1970, 45). Difficult decisions tend to move to the White House from the departments, from Congress, and from interest groups. Staffers are often faced with too many problems they must decide too quickly on the basis of too little information. Presidential staffers are in danger of getting into the details of administration while failing to address broader policy issues.

> Throughout the years 1966–1969, Budget Bureau staff tried their hand at dividing $53 million of "open space" funds among inner city and suburban localities while White House staff requested weekly reports on a housing program with a two year lead time. But in the same period, the [Budget] Bureau never got around to allocating funds for 12 pilot neighborhood center programs, and the White House never resolved the different definitions of "citizen participation" that were bringing poverty programs to a standstill (Wood 1970, 44).

A counterargument is that a great many policies involve more than one agency. White House staffers assert that many departments lack the flexibility to work easily together, let alone devise creative solutions to the many problems that arise. "Cabinet agencies," said Carter domestic aide Bert Carp,

> have most of the characteristics of independent nations. They have their own territories, and their own flags. They communicate with each other basically in writing, and have long historic disagreements that stretch so far back that nobody knows where they began. And to a large extent, there is an internal patriotism. Now sometimes when we get a couple of assistant secretaries over here, they can find a way to agree.[3]

---

[3.] As I mentioned in the preface, almost all of the uncited quotations in the book are drawn from interviews I have conducted myself. This is true of Bert Carp's statement and of all other uncited quotations in this chapter.

The White House becomes neutral territory where agencies can negotiate with each other, and if it should turn out that the matter is important enough to merit the president's attention, it can be moved up to his level.

The justification for White House involvement most frequently offered by White House staffers is the president's need to review decisions and alter them if necessary. "Until decisions get to the White House," Eisenhower aide Robert Merriam pointed out, "no one has looked at them from the president's point of view." The president's personal values may differ from those brought to bear at the departmental level, and the president may react differently to a policy proposal because of his wider responsibilities. A related argument is that the White House adds political considerations to the substantive judgment already reached. A Nixon staffer, speaking privately, conceded there might not be much difference between the White House and departmental perspectives, but he added that White House participation in decisions was legitimized by saying "we're giving it the political twist." All these arguments reflect the basic distinctions between the departments and the White House: the greater expertise and larger staff in the departments is contrasted with the greater sensitivity to presidential wishes and political currents in the White House.

*Generalists or Specialists?* What kind of expertise is needed to make domestic policy decisions? If the unique White House contribution is to weigh departmental recommendations against the political needs of the president, it follows that staff members ought to be generalists with political experience. Lawyers who have been active in presidential campaigns see themselves as qualified to evaluate domestic policy. Their analytic training allows them to elucidate the issues and present them for decision. They also know who the president's friends and enemies are.

In recent decades, about a third of the senior domestic advisers have been attorneys.[4] Ted Sorensen in the Kennedy White House, Joseph Califano and Harry McPherson in the Johnson administration, Nixon assistant John Ehrlichman, and Stuart Eizenstat of the Carter administration all had law degrees. But Robert Merriam of the Eisenhower staff, Martin Anderson and Edwin Harper from the Reagan administration, and Roger Porter of the Bush administration had gone to graduate school rather than law school. Two domestic aides, Johnson assistant Douglass Cater and Ford domestic adviser James Cannon, had been journalists;

---

[4.] The persons listed here are identified with the administration in which they held their most senior White House appointment. Several served in different capacities in other administrations.

two more, John Svahn and Gary Bauer of the Reagan administration, had held a series of political positions; and both Carol Rasco and Bruce Reed had prior experience with Governor Clinton.[5]

*The Danger of Disorder.* No policy process is altogether tidy. The challenges are to keep important issues from being smothered by a too-rigid organizational process, and to keep incipient disorder from verging into near chaos. In an area as complex as domestic policy, the latter occurs more frequently. Disarray is likely to assert itself if an administration is not much concerned with domestic policy, and it manifests itself whenever there is weak leadership or if there are so many persons with a piece of responsibility that no one is really in charge.

## The Evolution of Domestic Staffing

*A Few Generalists.* The practice of having a distinct domestic adviser, as opposed to generalists whose portfolios include some domestic responsibilities, originated in 1943 with the appointment of Samuel Rosenman as counsel to the president. Rosenman had worked with Franklin Roosevelt since FDR was governor of New York; then he had commuted to Washington while also serving as a member of the New York Supreme Court; finally he came to work in the White House full time as a domestic adviser and speechwriter. Roosevelt invented the counsel's title for him in recognition of his legal background (Hess 1988, 27, 244). When Rosenman resigned from the Truman administration in 1946, he recommended his part-time assistant, Clark Clifford, as his successor. When Clifford departed in 1949, after having orchestrated Truman's 1948 election victory, he recommended Charles Murphy, who had been his assistant (Clifford 1991, 75, 260). Murphy was assisted by five professionals, each of whom had specific responsibilities (Walcott and Hult 1995, 150).

Robert E. Merriam handled domestic policy for Eisenhower from 1956 onward.[6] (A list of the principal domestic advisers, beginning with Merriam, is in Box 6–1.) In addition, he handled coordination with state and local governments. He had only one staff member, Douglas Price. Because the domestic staff had only

---

[5] Rasco had worked in the Arkansas governor's office; Reed had much more extensive policy experience in the Democratic Leadership Council and Clinton's presidential campaign.

[6] Merriam was the first domestic adviser who was not the special counsel. Eisenhower began the practice, now common, of using the special counsel's office as a source of independent legal advice.

---

**Box 6–1  Domestic Advisers**

| President | Domestic Advisers | Years |
| --- | --- | --- |
| Eisenhower | Robert E. Merriam | 1956–1961 |
| Kennedy | Theodore C. Sorensen* | 1961–1963 |
| Johnson | Bill D. Moyers | 1963–1967 |
| | Joseph C. Califano Jr. | 1965–1969 |
| | Douglass Cater | 1965–1969 |
| | Harry McPherson* | 1965–1969 |
| Nixon | John D. Ehrlichman | 1969–1973 |
| | Kenneth R. Cole Jr. | 1973–1974 |
| Ford | James Cannon | 1975–1977 |
| Carter | Stuart E. Eizenstat | 1977–1981 |
| Reagan | Martin C. Anderson | 1981–1982 |
| | Edwin L. Harper | 1982–1984 |
| | John A. Svahn | 1985–1986 |
| | Gary L. Bauer | 1986–1989 |
| | Alfred H. Kingon | 1985–1987 |
| | Nancy Risque | 1987–1989 |
| | T. Kenneth Cribb Jr. | 1987–1989 |
| Bush | Roger B. Porter | 1989–1993 |
| Clinton | Carol Rasco | 1993–1997 |
| | Bruce Reed | 1997– |

*Sorensen and McPherson also served as counsel to President Kennedy and President Johnson, respectively.

---

two members, not much could be referred to the White House. In fact, Merriam wanted to keep things out of the White House whenever possible. "We tried to ask," Merriam recalled, "'Why do we have to decide this?' and 'Is this a presidential decision?' Usually, it was not."

Merriam was critical of later administrations, which brought more and more decisions into the White House. He thought they had made a terrible mistake. "Once you set up such a mechanism," he explained, "it tends to suck things into the White House." As a result, White House staffers end up having more work on their desks than they can deal with effectively.[7] In the Eisenhower administration many decisions were made in the Budget Bureau; later administrations

---

[7.] Note the agreement on this point between Robert Merriam and Robert Wood.

brought them into the White House. Bob Merriam handled only those matters in which President Eisenhower had some personal interest. He worked unostentatiously. As he put it, "You just untie the knots one at a time."

Kennedy's Theodore Sorensen also operated with a very small staff, but he had even wider responsibilities. As much as anyone in the modern era, he resembled earlier general-purpose aides such as FDR's Harry Hopkins. Not only did he serve as domestic coordinator, he also handled the special counsel's legal responsibilities, was John Kennedy's speechwriter, dealt with interest groups, and had some foreign policy and political responsibilities. As Merriam before him, he made do with a small staff by relying on the Budget Bureau and departmental staffs. Having himself handled broad responsibilities with only two assistants, he was skeptical of the need for larger staffs in succeeding administrations. In his eyes, the increase grew out of administration attempts at empire building, as well as distrust of agency heads and staffs.

*Sudden Growth with LBJ.*   The Eisenhower-Kennedy pattern of maintaining a very small domestic staff in the White House changed within a year of Johnson's becoming president.[8] In the Johnson White House, four staffs had something to do with domestic policy. Joseph A. Califano Jr. came from the Defense Department to be the principal domestic coordinator. Special Counsel Harry McPherson dealt with civil rights and urban affairs. Douglass Cater specialized in education and health policy. And Bill Moyers, who had been seeking ideas for domestic policy until he became press secretary in 1965, was actively concerned with policy until he left the White House in 1967. Further, Califano had a staff of seven, McPherson four, Cater three, and Moyers three. In place of two persons on the Eisenhower staff and three on the Kennedy staff, by 1967 there were twenty staff members dealing with domestic policy in the Johnson White House.

Lyndon Johnson had not been impressed with the earlier practice of having departments submit policy suggestions to the Budget Bureau, which in turn forwarded them to the White House. As he wrote in his memoirs:

> I had watched this process for years, and I was convinced that it did not encourage enough fresh or creative ideas. The bureaucracy of the government

---

[8.] Lyndon Johnson always liked to have large staffs. When his 1948 Senate election was being challenged, he assembled a roomful of lawyers to prepare. As majority leader of the Senate in the late 1950s, he also served as Conference chair, chair of the Policy Committee, and chair of the Steering Committee, and combined all four staffs into one giant staff that worked at his direction.

is too preoccupied with day-to-day operations, and there is a strong bureau-cratic inertia dedicated to preserving the status quo. . . . Moreover, the cum-bersome organization of government is simply not equipped to solve com-plex problems that cut across departmental jurisdictions (1971, 326–327).

Several of his advisers called his attention to the task forces commissioned by John Kennedy. Kennedy had used these primarily for campaign purposes. Under John-son, they became the principal mode of policy development.

The task forces were coordinated by Joseph Califano. As the administration gained experience, the task forces became a regular part of the annual policy cycle. Each spring, Califano and his assistants sought ideas from university and govern-ment sources. Together with proposals from other sources, the ideas were reviewed, first by senior White House staff members and then by Johnson and Califano, to determine which were worth the attention of new task forces. Task forces were appointed during the summer and worked during the early fall. They were instructed to concentrate on the substantive merits of the policy rather than its political feasi-bility, and to work in secret so the president could ignore any recommendations if he chose. In the late fall, the proposals were analyzed for budgetary implications, agency comments were gathered, and the proposals were forwarded to the president. At this point, the task force suggestions were only on the table for consideration. Johnson decided which ones to accept (Thomas and Wolman 1969; Hess 1976).[9]

As things turned out, the Johnson task forces did not become a permanent part of the Washington scene, but the practice of having major domestic policy decisions made in the White House was a lasting change. Robert Merriam had been right about the tendency of such an organization to suck things into the White House. The corollary is that it is easy to move the locus of decision mak-ing from the agencies to the White House but quite difficult to shift it back out to the agencies.

*A Single Domestic Staff.* Richard Nixon began with two counselors. He first appointed Daniel Patrick Moynihan, a Democrat, as assistant for urban affairs. Then the day after the inauguration, economist Arthur M. Burns agreed to join the administration as a special adviser (Reichley 1981, 69, 77). These appoint-ments gave Nixon one counselor (Moynihan) who could argue the liberal case and another (Burns) who could argue the conservative case. The idea was that

---

[9.] Some of the most important educational and housing programs emerged from task forces headed by John Gardner and Robert Wood, but task forces were not the only source of Great Society legislation.

Nixon would choose between the plans being presented. This arrangement did not last long. Nixon was not comfortable with conflict, preferring to look to a single source for ideas from which he could choose.

The twin counselor arrangement was still nominally in place when the family assistance plan (which would have made supplemental payments to the working poor) was devised in the summer of 1969. However, the in-house task group that submitted the formal option paper to the president was headed by a neutral person, Edward Morgan. As Morgan recounted this experience:

> This was really the project that created the pattern for the Domestic Council. The president generally knew what he wanted on this. He set down general guidelines. He knew that if the current system was projected, it was going to go bust. It would bankrupt the system. I was the person who headed up the task force on this. I had assistant secretaries from Labor, HEW [Department of Health, Education, and Welfare], someone from Budget, and one person from Moynihan's staff, and one person from Burns' staff. I don't mean to say that we did it all. We had departmental backup. We got figures from Labor, from HEW, from OEO [the Office of Economic Opportunity]. They had the best computer runs at the time, results of the experiments, and so forth. . . . The president gave his speech in mid-August. . . . The last time I remember celebrating was the Fourth of July weekend. I worked steadily from that time until the speech was given [on August 8].

About the same time, a Nixon-appointed Advisory Council on Executive Organization was at work. They reported in the spring of 1970, making two principal recommendations. One was to convert the Bureau of the Budget into the Office of Management and Budget, the other was to create the Domestic Council.

In the words of Nixon's reorganization plan, the Domestic Council was "to coordinate policy formulation in the domestic area. This cabinet group would be provided with an institutional staff, and to a considerable degree would be a domestic counterpart of the National Security Council." The NSC comparison was used repeatedly by Domestic Council staff members to explain what they were doing. As one staffer said:

> When the president came into office in '68, there was on the foreign policy and defense side a pretty well structured organization. . . . But on the domestic side, where there are probably more players and a greater variety of problems, there was not a structured policy development organization. And its always been my view that it works pretty much in parallel with the NSC with Kissinger on the one side and Ehrlichman on the other side.

This development took place under Nixon, but the desirability of keeping a domestic staff in the White House was widely recognized at the time. In fact, Hubert Humphrey had called for the establishment of a "national domestic policy council" in a Los Angeles speech on July 11, 1968, so a domestic staff would probably have been created regardless of who won the election. By 1972, the Domestic Council staff had twenty-eight members, slightly more than the twenty staffers in the Johnson administration. There were some variations in operating style, but the essential change was to consolidate all domestic staffers into a single powerful White House unit.

The Domestic Council was less influential during the brief Ford administration. President Ford's initial hope was that Vice President Nelson Rockefeller would serve as his domestic coordinator, and Rockefeller aide James M. Cannon was named to head the staff. But eleven months after his confirmation Rockefeller was off the 1976 ticket. The Domestic Council staff was divided into Nixon holdovers, Rockefeller appointees, and a few Ford appointees. It was not the source of ideas it had been during the Nixon years.

The Carter term was another period of strength for the domestic staff. Now called simply the Domestic Policy staff, it operated much as it had in the Nixon administration. It was headed by Stuart Eizenstat, who had a keen awareness of President Carter's thought patterns and was widely respected throughout the White House. The forty-one member staff was organized by areas of substantive responsibility—agriculture, energy, housing, human resources, drugs, and so on—and devoted much time to marshaling proposals that flowed upward to Eizenstat and then to the Oval Office.

*Councils and Near-Chaos.* The Reagan administration was not fertile ground for a domestic staff. Reagan's view was that government caused more problems than it solved, and this attitude set a limit to what any domestic staff could contribute. This ideological limitation was compounded by leadership and organizational considerations. The Office of Policy Development (OPD), as the domestic staff was called after yet another name change, was headed by four different men during the Reagan administration: Martin Anderson, Edwin Harper, John Svahn, and Gary Bauer. Anderson had close personal ties to Reagan, and Bauer brought mental agility to the office, but both seemed more interested in public advocacy than in the less glamorous work of policy craftsmanship. Harper, a veteran of the Nixon staff, had the requisite organizational skills, but he stayed on the job for only a short time.

Ronald Reagan had relied on cabinet government when he was governor of California. After Reagan entered the White House, his counselor, Edwin Meese, established six cabinet councils to re-create the president's preferred structure. Each was chaired by a cabinet member, and each dealt with a policy sector: economic affairs, commerce and trade, natural resources and environment, human resources, food and agriculture, and legal policy. The Office of Policy Development provided executive secretaries to these cabinet councils, thus retaining a toehold on power. But some of the councils rarely met, and those that did reported to Meese through the cabinet secretary. Organizationally, therefore, the Office of Policy Development was left with little to do.

In Reagan's second term, the six cabinet councils were reduced to two: the Economic Policy Council and the Domestic Policy Council. Whereas the six first-term councils gave outsiders an opportunity to choose the most favorable route into the White House, in the second term departments were compelled to come through a council with a clearly stated jurisdiction. Both cabinet departments and internal White House units (for example, OMB) were given seats on these councils. Having been granted equal organizational standing, the departments made fewer complaints about having to report to the president through a White House aide. Nominally, President Reagan chaired these councils. But in his absence, Treasury Secretary Baker chaired the economic council and Attorney General Meese chaired the domestic council. Thus advice to the president was coming through sources he trusted; but since these two cabinet officers were already very busy, they had little time for additional chores.

In addition to the councils and Office of Policy Development, second-term domestic proposals also emerged through the cabinet secretary (first Alfred Kingon, then Nancy Risque) and a very small Domestic Affairs office, headed by Kenneth Cribb, an erstwhile aide to Edwin Meese. With the Domestic Policy Council, Office of Policy Development, cabinet secretary, and Domestic Affairs all in play as the second term came to a close, it was not clear who, if anyone, was coordinating domestic policy.

*George Bush's Honest Broker.*  For most of the Bush administration, domestic policy making was largely handled by a single domestic staff. Roger Porter was appointed assistant to the president for economic and domestic policy. The cabinet councils were still used as forums for discussion from time to time, but the center of activity moved to Porter's office. President Bush used Porter as an honest broker, one who made sure that the departments, agencies, and other interested parties were fully involved in policy making; who arrived at tentative agreements with various actors on the president's behalf; and who could be trusted to convey others' views to the president without distortion. As Porter himself explained, "George Bush is the first president who has come into the presidency familiar with the concept of an honest broker. Gerald Ford became familiar with the concept, and ultimately I think Ronald Reagan became familiar with it. President Bush believes he has people on his staff who are performing this function, and this is the way he uses us." While Porter's role as a coordinator for Bush was clear enough, the activities of units reporting to Porter, the Office of Policy Development and the Office of Policy Planning, were less well defined.

*Lost in the Melee.* As the Clinton White House was being shaped, there was some talk of having Hillary Clinton serve as her husband's principal domestic adviser (Johnson and Broder 1996, 98; Drew 1994, 22). Instead, Hillary Clinton was put in charge of health care reform, and the domestic post went to Carol Rasco, who had worked in the health and human services area for Governor Clinton in Arkansas. On paper Rasco's Domestic Policy Council had power, but the action occurred elsewhere.

The 1993 economic package, put together by economic aides, captured Clinton's attention first. Health care, the domestic policy centerpiece, was securely in the hands of Hillary Clinton and Ira Magaziner. The national service bill was shaped by Eli Segal and his staff. The crime bill was managed by Rahm Emanuel. Vice President Gore headed a unit on reinventing government. Of all the domestic programs, only the welfare task force (co-chaired by domestic aide Bruce Reed) was substantially affected by the domestic staff. As time passed, the Domestic Policy Council faded into invisibility (Drew 1994, 348; Warshaw 1996, 197–202). Bruce Reed, who succeeded Rasco as the principal domestic adviser in Clinton's second term, was much better equipped to manage domestic policy, but the administration was distracted by other events, such as the Lewinsky affair.

## Coordination

*Multiple Departments.* "Any decision worth getting the president involved in," said Carter's chief domestic aide Stuart Eizenstat, "almost inevitably involves two or more departments. It just wouldn't get to his level if it was such a finite decision that only one agency was involved." Kenneth Cole, deputy director of the Nixon Domestic Council, made the same point implicitly in describing the business his group handled: "There isn't anything in the domestic area that we don't handle, and when we set this up we defined domestic as anything that wasn't obviously foreign. So there's quite a range. Busing. Housing. Use your imagination. Anything that's domestic. . . . There's one important qualification I should add here: anything that's domestic that merits the president's attention." The examples that Cole gave obviously go beyond the bounds of individual departments.

Take busing. Busing is used for the purpose of equalizing the racial balance in schools; but if schools are to be desegregated housing must also be desegregated, and housing policy involves HUD. Buses require adequate networks of roads, so Transportation may be involved. The desegregation orders came from the courts, and compliance is within the purview of the Civil Rights Division of the Department of Justice and the Civil Rights Commission. Since civil rights was such a hot political issue, politicians as well as substantive experts were watching it closely. And so it goes. If an issue is consequential enough to belong on the president's agenda, it quickly leaps across departmental boundaries.

*The White House as Neutral Turf.* The moment an issue embraces more than a single department, each affected department tends to safeguard its own interests and protect its own constituencies. Therefore, Eizenstat explained, the departments need "a neutral court that doesn't have any turf consideration or constituency allegiance to help those agencies work out their differences." If an issue can be resolved on the subpresidential level, then at least interdepartmental turf fights stay off the president's agenda. But that doesn't always happen, particularly if the cabinet officers are in disagreement. Any time cabinet members refuse to work out their differences, a domestic staffer has little choice but to present the question to the president. A Nixon aide recounted his experience:

> You see that one cabinet secretary says you've got to go this way, it's the only way. And the other secretary says that the worst thing you can do is to go that way. It has to lower—. . . I mean they are in direct conflict and I don't make the call on that. What I do say in my report is that Secretary A feels very strongly that the politics, the national interest, the budget, the long-term direction of the nation requires you to go this way, and he gives a, b, and c as his reasons. On the other hand, Secretary B says that's not true.

As this staffer began to say, the squabbling has to lower the standing of the secretaries involved, and it leads presidents to surround themselves with staff who can arbitrate as many of these interdepartmental fights as possible.

*Coordination Through Decision Processes.* Most of the domestic staff's coordination takes place when a decision is being made, especially when the president is going to make a decision. In view of the binding nature of a presidential choice, and the importance of issues that are worth presidential time and attention, extra effort may be made to make sure that all of the players have an opportunity to express their views. Which forum is chosen for this discussion depends on how decision processes are structured within a given administration.

Task forces are frequently used to achieve coordination.[10] If there is a strong domestic staff, as was the case in the Nixon and Carter administrations, the task force operates within that staff's framework. If there is not a strong domestic staff, as was the case in the Clinton administration, task forces may still be used for coordination, but they are appointed on an ad hoc basis. In the Nixon task forces, a Domestic Council staff member in charge of the subject would serve as executive secretary, and the task force membership would normally include persons from the agencies involved as well as from other parts of the presidency. One working group was described thus:

> Well, there were top people from OMB and some economists. We had top staff people, lawyers from the Treasury and from the Council of Economic Advisers, and economists from the Council of Economic Advisers who were familiar with the programs, particularly the financing of them. You know, it's kind of like we assign tasks to the people who are familiar with [programs in the area], and you say, will you develop something along these lines. And they come back to you and say, here's what we've got, and then the drafts go back and forth. And the Justice Department always had several good people because we were always talking about the law, and what can be done legally, and what cannot be done, particularly in this case.

Drafts flowing back and forth may not remove all of the differences between vying departments, but as the domestic staffer addresses the claims first of one department and then of another, many of the conflicts can be eased.

On many occasions, it is less important to ameliorate the interdepartmental tensions than to present the central questions. If a decision must go up to the president, Stuart Eizenstat explained, "we can at least narrow the decision by deciding some of the secondary and tertiary issues, and we can define the issue in a coherent form without ten agencies sending him ten different memos." Not only do the domestic staffers incorporate the views of multiple agencies, but they also obtain the reaction of White House units: OMB on the budget impact, the Council of Economic Advisers on the economic impact, and the legislative liaison staff on probable reaction on Capitol Hill. Hence the president has a lot of information in a single package.

This process, however, places the domestic staff in a gatekeeper role. For the staffers to be trusted to send in this single vital memo, they have to let all of the agencies know what is in the memo, make sure that the memo reflects the views

---

10. A variety of names are used for task forces. "Task groups," "working groups," and "interdepartmental groups" all refer to similar committees.

of each agency accurately, and ensure that the memo does not state the agencies' views in a way that reflects adversely on any particular agency. To do this properly requires extensive coordination with all the departments and executive agencies concerned.

A final point on the extent of coordination was made by Lynn Daft, Carter's thoughtful agricultural aide. "I think that if [something] is going to be a presidential matter, the [crucial] question is who all you want to involve in it before it goes to the president." Obviously, anything in the agricultural area would involve USDA, but who else? Take the question of meat imports:

> Since it has inflation overtones, you want the Council of Economic Advisers into it in a fairly major way. The Office of Consumers' Affairs will want to offer advice, although they don't have enough staff depth to give you a lot of help. It's pretty predictable where they're going to come out. If Fred Kahn's operation, the Council of Wage Price Stability, was in motion, you'd want to get advice from them. Treasury, with the secretary of the treasury in a fairly key advisory role, you want them involved. The State Department and the Office of the Special Trade Representative should both be involved.

Daft's point was that since a presidential decision was binding on the entire government, and since it was so difficult to alter once made, a domestic staff member ought to go to special lengths to make sure that every affected agency had a chance to state its position.

## Domestic Policy Activities

### Monitoring the Departments

If domestic policy is to be guided from the White House, the White House staff must know what the departments are doing. Perhaps top staff members are very carefully watching an issue of extreme political sensitivity. Or perhaps administration policy on an issue has long since been settled. In the first case, the administration wants to avoid letting anyone freelance (that is, act alone). In the second, the administration simply wants to avoid surprises. But in either case, the White House needs to be informed.

Most of the contact between any department and the White House is carried on by the assistant secretaries. The Department of Commerce, for example, has a secretary, a deputy secretary, five under secretaries, thirteen assistant secretaries, and three bureau chiefs. Some of the assistant secretaries have general administrative portfolios (for example, assistant secretary for administration or assistant secretary for congressional and intergovernmental affairs), but most have responsibilities for specific substantive areas (for instance, the assistant secretaries for the National Oceanic and Atmospheric Administration, Trade Development, and Patents and Trademarks). The secretary spends much of his or her time giving speeches, testifying on Capitol Hill, or dealing with general departmental administration; the assistant secretaries deal with day-to-day matters.

As the domestic staffs in the White House developed, there came to be a director, one or two deputy directors, and several assistant directors, each of whom had responsibility for particular substantive areas. (The formal titles vary a good deal from one administration to another.) Because of departmental organization, on the one hand, and domestic staff organization, on the other, the natural point of contact on most substantive matters is a departmental assistant secretary and the assistant director of the domestic staff dealing with that department. Consequently, most of the monitoring is handled by the assistant directors. More senior persons handle questions of high policy. As one of Nixon's assistant directors explained it:

> Clearly, the big gun is that the secretary weighs in with the president. However, as in any organizational conduct of affairs, that's the big gun and that's reserved. So the next one is that the secretary talks with [Nixon's principal domestic adviser John] Ehrlichman and that puts it in at the top level, or the secretary or assistant secretary talks to OMB. Another level is the White House or Domestic Council staff level. That's usually the assistant secretary talking to me or to my opposite number in OMB. That's the traditional way to do it.

When departmental–staff liaison is working well, the staff member has a good sense of which matters he or she needs to know about personally and which he or she should call to the attention of higher ranking staffers. Carter's Lynn Daft gave an example of a call he received from the Agriculture Department:

> I had a call from the under secretary of agriculture this morning on an issue that involves meat imports and action they propose to take. This is an issue that the president has recently touched and Eizenstat has recently touched. It comes to me in the vein that this is what we plan to do, and these are the likely effects. Does this sound o.k. to you? And my response is, yes, it sounds fine, let's go ahead.

Daft went on to explain the White House–department staff relationship was delicate. On the one hand, he wanted to have a very good rapport with the key departmental people so they would take him into their confidence and tell him things that they wouldn't tell most other people. On the other hand, he couldn't let them get the idea that he would always agree with them or serve as their resident lobbyist. Therefore, he had to explain to them very diplomatically from time to time that there were reasons he could not agree with them.

A Nixon aide pointed out that it took effort to maintain harmonious working relationships, but he was optimistic that it could be done.

> I think in fairness there is a constant battle to avoid agency paranoia and White House paranoia, and an intelligent approach with reasonably bright people can overcome a good deal of that. You can avoid this developing paranoia that the agencies hate us or they're out to sandbag us. You can avoid having the agency thinking that the White House is out to get them no matter what they do. Good people, I think, can overcome that. Some people don't, and you've got problems when you don't have good people. But I like to believe that with a conciliatory manner, you can sit down and talk with whoever's involved.

Sometimes, of course, the people are not so good. For example, when another member of the same staff was asked how she monitored activity in a large department, she replied: "Oh, it's easy. I have a contact over there. I call him and he tells me everything that's going on." It is naive to assume that a single source could be sufficient, but inexperienced or subpar personnel do show up occasionally on White House staffs.

The modest size of the domestic staff imposes another practical limit to monitoring. As one staffer put it: "John and I are all there are in this area. . . . Obviously, with only two people, we don't sit here and monitor everything that's going on in the entire Department of Agriculture or the Department of the Interior, or the Environmental Protection Agency, or the other agencies." As a practical matter, the staff members are able to find out some of what is happening in a few agencies, but of course they spend most of their limited time focusing on topics in which the president is interested.

But if the domestic staff cannot monitor government activity, who does? The standard answer is the Office of Management and Budget. The executive order creating these units stated that the OMB will be "the president's principal arm for the exercise of his managerial functions. The Domestic Council will be primarily concerned with what we do; the Office of Management and Budget will be primarily concerned with how we do it." The Domestic Council staff members' comments were more direct: "We watch out for the things the president has told us to watch out for, and they [OMB] watch out for the whole government." OMB, with a staff of 600, is much better able to track governmental activities than a domestic staff. But OMB has perhaps two dozen employees (exclusive of secretaries) working on natural resources while the Department of the Interior has more than 70,000. So, although some monitoring is done, it is at best incomplete.

## Fire Fighting

To a White House staff member, fire fighting does not conjure thoughts of a fire truck speeding down Pennsylvania Avenue. Instead, it means that something has gone wrong and that remedial action must be taken before further damage is done. "Putting out fires" or "fighting brush fires" have the same implications. Just as with a true brush fire, quick action is called for. If a small fire is allowed to spread, considerable damage may result. If small political problems are neglected, the administration may suffer substantial political damage.

Michael Uhlmann, who handled legal issues for Reagan's Office of Policy Development, said the OPD really had two functions. One was to assist the cabinet council process. But in addition,

> There are a whole host of issues that never quite rise to the level of full cabinet council deliberation, either because they are not important enough, or by their very nature, they are episodic in character and constantly changing from day to day. It is a case more of trying to keep those issues under control so that it doesn't become a big issue. If it is small by nature, keep it small.

Perhaps a more common source of fires is not the limited scope of the issues but their potential for crisis. "Given the nature of the issues I deal with, I spend a great deal of time on fire-engine chores," explained a Nixon staff member. "Busing, for example, can become a crisis issue with very little notice." When it does, the aide has to be able to set other things aside, deal with whatever problem has developed, and then return to normal business.

Still another Nixon Domestic Council aide gave an illustration of a brush fire that was ignited by Congress.

> One of the things that came across my desk concerned the budget for the Peace Corps. They are funded under the foreign appropriations bill. They were severely cut back by the Congress after spending at the level of the previous fiscal year under a continuing resolution. They were in real trouble. They would have had to discharge many employees, cut the programming schedule away back, and so on. My recommendation was that the president find loose money among other international agencies, and bail them out. When this Peace Corps budget matter came up, it took all my time for five or six days, and then the crisis was overcome, and that was it.

As with other fire-fighting tasks, this one monopolized time and attention but was of limited duration.

Putting out brush fires can be very simply described, but staff members devoted more time to this than to any other function. Why so? Some domestic staff members are dealing with politically sensitive areas. One Nixon staffer was dealing with the environment. "Congress," he said "is just red hot on this issue. There were 948 environmental bills, I think, submitted in [the present] Congress. And there are lots of fires. So that's probably half of my time spent just on discrete problems." A more general answer has to do with the large number of agencies in the federal government and with the recurring deadlines that they all confront. Because of the multiplicity of agencies and deadlines, special effort is often required just to get things done on time.

## Information Gathering in Domestic Policy

The domestic staffers form the junction between the president and all the domestic agencies. A great deal of information arrives on their doorstep, and they need to extract the material that should be forwarded to the president. "The most important thing we do," said Carter deputy director Bert Carp, "is to take the mass of paper that pours in here from a bureaucracy which inevitably confuses length with persuasiveness and boil it down into pieces of paper that a president might conceivably read." Carp's comment echoed a statement made eight years earlier by a Nixon staffer: "The first thing I'd say [we have to do] is to write as simply and clearly as possible. In other words, give [the president] a range of options, but do it without his having to read through reams and reams of material, and without his having to become an expert in any particular field. We do this by applying our judgment, and our judgment as experts in the field." This involves more than just condensing the incoming information. The material forwarded to the president or his immediate assistants must be clear and concise, and it must focus on the choices the president has to make.

The White House lies at the intersection of substantive and political forces; this position affects the type of information gathered by domestic staffs. Any policy decision must have substantive merit. It must deal effectively with the issue at hand. At the same time, the policy must be politically viable. A meritorious policy that cannot be put into effect does not help any president. Stuart Eizenstat recalled that Ted Sorensen had told him when he assumed his position "that if I performed it the way he performed his somewhat comparable role, the academicians would think I was a politician, and the politicians would think I was an academician.[11] That," he continued, "is not too far off. That is to say, I had to help factor in the political content to decisions, but I did not feel that I was a politician, a campaign aide. My job was to help develop policy. [But to do that] I served as a link between the substantive people and the political people."

The conversation of domestic staff members is filled with talk of balancing substantive and political considerations. The option papers they write have the same character. Simon Lazarus had been the key domestic staffer on a Carter task force dealing with civil service reform.

> When we began going over the proposals, we found we had to make some decisions about excluding some of the things in the original package because they were too heavy politically. For example, a proposal to change the mode of evaluating the comparability of federal pay and the pay of people in the private sector was a proposal we ultimately knocked off. . . . We discovered that the proposal for changing the procedures for disciplining people as drafted by the Civil Service Commission was unconstitutional, so we had to undertake a crash project to get them rewritten. . . . Frankly, I was so worried about it that I got both the Justice Department and my former law firm to undertake the same project simultaneously on a pro bono basis in the hope that at least one of them would come through. In fact, the private law firm did and the Justice Department didn't. . . . One of the central premises of the whole effort was that it could not pass if the entire labor movement were against it. [But] we didn't want to write something that was such a soft package that the entire labor movement would endorse it because among other things, it wouldn't do any good. . . . So I think we did basically the kinds of things you would expect a policy staff to do.

This was not simply gathering information. At one point, Lazarus was making judgments about whether a provision would pass muster on Capitol Hill. At another, he was a lawyer who saw an urgent need to redraft some provisions so they would meet tests of constitutionality. At still another, he was negotiating with the labor unions about language that the president might use in submitting legislation. Neither substantive nor political interests could be neglected if he was going to do his job.

Once the domestic staff members have the information, how is it passed along to the president? Part of the answer, of course, is that the staff members do a lot

---

[11.] The "academicians" Eizenstat mentions here are substantive experts. Some had held academic positions, others had won academic honors during their college careers.

of writing and rewriting, working over option papers until the underlying issues are clear and presented in the sort of language the president prefers.[12] But a more important element is the person through whom the information is passed to the president. In Lynn Daft's judgment:

> Of the things that shape the work of this staff, far and away the most important is the personality, skills, and experience of Stu Eizenstat plus his relationship with the president. Eizenstat has worked with the president for some time. He knows him well. He is one of the fairly limited number of people who have, who really have the confidence of Carter.

An almost identical point was made by a member of Nixon's staff:

> You really only get good communication with the president if you're performing very well—and to perform very well, you've got to have good communication. So the key is the guy who's running the Domestic Council. If he's got the president's confidence, and the president has a good working relationship with him, the council can be potent and effective because it will have this communication. Without it, I think you might as well take the Domestic Council out of the White House.

If the president respects the head of the domestic staff, he will study the information gathered by the staff, allowing it to illuminate the questions before him. But if he is skeptical when he begins to read, he may discount even the most carefully prepared document.

## Decision Making in Domestic Policy

Papers proposing decisions to be made by the president rarely show up unheralded on the desks of his principal advisers. Either they result from the discussions of study groups (often created because of presidential interest in a given program) or they come in from cabinet departments. If the president allows the

---

[12.] If presidents are not receiving information in the form they wish, they let the staff members know. For example, early in the Carter administration (February 1977), Stuart Eizenstat was submitting brief notes on domestic developments. These included such economic indicators as the wholesale price index, sales of new one-family homes, basic money supply, and so on. One came back with a note from President Carter: "Stu—This is the driest report I've ever had to read. A dictionary would be more interesting. Let someone assess it & give me the significant points, data, trends, etc. each week. J. C." (Eizenstat Files, Box 316, Carter Library).

departments freedom of action in their own areas, or if he just finds their arguments persuasive, the proposals are likely to be adopted as administration policy. "In this administration," said Carter aide Bert Carp, "cabinet government has meant that the secretaries have control over their agencies, except to the extent that the president himself disagrees with what they want to do. And if [the domestic staff] disagrees with [the secretary] we can't do a damn thing about it except advise the president and let him make up his own mind." The movement of proposals from agencies to the president has the effect of involving a great many people in the early stages of a decision, although the number decreases as the proposal moves closer to the Oval Office. Craig Fuller, cabinet secretary during the first Reagan administration, said that the cabinet councils had that effect.

> If you imagine a process by which you have a triangle, large at one side, with the larger number of people involved in the formulation process, it continually narrows so you are left just prior to the decision with the president meeting with eight or nine cabinet officers, hearing the views of his cabinet on which of the three or four different options he must decide from. The final decision process, of course, involves the smallest number of people, and it may be that the president makes the decision in the room. Usually, he makes a decision after the discussion, maybe without any additional information, or maybe with information from any one of that core group I just described.

A consequence of widespread involvement, according to Reagan aide Michael Uhlmann, is to increase the stability of the decision once it is made. This would apply to other administrations as well. If a proposal moves from a department to a domestic staff aide to Bert Carp to Stuart Eizenstat and finally to the president, as happened in the Carter administration, everyone from the agency up to the president is going to understand the arguments pro and con. Consequently a decision is less likely to be challenged when it is made.

On many occasions, issues are decided without the president's involvement. Policies on which opinion is divided are more likely to go to the president, Eizenstat assistant David Rubenstein explained, while those on which aides are agreed may not be referred to the president at all.

> Let's say a congressman calls me up, and says he wants to add thirty million dollars to a project. I call the Office of Management and Budget, and say I think it's a good idea if we add thirty million dollars for these reasons. If they agree, we would probably go ahead and do it and not tell the president, although I would probably tell Stuart to make sure he thought it was o.k. But if that same thing came along, a congressman called with this request, and

OMB said no, I would talk to Stuart about it, and if he thought it was a good idea, we would take it to the president, saying, "Look, Congressman X wants this thirty million dollars; he's useful to us; OMB says no; what do you want to do?"

Danny Boggs, who chaired the Reagan cabinet council on energy, made a similar point. If the president did not attend a meeting himself and there was a consensus among those who did, a paper would be sent to the president telling him of the recommendations and the reasons for it. If the participants were split, he said, a similar paper would be prepared giving the pros and cons of the proposed action, except at the end it would say that group *a* feels this way and group *b* feels another way.

Another factor relating to whether a staff member will make a decision himself or refer it upward is the degree of his own knowledge of the president's preferences. For example, Robert Carleson's experience with Governor Reagan began thirteen years before Reagan entered the White House. He said, "I would guess that I would be more apt to make decisions than others, particularly in the general welfare area, because I have been with the president long enough to know what he wants." Finally, given the complexity of domestic political decisions, aides rarely take dogmatic positions. That did happen in the Reagan administration, though. Martin Anderson, Reagan's first domestic adviser, said that one of his criteria was whether a proposal was "in basic philosophic compliance with Ronald Reagan's positions. Ronald Reagan has made it clear for decades where he stands on issues. The time for debate is past. The question is how do we implement it. I don't want to sit through debates on every aspect of policy. I've done that." More frequently, an adviser will maintain a degree of flexibility.

If the president's principal domestic adviser has standing with the president (as is usually the case), outside agencies often attempt to coopt him as their advocate. David Rubenstein gave an unusually candid account of agencies' desire to enlist his boss, Stuart Eizenstat.

Before a department secretary ever makes a recommendation, he will know what the interest groups want, and will probably have a recommendation that's somewhat consistent with what they want. He will then try to line up Stu to support his position because the general view was, rightly or wrongly, that if Stu Eizenstat supported their position, chances were they were going to win in front of the president. What they would try to do, knowing they couldn't get OMB to support their position was to try to line Stu up, get Stu to be the person who would argue with OMB, and then when he couldn't get that far with OMB, he would draft a memo that would go to the president making sure that his view and the agency's view was more favorably presented than if OMB had drafted the memo, or if the agency had drafted the memo without Stuart's involvement, and then OMB had put a cover memo on top that basically killed the position.

## Exercising Influence in Domestic Policy

Once the president makes a decision, how does the White House build support for it? That depends on who has to take what kind of action. Within the White House, a decision by the president normally stops discussion of a matter. If a senior staff member feels the decision was made too casually, or without information that should be brought to the president's attention, he may see to it that further staff work is done before the decision is implemented. For example, H. R. Haldeman, who had to deal with ill-considered orders Nixon issued when he was angry, felt "it's the obligation of the senior staff person dealing with any such kind of situation not to carry out the order until it has been at least reviewed once and then reordered by the president on the basis of making the right decision for the right reasons instead of for the wrong reasons" (Kernell and Popkin 1986, 21). Once a presidential decision has been verified, though, presidential wishes are commands to the White House staff.

Outside the White House the situation is different. Others must be persuaded to support the presidential decision. The nature of this persuasion depends on whether the decision concerns an administrative or legislative matter. An administrative decision carries with it the danger that a White House instruction will disappear in the bureaucracy without much action being taken. If important legislation is involved, there is less danger the decision will be neglected because the legislative liaison staff will follow it.

Several techniques are used to ensure agency support of an administration policy. The most important is to include the agency in the determination of the policy, so agency staffers know that their views have been carefully considered before the decision is made. "I've never really had to think of strategies [to gain agency support]," said Carter aide Alfred Stern, "since we've been very careful about consultation on the way up." Reagan staffer Michael Uhlmann made a similar point in discussing the cabinet councils:

> Of course, you want policy to drive the system because it is of concern to the president either personally or politically. . . . It very often happens [there are] a number of conflicting views among the departments. [But] the departments must pass their views through the filter of some of their peers, and

through the filter of other departments which have different points of view before a decision is made.

Thus, the departments already know that the president has the matter under advisement. They know what options have been presented and what arguments have been made for each one.

Sometimes there is bargaining between the White House and the agencies concerning the nature of a decision. The key here is that the president makes decisions on a number of basic points. These fundamental considerations may be the options that have been presented to him, or they may simply be things that he cares about. At the same time, there's lots of room for negotiation about other matters. Something that is trivial from the president's point of view may be of extreme importance to, say, the Interior Department and the interest groups with whom the department must deal. A Nixon aide recalled one negotiation:

> Three departments were concerned with this in a major way. They were all not necessarily with an institutional position they had to protect, but with a broad constituency they had to deal with, and so it made a great deal of difference to them and to their constituencies just what course things were going to take, and I would say that there was some hauling and pushing. This resulted in lesser compromises than made a difference to the president. In other words, the big policy options were not compromised. . . . But once the presidential decisions are made, there are a myriad of details, regulations and everything else where you can still make trade-offs between departments. The result is that everybody doesn't get killed over something.

If the policy has been modified so as to make it easier for the department to deal with its constituency, the department is going to be a good deal more energetic in administering the policy.

Beyond this, there are some formal and informal techniques that can be used. One formal approach mentioned by Reagan aide Robert Carleson is to create an implementation working group, "either chairing it myself, or assigning it to someone who is interested in making [the policy] work." If the domestic staff member has good working relationships with the agencies, these lines of communication can be used to pass messages along and monitor progress of a new program. "You develop relationships with certain people in the departments, frequently [with] . . . the congressional affairs, the public affairs, the assistants to the secretary, people that you tend to deal with a lot," explained Reagan assistant Danny Boggs. "You develop relationships with some of the substantive people, and tell them this is the way it's going to be. You have to develop a kind of feeling for which ones you can talk to directly, and which ones have to be handled through the department."

Finally, there are times when subtlety just doesn't work. Then White House staffers have to resort to calling meetings, doing a little desk pounding, and insisting on action. An assistant director of Nixon's Domestic Council remembered one such case.

> I got into going to meetings, and sending out memoranda to anybody whose job it was to make some progress on this thing. It didn't happen, because there was a bureaucratic process of regulations and sign-offs, and . . . [nothing was] happening. And we ended up calling in the procurement officers and saying, "I don't care . . . whether those regs are there. You know they're coming. So start telling everybody that this is what we want to happen." . . . We just kept hammering and hammering on enough people until it finally eked its way out into the bureaucracy and some things started to happen.

When dealing with Congress, White House staffers are in a rather different situation. Here the assistants to the president for domestic policy have been intensely involved in strategy, particularly in the Nixon, Carter, and Bush administrations. Roger Porter described his activities on a typical day during the first year of the Bush administration.

> My schedule today is instructive. I held a strategy meeting on minimum wage to decide how we're going to work the Hill. When it concluded, I went down and talked to Vice President Quayle about it. An hour later I held a meeting on food safety legislation to decide what position and actions we would take. We discussed a fact sheet, a legislative statement, decided who was going to talk to particular senators and representatives, and what our strategy was going to be for both the House and the Senate.

Stuart Eizenstat estimated that during the third year of the Carter administration he spent 25 percent of his time on the Hill. These ranking domestic aides are vital participants because they can discuss the contents of individual pieces of legislation in some detail, and they are also aware of the relation of the individual bills to the total legislative program. Lower ranking members of the domestic staffs can discuss the merits of legislation in their own areas, and the congressional relations personnel know what bills are moving on the Hill, but the top domestic assistant is likely to be the one who best combines both perspectives.

Yet another example of domestic staff involvement in launching legislation comes from the civil service reform legislation submitted in 1978. This was important in light of President Carter's emphasis on government efficiency. The drafters' key assumptions were that the bill would not pass if it were opposed by labor, and that it would not be effective if it were so weak that every labor organization endorsed it. So, in addition to working things out with the affected departments and agencies, White House staffers arrived at an understanding with the AFL-CIO (whose membership included the largest and most moderate of the federal employee unions) that the AFL-CIO would oppose individual parts of the legislation but would not oppose the bill as a whole if those parts were adopted. As domestic staff member Simon Lazarus recounted the effort:

> This was all very delicate. The words in the president's message sending the original package up to the Hill were all negotiated out with the AFL-CIO. So we were very much involved during this period. Then we were involved in the drafting of the legislation, and getting comments from the agencies, and changing the legislation, and drafting the speech the president gave at the National Press Club to kick off the submission of the bill to Congress. Then we were involved in briefing the press, and trying to explain why this was such a terrific thing. Then we all went to work on the task force [that handled the bill as it moved through Congress].

Obviously, much administration effort is expended in shaping legislation to improve its chances of moving through the congressional labyrinth.

## Summary

*Actors.* In domestic policy, fiefdoms in welfare, education, transportation, civil liberties, public safety, energy, and many other areas must be dealt with. The White House has handled this challenge in several different ways: a few generalists early on; task forces under Johnson; domestic staffs during the Nixon, Ford, and Carter administrations; multiple decision centers under Reagan; a domestic staff again under Bush; and constantly shifting arrangements under Clinton. With so many conflicting interests coordination is difficult, but the departments often need the neutral turf offered by the White House to reconcile their differences.

*Domestic Policy Activities.* Two distinctive domestic activities stem from the complexity of the domestic policy environment. Because so many agencies are engaged in the implementation of domestic policy, some monitoring of their activities is necessary. This means White House–departmental relations must be nurtured so that departmental personnel will trust staff members enough to speak frankly, but without concluding that the White House staff is subject to their control. The large number of agencies, along with the frequency of governmental deadlines, means that some things will fall into the cracks. As a matter of necessity, domestic staffers are going to spend time putting out fires to keep small problems from getting out of hand.

*Common Activities in a Domestic Policy Environment.* The White House is above all the place where calculations of substantive merit and political advantage intersect. Hence information gathering involves searching for technically appropriate solutions and forming judgments about political viability. As information is moved from the advocacy departments to the ultimate decision makers, there is an emphasis on neutral writing and on the maintenance of policy splits so all parties can be confident that their positions will be fairly judged by the president. Once a decision has been made, enough room for maneuver remains within the presidential parameters that staffers can enlist agency cooperation on the points that are most important to them. Still, success in passing legislation and in implementing new domestic policies generally requires both presidential skill and presidential luck.

In this chapter and in the four preceding, we have seen how the major units of the presidency have adapted themselves to the needs of individual presidents, and at the same time adapted themselves to the contours of the political environment. This dual adaptation has helped each president accomplish his own tasks, and has linked the presidents to the larger world of political institutions in which they are situated.

We turn now to the question of what recent presidents have been able to accomplish, given their skills, the resources at their disposal, and the challenges they faced.

# 7. Samples of Presidential Accomplishment

There has been much, indeed too much, discussion of presidential failure in recent decades. Consider the following. Shortly after he left the presidency, a panel of historians found Dwight Eisenhower to be tied with President Chester Alan Arthur, next to the bottom rank of "average" presidents. John Kennedy's own staff complained that he was unwilling to attend meetings and read reports he had asked for himself. Lyndon Johnson was very difficult to work for, frequently belittling loyal aides, and Richard Nixon constantly imagined that he was surrounded by enemies. Gerald Ford could not win the 1976 election, and George Bush could not win the 1992 election. Jimmy Carter was negatively portrayed in the media. Ronald Reagan's approval ratings were so low in his third year that as his campaign managers began work on his reelection planning Walter Mondale was running ahead of Reagan in the polls. And Bill Clinton was the only president to be impeached in the twentieth century.

These statements are all negative, and they are all true. But before concluding that the presidency is in trouble, notice the nature of these statements. The nine presidents are being evaluated in seven different ways. Eisenhower was thought to be wanting by a group of historians. Kennedy was criticized for the absence of an orderly executive process. Johnson and Nixon were being evaluated through the lens of personality. Ford and Bush lacked the political laurels that come with reelection. Journalists reached a negative judgment about Jimmy Carter. Reagan's public support was low during an economic downturn early in his administration. And Clinton ran afoul of a constitutional process. When there are so many different ways to evaluate presidents, almost every president fails to pass certain criteria for success.

The crucial point here is that a president can be an utter failure by one criterion and a considerable success by another. Eisenhower made important improvements in the institutional presidency. The policy processes in the Kennedy White House were often much too casual, yet Kennedy's approval ratings were consistently high. Neither Johnson nor Nixon was an admirable human being, but Johnson was very successful in passing domestic legislation, and Nixon's foreign policy was shaped by long-range vision. Ford's straightforward honesty enabled him to restore public confidence in government. Both Carter and Bush followed successful policies in the Middle East, Carter in the Camp David and subsequent negotiations, Bush in Desert Storm and in encouraging Israel to negotiate with Arab countries and factions. Both Reagan and Clinton won substantial victories when they ran for reelection. A claim of success or a concession of failure by one criterion says nothing about a president's attainment according to another criterion.

Notwithstanding these differences, global judgments are often rendered on the basis of specific criteria. If a president wins reelection, he is successful regardless of anything else he may have done. If a president fails to win reelection, he is a failure regardless of anything else he may have done. Similarly, if a president has high approval ratings, or a pleasant personality, or a high rating from historians, he is thought to have done well. And if a president has low approval ratings, or an unpleasant personality, or a low rating from historians, he is thought to have done poorly.

There is another point as well. Using a dichotomous criterion encourages labeling one president as a success and another as a failure. For example, if a president is judged on the basis of reelection or defeat, or if a president's approval rating is categorized as "good" if above 50 percent and "bad" if below 50 percent, then restricting the possibilities to reelected/defeated or good/bad makes it more likely that we will view a president as completely successful or completely unsuccessful.

If, on the other hand, we inspect a wider range of alternatives, we increase the likelihood of more nuanced judgments. If we ask whether a president passed several criteria, then we allow for the possibility that he will have passed some of them and failed others. Likewise, if we look across the whole range of challenges facing a president, it turns out that presidents are very likely to do well at some things, to do poorly at others, and to achieve partial success with still others.

Since the record of all administrations is composed of successes, failures, and mixed outcomes, we will examine one of each type for the presidencies from Eisenhower through Clinton. These samples should provide a better sense of what kinds of experiences and evaluations await chief executives as their terms begin.

## *Dwight D. Eisenhower*

### A Modified Containment Policy

In the spring of 1953, three different approaches to foreign policy were being advocated by various Republican leaders.[1] President Eisenhower suggested that teams of analysts study the full implications of approach and then make the best possible case for it. The teams worked with few breaks from eight in the morning until midnight for about five weeks. Their reports were presented to the president, the National Security Council, the Joint Chiefs of Staff, and other administration leaders on July 16.

The three policies varied most in the assumptions they made. Team A was led by George Kennan, a highly respected diplomat who had developed the containment policy during the Truman administration. Containment assumed that if the Soviet empire were simply prevented from expanding, the costs of the USSR's efforts to challenge the West would ultimately weaken it. Western pressure was also expected to debilitate the Soviet system. Therefore time was on the side of the West, not the communists. Team A asserted that the United States had the economic capacity needed to carry out this policy. As was consistent with Eisenhower's known preferences, they also argued for a expense level the country could sustain over time.

Team B argued for a different form of containment. Its members argued for drawing a line around the Soviet empire, then relying on the threat of general war to keep the Soviets within that orbit. This approach relied to a much greater degree on unilateral U.S. action. Team B's approach was less flexible and, since the United States had to be prepared to fight a general war at any time, its recommendations were more expensive.

Team C analyzed and argued for a rollback policy that would shrink the communist-dominated area in Eastern Europe and in Asia. Team members assumed that communist powers would never adopt true co-existence, that time was working against the West, and that the trend of growing communist strength must be reversed by aggressive action. They recognized that aggressive policies carried a substantial risk of war but argued that American policy had been too cautious for too long.

The three teams had no sooner finished than President Eisenhower stood up. After praising the team members for as fine a staff job as he had ever seen, he

---

[1.] This case is based on Bose 1998b, chap. 1; Bowie and Immerman 1998, chaps. 8–9; Pach and Richardson 1991, 77–80; and Ewald 1981, 169. Unless otherwise indicated, all information and quotes will come from these sources. A similar citation will appear at the beginning of each case.

spoke spontaneously for about forty-five minutes. Eisenhower analyzed the similarities and differences in the proposed policies. In saying that another global war would destroy individual freedom, he clearly signaled his opposition to a rollback policy. Eisenhower's logic and command of the subject matter so impressed George Kennan that he said "in summarizing the group's conclusions, President Eisenhower showed his intellectual ascendancy over every man in the room."

This exercise, dubbed Project Solarium after the White House room where the discussions began, was certainly a *success*. Thorough analyses of the alternatives were followed by candid discussion of their merits. Papers flowed from Project Solarium to the NSC staff, from there to the planning board, and from there to two meetings of the National Security Council. On October 30, President Eisenhower approved a Basic National Security Policy. Portions of the work of each team appeared in that final document, but essentially it endorsed Kennan's containment policy, modified to reflect Eisenhower's Great Equation: balancing requisite military strength with healthy economic growth.

The modified containment policy remained in effect throughout the Eisenhower administration. Four decades later, this Truman-Eisenhower policy was ultimately vindicated with the collapse of the Soviet Union.

## The 1957–1958 Recession

On October 14, 1957, President Eisenhower met with Treasury Secretary Anderson, CEA Chair Saulnier, and Federal Reserve Chairman Martin; he learned that a recession was in the offing.[2] Eisenhower had heard similar news in September 1953. From then through May 1954, relying on the guidance of then CEA Chair Arthur Burns, he had coped with the recession rather well. But in 1957–1958, there were several important differences.

While the 1957–1958 recession was shorter than that of 1953–1954, the unemployment rate was higher: 6.8 percent as compared with 5.5 percent. Unemployment more than doubled between October 1957 and February 1958. Prices were rising in 1957–1958 while disposable income declined. Consequently, the 1957–1958 recession impinged more sharply on Americans' personal lives.

Important changes had taken place among the economic advisers. Arthur Burns had departed, as had Gabriel Hauge, another able economic assistant. The man Eisenhower most respected on his second-term economic team was Trea-

---

[2.] This case is based on Eisenhower 1965; Sundquist 1968; Ewald 1981; Ferrell 1981; Ambrose 1984; and Pach and Richardson 1991.

sury Secretary Robert Anderson. "We face a choice," Anderson counseled, between "preventing a little more unemployment and preserving the value of the dollar. I favor the second course. Because if inflation ever starts snowballing, it will require so much unemployment to stop it that even a Dwight Eisenhower couldn't survive politically."

Arthur Burns was on the opposite side of this argument. In February 1958 he wrote that since he could see no evidence of an early recovery, he favored a tax cut. In the Anderson-Burns dispute, Secretary Anderson had the advantage of appealing to Eisenhower's own strongly held attitudes. As Eisenhower wrote in his diary: "(1) We believe in a private enterprise rather that a 'government' campaign to provide the main strength of recovery forces. (2) We want to avoid a succession of budget deficits because of the inflationary effect. (3) We prefer to limit [any] . . . expenditures to projects that are useful and needed." By spring, economic growth had resumed, and in Eisenhower's words, "the storm was over."

Not quite. In 1954 Congress had been in Republican hands, but now there was a Democratic majority. Hubert Humphrey, for example, spoke out against the "planned, premeditated, predesignated recession of this administration." Many Democrats joined his attack. More importantly, Congress passed some bills to demonstrate a desire to protect citizens from the harsh winds of the recession. Among these was a farm bill. Although legislation had passed earlier in the Eisenhower administration to phase out farm subsidies and move to a free market, Congress had been delaying the bill's implementation. In March, Democrats and farm-state Republicans passed a bill that would extend price supports for another year. On March 31, Eisenhower vetoed the bill. Democrats and farm-state residents attacked Eisenhower for his devotion to economic abstractions rather than needy farmers.

Recovery began in April 1958, but it was slower than usual, and the recession hardly abated at all in many agricultural areas. Democrats used the farm recession to portray the Republicans as heartless. And whatever the economic arguments, the Democrats won the political contest in November, picking up thirteen seats in the Senate and forty-eight in the House. Many of the Republican losses came in farm states.

As long as one concentrates on inflation, this record might be called a success. The increase in inflation dropped from 3.3 percent in 1957 to 2.8 percent in 1958. But in a broader sense, Eisenhower's handling of the 1957–1958 recession was a *failure*. The unemployed of course suffered, and many with jobs faced economic hardships. For this, the administration paid a very high political price in the 1958 congressional elections.

### The 1957 Civil Rights Bill

The civil rights movement had begun to gather force by the late 1950s, but the federal government still had very little power to act on civil rights matters.[3] Attorney General Herbert Brownell decided to submit a bill to remedy this situation. It had four parts:

1. Creating a presidentially appointed civil rights commission.
2. Creating a civil rights division in the Department of Justice.
3. Giving the attorney general power to seek injunctive relief against obstructions of constitutionally protected civil rights. This was a key provision because the Justice Department could use civil procedure rather than criminal law. Civil law allowed injunctions to be sought *before* violations took place; criminal proceedings could begin only after the fact. Even more important, injunctions could be issued by judges, whereas criminal trials in the South depended on all-white juries.
4. Allowing the attorney general to go into federal court to seek relief for blacks who were deprived of their right to vote in federal elections.

This bill was passed by the House in 1956. But it had no hope that year in the Senate, where southern conservatives (all Democrats at the time) could use the filibuster and committee power to prevent any civil rights legislation. Still, President Eisenhower (who was personally more interested in voting rights than in broader issues of civil rights) endorsed the bill during the 1956 campaign, and he called for its passage in his 1957 State of the Union Message. The House quickly repassed the bill and sent it to the Senate. Vice President Nixon was presiding; in an unusual parliamentary maneuver, he sent the bill directly to the Senate floor, bypassing the Judiciary Committee, where southerners could have buried it.

Southerners were quite angry. Sen. Richard B. Russell of Georgia, the de facto leader of the Southern Democrats, described the bill as "a cunning device [to use] the whole might of the federal government . . . to force a commingling of white and Negro children." President Eisenhower met Russell on July 10. He told Russell that although he understood the problems facing the South, he would insist on protecting the citizen's right to vote. On July 16 Eisenhower released a statement listing four essential objectives. Giving the attorney general the right to seek injunctive relief for civil rights transgressions was not among them. With Eisen-

---

[3.] This case is based on Ambrose 1984, 406–410; Pach and Richardson 1991, 145–150; Eisenhower 1965, 155–161; and especially on Brownell 1993, 217–226.

hower no longer supporting the third part of the bill, the Senate voted on July 24 to delete it.

Then, on August 2, the Senate added another amendment guaranteeing a trial by jury to those accused in criminal contempt cases. This, together with the elimination of the attorney general's power to seek injunctive relief, reversed the intent of the legislation. The trail-by-jury amendment was later modified, but the resulting legislation was now much weaker.

The efforts to pass the Civil Rights Bill of 1957 brought *mixed results.* On the plus side, it was the first civil rights legislation passed since Reconstruction. The bill was followed by considerably broader legislation in 1960 and 1964. But the final 1957 bill was much weaker than what was drafted by Attorney General Brownell, and it was weaker than it might have been if President Eisenhower had been willing to fight for it.

## John F. Kennedy

### The American University Speech

In many ways, the Cuban Missile Crisis was a transforming event.[4] After that, John Kennedy no longer needed to demonstrate his competence in international affairs. Even more important, this first and (thankfully!) only nuclear confrontation had a sobering effect on both Chairman of the USSR Council of Ministers Nikita S. Khrushchev and President Kennedy. They were now anxious to reduce international tensions, and to some degree, they reached out to each other.

Private negotiations were discouraging to both men. Khrushchev felt he had been misled; Kennedy was anxious for a nuclear test ban treaty but could see few signs of Soviet interest. Their domestic situations were also difficult. Russian hard-liners accused Khrushchev of being too soft with the West; American hard-liners accused Kennedy of being too soft with the USSR.

Wishing to convince the Soviets that the United States was sincerely interested in a test ban treaty, President Kennedy decided to make a speech emphasizing peace that would be delivered before the Communist Party Central Committee meeting in mid-June. A June 10 commencement address at American University was selected as the venue. Before leaving on a trip to Honolulu, Kennedy instructed speechwriter Ted Sorensen to stay behind to work on the speech. Sorensen met Kennedy with a draft in San Francisco, and final editing took place as *Air Force One* flew back to Washington.

---

[4.] This case is based on Schlesinger 1965, 897–902; Reeves 1993, 510–514; and especially on Sorensen 1966, 822–829.

The speech began by referring to a practical peace "based not on a sudden revolution in human nature but on a gradual evolution in human institutions. . . . [I hope Soviet leaders] adopt a more enlightened attitude. . . . [But] we must reexamine our own attitude." Kennedy then focused on the common interests of the United States and the USSR.

> Among the many traits the people of our two countries have in common, none is stronger than our mutual abhorrence of war. Almost unique among the major world powers, we have never been at war with each other. . . . We must deal with the world as it is, and not as it might have been had the history of the last eighteen years been different. We must conduct our affairs in such a way that it becomes in the Communists' interest to agree on a genuine peace. . . . In the final analysis our most basic common link is the fact that we all inhabit this planet. We all breathe the same air. We all cherish our children's future. And we are all mortal.

The final rhetoric was a rededication to peace. "We shall do our part to build a world of peace where the weak are safe and the strong are just. We are not helpless before that task or hopeless of its success. Confident and unafraid we labor on—not toward a strategy of annihilation but toward a strategy of peace."

At the very end, President Kennedy made two announcements. First, important because neither country was then conducting nuclear tests, was a decision made by Kennedy that the United States would not be the first to resume testing. Second, he announced that Premier Khrushchev had agreed to receive emissaries in Moscow to negotiate a nuclear test ban treaty.

The American University speech was a *success,* particularly in its impact overseas. In England the *Manchester Guardian* called it "one of the great state papers of American history." The full text was published in Russian papers; the Soviets ceased their customary jamming of the Voice of America so the president's speech could be heard by the people of the USSR. And the Moscow negotiations, closely monitored by President Kennedy, led to a limited nuclear test ban treaty, which was initialed just six weeks after the speech.

## Medicare

John Kennedy wanted Medicare.[5] Health care for the elderly had been debated for over a decade; Kennedy had supported it as a senator; it had been an issue in his

---

[5.] This case is based on Sorensen 1966, 383–385; Sundquist 1968, chap. 7; Ripley 1972, 7–8, 22; O'Brien 1974, 147; and Reeves 1993, 327–328.

presidential campaign. Kennedy submitted a Medicare bill to Congress, and designated it as a priority item in 1962.

Interest groups were active on both sides. The American Medical Association had campaigned against "socialized medicine" for years and waged an expensive fight against Medicare in 1962. Medicare's principal proponent was the National Council of Senior Citizens, subsidized by organized labor and the Democratic National Committee and coordinated by the White House.

In May President Kennedy gave an impassioned speech to a pro-Medicare rally in New York's Madison Square Garden. He was cheered by the assembled enthusiasts, but he was less successful in reaching the uncommitted. Medicare, however, faced more serious obstacles than a subpar speech. Majorities in both the House and the Senate were against it. In the House Ways and Means Committee, Chairman Wilbur Mills, Southern Democrats, and Republicans all opposed it. Opponents were not quite as strong in the Senate, but were nonetheless a majority.

Although Representative Mills was personally opposed, he suggested to House Majority Leader John McCormack that Medicare's chances might be improved if it were introduced in the Senate first. If a Medicare bill should pass the Senate, then the House might be more disposed to act favorably. Gaining Senate passage required two things. First, a majority was needed; and since a third of the Democrats opposed Medicare, Republican votes had to be obtained. Sen. Clinton Anderson, leader of the pro-Medicare Democrats, therefore negotiated with Sen. Jacob Javits, a pro-Medicare Republican, to write a bill that would get some Republican support.

The next need was tactical, to identify a House-passed measure to which the Anderson-Javits bill could be attached as an amendment. Prior House passage meant the bill would go to conference, and then back to the House floor as part of the conference report. The bill decided upon was the House-passed welfare bill. Senator Anderson offered his amendment to attach Medicare to the welfare bill on July 17.

Thirty-nine Northern Democrats, four Southern Democrats, and five Republicans voted for Medicare. Two Northern Democrats, nineteen Southern Democrats, and thirty-one Republicans voted against. The proponents were just two votes shy of a fifty-fifty tie that Vice President Johnson could have broken by voting for Medicare.

President Kennedy was angry and deeply disappointed. But even if the Senate vote had been affirmative, the problem of how to get the bill through the House would have remained. And in the House, the bill never even got out of the Ways and Means Committee.

The Medicare outcome was a *failure* for the Kennedy administration. The fundamental problem was that liberal Democrats lacked the votes for passage, particularly in the House. The partisan division of the House was 263 Democrats to 174 Republicans, but the ideological division was 224 conservatives to 213 liberals. Whenever the Democrats lost a handful of votes, Kennedy could not prevail. In fact, Medicare did pass in the Great Society Congress in 1965. Larry O'Brien, who coordinated legislative liaison for both Kennedy and Johnson, believed "that if Kennedy had lived, he would have defeated Goldwater by a margin similar to Johnson's . . . and would have achieved a legislative record in 1965–66 comparable to Johnson's."

## Laos

On March 23, 1961, John Kennedy appeared on television standing before a map of Laos.[6] The new president had learned "that from December 20 to the present date . . . [the area] the communists control [has expanded to] a much wider section of the country." A Soviet airlift, he continued, was bringing troops and supplies from North Vietnam.

   None of the options facing the president was very attractive. One was to let events take their course, which would have allowed Laos to be absorbed into the communist orbit. A second was to ask Americans to do the fighting Laotians were unwilling to do, to send troops halfway round the world to struggle in the mountains and jungles of a small, landlocked country. A third was to neutralize the country, to abandon the idea of a western-oriented Laos while preventing communist domination. After considering the likely results of each policy and assessing the capabilities of the various Laotian factions, Kennedy opted for neutrality as the least undesirable alternative.

   How was neutrality to be brought about? If Laos would fall under communist power in the natural course of events, why should the USSR, China, or Vietnam acquiesce to a neutral outcome? To accomplish this would require some additional U.S. action. Therefore, President Kennedy's policy became a combination of the "fight" alternative and the "neutral" alternative. Specifically, the United States preferred a neutral outcome, but if the hostile powers were to reject this, then the United States, however unwillingly, would send troops to defend Laos. Kennedy sent messages explaining this to China and, by three separate channels, to the Soviet Union. In the process, both Great Britain and India also learned about U.S. policy. Finally, to make the threat of American force credible, one

---

[6.] This case is based on Schlesinger 1965, 323–340, 512–518; Sorensen 1966, 721–731; and Reeves 1993.

marine unit was landed in Thailand, and more Marines were made ready to move to Thailand if need be.

With all this done, Great Britain and the USSR (as co-chairs of the 1954 Geneva Conference) convened fourteen-nation talks in May on the future of Laos. These talks were suspended while Kennedy and Khrushchev met in Vienna in June 1961. Here Kennedy repeatedly reminded Khrushchev that it was not in either country's interest to fight over a small country of little strategic value. Special Ambassador Averell Harriman conducted the most important negotiations thereafter, sometimes with Laotians and sometimes with Soviets. Finally, in October, the warring factions in Laos (who were often unresponsive to the wishes of outside powers) agreed in principle to a division of power.

Laotian fighting resumed with a Pathet Lao attack (support by the North Vietnamese) in May 1962. Once again, U.S. forces were moved into position, this time including marines, army troops, naval forces, and air forces. Having been shown that the United States was serious, the Laotian factions agreed to a coalition government in June. On July 23, a fourteen-nation Declaration on the Neutrality of Laos was formally agreed to in Geneva, and by December all U.S. troops were out of Laos.

Kennedy's Laotian policy led to *mixed results.* Combining a show of force with persistent diplomacy, Kennedy was able to keep the United States out of a war that would have been hard to fight. But agreement or no agreement, fighting continued between the Laotian factions. And Laos was used as a supply route for Vietnam. What good did it do to have part of the jungle neutralized when there was a hot war going on elsewhere in the same jungle?

## Lyndon B. Johnson

### Federal Aid to Education

For decades, federal aid to education bills had been defeated by three powerful congressional factions.[7] Catholics objected to a program that would benefit only public schools while they faced increasing costs in their own parochial schools. Southern Democrats were afraid that federal aid would be an opening wedge to desegregation. Many Republicans opposed the tax increases that would have been needed, and they were also fearful that federal aid would lead to less local control

---

[7.] This case is based on Bailey and Mosher 1968; Goldman 1969; Eidenberg and Morey 1969; McPherson 1972; Thomas 1983; Cater 1977; Graham 1981; and Bornet 1983.

over schools. The political challenge facing the Johnson administration was how to outflank this long-successful coalition.

The odds favoring federal aid to education increased substantially with the 1964 election. The Northern Democrats gained 41 members, for a total of 194. Many of them favored educational aid, and being only twenty-four votes shy of an absolute majority, they could provide most of the needed votes.

Political craftsmanship can be seen by considering the hitherto opposed groups. One element of the bill required school districts to provide "shared-services" for children enrolled in private nonprofit schools. Catholic leaders had agreed that aid to disadvantaged children could be distinguished from the general aid to which they had been opposed. Hence the United States Catholic Conference supported the bill: "We look with favor upon [the bill's] provisions and hope they can be worked out successfully." So one key group of opponents had been converted into supporters.

The formula for aid distribution was important to Southern Democrats.[8] The federal government would provide aid based on the number of low-income (less than $2,000 annually) families per state multiplied by 50 percent of that state's average per pupil expenditure. Under this formula, the largest amounts of funds would go to inner-city and rural southern districts where schools were most in need of improvement and where, not coincidentally, there were large concentrations of Democratic members of Congress. The White House was able to show that under this formula the South would fare as well as or better than it would have under any alternative. This argument did not persuade all Southern Democrats, but enough of them became supporters to create a potential majority.

The Republicans were left with the task of opposing the 1965 bill. Although the contingent included some very astute legislators, they just didn't have the votes. Early in the House debate, Charles Goodell of New York raised crucial questions: Did the bill authorize a person on the public payroll to teach in parochial schools? Wasn't the argument that the bill could be improved later one that would justify passing anything? Why not use a more equitable distribution formula? The debate on these matters was lively, but the Republicans were in the minority. By early spring, the bill became law.

Passage of federal aid to education was a *success*. Politically, the Johnson administration took advantage of its abnormal majority to overcome the anti–federal aid coalition. Substantively, it provided an infusion of federal cash

---

[8.] The 1964 Civil Rights Act prohibited the use of federal funds for segregated facilities, so the argument that educational aid would be the "entering wedge" for desegregation was now moot.

just when school systems needed more buildings and teachers to educate the huge baby-boom generation.

## A War Without Taxes

Wars are expensive, and the pressures generated by wartime government spending leads to inflation.[9] Drawing on these lessons of past wars, Harry Truman had recommended raising taxes and had instituted wage and price controls early in the Korean War. Lyndon Johnson did neither when he escalated the Vietnamese conflict in 1965. Instead Johnson attempted to fund the war and his expensive, new Great Society programs without asking for tax increases.

By December 1965, economists saw a need for action to prevent the economy from overheating. Believing that expenses of the Vietnam War were likely to be much larger than advertised, the Federal Reserve announced an increase in the discount rate from 4.0 to 4.5 percent on December 5. On December 17, CEA Chair Gardner Ackley sent Johnson his private view that if the budget were $115 billion, "there is little question in my mind that a significant tax increase will be needed to prevent an intolerable degree of inflationary pressure." Sensing that Johnson was not ready for a tax increase, Budget Director Charles Schultze proposed a strategy of calculating the defense budget on the *assumption* that the war would be over by June 30, 1967. Making this assumption was an economic signal that the cost of the war was understated, *and* understated by an unknown amount.

Johnson followed the Schultze strategy but did nothing to call general attention to the inadequacy of existing revenues. Instead, his Budget Message said, "Both [military and domestic] commitments involve great costs. These are costs we can and will meet. . . . The struggle in Vietnam must be supported. The advance toward a Great Society at home must continue unabated." Not only was Johnson skeptical about raising taxes, but his suspicion that Congress would not pass a general tax increase was confirmed by leading legislators. Johnson asked for some small adjustments in existing taxes. Congress passed these, but that was all.

By the end of 1966, his economic advisers recommended a 6 percent tax surcharge to go into effect July 1, 1967, together with some measures to soften its effect. President Johnson concluded that he could no longer put off a tax increase, and he announced his intentions in the State of the Union Message. By summer, the inflationary pressures were more serious than anticipated. On August 3 Johnson asked Congress to enact a two-year surcharge of 10 percent (up from the earlier 6

---

[9.] This case is based on King 1985; Kettl 1987; Califano 1991; and Carroll 1995.

percent). Congress took nearly a year to act. Wilbur Mills refused even to report the bill from his Ways and Means Committee. Finally, the Senate attached the surtax to a bill the House had already passed, thus sending the surtax to a conference committee. President Johnson agreed to a $6 billion spending cut as the price of getting the surtax, and it went into effect on July 1, 1968.

The two-and-a-half-year delay in raising taxes was a serious *failure*. According to Richard Carroll's analysis, the increase in inflation during the Johnson administration was greater than in any other administration since World War II. It would be too simple to attribute this to the president's reluctance to ask for more taxes. Reluctant he was, but Johnson also received conflicting economic and political advice and faced a Congress that was slow to act. Still, by the time the tax increase took effect, inflation was so firmly established that it persisted for well over a decade.

### Dominican Intervention

The Dominican Republic had little experience with democracy.[10] Its twentieth-century experience included occupation by U.S. Marines from 1916 to 1924 and dictatorship by Rafael Trujillo from 1930 until his assassination in 1961. In 1965, the island country was led by one Donald Reid Cabral, whose government collapsed after he alienated one Dominican faction after another. Amid the chaos that followed, Lyndon Johnson responded to a plea from the U.S. ambassador by sending in marines.

What Lyndon Johnson wanted to avoid was clearer than what he wanted to achieve. He most wished to avoid "another Cuba," a communist regime that would take cues from Moscow. He also opposed any return to the sort of government Trujillo had led. But while he wanted to avoid a far-left or far-right outcome, it wasn't obvious what results were likely, or even what the situation was.

After the coup against Reid Cabral on April 24, there were military factions supporting the rebels and other military factions opposing the rebels, with occasional clashes between them. (One couldn't speak of pro-government forces since there was no government to be found.) In addition, the rebels distributed weapons to their sympathizers. A U.S. aircraft carrier with marines on board was stationed offshore on April 25, but for a couple of days it didn't look as though U.S. intervention would be needed. Then on April 28 there was more gunfire in Santa Domingo, and the U.S. ambassador cabled that "you must land troops

---

[10.] This case is based on Geyelin 1966, chap. 10; Bornet 1983, 174–178; Hammond 1992, 23, 180.

immediately or blood will run in the streets, American blood will run in the streets." In response, Johnson ordered the marines ashore.

Landing a few hundred marines to stabilize an uncertain situation would cause little comment. But next Johnson sent in the rest of a marine battalion, and then the 82nd Airborne Division and other units, for a total force of 22,000. This was the same number of U.S. troops as were in Vietnam at the end of 1963, quite a sizable force for a relatively small country.

This move could have been portrayed as an action needed to reduce risks. There was a danger of harm to American citizens. There was a further possibility that far-left (or far-right) militants could take advantage of the chaotic situation to establish themselves as the government. The probabilities of these dangers were unknown at the time Johnson had to act. Even so, he could have defended his actions by saying that he couldn't run *any* risk of American bloodshed or the establishment of a left-wing dictatorship.

The troop deployment, however, was not justified this way. Speaking on national television on May 2, President Johnson claimed that "communist leaders, many of them trained in Cuba, seeing a chance to increase disorder, to gain a foothold . . . really seized [a popular democratic revolution] and placed [it] into the hands of a band of communist conspirators." Unfortunately for the believability of this explanation, there were no communists to be found.

The Dominican intervention led to a *mixed outcome.* Possible dangers were avoided. There were no American casualties. Dictatorial government was not only avoided, but in time the Dominican Republic moved in a more democratic direction. But this "hasty and ill-considered involvement" generated worries about Johnson's foreign policy skills. Where else would he imagine that communists were at work? And if he did, would his appeal to force be disproportionate to the threat?

## Richard M. Nixon

### Opening Relations with China

In October 1967 Richard Nixon published an article in *Foreign Affairs,* which read in part:

> Any American policy toward Asia must come urgently to grips with the reality of China. . . . Taking the long view, we simply cannot leave China outside the family of nations, there to nurture its fantasies, cherish its hates and threaten its neighbors. . . . [We must] persuade China . . . that its own national interest requires a turning away from foreign adventuring and a turning inward toward a solution of its own domestic problems.

After he entered the White House sixteen months later, Nixon followed this new policy with real determination.[11]

President Nixon's pursuit of China took several forms. First, he asked several foreign leaders—Charles DeGaulle of France, Yahya Khan of Pakistan, and Nicolae Ceausescu of Romania—to tell the Chinese that the United States was interested in renewed contact. Second, the president included a number of signals in messages he sent. For example, the United States began to use the country's official name, the People's Republic of China, in place of "Communist China." Perhaps most important, the administration instituted several policy changes. President Nixon announced that henceforth the United States would support allies with money and materiel, but not with troops, and that U.S. troops would gradually be withdrawn from Vietnam. These changes convinced the Chinese that the United States was more interested in departing from the Asian mainland than in expanding a military presence.

In April 1971 these efforts yielded results. The Chinese sent word of their willingness to receive an envoy for high-level talks. Nixon decided to send Henry Kissinger. In July, Kissinger left for Beijing in total secrecy. For two days, he and Zhou Enlai got to know one another and reached agreement on some crucial issues in Sino-American relations. On July 15, it was announced that President Nixon had been invited to Beijing, and had accepted with pleasure.

Shortly after the Nixon party arrived in Beijing in February 1972, Mao Zedong sent word that he would like to see the president. The discussion between Mao, Zhou, Nixon, and Kissinger did not last long, but Mao and Nixon showed familiarity with each other's writings, and Mao indicated which topics were of concern to him. Mao did not meet with any American again, but his quick reception of President Nixon signaled that the new Sino-American relationship had his blessing.

Thereafter, negotiating sessions alternated with the public events that were fully covered by television and print media. Broadly speaking, general topics were discussed by Nixon and Zhou. Kissinger and Deputy Foreign Minister Chiao Kuan-hua dealt with the wording of the final communiqué. Taiwan was the most difficult topic. The crucial passages of the compromise read: "The government of the People's Republic of China is the sole, legal government of China [and] Taiwan is a province of China. . . . The United States . . . reaffirms its interest in a peaceful settlement of the Taiwan question by the Chinese themselves." In a closing toast Nixon declared, "This was the week that changed the world."

Opening contact with China was a *success* for President Nixon's foreign policy. His trip to Beijing recognized that the USSR and China were not a single mono-

---

[11.] This case is based on Kalb and Kalb 1974; Reichley 1981; and Small 1999.

lithic bloc. In the short term, this increased both the USSR's and China's interest in better relations with the United States. In the longer term, it was an important step in replacing the cold war with détente, and in bringing China back into the international community.

## Economics in the Service of Politics

"Nowhere," writes Joan Hoff, "was [Richard Nixon's] aprincipled pragmatism more evident" than in economics.[12] Obviously, Nixon—who followed six different fiscal policies in as many years—was inconsistent. Nixon's economics, however, can be seen as a product of his overriding concern with politics, the difficulty of the economic challenges he faced, and the lack of economic theory appropriate to the situation.

Nixon's economic advisers in 1970—George Shultz, Paul McCracken, and Herbert Stein, all preferred to rely on market forces to shape the economy rather than government action. It was hardly a surprise, therefore, that the 1970 Nixon program called for a gradual approach intended to wring inflation out of the economy, and to do so gently enough to avoid the danger of recession.

As time passed, however, a counterargument was heard with increasing frequency. It held that some type of incomes policy (governmental activity directed at wage and price decisions made in the private sector) ought to be used to deal with inflation. Some of this criticism was coming from the business community and conservative economists, normally administration allies, so it commanded attention.

Into this controversy in December 1970 came John Connally as secretary of the treasury. A Democrat who had served three terms as governor of Texas, Connally was articulate, forceful, and colorful. Nixon was drawn to him, so much so that Connally quite rapidly became Nixon's most important economic adviser. And since Connally had no fixed convictions on economics, he was likely to reinforce the political argument that the state of the economy was threatening Nixon's reelection.

On August 15, 1971, Richard Nixon announced that wage and price controls would be put into effect. Allen Matusow explained the reasons for the switch from gradualism: "Not an economist but a politician, Nixon simply refused to bet his reelection on good times that seemed a dimming prospect. Moreover, he abandoned gradualism only after practically every prominent Democrat, most pro-

---

[12.] This case is based on accounts in Safire 1975; Reichley 1981; McCracken in Hargrove and Morley 1984; Stein 1985; Weatherford 1988; and Matusow 1998.

fessional economists, a growing number of Republicans, much of the corporate community, his own CEA, [Federal Reserve Chairman] Arthur Burns, and the public demanded that he do so" (1998, 116).

Prices were held down by the wage and price controls. The consumer price index rose by only 3.4 percent during both 1971 and 1972, the lowest increase of the 1970s. Unemployment, however, had risen again to 5.9 percent during 1971. This violated Richard Nixon's central economic imperative: that nothing should threaten his reelection. Therefore Nixon ordered an increase in the rate of government spending. The inflationary pressure generated thereby was held back by the controls, but of course added to the pressure being generated in the private sector.

In January 1973, President Nixon gave instructions to replace mandatory controls with voluntary guidelines. With all the pressures that had been built up, these guidelines were quickly overwhelmed. All in all, the consumer price index increased 8.8 percent in 1973 and 12.2 percent in 1974. Economist Allen Blinder estimated that 1974 prices were about 1 percent higher than they would have been if no controls had been used at all.

The wage and price controls were conceded to have been a *failure*. The Nixon administration had the second-highest inflation rate and the greatest increase in the unemployment rate of any administration since World War II. Nor did these moves have their desired political effect. Nixon was easily reelected, but voters' comments about economics were far more pro-Democratic than usual.

## Reacting to the Charlotte-Mecklenberg Decision

In his 1968 presidential campaign, Richard Nixon was positioned in the middle, between the segregationist governor of Alabama, George Wallace (running as a third-party candidate), and the long-time champion of civil rights, Vice President Hubert Humphrey.[13] Similarly, he was in the middle on desegregation. He did not interpret the Supreme Court's "all deliberate speed" standard as allowing any halt to desegregation *or* requiring immediate implementation regardless of the cost to individuals.

The Nixon administration's record on desegregation was quite mixed. Tilting negatively, Nixon was said to have instructed that nothing be done in the South without checking with Harry Dent, a conservative South Carolinian. Also, the director of the Department of Health, Education and Welfare's Office of Civil

---

[13.] This case is based on Reichley 1981, chap. 9; Safire 1975, 480–485; Small 1999, 172–174; and Haldeman 1994, 275–276.

Rights was dismissed.[14] On the positive side, Nixon produced a statesmanlike analysis distinguishing between de jure segregation resulting from some deliberate act, such as the creation of dual school systems, and de facto segregation caused by housing patterns. George Shultz also established some remarkably effective biracial advisory councils in the South. Over four years the proportion of black children attending totally black schools in the South declined from 68 percent to 8 percent.

On April 20, 1971, the Supreme Court ruled unanimously that the busing of children to a school away from their neighborhood could be used throughout a unified school district consisting of the city of Charlotte, North Carolina, and surrounding Mecklenberg County. The decision was moderate, giving courts broad latitude to decide on the remedy for any particular community, and stating that since the Constitution did not mandate "that every school in every community must always reflect the racial composition of the school system as a whole," an overall racial balance could not be required. Still, newspaper headlines and lead broadcast stories declared that countywide busing had been legalized (even required), and this set off alarm bells.

The same day, President Nixon instructed Press Secretary Ron Ziegler to say it was "the obligation of the local school authorities and the district courts to carry out the mandate of the court," but not to go any further than that. The next morning he met with his assistant for domestic affairs, the Health, Education and Welfare secretary, and the attorney general to instruct them to follow the court decision exactly, but not to go one step beyond it. After a month's study of the decision, Nixon agreed that "if we can keep our liberal writers convinced that we are doing what the Court requires, and our conservative southern friends convinced that we are not doing any more than the Court requires," that might be enough "to walk this tight rope until November, 1972."

Public opinion was decidedly opposed to busing and was too intense for this cautious approach alone to be viable. In March 1972 Nixon made a television address proposing two pieces of legislation. The Equal Educational Opportunities Act would provide $2.5 billion to improve poor schools, and it would prohibit busing except as a last resort. The Student Transportation Moratorium Act would suspend busing until July 1, 1973, or until Congress passed the Equal Educational Opportunities Act. There were constitutional problems with these proposals: if equal education was a constitutional right, how could efforts to achieve it be suspended? The proposals went nowhere, but they allowed Nixon to indicate sympathy with busing opponents.

Richard Nixon's reaction to *Charlotte-Mecklenberg* was at best *mixed*. This was a difficult issue, and he was circumscribed by the intense feelings on both sides.

---

[14] The director, thirty-two years old at the time, was Leon Panetta. He ultimately became Clinton's White House chief of staff.

Hence, his caution is understandable. However, his approach did no more than buy time. He did not propose any inventive alternative around which a consensus might have developed.

## Gerald R. Ford

### Cutting Taxes, Cutting Spending

Economic policy was the area with which Gerald Ford was most familiar.[15] As an undergraduate Ford had contemplated a career as an economist. He spent years as a member of the House Appropriations Committee, where he gained a mastery of the budget equal to that of civil servants with years of OMB experience. In the judgment of Nixon CEA Chair Paul McCracken, of all the presidents, Ford was the most interested in economics. And Ronald King concluded that of all the post–World War II presidents Ford was the most concerned with long-term economic policy.

The first economic threat Ford had to face was a jump in the rate of inflation. But soon the administration found itself in the midst of a sharp recession, so had to devise countercyclical policies. In both these instances, the Ford administration was reacting to ominous changes in the economic environment, and in both instances, its prescriptions were rather conventional.

A more interesting example of considered policy choice came in 1975 as the economy began to recover from recession. CEA Chair Alan Greenspan developed a thesis that captured Ford's attention. While total federal spending had been relatively stable in comparison with the gross national product, spending on social services (such as Social Security, Medicare, and so forth) had been outpacing general economic growth. The increase in social services had been made possible by the reduction in defense spending, and therefore could be continued only with further defense cuts or with increases in taxes. Since neither of these alternatives was palatable, Greenspan argued that the rate of growth of human resource spending should be cut in half, specifically, from 11 percent to 5.5 percent. This was *not* cutting spending, it was slowing the rate of growth.

In July 1975, Gerald Ford began a series of confidential meetings with five of his closest advisers to plan concrete steps.[16] The result was a proposal of a permanent tax cut of $28 billion to go with spending cuts of $28 billion, announced

---

[15.] This case is based on Ford 1980; Reichley 1981; Stein 1985; Porter 1988; Ippolito 1990; King 1993; Cannon 1994; and Carroll 1995.

[16.] The advisers were Chief of Staff Donald Rumsfeld; Dick Cheney, Rumsfeld's assistant and successor; Alan Greenspan; OMB Director James Lynn; and OMB Deputy Director Paul O'Neill.

by Ford on October 6. This was a thoughtful approach that favored the free market. By moving these funds from the public to the private sector, it would allow more decisions to be made by market forces, and it would also restrain inflation. Congress did not approve Ford's plan. On December 16, Congress passed a simple extension of a temporary tax cut passed earlier to counter the recession. President Ford promptly vetoed the bill because it did not contain any reference to spending limits. His veto was sustained. A compromise bill then passed that included an ambiguously worded statement saying that Congress would consider spending limits. Gerald Ford did not get what he wanted, but by using the veto he was able to get an approximation of what he wished. Thereby he was able to restrain the increase in spending and reduce inflationary pressure.

This could be called a *success,* not because President Ford obtained the tax cuts and spending cuts he recommended, but because of the relative success of his economic strategy. According to Richard Carroll's analyses, Ford was the third most successful of all postwar presidents in reducing the rate of inflation and the most successful in reducing the growth rate of the federal budget. In both these respects Ford was much more successful than his predecessor, Richard Nixon, or his successor Jimmy Carter, both of whom had to deal with a similar economic environment.

## Angola

There were few heroes in post-colonial Africa, and the political situation of the continent was very complex.[17] As the colonial powers withdrew, there were contests between local, often tribal-based, factions, sometimes accompanied by external interventions. When Portugal withdrew from Angola (located on the southwest African coast) in 1975, the three factions that had been fighting for independence turned their attention to which would rule the country. All three were supported by outside powers.

Faction A (Popular Movement for the Liberation of Angola) was supported by the Soviet Union and Cuba. Faction B (National Front for the Liberation of Angola) was supported by China and, covertly, by the United States. Faction C (National Front for the Total Independence of Angola) was supported by the United States and France.[18] Each of the three factions was also supported by African states. Faction A was supported by Mozambique, another former Portuguese colony. Faction B was supported by neighboring Zaire. Faction C was supported by South Africa, which had closer ties to the West. And hovering behind the

---

[17.] This case is based on Osborne 1977; Ford 1980; and especially Greene 1995.

[18.] The names of the factions reflect their origin in the struggle against Portugal.

various states were private businesses interested in Angolan oil, diamonds, and other natural resources.

The United States did not want to see the establishment of a Soviet satellite in Africa. Containment, which had been American policy for some time, meant that the USSR should be confined to its own borders and existing areas of influence. In order to try to prevent Faction A from becoming the Angolan government, Secretary of State Kissinger recommended sending funds through the CIA to Factions B and C. This covert approach was taken without notifying either Congress or the American public. As soon as Faction B received funds, it used them to attack Faction A with the assistance of army troops from next-door Zaire. Faction A thereupon appealed to its patrons and received arms from Russia and troops from Cuba. This support enabled Faction A to defeat Faction B in subsequent battles.

The American activity became public in the fall, after South African troops crossed into Angola. Sen. Dick Clark, D-Iowa, went to Africa to investigate reports of cooperation between South Africa and the CIA. When Senate investigation revealed the U.S. involvement, Senator Clark offered an amendment to the defense appropriations bill prohibiting the use of funds "for any activities involving Angola directly or indirectly." It passed the Senate on December 18 and was confirmed by the House on January 27, 1976. In both cases, most of the Democrats and half of the Republicans voted for the cut-off of funds.

President Ford protested that "resistance to Soviet expansion by military means must be a fundamental element of U.S. foreign policy. There must be no question in Angola or elsewhere in the world of American resolve in this regard," but it was to no avail. In 1975, North Vietnam had completed its conquest of South Vietnam, and there was no congressional willingness to support any foreign involvement that even hinted at another Vietnam. And 1975 was also the year in which Congress was conducting a extended investigation into covert operations by the CIA. To undertake a CIA-sponsored operation in this climate was folly.

In sum, U.S. involvement in Angola was clearly a *failure*. Not only did Congress terminate U.S. support for this operation, but its action suggested an unwillingness to embark on other foreign activities.

## A Balanced Budget?

In his 1976 State of the Union Message, Gerald Ford held out two prospects.[19] One was a balanced budget. "We can achieve a balanced budget by 1979," President

---

[19.] This case is based on Reichley 1981; Porter 1988; King 1993; Cannon 1994; and Carroll 1995.

Ford said, "if we have the courage and wisdom to continue to reduce the growth of federal spending." His assertion was based on the October proposal to cut taxes and spending at the same time. By January, a full budget had been developed. The plan listed specific amounts for all the budget items so that the budget would be balanced in just three years. Ford's reference to a balanced budget, therefore, was not empty rhetoric but a concrete proposal.

Ford's other goal was to create jobs. The federal government, Ford argued, cannot create large numbers of jobs itself, but it can

> create conditions and incentives for private business and industry to make more and more jobs. Five out of six jobs in this country are in private business and industry. Common sense tells us this is the place to look for more jobs and to find them faster. . . . To achieve this we must offer the American people greater incentives to invest in the future. My tax proposals are a major step in that direction.

To Ford and his economists, solid job growth required an increase in productivity; greater productivity allows an employer to pay workers more without generating inflationary pressure. To obtain productivity, investment in the technology that enables each worker to produce more is needed. And to obtain greater investment, more savings are needed. There were two ways to increase savings: to reduce government debt so the government would not compete with business as much for available capital, and to restructure corporate taxation to allow more cash to flow to investments. This is what Gerald Ford was talking about when he said that "my tax proposals [will] offer the American people greater incentives to invest."

Job creation is never a trivial political matter, but it was vital in 1976. Unemployment tends to remain high after the economy has begun to recover from a recession. Even though the economy had begun to expand in May 1975, the mean unemployment rate for 1976 was 7.7 percent. However, organized labor, which had the greatest interest in reducing unemployment, was skeptical of the Ford approach. Instead of a long-term plan that *might* produce jobs and control inflation eventually, the unions preferred programs that would reduce unemployment as quickly and as directly as possible through government spending. And business interests were less supportive of restructuring corporate taxation than of lowering corporate tax rates to increase cash flow. The Ford administration was politically weak to begin with, and when it presented a plan opposed by both labor and business, it faced formidable obstacles.

In spite of Gerald Ford's economic expertise and his unusual dedication to long-term economic development, his plans were ignored by Congress. Turned out of office in 1976, he had no opportunity to work toward a balanced budget in 1979. Such meager results would stamp this effort as a *failure*. The claim that this outcome might be regarded as *mixed* must rest on a comparison of Ford's economic policy with the overly politicized economics of his predecessor, the ineptitude of his successor, and the profligate spending of the 1980s. Although Gerald Ford's years in the White House were brief, they were long enough for him to contribute an instructive might-have-been to U.S. economic history.

## *Jimmy Carter*

### Camp David

Jimmy Carter's invitation to Israeli prime minister Menachem Begin and Egyptian president Anwar Sadat to meet with him at Camp David in September 1978 was a high-stakes gamble.[20] The two men disliked one another; their positions were irreconcilable; Begin had a lawyer's preoccupation with details while Sadat was concerned with broad principles. Carter, however, was a devout Baptist deeply interested in the Holy Land, an idealist who wanted to bring peace, and a politician who sensed that Sadat was ready to make a deal.

After the first two days, there was a continual stream of separate meetings. The Americans dealt most seriously with President Sadat on the Egyptian side and with Begin's subordinates (Foreign Minister Moshe Dayan, Defense Minister Ezer Weizman, and Attorney General Aharon Barak) on the Israeli side. President Sadat was more willing to reach an agreement than his subordinates, and the other Israelis were more flexible than Prime Minister Begin. While President Carter met with the heads of the delegations other Americans were meeting with Israeli or Egyptian negotiating teams.

What were the key developments? On the fourth day, Carter revealed Sadat's plans to Begin. The Egyptians would not compromise on sovereignty or land (that is, the Sinai peninsula must be returned), but they were willing to be flexible on other issues. That same evening work began on an American proposal. This was shown to the Israelis first. In the course of discussion, Carter revealed his own priorities: the question of sovereignty over the West Bank and Gaza need not be settled at Camp David, but the matters of Israeli settlements and withdrawal from the Sinai peninsula should be. Both these revelations hardened the Israeli negotiating position.

On the eleventh day, President Carter learned that the Egyptian delegation intended to leave. He went to Sadat's cabin and told him that if he walked out it

---

[20.] This case is based on Carter 1982, Brzezinski 1983, Vance 1983; Quandt 1986, 1994; Telhami 1989, 1990; and Saunders 1994.

would end the relationship between the United States and Egypt, as well as their personal relationship. These strong threats were successful. Sadat had been more cooperative than Begin, but at this crisis point, it was Sadat whom Carter was willing to intimidate.

The next evening another crucial negotiating session took place, this time involving Carter and Vance on the American side and Begin, Dayan, and Barak for the Israelis. Crucial issues needed to be resolved. On the question of the Sinai settlements, Begin finally agreed to a Knesset (the Israeli parliament) vote on the question, "If agreement is reached on all other Sinai issues, will the settlers be withdrawn?" The matter of the West Bank and Gaza settlements proved more intractable. Carter and Vance believed they had Begin's agreement to a prohibition on further settlements during the period of negotiations on Palestinian autonomy. This was to be confirmed in a letter from Begin to Carter. But when the letter arrived, it stated that the freeze would be effective only for the three months of the Israeli-Egyptian negotiations. President Carter told Israeli attorney general Barak, but *not* Prime Minister Begin, this was unsatisfactory. Thereby Carter did not force Begin to choose between a freeze on settlements and an agreement.

Could Carter have exerted pressure more equitably on the Israeli and Egyptian delegations? Unquestionably. But in sensing the nature of an agreement that the Israelis and Egyptians were willing to make, and in leading Begin and Sadat from their existing deadlock to a Nobel Peace Prize, he certainly achieved *success*.

### An Ineffectual Fight Against Inflation

Jimmy Carter did not much like economics.[21] "His voice went flat when the subject came up," one adviser recalled. "You didn't even have to hear the words to know what was being discussed." This was ill-starred since President Carter was confronted with serious economic challenges: inflationary pressures, relatively high rates of unemployment, and sharp increases in oil prices. Unfortunately, inconsistency in administration policies exacerbated these difficulties.

The 1977 Carter program was designed to stimulate the economy. It called for a small tax reduction, considerable spending on jobs programs, and a one-time rebate of $50 per taxpayer (later withdrawn). This was patterned after the Kennedy administration's expansion of the economy, but it had different effects. Kennedy acted after eight years of Eisenhower's economic restraint, but the core inflation rate when Carter entered office was already 6 percent. Hence the Carter

---

[21.] This case is based on Rattner 1980; Stein 1985, 216–233; Biven 1991, 1994; Anderson 1993; King 1993, chap. 12; Schultze 1994; and Carroll 1994.

stimulus and other domestic programs reignited inflationary forces, and the Carter administration was never able to contain them.

President Carter's 1978 proposals began with further stimulation and edged toward restraint as the year went on. His proposed tax reform bill was stimulative; what Congress passed was very different, but still stimulative. In April, however, Carter extended the Council on Wage-Price Stability, which was about to expire, and began a modest program to monitor inflationary pressures. In October the administration announced a package including voluntary wage and price restraints, regulatory reform, and a novel proposal for real wage insurance.

Inflation dominated the scene in 1979, and a sharp surge in oil prices reinforced tendencies that were already present. OPEC had announced a 14 percent increase from $12.70 a barrel in December 1978 to $14.54 in October 1979; with the decline in oil production following the Iranian revolution, world oil prices were as high as $30 a barrel by December 1979. The administration's wage-price guidelines were impotent in the face of pressures such as these, and the consumer price index rose 13.3 percent during the year. In October, President Carter made his most important single economic decision, appointing Paul Volcker to head the Federal Reserve. Unlike the administration, Volcker would not vacillate. He immediately announced a focus on restricting the growth in the money supply. Although it was not yet apparent, Volcker's tight-money policy would eventually end the inflation begun during the Vietnam War.

By 1980, Carter had moved almost completely from stimulus to restraint, but the economic news did not improve. Consumer prices increased 12.4 percent during the year. This was the first time since World War I that the country had experienced two consecutive years of double-digit inflation. Administration economists had tried, but as economist Barry Bosworth recalled, "Each time a policy was developed, the policy was too weak for the problems that appeared."

The Carter economic policy was a *failure*. Richard Carroll's overall rankings place Carter's economic performance in historic perspective: "Truman ranks first in overall performance, significantly ahead of Kennedy, who is in second place, and Ford, in third. There is a large drop-off to fourth, fifth, and sixth places for Eisenhower, Reagan, and Johnson. For seventh and eighth places, there is another large drop-off for Nixon and Bush. Finally, there is precipitous drop to ninth place, held by Carter" (1995, 212).[22]

---

[22.] These overall rankings should not be confused with a president's performance in particular economic areas, such as Ford's reduction in the growth rate of the federal budget, that have been discussed previously. These rankings are weighted averages of forty economic indicators for each president. Carroll is careful to point out that the ranking refers

## The National Energy Act of 1978

Jimmy Carter made two crucial decisions about energy legislation.[23] One was to deliver legislation within ninety days of his inauguration. The other was to put designated Energy Secretary James Schlesinger in charge. Schlesinger, in turn, instructed his small staff to work alone. The proposed legislation included direct conservation measures such as tax credits for home insulation, and aimed at further conservation through gradual increases in the prices of oil and natural gas. But since the plan had been drafted in secret within a short time frame, most critical issues had to be worked through after the bill had been sent to Congress.

Broadly speaking, the House was more sympathetic to energy consumers, and the Senate was more hospitable to energy producers. Democrats leaned toward continued regulation of energy prices (a government mechanism); Republicans leaned toward deregulation (a market mechanism). Moreover, there were so many additional divisions within these broad groupings that passage of any legislation was unlikely.

The bill went first to the House, where it passed due to the strong leadership of Speaker Thomas P. (Tip) O'Neill and to cooperation between the White House and key congressional allies. O'Neill set up a special procedure whereby the bill was referred first to the substantive committees and then to an ad hoc super committee, all with short deadlines so that floor action could take place before the August recess. There were some minor adjustments on the floor to make the bill more palatable to one group or another, and some relatively close votes, but all save one of the major provisions emerged from the House intact.

Things were different in the Senate. Part of the legislation went to the Energy and Natural Resources Committee and part to the Finance Committee. Energy and Natural Resources deadlocked on the question of phased decontrol of natural gas prices, so the committee sent its portion of the bill to the floor without a committee recommendation. The Finance Committee removed all the taxes intended to encourage conservation and replaced them with tax credits intended to stimulate production as well as conservation. Phased decontrol of natural gas

---

to the performance of the economy while the administration is in office. Because the effects of any administration policy take at least a year to have their impact, he assigns the first year of the next term to the preceding president. Therefore the Carter term is 1978 to 1981, not 1977 to 1980.

[23.] This case is an abbreviated version of Kessel 1984b, chap. 1, which draws on Cochran 1981; Jones 1979; Malbin 1983; Nivola 1979; and Sinclair 1981.

prices passed narrowly on the Senate floor, and the substitution of tax credits for taxes won by a larger margin.

Since the House and Senate had passed different bills, the task of the conference committee was difficult. Moreover, Finance Chair Russell Long, D-La., had obtained Senate instructions giving him wide latitude on tax negotiation, and he would not negotiate on taxes until he was satisfied on natural gas pricing. Some Democrats were unwilling to consider any form of deregulation, while some Republicans would accept only immediate and complete deregulation. Therefore a shaky centrist coalition had to be constructed in favor of phased deregulation. This compromise barely passed, but negotiation on taxes could now begin. Agreement dropping two of the three administration-proposed taxes was reached in October. The final legislation, by now much more favorable to energy producers, survived a Senate filibuster and a 207 to 206 vote on a House rule to pass on the final day of the congressional session.

This outcome was *mixed.* By submitting legislation early in the session, the administration left enough time for Congress to pass legislation on a critical 1970s issue. But by failing to determine what kind of bill might pass, and because the Senate was more sympathetic to energy producers, the administration got a very different bill than it wanted. In 1979, a more experienced Carter administration submitted another energy bill. This time Carter officials and congressional leaders carefully negotiated the content of the bill in advance and consequently were much more successful.

## *Ronald Reagan*

### A Start on Nuclear Disarmament

Soviet-U.S. arms control negotiations involved three types of weapons.[24] First were the strategic arms—the land-based, submarine-based, and airborne intercontinental ballistic missiles—that had been targeted on the USSR and United States for some time. Second were intermediate-range ballistic missiles (IRBMs) deployed by the Soviets in the 1970s and aimed at Western Europe. These were countered in the 1970s by European missiles and in the early 1980s by U.S.-supplied IRBMs on Western European soil. The IRBMs came to be referred to as the intermediate nuclear force (INF). Third was the Strategic Defense Initiative (SDI) proposed by Ronald Reagan in 1983. To Reagan, this was a shield that would protect the United States,

---

[24.] This case is based on Rice 1990; Cannon 1991, chap. 21; Oberdorfer 1991; and Wohlforth 1996.

and ultimately other countries, from incoming missiles. To many American scientists, however, SDI would, *at best*, take a very long time to develop. To the Soviets, SDI would allow the United States to launch a missile attack while protecting itself from a counterattack, and thus was an offensive weapon.

Although Reagan had privately expressed interest in negotiations in 1981, there were no serious developments until Mikhail Gorbachev came to power in 1985. Gorbachev, confident and energetic, believed the USSR needed fundamental reform. Even more important, he knew the precarious Soviet economy required a reduction in the state's huge arms expenditures. He therefore instructed his associates to try very hard to achieve arms control. By July, arrangements had been made for a Reagan-Gorbachev meeting in Geneva in November, and both sides engaged in serious preparations.

Few agreements were reached at the Geneva meeting. The most important development at Geneva was that Reagan and Gorbachev found they respected one another, even though they disagreed. In their initial meeting, Reagan discovered a warmth in Gorbachev that was distinctly lacking in the other Soviet leaders he had met. Gorbachev did not like some features of Reagan's style, but he could see that Reagan was a person of stature who could make decisions. Further, Reagan and Gorbachev personally arranged two future summit meetings, one in Washington and the other in Moscow.

In fact, the next meeting took place in Reykjavik, Iceland, in October 1986. Reagan, expecting the meeting to be a planning session for the 1987 Washington summit, was met with a serious proposal for a 50 percent cut in missiles, tied to the elimination of SDI. President Reagan had no problem with the deep cut in missiles, but he was very angry about the proposed elimination of SDI. General Secretary Gorbachev's position was that SDI could be explored in a laboratory; but Reagan saw nondeployment as denying the United States its best means of defending itself. The result was that the Reykjavik summit failed over this single issue.

The momentum of Reykjavik was not lost. In February 1987 Gorbachev "unlinked" the intermediate nuclear force question from the ICBMs and SDI. INF was the simplest of the three weapons systems to agree upon, and Reagan quickly accepted. Some problems remained—for example, older U.S. missiles in West Germany—but the North Atlantic Treaty Organization and the USSR agreed on a concept called "double global zero." This meant that both sides would dismantle all their short-range and medium-range missiles. Secretary of State George Shultz and Foreign Minister Edward Shevardnadze, both of whom had played enormously important roles in bringing Reagan and Gorbachev together, held two preparatory meetings to work out final details. The Intermediate Nuclear Force Treaty was signed at a summit meeting in Washington in November 1987.

The INF Treaty was a *success*. It was the first treaty to call for the reduction of nuclear forces, and thus the first dividend of the end of the cold war. It is unlikely that agreement could have been reached without Reagan and Gorbachev. Both were sure of themselves and willing to take bold steps. They were very different types of men, but they ended up as good friends, proud of their joint contribution to history.

## The Cost of Reaganomics

At the core of Ronald Reagan's ideology was a set of strongly held attitudes.[25] Those with the greatest impact on his economic policy were: taxes should be reduced; American military forces should be strengthened; the budget should be balanced. The incompatibilities between these elements led economists to ask how he was going to do all three at once. As Alan Greenspan pointed out, however, these priorities were ordered. Tax reduction was the most important; spending to increase military strength was next most important; the balanced budget was the least important. Weatherford and McDonnell make the same point. The relative unimportance of budget balancing led to the "tax cuts and defense-spending increases to which Reagan attributed higher priority." Once in office, Reagan pushed right away for tax cuts and more defense spending, but a balanced budget never materialized.

Since spending came first in the 1981 legislative sequence, let's begin with defense spending. The Reagan administration came to power pledged to make up for the Carter administration's neglect. In the latter part of the Carter administration, however, the defense budget had been increased. So when President Reagan agreed with Defense Secretary Caspar Weinberger's argument for a 7 percent increase, the actual result was a 17.5 percent increase in fiscal 1981 and a 17.1 percent increase in fiscal 1982. There were some cuts in nondefense spending, but when the nondefense cuts were combined with the defense increases, the result was an increase in total spending.

The major vehicle used for enactment of Reagan's budget preferences was reconciliation, a device that forces appropriations to remain within their budget goals. There was no real problem in the Senate, which had a Republican majority. The test came on a rules vote in the House, where there was 51-seat Democratic majority. On June 25, a solid Republican Party combined with 29 conservative Democrats to

<hr />

[25.] This case is based on Barrett 1983; Huntington 1983; Stockman 1987; Smith 1988; Tobin 1988; Weatherford and McDonnell 1990; Peterson and Rom 1988; Cannon 1991; and Carroll 1995.

win by a narrow 217 to 210 vote. The following day, this Reagan majority prevailed on the reconciliation vote 217 to 211. Congress gave final approval to the package just over a month later.

The legislative conduit for tax cuts was the Kemp-Roth bill. It reduced individual income tax rates 5 percent in 1981, 10 percent in 1982, and another 10 percent in 1983. As was true with the spending cuts, it encountered little trouble in the Republican Senate, and it passed the House with a Reagan majority of virtually all Republicans and forty-eight mostly conservative Democrats. The resulting tax cut was $162 billion, by far the largest since World War II. When substantial increases in spending were coupled with a huge tax cut, the effect was just the opposite of a balanced budget.

Passage of these bills was a real political success. It was a masterful combination of good legislative politics, good interest group politics, and a good public relations campaign. At the same time, it was an undoubted policy *failure*. There was more to the Reagan economic policies than their initial spending and taxing decisions, but of all modern presidencies the Reagan administration produced the highest average debt growth and the largest increase in the debt as a percentage of the gross domestic product (GDP). In fact, the Reagan administration increased the national debt more than *all* of its predecessors put together.

## A Diminished Government?

"Government is not the solution to our problem," said Ronald Reagan in his inaugural address, "Government is the problem. . . . It is my intention to curb the size and influence of the federal establishment."[26] With statements such as these, a considerable transformation in federal programs might have been expected. What did happen? We can't look at all federal programs, but we can survey some of the more expensive.

The administration and Congress compromised in 1983 on measures to insure the solvency of *Social Security*. These steps included higher payroll taxes, taxation of some Social Security benefits, and a gradual increase in the retirement age from sixty-five to sixty-seven.

There were no major changes to *Medicare*, but a cost-containment procedure known as diagnostic related groups was put in place limiting the amount paid to hospitals for any given procedure. President Reagan recommended and signed a bill to protect beneficiaries from the costs of catastrophic illness, to be funded

---

[26.] This case is based on Palmer and Sawhill 1984; Weaver 1988; Kosterlitz and Moore 1988; Ippolito 1990; and Hager and Pianin 1997.

by increases in Medicare premiums. This increase was repealed within a year because of beneficiaries' protests against the increased premiums.

Growth in the costs of *Medicaid,* a state-administered program to provide medical care to the poor, was slowed somewhat. Rates were reduced on reimbursement to the states, and the states were given increased flexibility in administering the program. Changes in the eligibility for AFDC (Aid to Families with Dependent Children) reduced the number eligible for Medicaid because the two programs were linked.

*Unemployment compensation* was reduced by changes to extended benefits and supplemental benefits. Extended benefits provide longer coverage for areas with high unemployment. Federal costs were reduced by changing the point at which these went into effect. Supplemental benefits provide longer coverage during recessions. These were less generous during the 1982 recession and were phased out during Reagan's second term.

Benefits provided by *food stamps* were cut through some marginal adjustments, and then eligibility was tightened by changing the income threshold. In 1985 Congress increased the number of participants by changing the way in which the maximum income was calculated.

*Supplemental Security Income* (SSI), a program providing additional income to poor elderly, blind, and disabled persons, had its requirements altered through various technical adjustments. The net of the adjustments was to increase SSI outlays by 9 percent by 1985. Further adjustments during the second term also increased SSI payments.

Domestic spending in other areas was sometimes increased (agriculture and antidrug activities) and sometimes decreased (energy). There were also a very few programs that were actually eliminated. Revenue sharing, a major initiative of the Nixon administration, was eliminated, as were block grants for community services. The Comprehensive Employment and Training Act was terminated in 1981 and replaced in 1982 with the Jobs Training Partnership Act, which did not provide public service jobs. Otherwise, federal programs remained in force.

Obviously, the changes in government programs had a *mixed outcome.* President Reagan contributed a rhetoric that was critical of welfare programs. Yet some were part of the Reagan administration's own safety net, others were defended by Congress, and almost all had groups of supporters for whom the programs were very important. When Reagan flew back home to California in 1989, domestic policy had not been fundamentally changed from what he inherited in 1981, when he came to Washington.

## George Bush

### German Reunification

With the collapse of Soviet domination of Eastern Europe in 1989, the most important geopolitical question was the future of Germany, which had been partitioned after World War II into the Federal Republic of Germany (West Germany) and the German Democratic Republic (East Germany).[27] President Bush wanted to see a reunited Germany that would remain in NATO. NATO gave the United States a role in European security, and U.S. military bases were located in Germany.

The facts of Germany's past challenged prospects for reunification. France had been invaded by Germany in 1870, 1914, and 1940, and Britain and Russia had fought two exhausting world wars against Germany. President Mitterrand was fearful that France would be dominated by a larger Germany, and he wanted to move slowly. British Prime Minister Thatcher did not want to commit to a stance on unification until the implications were explored in a larger context. Soviet general secretary Gorbachev was in the most difficult position of all. Not only were there memories of Russia's 1940–1945 war with Germany and of the animosities of the cold war, but he was caught in the middle. He was aware of the manifest wishes of the German people, but right-wing Soviet politicians and Russian military leaders were adamant that a reunited Germany not become tied to the West.[28]

In the seven months beginning in December 1989, Bush held three meetings with Chancellor Helmut Kohl of West Germany, two meetings with Mitterrand, one meeting with Thatcher, and two meetings with Gorbachev; he attended two more meetings where most Western leaders were present. In addition, Secretary of State Baker made numerous trips, foreign ministers and heads of state came to Washington, and there were many phone calls. Bush's first contact, immediately after a December meeting with Gorbachev, was with Germany's Kohl. Their conversations revealed that both men wanted to see a reunited Germany functioning as an active member of NATO.

The process for negotiation was devised by the State Department: "Two-plus-Four." The two were the two Germanies; they were to determine whether

---

[27.] This case is based on Beschloss and Talbott 1993, chaps. 7–11; Baker 1995, chaps. 12, 14; and Bush and Scowcroft 1998, chaps. 8, 10–12.

[28.] Gorbachev's position was further complicated by Baltic independence movements, arms control talks, and trade negotiations, all of which were going on simultaneously with the discussions about Germany.

they wanted to be reunified and how they would proceed. The four were the USSR, Great Britain, France, and the United States; they would become involved whenever external questions arose. Practically speaking, both Germanies had to agree on the structure of their future government. The USSR, United Kingdom, France, and United States had legal rights as the victorious powers in World War II, but more important, limiting participation to just these four countries mooted any question of which other nations might be involved. By February, Secretary Baker had sold the Two-plus-Four idea to the other powers. And on March 18, a pro-unification party allied with Chancellor Kohl won East German elections by a large margin. This made it clear that reunification would take place very rapidly.

American activities in the ensuing meetings can be summarized as encouraging Chancellor Kohl to proceed with German reunification, calming British and French anxieties over the implications of reunification, assuring General Secretary Gorbachev that NATO would restrain Germany rather than threaten Russia, and providing Gorbachev with arguments he could use against his domestic opponents. At a May 31 meeting in Washington, Gorbachev conceded to Bush that a united Germany would have the right to decide for itself to be a NATO member, and once Gorbachev had faced down critics at a Communist Party Congress, Gorbachev and Kohl agreed on July 16 that Germany would be a member of NATO.

These complex negotiations were *successful*. Americans had nothing to do with the decisive East German elections, and they were not present when Gorbachev and Kohl reached their final agreement. But the Bush foreign policy team had done everything possible to facilitate negotiations, and the result was exactly what the Americans wanted.

## A Weak Recovery

In foreign policy, George Bush was surefooted and decisive, but in economics, he was uncertain and frequently delayed taking action.[29] This behavioral pattern was costly in the fall of 1991 because the economy presented the Bush administration with a real challenge. A recession had lasted from July 1990 until March 1991, but the indicators brought into question whether it was really over. Growth in the GDP was a weak 1.8 percent in the second quarter, and had fallen to 1.0 percent in the third quarter. Thus the 1992 possibilities still included a vigorous

---

[29.] This case is based on Duffy and Goodgame 1992, 245–260; Woodward 1992; Hershey 1991, 1993; and Carroll 1995.

recovery (political nirvana in 1992), but there was a danger of falling back into recession (political disaster in 1992).

The question was what the administration should do. Treasury Secretary Brady, relying on his personal business experience, believed the economy would recover. "I feel it in my bones," he declared. CEA Chair Michael Boskin had seen third quarter data suggesting that the economy was stalling, but Chief of Staff Sununu kept him away from President Bush. Boskin ultimately had to threaten to resign before he got to see Bush in late November. Boskin advocated using the average fiscal stimulus (about $75 billion) employed by previous administrations when emerging from recessions. Bush decided not to do anything.

In his 1992 State of the Union Message President Bush declared that he was opposed to hard times, but his economic proposals were a little of this and a little of that. Most dealt with taxes: a $500 increase in personal exemption (dropped just a week later); a couple of items dealing with real estate, for example, permitting first-time home buyers to make tax-free withdrawals from IRAs; changes in the alternative minimum tax; and a cut in capital gains. The only item aimed directly at job creation was an investment tax allowance.[30]

The economic effects of this presidential inertness were not encouraging. GDP growth was 4.2 percent in the first quarter of 1992, 3.9 percent in the second quarter, and 2.9 percent in the third quarter. Recovery from the recession was taking place, but at too slow a rate to cut into joblessness. Unemployment, which continued to increase after the recession was over, had reached 7.3 percent in December 1991, peaked at 7.8 percent in June 1992, and lingered at 7.4 percent when votes were cast in November 1992.

There was another consequence of George Bush's indecision. Indecision led to inarticulateness, and the president's effective silence allowed his critics to define economic circumstances as being much worse than they really were. A slow rate of growth and high unemployment are never good for an incumbent seeking reelection, but when an articulate challenger is allowed to define the situation, the result is sealed.

George Bush's stewardship of the economy in 1991–1992 was a *failure*. Carroll's analyses reveal that the average GDP growth rate and the average employment growth rate for the Bush administration were the worst since World War II. We now know that the recovery of 1991 was the beginning of the longest economic expansion on record, but its early months were too tepid for voters to give President Bush a chance to do better in a second term.

---

[30.] Nothing came of all this. Democrats added a couple of their favored taxes to two legislative packages, and Bush vetoed both of them.

## The Education President

During the 1988 presidential campaign, Vice President Bush announced his desire to become the "Education President."[31] He took steps toward this goal early in his administration. In his initial State of the Union Message, he made some educational proposals, including a plan to designate merit schools, a program of awards for each state's best teachers, and a plan to name National Science Scholars. In September, he asked the nation's governors to meet with him in an "education summit" at the University of Virginia. Because 94 percent of educational funding came from state and local sources, gubernatorial cooperation was essential.

Six goals to be achieved by 2000 were presented at the summit. They were:

1. American students must rank first in the world in math and science.
2. All children must be ready to learn when they start school.
3. Students must be provided with safe drug-free schools so they can learn.
4. The dropout rate must be reduced and the performance of "at risk" students improved.
5. The training necessary for a competitive work force must be provided.
6. Qualified teachers must be recruited and retained.

These goals were laudable, but all could be questioned. For example, American students did not do well in international competition on math and science. Governor Clinton of Arkansas said the goal of ranking first was not achievable, and he suggested that the United States aim for comparability with major trading partners. It would be difficult for poor children to be ready to learn unless there were a massive increase in expensive preschool programs such as Head Start. It would be hard to eliminate drugs from schools as long as they were pervasive in society. And so on.

But if the goals were ambitious, they were nonetheless agreed to. Staff members of the National Governors' Association continued to work with Bush domestic aide Roger Porter to refine the goals. The reference to qualified teachers was dropped, and a program of testing in the fourth, eighth, and twelfth grade was added. Reduction of the dropout rate was translated to increasing the high school graduation rate to 90 percent. With these changes, the six goals were included in the 1990 State of the Union Message, and they were unanimously endorsed by the governors at their February 1990 meeting.

---

[31.] This case is based on Thompson and Scavo 1992; Quirk 1991; Ingwerson 1990; and Fiske 1990.

The Bush administration, however, did not submit specific legislation centering on these six goals. Rather, aspects of the program were incorporated into various congressional bills. The Senate passed two of its bills in February 1990, and the House, after a partisan fight was resolved, passed a single measure in July. The House passed one Senate bill creating math and science scholarships, but that was the only part of the program that became law. Just before the end of the session, Roger Porter and the Senate and House conferees worked out a compromise for the balance of the legislation. It passed the House, but Jesse Helms prevented it from being considered in the Senate. Consequently, it died.[32]

Education 2000 led only to *mixed results*. President Bush obtained gubernatorial support for his goals—though goals to be reached after most of the governors would have left office didn't ask much of them. And Congress did provide some new scholarships in mathematics and science. Otherwise there was some publicity, but not the action needed to turn the goals of Education 2000 into accomplishment.

## Bill Clinton

### 1993 Deficit Reduction

President Clinton entered office committed to deficit reduction; investment in education, research, and infrastructure; spending to stimulate economic growth; health care reform; and a middle-class tax cut.[33] Since all these programs required money, they conflicted with one another. Therefore Clinton had to decide which elements to emphasize. Though their individual positions varied, his economic advisers—Bentsen and Summers of Treasury, Panetta and Rivlin of OMB, Tyson and Blinder of CEA, and Rubin and Cutter of the new National Economic Council—all favored deficit reduction. President Clinton became convinced that this was the most effective step he could take. *If* the reduction were large enough to convince the Federal Reserve and the bond market that the administration was serious, then deficit reduction would lead to lower interest rates. Lower interest rates would stimulate greater investment in the private sector, and this, in turn, could lead to greater productivity. Any lessening of the federal debt also has the long-term advantage of lowering the

---

[32.] A somewhat different bill was put together in the 1991–1992 session by new education secretary Lamar Alexander. It was also blocked by Senate Republicans who defeated a cloture vote.

[33.] This case is based on Woodward 1994, chaps. 11–16; Balz and Devroy 1993a; Ifill 1993b; Rosenbaum 1995; Sinclair 1996; and Weatherford and McDonnell 1996b.

proportion of the budget required for debt service, and this allows greater flexibility in dealing with other public problems.[34]

Once this decision was reached, President Clinton and his advisers searched for tax increases and spending cuts that would add up to a cut of $140 billion in the projected 1997 deficit. Many possibilities were examined both on economic grounds (How much money would be involved?) and political grounds (Who would be helped? Who would be hurt?). The president and his economists worked many hours, taking one budget item at a time, and Treasury and OMB staffers worked overnight to produce fresh estimates. In the end three of the five original goals were included in the economic package, but deficit reduction dominated. President Clinton recommended a net deficit reduction of $473 billion over the next five years, $230 billion of investments, and a stimulus package with spending of $16 billion. Health care was to be submitted later, and the middle-class tax cut disappeared entirely.

Congressional approval was hard to come by. It required five steps: approval of the stimulus package as a supplemental appropriation, the passage of a budget resolution, the crafting of committee bills consistent with the budget resolution, the adoption of a reconciliation bill incorporating all the committee bills, and the production of a conference report resolving Senate-House differences. The administration followed a straight party-line strategy, which meant that any Democrat who wanted something special could bargain, and a great many did. The stimulus package died in the Senate. (Republicans had no sympathy for Clinton's approach, and Democrats did not have the votes to obtain cloture.) A BTU tax (a broad-based energy tax) was opposed by some Senate Democrats. It was replaced by a gas tax to get the bill out of the Senate Finance Committee, and some proposed benefits were cut to compensate for the loss of revenue that the BTU tax would have generated. It was difficult to write a conference report that would be accepted by both the House and the Senate, and it passed by the narrowest possible margins, 218 to 216 in the House and 51 to 50 in the Senate.

---

[34.] It is important to understand the difference between the federal deficit and the federal debt. The *deficit* is the amount by which total budget outlays exceed total revenues in a single fiscal year. The *debt* is the amount the government owes because of the accumulation of yearly deficits and surpluses. Deficit reduction does not lead to debt reduction because the remaining deficit adds to the existing debt. Deficit reduction can be helpful in managing the debt in two ways. First, the debt is not as large as it would have been if the deficit were not reduced. Second, if the rate of growth of the debt is slower than the rate of growth of the economy, then the debt is easier to service. If there is a surplus, of course, then funds can be applied directly to debt reduction.

In spite of the political difficulty of passing this budget package, it was an economic *success*. Together with the Bush budget agreement passed in 1990, it led to balanced budgets in Clinton's second term. Moreover, it contributed to the economic expansion that lasted into the new century.

## The Clinton Health Care Bill

In the health care battle of 1993–1994, there was real need on one side and real impediments on the other.[35] In 1992, there were 35 million Americans without any health insurance, and millions more who might lose their coverage if they changed jobs. But health care touched so many different segments of American life that there was bound to be intensive lobbying to protect the diverse interests—and there was no consensus on how health care should be handled.

President Clinton appointed Hillary Clinton and Ira Magaziner to head a health care task force. Both had histories of achievement, but both were inflexible, and neither had any experience making policy at the federal level. The Clinton-Magaziner task force was very large and cumbersome. The task force proceeded in secret, and many of its own members didn't know what was being decided.

Relations with outside groups posed continuing problems. For example, the Business Roundtable, probably the most important business group in the country, had a meeting with Hillary Clinton. At one point Ralph Johnson, CEO of Johnson & Johnson, said, "You've said that these regional alliances . . . aren't regulatory bodies, but as I hear what Mr. Magaziner says . . . they sound like regulatory agencies to me." Hillary Clinton slammed her hand on the table and replied, "I said they were purchasing cooperatives, and that's what they're going to be!" Time and again, Mrs. Clinton and Mr. Magaziner had opportunities to enlist potential allies but instead drove them into opposition.

There were also a number of delays. The original deadline for drafting the legislation had been April 30, 1993, but President Clinton was unable to announce his health care plan until September 22, and Congress could not act until 1994.

The proposal was long (1,342 pages) and complex. The key points were managed competition, universal coverage, and employer mandates. Consumers would choose among competing health plans that would be made available to them through health alliances in their states. Everyone would be required to enroll, with universal coverage to be achieved by 1999. The cost would be covered

---

[35.] This case is based on Fein 1992; Clymer, Pear, and Toner 1994; Ellwood 1994; Quirk and Hinchcliffe 1996; Sinclair 1999; and particularly on Johnson and Broder 1996.

by requiring employers to pay 80 percent of their employees' coverage, cutting the growth of Medicare expenses by 65 percent, cutting the growth of Medicaid expenses by 75 percent, and enacting various new taxes.

Because of the many interests involved, the bill was referred to five different committees in Congress. Of these, House Energy and Commerce, House Ways and Means, and Senate Finance were crucial because they were most representative of their respective chambers. There was not enough Democratic support on House Energy and Commerce to assemble a majority. The bill crept out of House Ways and Means with a 20 to 18 vote, hardly a ringing endorsement. There was no consensus on the Senate Finance Committee either. The vote was 12 to 8 in support of a bill without employer mandates and with only a "goal" of universal coverage. With backing this weak, it proved impossible to craft a bill that had any real hope of passing the House or the Senate.

The Clinton-Magaziner health care proposal was a *failure*. As the physician Robert Ellwood, one of the leading proponents of reforming health care financing, said: "No one killed health care reform. It died in the White House. . . . Unfortunately, we did not get managed competition out of the White House. . . [but only] an elaborate regulatory scheme."

## NATO Expansion

While visiting Washington in 1993, Polish president Lech Walesa and Czech president Václav Havel asked President Clinton about the possibility that their countries could join NATO, and in 1994 Clinton stated that "the question was no longer whether NATO will take on new members, but when and how."[36] By 1995, without much formal review or analysis, it had become American policy to encourage the expansion of NATO, and in 1997, the Clinton administration was moving aggressively to implement this policy.

There were two defensible reasons why NATO should expand by inviting the Czech Republic, Hungary, and Poland to become members. The first was that these countries *wanted* to be identified with the West rather than continuing to be part of the Russian sphere of influence. By joining NATO, they would at once gain military and political ties to the West, and presumably would expand economic and cultural ties as well.

The other argument (though rarely articulated) was that NATO should take advantage of Russian weakness to move closer to the Russian border. Then if Rus-

---

[36.] This case is based on Dean 1997; Apple 1997a; Friedman 1997a, 1997b; Kennan 1997; and Myers 2000.

sia were to become aggressive sometime in the future, NATO could bring the battle and destruction closer to Russia itself.[37]

A curious feature of the 1997 expansion was the lack of political debate over such an important change. Questions were raised in the press rather than in administration documents, NATO councils, or Senate debate.

George Kennan, the diplomat and historian who had originated the containment policy, said that NATO expansion could be "the most fateful error of American policy in the entire post–cold-war era." Just when Western resolve and Russian courage had led to the collapse of the Soviet empire, this step would tend to "inflame the nationalistic, anti-Western and militaristic tendencies in Russian opinion, . . . impel Russian foreign policy in directions decidedly not to our liking, and . . . make it much more difficult . . . to secure ratification of the Start II [nuclear disarmament] agreement."

Another question was what benefit NATO would obtain by adding these three countries to its membership. It is easy to understand why the Czech Republic, Hungary, and Poland would prize a guarantee of defense by NATO forces, but how much more secure would the United States, the United Kingdom, Germany, and other NATO countries be because Czech, Hungarian, and Polish forces were available to take part in the common defense?

Whatever the merits of these arguments, NATO members gathered in Madrid in July 1997 and issued invitations to the three countries. In due course, three countries from Central Europe were added to the North Atlantic Treaty Organization.

This was a *mixed outcome.* On the positive side, President Clinton got exactly what he wanted. He was able to shape U.S. and NATO policy so that the Czech Republic, Hungary, and Poland became members of NATO. But on the negative side, Russia was not entirely cooperative in subsequent crises over Iraq and Kosovo; the Start II treaty to further reduce the number of nuclear warheads, signed in 1993, was not ratified by the Russian Duma until 2000; and President Vladimir Putin mounted a strong diplomatic campaign against a proposed U.S. national missile defense.

## Success and Failure

No president accomplishes as much as he hoped when he took his oath of office. Nor is he able to do as much as the voters expected of him when they cast their

---

[37.] A third argument was that with the end of the Cold War, NATO had to find some new role or it would fall apart from disuse. As things developed, NATO discovered a new military role on its own, bombing to bring the Bosnian war to an end in 1995, and bombing again to end the war in Kosovo in 1999. These two military actions certainly gave NATO something to do, but they had little to do with NATO expansion.

ballots. But equally surely, he finds success in some of his endeavors, even though he fails in others and reaches indeterminate outcomes in still others. We have seen that this mixture of successes, failures, and mixed outcomes applies to all chief executives.

What leads to success or failure? Since we have surveyed only a limited number of cases, it would be premature to speak of patterns of presidential behavior. Still, we have seen enough to begin to form some *preliminary* impressions. In every case of presidential success, the subject has been something about which the president cared deeply: Eisenhower and national security policy, Johnson and education, Nixon and foreign policy, Carter and peace in the Middle East, and so forth. This may not be a requirement for presidential success, but if a president devotes attention to a subject it makes things easier. A second consideration is presidential expertise. If a president has enough personal experience with the subject to sense what is more or less consequential, this also helps. In these cases, Eisenhower, Nixon, and Bush had developed expertise in foreign policy, and Ford had done so in economics. The third characteristic is more diffuse, but often a president has some personal attribute that allows him to achieve in a particular area. The well-honed political skills of Lyndon Johnson and Bill Clinton allowed them to see how policy goals might be achieved. John Kennedy was confident enough to send an open signal of his desire for peace, and both Kennedy and Reagan were confident enough to take risks to reduce nuclear threats. Jimmy Carter's determination allowed him to press on at Camp David, and George Bush's skill as a conciliator brought a deftness to his negotiations about German reunification. These are only impressions, but presidential concern, presidential expertise, and presidential personality all provide clues about presidential success.

When it comes to failure, the picture is more fragmented, but again there are some impressions. If expertise facilitates success, absence of expertise contributes to failure. Neither Carter nor Reagan showed appreciable expertise about economics, and both ran into serious problems. Lack of expertise may have played a role in the mixed outcomes of Eisenhower and the 1957 Civil Rights Bill, Johnson and the Dominican Republic, and Clinton and NATO expansion. A second factor is the absence of political power. Whatever the merits of Kennedy's Medicare proposal or Ford's request to send aid to a pro-Western faction in Angola, the presidents simply didn't have the votes to move the proposals through Congress. A third factor is that a president may assign a higher priority to some other consideration. Lyndon Johnson wanted to win in Vietnam and pass Great Society legislation, and he was afraid that calling attention to the government's lack of revenue might threaten these goals. Richard Nixon was more concerned with getting reelected in 1972 than in economic policy. A fourth factor is that an environmental challenge may be too great: a foreign leader who resists American policy or a recession that is not followed by a quick recovery. Finally, of course, ineptitude plays a role, although the clearest cases we've seen of that—Carter's inability to handle the economy, Bush's indecision on the economy in the fall of 1991, and the Clinton-Magaziner fiasco on health care—all dealt with subjects that would have been difficult for anyone to handle successfully.

These impressions are useful, but the number of cases is still limited. Moreover, our sample of presidential accomplishment is not representative. The cases were deliberately chosen so we could examine one success, one failure, and one indeterminate outcome for each president. When we turn to a larger set of cases in the next chapter, we shall see that successes come more often than failures. Then we will be in a better position to speak about patterns of presidential accomplishment.

# 8. Patterns of Presidential Accomplishment

Dipping into the records of recent presidents, we have found instances of success, failure, and mixed outcome. Thus we learned that no president experiences either uninterrupted good fortune or total disaster. In this chapter, we want to look for broader patterns. To that end, we shall first ask: What issues do most presidents address? And what kinds of actions do presidents take? Then, taking a larger set of presidential cases, we shall ask about the balance between failure and success in the presidencies of the past half-century.

## *The Presidential Agenda*

Successive presidents confront many of the same issues. Regardless of the expectations an individual brings to office, he discovers that he must deal with an ongoing presidential agenda. The agenda may change, and there is room for individual interests and novel problems. But it continues to define a substantial part of every president's workload.

Foreign policy and economic policy come with the office and may leave little room for a president to maneuver; domestic policy allows a little more discretion. Since the end of World War II, every president has had to deal with the Soviet Union or its successor states. The use of U.S. troops abroad, in war and times of crisis, has been part of every presidency. Levels of defense spending have occupied presidents in a major way, whether they were being adjusted upward to contend with international threats, downward when danger subsided, or simply because they were such a large element of the total budget. Nuclear arms, nuclear power, and the control of arms races have been constant items on the presidential agenda. Every president has been concerned with Europe and the Middle East, although the specific problems have differed from one administration to the next. Every president has dealt with problems and opportunities in Asia. Central American crises have often commanded presidential attention, and every president from Eisenhower to Clinton has had to deal with Cuba.

Presidents cannot escape demands of the economy. Every president except Kennedy (after the first year), Johnson, and Clinton had to contend with recession or unemployment. Every president had to confront inflation until the Federal Reserve reduced it early in the Reagan administration.[1] Presidents have been constantly concerned with fiscal policy. Every president has made decisions to increase or decrease various taxes. Every president has been concerned about levels of federal spending, though Democratic presidents have been more likely to favor spending to stimulate growth and Republican presidents have been more likely to rein in spending to reduce inflation and the pressure on interest rates. All presidents are concerned about budgets because of the annual budget cycle. International trade and trade imbalances have grown in salience as more Americans have been affected by the international economy. Other economic concerns—labor disputes, Social Security, regulation—show up from now and then, but are not perennial items on the economic agenda.

No single domestic topic has commanded continual attention in the same way as relations with the Russians or taxes and spending, but half a dozen have turned up with some frequency. Civil rights, health care, welfare, and environmental protection are all staples on the presidential agenda. Presidents also frequently take positions on education, crime, or drugs, but since education and law enforcement are primarily local responsibilities, subsidies and symbols are the principal components of federal action. Republican presidents are more likely to initiate state-related programs such as revenue sharing, and Democratic presidents are more likely to be concerned with urban policy, antipoverty programs, and national service. Finally, there are some topics that occasionally turn up. These include human resources, transportation, agriculture, energy, and increasingly in recent years, child care and medical leave for family crises. Given the variation in domestic policy, it affords more scope than foreign and economic policy for personal and partisan differences.

---

[1.] Inflation was thought to be under control because it was so much lower than it had been in the Carter administration. But the "modest" inflation of the 1980s and 1990s (averaging 3.5 percent between 1983 and 1997) was actually higher than the "unacceptable" inflation of the Eisenhower and Kennedy years.

Because the same types of problems remain on the agenda from one president to the next, it follows that incoming presidents should pay careful attention to the policies of their predecessors. Yet they often do not. Politics gets in the way of good policy development. After a candidate has crisscrossed the country denouncing his predecessor's policies, he naturally concludes they were mistaken. When incoming staff members come to be briefed by their outgoing counterparts, they arrive thinking they have little to learn. After all, haven't they just won an election?

Yet successful policies have often reflected continuity from one administration to the next. Eisenhower adapted Truman's containment policy to fit his reading of strategic and economic constraints, and elements of this policy ultimately led to the collapse of the Soviet Union in the 1990s. Nuclear threats have been reduced by test bans, strategic arms limitations, and strategic arms reduction treaties pursued by successive presidencies. Several administrations have urged peace negotiations between Israel and surrounding Arab states. On the domestic front, there has been continuing governmental attention to the link between smoking and cancer since it was first publicized by the surgeon general in 1964. The U.S. environment has been improved by the gradual strengthening of clean air and clean water legislation. It was the *combined* actions of the Bush and Clinton administrations—the 1990 budget agreement and the 1993 budget package—that brought deficit spending under control in the 1990s. Although both presidents later said that their tax increases were mistakes, and both condemned the other's economics, the actions of both administrations were integral to success. Robert Reischauer calculated that 49 percent of the savings that ultimately balanced the federal budget came from Bush's 1990 budget agreement, another 40 percent came from Clinton's 1993 budget package, and only 11 percent came from the 1997 balanced-budget agreement (Rosenbaum 1995).

Of course, various policies fail, and these should be modified or dropped altogether. All new administrations should conduct a thorough policy review. But as they decide on the direction of their own policy initiatives, they should consider staying with existing policies that make sense. Whether their predecessors are political opponents or not, they are intelligent persons who have done their best to cope with complex situations. Their policies are often worth maintaining.

## *Presidential Actions*

What leads a president to take a particular action? It may be many things: a foreign crisis will not wait; adverse economic circumstances force action; a president believes a move will improve his chances for reelection; an important political ally importunes him; or he receives a compelling option paper from his aides. But on a more general level, recall the argument from Chapter 6 that the White House lies at the intersection of substantive and political forces. The presidency is preeminently an institution where good public policy and partisan advantage must be balanced. The cognitive prerequisite for effective public policy is *expertise.* The cognitive prerequisite for partisanship (or ideology) is *attitude strength.* To understand presidents' decisions, therefore, we must consider expertise and attitude strength.[2]

For our purposes, expertise means an objective facility in processing information (and thus differs from a subjective belief in one's own competence). Expertise can be learned (and thus differs from intelligence, which is established early in life). This learning results from "an extended adaptation to the demands of naturally occurring situations" (Ericsson and Charness 1994, 732). Professionals improve their expertise in this way.[3] "Experts in a particular domain are simply more efficient and organized in their attentional capacities and consequently stay more informed, more organized and more opinionated" (Fiske 1993, 249). But because experts develop their memory and organizational skills "to meet specific demands of encoding and accessibility in specific activities in a given domain . . . their skill does not transfer from one domain to another" (Ericsson and Charness 1994, 736). A specialist on agriculture, in other words, is unlikely to manifest expertise on Middle Eastern politics, and vice versa. And if a president has developed genuine expertise of his own, it is likely to be within a single policy area in which he has been immersed for some time.

A clear illustration of the domain specificity of presidential expertise comes from the administrations of Dwight Eisenhower and Lyndon Johnson. Eisenhower was an expert in foreign policy, Johnson was not. In a careful comparison of their decisions on whether the United States should become involved in Vietnam, John Burke and Fred Greenstein showed that Eisenhower proceeded with great care, gathered information from multiple sources, and decided against U.S. involvement. Johnson relied instead on his assessment of his political support, and opted for a major expansion of U.S. involvement (Burke and Greenstein 1989). But if Eisenhower and Johnson are compared on the matter of civil rights, the balance is different. In this policy area Johnson had expertise and Eisenhower did not. As president, Johnson provided critical leadership in changing national

---

[2.] I should like to thank Jon Krosnick for his help in thinking about these variables.

[3.] It has been estimated that the time interval between scientists' and authors' first publications and their most valuable contributions averages more than ten years (Ericsson and Charness 1994, 738).

attitudes toward civil rights whereas Eisenhower had worried about moving too quickly.

In fact, it is difficult to be certain about the presence or absence of presidential expertise. Expertise is most easily ascertained in activities such as chess where ratings exist. Grand masters can be evaluated and differentiated by inspecting their ratings (Ericsson and Charness 1994, 731). In evaluating presidents, we have only impressions arising from their records in office. On this basis, it would appear that Eisenhower was expert in foreign policy, Johnson in civil rights, Nixon in foreign policy, Ford in economics, and Bush in foreign policy. The absence of expertise can be seen with Eisenhower in civil rights, Johnson in foreign policy, Carter in economics, Reagan in both economics and domestic policy generally, and Clinton (especially at the beginning of his administration) in foreign policy.

These impressions again emphasize that both expertise and its absence are specific to the policy domain in question. When we consider the three broad areas of foreign policy, economics, and domestic policy within the administrations of nine presidents, we obtain twenty-seven president-domain combinations. In only five of these cases do we see expertise, and in only six more the absence of expertise. The majority of cases, in which we see neither, are the *normal* circumstances, in which the president enters office without expert standing but over time learns enough to function in various policy areas. Expertise is customarily passed along by the head of the relevant organizational unit. For example, Carter was advised on international questions by Zbigniew Brzezinski, and Clinton was coached on economics by Robert Rubin. In normal circumstances, the conversation is between an expert adviser and a generalist president. As time passes, the president becomes much more competent than when he entered office, even if he does not develop the expertise of a specialist.

A second key to presidential actions is the presence of *strong attitudes*. For some time it has been thought that stronger attitudes would more likely lead to action (Newcomb, Turner, and Converse 1965, 118). Recent work spells out the relationship between attitudes and action in more detail. Strong attitudes tend to be more stable over time and are more resistant to attack. In addition, strong attitudes "make it more likely that certain information will come to mind, or that certain decisions will be rendered" and "strong attitudes should be more likely to [guide behavior]" (Krosnick and Petty 1995, 2–3). Weak attitudes have the opposite effects.

Just why strong attitudes have these properties is less clear. It appears that attitude strength is multidimensional, but research on other characteristics related to it has not produced consistent results. A subset of four attributes, however, can be isolated from the larger constellation. These four attributes are strongly cor-

related with each other, and are all related to attitude strength. They are importance (the significance attached to an attitude), certainty (the degree of confidence
a person has in an attitude), amount of thought devoted to the attitude object,
and extremity (the extent to which an attitude departs from neutrality) (Krosnick
et al. 1993). Two of these are quite consequential in presidential decisions. If an
attitude object is important to a president, the odds are increased that it will be
part of his personal agenda. If a president is certain, he will be less hesitant in
the face of incomplete information and conflicting arguments. Presidents who
were motivated by strong attitudes would include Eisenhower with respect to economics and the Interstate Highway System, Johnson on education, Nixon on law
and order, Ford on economics, Carter on human rights, and Reagan on several
topics (defense spending, taxes, and so on).

An elementary theory of presidential behavior can be constructed by cross-
classifying expertise and attitude strength.[4] This approach rests on two considerable simplifications. First, we have chosen to characterize expertise as present or absent and attitude strength as strong or weak; for a better picture of
reality, the variables should be represented by continua ranging from great
expertise to no expertise, and from very strong attitudes to very weak attitudes.
Most presidents would fall somewhere in the middle of these scales, with varying amounts of expertise, depending on topic, and a mix of strong attitudes
on some topics and moderate to weak attitudes on others. By dichotomizing the
continua patterns become apparent, but we lose important detail in the process.
Second, by using impressions of the presidents' own expertise and attitude
strength, we exclude the attributes of the close associates with whom the president works. In particular, we leave out the adviser-supplied expertise on which
all presidents depend. This omission is helpful in estimating the presidents' own
contributions, but once again we have simplified reality. The patterns displayed
in Figures 8–1 and 8–2 are suggestive, but these simplifications should be borne
in mind.

What general patterns of action are likely to be associated with the various levels of expertise and attitude strength? When presidents have both expertise and
strong attitudes, they have both the knowledge to craft appropriate policies and the
motivation to put them on the national agenda. With this combination, indicated

---

[4.] What do I mean by calling this an "elementary" theory? It could have equally well been
called a simple theory, a rudimentary theory, a limited theory, or a partial theory. I think it
is striking that these two dimensions alone allow us to understand a number of actions that
presidents take. At the same time, this theory does not reach many other vital topics, such
as the role of the presidential staff or the constraining effects of the political environment.

**Figure 8–1   Types of Presidential Behavior**

|  | Strong Attitudes | Weak Attitudes |
|---|---|---|
| *Expertise Present* | Policies well designed to move in preferred direction | Pure policy politics; relatively few new initiatives |
| *Expertise Absent* | Partisan and/or ideological politics | Trial and error or drift |

in the upper left quadrant of Figure 8–1, we should expect the administration to have designed policies that would move toward the president's preferred goals. Having strong attitudes, but not having developed expertise, the combination in the lower left quadrant of Figure 8–1, is quite a common situation in Washington. Depending on whether the attitudes coincide with partisan divisions, this combination produces pure ideological politics, pure partisan politics, or both. In either case, rhetoric is placed in the service of ideological goals.

It is harder to make predictions about policy in areas where the president's attitudes are weakly held. In such cases presidents lack the motivation that comes with feeling that a subject is important. In fact, a combination of high expertise and weak attitudes, the pattern in the upper right quadrant of Figure 8–1, is rare. It is unusual not to have developed strong attitudes in the course of acquiring expertise, but this *could* happen. In this case the president could use his knowledge for appropriate system maintenance, but he would be unlikely to launch new initiatives in the absence of a crisis or some other stimulus. The combination in the lower right quadrant of Figure 8–1, weak attitudes with a lack of expertise, presents a number of possibilities. One is that the administration will proceed by trial and error. The citizenry can always hope that an administration will hit on a productive policy, recognize its virtues, and stick with it. Another possibility is that the president will allow policy to drift along, which may not cause any harm as long as nothing goes wrong. And *if* there is an expert staff member who can make a skillful presentation of a policy position, there is a chance that the president may acquiesce because he is convinced and doesn't care very much personally. If presidential indolence clears the way for good staff-driven policy, the results may be surprisingly propitious.[5]

Instances of all these behaviors are shown in Figure 8–2. The combination of expertise and strong attitudes (the upper left quadrant) is exemplified by Eisenhower's adoption of a modified containment policy vis-à-vis the Soviet Union and by Ford's 1976 presentation of a plan to balance the federal budget in three years. Both policies were skillfully crafted to achieve particular goals. We can't be sure of the efficacy of Ford's budget proposal, as it was never implemented, but Eisenhower's modified containment policy certainly worked.

Strong attitudes without expertise (the lower left quadrant) are the stuff of straight partisan fights, staples of Washington politics. This combination is represented by Johnson's victory on federal aid to education and by Reagan's substantial 1981 tax cut. Johnson had long believed in the value of education, and Reagan had strong attitudes about the virtues of tax cuts, but neither man could be said to be an expert on the subject matter.

To develop expertise without having strong attitudes, the combination in the upper right quadrant of Figure 8–2, is unusual. George Bush, however, as a foreign relations expert who had some weak attitudes, provides an example. In the

**Figure 8–2  Examples of Presidential Behavior**

|                      | Strong Attitudes                                               | Weak Attitudes                          |
|----------------------|---------------------------------------------------------------|-----------------------------------------|
| *Expertise Present*  | Eisenhower modified containment<br><br>Ford balanced budget proposal | Bush international system maintenance    |
| *Expertise Absent*   | Johnson federal aid to education<br><br>Reagan tax cut and deficit | Carter economic policies<br><br>Clinton policies toward Haiti |

---

5. One way to contend with the difficulty of predicting actions when presidents have weak attitudes is to subdivide these cases into presidents with a need for achievement (abbreviated as *n* Achievement) and presidents lacking such motivation. A person with high *n* Achievement wants to succeed, will try harder, will persist longer, and is a moderate risk-taker (McClelland 1961, 43–46). Thus within the cases of low expertise and weak attitudes, a president with high *n* Achievement might try first one thing, then another in the hope of accomplishing something, whereas a president with a low *n* Achievement might be contented to drift.

case of Panama's Manuel Noriega and Iraq's Saddam Hussein, who had challenged him personally, he had strong attitudes and acted on them. But otherwise, he generally acted to sustain the status quo and devoted a lot of time to system maintenance.

Weak attitudes without expertise, the lower right quadrant, opens doors to a number of possibilities, including policy making by trial and error. Trial and error certainly describes Jimmy Carter's method of formulating economic policies. The same is true of Bill Clinton's multiple changes of mind about Haiti: first Haitian refugees would be admitted to the United States, then Haitian refugees would be returned to Haiti, then Haitian refugees would be taken to the U.S. base at Guantanamo, Cuba, and so on.

Obviously, expertise and attitude strength do not account for all presidential behavior, but these two variables are a good place to start in analyzing the record.

## *Types of Presidential Failure*

At this point we are ready to attempt a more complete examination of the successes, failures, and indeterminate results achieved by the nine presidents who served during the last half-century.[6] In judging whether a policy was a success, a failure, or indeterminate, I asked whether the policy was accepted by the other decision makers involved and whether the effects of the policy were desirable. Criteria of acceptance include Congress's passage of appropriate legislation and foreign allies' willingness to follow American initiatives. In judging the desirability of the policy results, I gave some weight to what the incumbents were trying to accomplish. I considered available hard data (unemployment rates, for example), and I also took into account the results of the policy, both short term and those that became evident with the passage of time.

The most damaging failures—Nixon's Watergate and Clinton's impeachment—were primarily the responsibility of the presidents themselves. Nixon was not personally involved in the Watergate break-in; but rather than discharging the persons responsible, he established a policy of stonewalling. Clinton deceived

---

6. The record I examined was a 47,000-word summary of these administrations that I wrote for an earlier draft of this book. Although it was dropped in order to reduce the overall length of the book, it was a convenient account to consult. There were 161 policies discussed in the sections on foreign policy, economic policy, and domestic policy. I classified each of these as a success, a failure, or indeterminate. While indeterminate (i.e., mixed) outcomes were discussed in Chapter 7, they were comparatively infrequent. Consequently, we shall focus on successes and failures.

everyone about his relationship with Monica Lewinsky. In both cases, presidents invited disaster by lying about what had taken place. Watergate arrested the policy initiatives of one administration, and its legacy of distrust made it harder for succeeding administrations to build support for their programs. Clinton's impeachment permanently stained his reputation and reinforced citizens' distrust of the government.

Moving beyond these two exceptional cases, the first group of failures consists of international policies that foundered before achieving hoped-for results. In many cases, these were programs undertaken by U.S. administrations rather than necessary responses to foreign events. The first case is Eisenhower's approval of a 1953 CIA-sponsored coup to restore the shah to the Iranian throne. At the time, the result appeared to be the presence of a friendlier government in an important country. But resentment in Iran of the American interference ultimately made it much more difficult for later presidents to deal with the Iranians. The 1961 Bay of Pigs expedition, an attempt to unseat Castro in Cuba, was an immediate military disaster. Kennedy also initiated substantial U.S. involvement in Vietnam, and Johnson escalated the conflict to full-scale war. Americans lost their stomach for the costs of the war whereas the North Vietnamese were willing to endure much greater hardship. Reagan abided American casualties in Lebanon without any compensating advantage, and he undertook a small war of his own in encouraging contras to attack the Nicaraguan border. He also approved an unsuccessful arms-for-hostages policy with Iran, which in time became an element in the Iran-contra scandal. Clinton paid almost no attention to the U.S. troops who were in Somalia as part of the UN's peacekeeping efforts, then withdrew the troops after they suffered casualties.

A second class of failures consists of inadequate responses to events. Three of these concerned foreign policy. Carter was unable to build Senate support for the SALT II Treaty in 1979 (even before the Soviet invasion of Afghanistan made it impossible to proceed). Until he was leaving office, Carter was also unable to secure the freedom of sixty-six diplomats seized in Tehran in 1979. And the Clinton administration gave only sporadic attention to nuclear disarmament.

Many more of the inadequate responses concerned economic challenges. The Eisenhower administration did not handle either the 1958 recession or the more modest 1960 recession nearly as well as it had the 1954 recession. Lyndon Johnson's decision not to ask for wage and price controls when the Vietnam War was expanded, together with his subsequent delay in asking for a tax increase, unleashed an inflation that lasted for more than a decade. Nixon's economic policies were designed to aid his reelection; after wage and price controls were removed, both inflation and unemployment returned. Ford could not cope with the 1974–1975 recession soon enough to permit his reelection. Although the Ford administration did well in 1976, the Carter administration's spending reignited inflation soon thereafter, and this was coupled with unemployment in the 1980 recession. Reagan's failure to restrain spending commensurately with his 1981 tax cut produced a deficit twice as large as that of all of his predecessors taken together. And Bush did not think the 1991 recession required a vigorous response. Of the nine presidents, only Kennedy and Clinton were fortunate enough to escape severe economic challenges.

The Johnson administration never devised a way of coping with the urban riots of the "long hot summers" of the late 1960s. In spite of Canadian complaints about acid rain resulting from industrial emissions in the United States, Ronald Reagan refused to support clean air legislation. He left response to the outbreak of AIDS to the surgeon general, and his administration was also marked by the costly savings and loan and Department of Housing and Urban Development scandals. Beyond this, it is hard to match domestic challenges with inadequate responses by the administration. There is not enough consensus on what constitutes a problem that is serious enough to demand administration action. For example, a case could be made that George Bush should have addressed inadequacies in health care in the United States, but his defenders could argue that reform would have been too difficult to attempt when he was facing a Democratic Congress.

The final category of failed policy is comprised of things presidents tried to do, only to be blocked by political opponents in Congress. Kennedy got a fair amount of legislation through Congress, but he lacked the congressional votes to obtain his major goals, such as Medicare, aid to education, and the creation of a Department of Urban Affairs. Nixon submitted some far-reaching legislation, but he was not able to get his Family Assistance Plan, health care, or cabinet reorganization through Congress.[7] Carter likewise failed to get welfare reform or health care legislation. Clinton failed to get health care from the 103rd Congress, which was Democratic; and after Republicans took control in the 104th Congress, he had to be satisfied with less consequential legislation.

It's worth noting that Kennedy, Nixon, Carter, and Clinton were unable to get major health care legislation, though all tried, and Nixon and Carter were unable to get welfare reform.[8] Thus, an inability to obtain health or welfare legislation

---

[7] Ford was so weak politically that his administration really couldn't contemplate major initiatives.

[8] Whether Clinton will be said to have achieved welfare reform depends on the success of the program that was substituted for the terminated Aid to Families with Dependent Children. The early results of the welfare-to-work program do not bear out either the predictions of proponents or the fears of opponents.

may result as much from the intractability of these policy areas as from difficulties in individual administrations.

## Instances of Presidential Success

To examine successes, we shall consider one president at a time. Dwight Eisenhower's international endeavors included settling on a modified containment policy and stable defense financing, getting the United States out of the Korean war, and keeping the United States out of possible wars in Vietnam and over the Chinese offshore islands of Matsu and Quemoy. Although he failed to cope satisfactorily with economic problems in his second term, the 1954 recession was very carefully handled. And while his domestic program was modest, the St. Lawrence Seaway and Interstate Highway System have been facilitating travel for decades.

In the Cuban Missile Crisis, John Kennedy defended American interests and kept the world back from the nuclear threshold. In the aftermath, he reached out to the Soviet Union in his American University speech, following which the Limited Test Ban Treaty was swiftly concluded. With the help of economic stimuli, the United States recovered rapidly from the 1960 recession, and the Trade Expansion Act in 1962 laid a foundation for an expansion of international trade. Kennedy's 1963 tax cut proposal (passed after his death) aided a period of sustained growth in the U.S. economy. Though he lacked the votes in Congress to get his most-preferred legislation, he obtained manpower development and some other important programs, shepherded the nation through desegregation crises at the Universities of Mississippi and Alabama, and submitted major civil rights legislation in 1963.

Lyndon Johnson shares credit with Kennedy for the tax cut and civil rights legislation that Kennedy submitted and Johnson fought for and signed. In his own right, Johnson obtained the Economic Opportunity Act in 1964, and then the flood of legislation from the Great Society Congress: Medicare, Medicaid, aid to education, the creation of the Department of Housing and Urban Development and the Department of Transportation, Model Cities, motor vehicle and highway safety, clean air and clean water, highway beautification, a new national park, and the National Endowments for the Humanities and Arts. The 90th Congress did not match this outpouring, but the Corporation for Public Broadcasting was created, truth in lending legislation was passed, and two more national parks were created.

Richard Nixon brought a vision of a post–cold war world to the White House, and he took important steps in this direction. His trip to China began the opening of relations with that huge power; the SALT I Treaty accelerated efforts to control the danger of nuclear war; Henry Kissinger's shuttle diplomacy began active U.S. efforts to bring peace between Israel and its neighbors. President Nixon's 1970 State of the Union Message was largely devoted to the environment, and much environmental legislation was passed during his administration. Revenue sharing helped states struggling with the financial problems of providing institutions adequate for the explosive population growth that was the baby boom. The Philadelphia Plan opened job opportunities for African Americans; and though little publicity attended the accomplishment, substantial progress was made in finding minority jobs and in implementing school desegregation throughout the South.

The presidency of Gerald Ford was too brief for substantial accomplishment, but the Vladivostok Agreement provided a further check on nuclear weapons. The Helsinki Accords were of considerable help to human rights advocates in Eastern Europe. Economically, Ford was successful in reducing the growth of federal spending, and he managed to slow the rate of inflation in 1976.

Although he had little background in foreign policy, Jimmy Carter's determination to work for peace brought two signal achievements. He brought about ratification of the Panama Canal Treaties, and he persuaded the heads of the Israeli and Egyptian governments to sign a peace treaty. The complex 1979 energy bill was maneuvered through the Congress, as was civil service reform, and the Departments of Energy and Education were established.

To the surprise of many who listened to his anticommunist rhetoric, and to foreign policy professionals who thought that the Soviet Union would never agree to reduce its strategic forces, in the last year of his presidency Ronald Reagan concluded a treaty reducing intermediate-range nuclear forces. He also reordered spending priorities to his liking (more on defense, less on domestic programs) and could point to real economic growth after 1982. Bipartisan negotiations with congressional leaders led to an important agreement putting Social Security financing on a firmer basis.

George Bush's great interest in foreign policy led to several accomplishments. A series of American-Russian agreements sealed the end of the cold war by binding both states to the reduction of conventional as well as nuclear forces. When he felt challenged, first by Manuel Noriega and then by Saddam Hussein, Bush used military force with decisive effect. The prestige the United States gained in the Gulf War victory was then employed to encourage further negotiations between Israel and the Palestinians. Domestically, Bush obtained the 1990 Clean Air Act and the Americans with Disabilities Act, as well as some less-publicized legislation.

Bill Clinton came to the presidency determined to focus on the economy, and the economy was his great success. He made courageous decisions on deficit reduction at the outset, and, with the help of the longest economic expansion since World

War II, was able to submit the first balanced budget in a full generation. His records in foreign policy and domestic policy were mixed, but in both these areas, there were some accomplishments. Clinton obtained approval of the North American Free Trade Agreement (NAFTA), the Uruguay Round of the General Agreement on Tariffs and Trade (GATT), and the Chinese trade agreement, and working through NATO, saw both the war in Bosnia and the ethnic slaughter in Kosovo brought to an end. Domestically, he signed legislation mandating family and medical leave, the Brady Bill (requiring background checks of hand gun purchasers), the 1994 crime bill, some focused health care initiatives, and an increase in the minimum wage.

## What Does This Tell Us?

What can be learned from this record? The most important lesson is that presidential successes come more often than presidential failures. Success dominates failure by a ratio of three to two. Including the indeterminate outcomes, there are nearly as many successes (48 percent) as failures (32 percent) and mixed outcomes (20 percent) put together. (For a consideration of measurement issues, see Box 8–1.) In light of claims that recent presidencies have been failures, this finding is consequential.

This ordering of frequencies—successes first, failures next, and mixed outcomes last—clearly applies to both economic and domestic policy, and almost applies to foreign policy. The three categories are more equally distributed in foreign policy (40 percent successes, 29 percent failures, 31 percent mixed outcomes), and there was one more mixed outcome than failure. This same ordering holds for most individual presidents.[9] Hence we can conclude that the ordering is authentic.

Each president's successes have not been limited to a single policy area. By my rough reckoning, Eisenhower, Kennedy, and Clinton accomplished something in foreign policy, economic policy, and domestic policy. Johnson, Nixon, Ford, Carter, Reagan, and Bush did so in two of the three policy areas.[10] Every president has left office with notable fulfillment in more than one policy area.

---

[9.] When the analysis gets down to the level of individual presidents, two things seem to be happening. There is some genuine variation from president to president. But at the same time, the measurement becomes less dependable. Estimates become more robust as the $N$ increases, but they become more fragile as the $N$ is reduced.

[10.] For the record, I don't think there were signal achievements by Johnson in foreign policy, by Nixon or Carter in economics, or by Ford or Reagan in domestic policy. Bush's record in economics was indeterminate; his courageous 1990 decision to seek a budget deal was positive, but his inadequate response to the 1991 recession was negative.

**Box 8–1   A Note on Measurement**

Although questions can be properly raised about the classification of any one case as a success, a failure, or mixed outcome, the measurement used here is quite robust.

The measurement does not assume that all of the individual cases have been classified correctly. I might well have been mistaken, for example, in classifying Kennedy's inability to pass Medicare as a failure and Ford's inability to get Congress to pass his balanced budget as a mixed outcome. But the assumption is that compensating errors will correct for whatever individual mistakes have been made. We are working with a scale composed of three magnitudes, $a$, $b$, and $c$. Now let us say that with an error-free classification, cases 1, 2, and 3 are known to belong in magnitude $a$; cases 4, 5, and 6 are known to belong in magnitude $b$; and cases 7, 8, and 9 are known to belong in magnitude $c$. In an actual classification, however, an observer assigns cases 1 and 2 to $a$, and case 3 to $b$, case 4 to $a$, case 5 to $b$, and case 6 to $c$, cases 7 and 8 to $c$, and case 9 to $b$. In this instance, the observer has made four classification errors out of a possible nine, but there are compensating errors. That is, in the error-free distribution, there are three cases assigned to $a$, three cases assigned to $b$, and three cases assigned to $c$. And because the mistakes made by our hypothetical observer exactly compensate for each other, in this instance there are also three cases assigned to $a$, three cases assigned to $b$, and three cases assigned to $c$. Thus, the distributions are the same.

Although it would be unusual for classification errors to exactly compensate for each other, the likelihood that they would approach the error-free classification increases as the number of cases increases. The number of presidential cases we are working with (161) does not give us the same confidence we would have if we were working with, say, 582 cases, but the number is high enough to provide a robust distribution.

It is necessary that the errors be random, some in one direction and some in another, rather than systematic. Hence the reader should satisfy himself or herself that I have treated Republican presidents the same as Democrats, liberal presidents the same as conservatives, right-handed presidents the same as left-handers, and so on. As long as the classification is free from systematic bias, we can rely on the reported distribution.

A final point to recall is this. One can rely on compensating errors if one is seeking robust distributions (the number of cases in each magnitude). However, it will not work in an analysis that requires correlations or some form of causal analysis.

Presidents are not always successful. Failures are a part of every president's record. But rather than global statements that "this presidency was successful" or "that presidency was a failure," we should attend to the balance between success and failure. We do not argue that presidents have been omniscient or omnipotent. Rather, and more significantly, these nine presidents, with all their human strengths and human weaknesses, have been successful more often than not.

Why should U.S. presidents invariably have mixed records? Recall the argument about accomplishment from the conclusion of Chapter 1: an individual president begins with a set of policy skills, takes the power he has (or lacks) to build support with the electorate and Congress, considers what he regards as good public policy, and then arrays his resources against the challenges he faces in each policy arena. Now consider the variation that is possible with all of these concepts. As far as the presidents are concerned, the key considerations are expertise and attitude strength. Expertise, as we have seen, varies from one policy area to another, and attitudes about what constitutes good public policy change from one president to the next. Presidential power certainly varies; some presidents have supporting majorities in Congress and enjoy public approbation; some do not. And power increases or decreases within individual administrations. Finally, the challenges a president faces in each policy arena vary from one president to the next, as does the skill each unit of the presidency exhibits in working in different sectors of the political environment. Probabilistic logic tells us that sometimes the combination of all these factors is going to lead to success and that at other times the combination will lead to failure. The probability that a president will experience success (or failure) in *every* venture is so tiny that it can be dismissed.

Why recent presidents have had a larger proportion of successes than failures is a more difficult question, but the answer is encouraging. The difficulty arises because analysis depends on the *values* of the concepts, and not on the *nature* of the concepts themselves. For there to be more successes than failures, the values must be positive more frequently than negative. Positive values mean the president must have access to relevant expertise, have enough support from the public, be able to work effectively with the other institutions in the presidential environment, and so forth. Negative values mean the opposite. Whether there are more positive than negative values can be demonstrated only by empirical examination, and here the balance of successes to failures tells us there have been more positive than negative values among the concepts linking presidents to accomplishment.

In sum, U.S. presidents are neither irreproachable heroes nor base scoundrels, but skilled politicians who bring experience and occasionally expertise to the White House. The tasks before them are sufficiently complex that they must be learned, but the institutional presidency supports the individuals and helps in the bargaining needed to win the support of others in the political environment. The outcome is likely to be mixed, with more successes than failures. Barring drastic change, this pattern should continue into the foreseeable future. If Americans modify their expectations accordingly, they will be less likely to be disappointed in presidents and more likely to be fair in evaluating their accomplishments.

# References

Aberbach, Joel D., and Bert A. Rockman. 1976. "Clashing Beliefs within the Executive Branch: The Nixon Administration Bureaucracy." *American Political Science Review* 70 (June): 456–468.

Aldrich, John H. 1980a. *Before the Convention: Strategies and Choices in Presidential Nomination Campaigns.* Chicago: University of Chicago Press.

———. 1980b. "A Dynamic Model of Pre-Convention Campaigns." *American Political Science Review* 74 (September): 651–669.

———. 1993. "Presidential Selection." In *Researching the Presidency: Vital Questions, New Approaches,* ed. George C. Edwards III, John H. Kessel, and Bert A. Rockman. Pittsburgh: University of Pittsburgh Press.

Allison, Graham T. 1971. *Essence of Decision: Explaining the Cuban Missile Crisis.* Boston: Little, Brown.

Ambrose, Stephen E. 1983. *Eisenhower: Soldier, General of the Army, President-Elect, 1890–1952.* New York: Simon and Schuster.

———. 1984. *Eisenhower: The President.* New York: Simon and Schuster.

———. 1987. *Nixon: The Education of a Politician: 1913–1962.* New York: Simon and Schuster.

Anderson, James E. 1993. "Managing Macroeconomic Policy: The Carter Experience." In *The Presidency Reconsidered,* ed. Richard W. Waterman. Itasca, Ill.: Peacock, 247–273.

Anderson, James E., and Jared E. Hazleton. 1986. *Managing Macroeconomic Policy: The Johnson Presidency.* Austin: University of Texas Press.

Anderson, Patrick. 1968. "The New Defense Secretary Thinks Like the President." *New York Times Magazine,* January 28, 20–21, 70, 72–75.

Apple, R. W., Jr. 1986. "The Reagan News Conference: A Comparison." *New York Times,* January 9, 10.

————.1993. "Clinton's Refocusing." *New York Times,* May 6, 10.

————.1997a. "Road to Approval is Rocky, and the Gamble is Perilous." *New York Times,* May 15, 1, 8.

————.1997b. "The Slowly Rising Price of Delay and Foul-Ups." *New York Times,* October 8, 12.

Applebome, Peter. 1991. "Clinton Record in Leading Arkansas: Successes, But Not without Criticism." *New York Times,* December 22, A15.

Armstrong, Scott. 1980. "Carter Held Hope Even After Shah Lost His" (a series of six newspaper articles). *Washington Post,* November, 25–30.

Arterton, F. Christopher. 1984. *Media Politics.* Lexington, Mass.: Lexington.

Auger, Vincent A. 1997. "The National Security Council System after the Cold War." In *U.S. Foreign Policy After the Cold War,* ed. James M. Lindsay and Randall B. Ripley. Pittsburgh: University of Pittsburgh Press.

Ayers, B. Drummond, Jr. 1992. "Despite Improvements, the Schools in Arkansas Are Still Among Worst." *New York Times,* April 1, A14.

Bailey, Stephen K., and Edith K. Mosher. 1968. *ESEA: The Office of Education Administers a Law.* Syracuse, N.Y.: Syracuse University Press.

Baker, James A., III, with Thomas M. DeFrank. 1995. *The Politics of Diplomacy: Revolution, War and Peace, 1989–1992.* New York: Putnam.

Balz, Dan. 1997. "Just Show Them the Money." *Washington Post National Weekly Edition,* May 12, 11.

Balz, Dan, and Ann Devroy. 1993a. "The Making of an Economic Package." *Washington Post National Weekly Edition,* March 1–7, 12–13.

————.1993b. "The Training Wheels Have Come Off." *Washington Post National Weekly Edition,* June 5–11, 12.

Barber, James David. 1977. *The Presidential Character: Predicting Performance in the White House,* 2d ed. Englewood Cliffs, N.J.: Prentice Hall.

————.1992. *The Presidential Character: Predicting Performance in the White House,* 4th ed. Englewood Cliffs, N.J.: Prentice Hall.

Barilleaux, Ryan J. 1988. "Presidential Conduct of Foreign Policy." *Congress and the Presidency* 15 (Spring): 1–23.

Barilleaux, Ryan J., and Mary E. Stuckey. 1992. *Leadership and the Bush Presidency: Prudence or Drift in an Era of Change?* Westport, Conn.: Praeger.

Barone, Michael, and Grant Ujifusa, eds. 1983. *Almanac of American Politics 1984.* Washington, D.C.: National Journal.

Barrett, Laurence I. 1983. *Gambling with History: Reagan in the White House.* Garden City, N.Y.: Doubleday.

Barringer, Felicity. 1999. "Journalism's Greatest Hits: Two Lists of a Century's Top Stories." *New York Times,* March 1, C1, C13.

Beck, Nathaniel. 1982. "Parties, Administrations, and American Macroeconomic Outcomes." *American Political Science Review* 76 (March): 83–93.

Benda, Peter M., and Charles H. Levine. 1986. "The 'M' in OMB: Issues of Structure and Strategy." Paper presented at the annual meeting of the American Political Science Association, Washington, D.C., August 28–31.

Bennet, James. 1997. "Clinton Presents '98 Budget, and a Goal." *New York Times,* February 7, 1, 10.

————.1998. "President Offers the First Budget to Balance in Nearly 30 Years." *New York Times,* February 3, 1, 16.

Bennett, W. Lance, and David L. Paletz, eds. 1994. *Taken by Storm: The Media, Public Opinion and U.S. Foreign Policy in the Gulf War.* Chicago: University of Chicago Press.

Berman, Larry. 1977. "The Office of Management and Budget That Almost Wasn't." *Political Science Quarterly* 92 (Summer): 281–303.

————.1979. *The Office of Management and Budget and the Presidency, 1921–1979.* Princeton: Princeton University Press.

————.1988. "Lyndon B. Johnson: Paths Chosen and Opportunities Lost." In *Leadership in the Modern Presidency,* ed. Fred I. Greenstein. Cambridge: Harvard University Press, 134–163.

———— ed. 1990. *Looking Back on the Reagan Presidency.* Baltimore: Johns Hopkins University Press.

Berman, Larry, and Emily O. Goldman. 1995. "Clinton's Foreign Policy at Midterm." In *The Clinton Presidency: First Appraisals,* ed. Colin Campbell and Bert A. Rockman. Chatham, N.J.: Chatham House.

Berman, Larry, and Bruce W. Jentleson. 1991. "Bush and the Post–Cold-War World: New Challenges for American Leadership." In *The Bush Presidency: First Appraisals,* ed. Colin Campbell and Bert A. Rockman. Chatham, N.J.: Chatham House.

Berry, John M. 1996. "A Power Struggle at the Fed." *Washington Post National Weekly Edition,* July 15–20, 20–21.

Beschloss, Michael R., and Strobe Talbott. 1993. *At the Highest Levels: The Inside Story of the End of the Cold War.* Boston: Little, Brown.

Biven, W. Carl. 1991. "The Process of Economic Advice in the Carter Administration." Paper presented at the annual meeting of the American Political Science Association, New York, August 31.

————.1994. "Economic Advice in the Carter Administration." In *The Presidency and Domestic Policies of Jimmy Carter,* ed. Herbert D. Rosenbaum and Alexej Ugrinsky. Westport, Conn.: Greenwood.

Bond, Jon R., and Richard Fleisher. 1990. *The President in the Legislative Arena.* Chicago: University of Chicago Press.

Bornet, Vaughn Davis. 1983. *The Presidency of Lyndon B. Johnson.* Lawrence: University Press of Kansas.

Bose, Meena. 1998a. "Words as Signals: Drafting Cold War Rhetoric in the Eisenhower and Kennedy Administrations." *Congress and the Presidency* 25 (Spring): 23–41.

————.1998b. *"Shaping and Signaling Presidential Policy: The National Security Decision Making of Eisenhower and Kennedy."* College Station: Texas A&M Press.

Bowie, Robert R., and Richard H. Immerman. 1998. *Waging Peace: How Eisenhower Shaped an Enduring Cold War Strategy.* New York: Oxford University Press.

Bowles, Nigel. 1987. *The White House and Capitol Hill: The Politics of Presidential Persuasion.* Oxford: Clarendon Press.

Bradsher, Keith. 1995. "Gap in Wealth in U.S. Called Widest in West." *New York Times,* April 17, 1, C4.

Brauer, Carl M. 1986. *Presidential Transitions: Eisenhower Through Reagan.* New York: Oxford University Press.

———.1988. "John F. Kennedy: The Endurance of Inspirational Leadership." *In* Leadership in the Modern Presidency, ed. Fred I. Greenstein. Cambridge: Harvard University Press.

Brinkley, Joel. 1992. "Clinton Remakes Home State in Own Image." *New York Times,* March 31, A1, A10.

Brinkley, Joel, and Stephen Engelberg, eds. 1988. *Report of the Congressional Committees Investigating the Iran-Contra Affair,* abridged ed. New York: Times Books.

Broder, David S. 1966. "Consensus Politics: End of an Experiment." *Atlantic,* October, 60–65.

———.1972. *The Party's Over: The Failure of Politics in America.* New York: Harper and Row.

———.1980. *Changing of the Guard: Power and Leadership in America.* New York: Simon and Schuster.

———.1987. *Behind the Front Page: A Candid Look at How the News is Made.* New York: Simon and Schuster.

———.1990a. "Bush's Skills as Negotiator Are First-Rate." *Columbus Dispatch,* May 9, 11A.

———.1990b. "Some Newsworthy Presidential CPR." *Washington Post National Weekly Edition,* June 4–10, 4.

Broder, John M. 1999. "In U.S., A Vocal Dove Turned Hesitant Hawk." *New York Times,* March 28, 1, 15.

Brodie, Fawn M. 1981. *Richard Nixon: The Shaping of His Character.* New York: Norton.

Brody, Richard A. 1991. *Assessing the President: The Media, Elite Opinion, and Public Support.* Stanford, Calif.: Stanford University Press.

———.1994. "Crisis, War, and Public Opinion." In *Taken by Storm: The Media, Public Opinion and U.S. Foreign Policy in the Gulf War,* ed. W. Lance Bennett and David L. Paletz. Chicago: University of Chicago Press.

Brody, Richard A., and Simon Jackman. 1999. "The Lewinsky Affair and Popular Support for President Clinton." Paper presented at the annual meeting of the Midwest Political Science Association, Chicago, April 15–17.

Brownell, Herbert, with John P. Burke. 1993. *Advising Ike: The Memoirs of Attorney General Herbert Brownell.* Lawrence: University Press of Kansas.

Browning, Rufus P. 1968. "The Interaction of Personality and Political System in Decisions to Run for Office: Some Data and a Simulation Technique." *Journal of Social Issues* 24 (July): 93–109.

Brownstein, Ronald. 1986. "Getting an Early Start." *National Journal,* November 29, 2876–2881.

Brendon, Piers. 1986. *Ike: The Life and Times of Dwight D. Eisenhower.* London: Secker and Warburg.

Brinkley, Joel. 1988. "Reagan to Close Terms Mostly by Summing Up." *New York Times,* January 17, 10.

Bryner, Gary C. 1995. *Blue Skies, Green Politics: The Clean Air Act of 1990 and Its Implementation.* Washington, D.C.: CQ Press.

Brzezinski, Zbigniew. 1983. *Power and Principle: Memoirs of the National Security Adviser, 1977–1981.* New York: Farrar Straus Giroux.

Burden, Barry, and Aage C. Clausen. 1998. "The Unfolding Drama: Party and Ideology in the 104th House." In *Great Theater: The American Congress in the 1990s,* ed. Herbert F. Weisberg and Samuel C. Patterson. New York: Cambridge University Press.

Burke, John P. 1992. *The Institutional Presidency.* Baltimore: Johns Hopkins University Press.

Burke, John P., and Fred I. Greenstein. 1989. *How Presidents Test Reality.* New York: Russell Sage Foundation.

Burns, James MacGregor. 1960. *John Kennedy: A Political Profile.* New York: Harcourt Brace.

Bush, George, and Brent Scowcroft. 1998. *A World Transformed.* New York: Knopf.

Califano, Joseph A., Jr. 1991. *The Triumph and Tragedy of Lyndon Johnson: The White House Years.* New York: Simon and Schuster.

Campbell, Colin. 1986. *Managing the Presidency: Carter, Reagan, and the Search for Executive Harmony.* Pittsburgh: University of Pittsburgh Press.

———.1991. "The White House and Cabinet under the 'Let's Deal' Presidency." In *The Bush Presidency: First Appraisals,* ed. Colin Campbell and Bert A. Rockman. Chatham, N.J.: Chatham House.

———.1995. "Management in a Sandbox: Why the Clinton White House Failed to Cope with Gridlock." In *The Clinton Presidency: First Appraisals,* ed. Colin Campbell and Bert A. Rockman. Chatham, N.J.: Chatham House.

Campbell, Colin, and Bert A. Rockman, eds. 1991. *The Bush Presidency: First Appraisals.* Chatham, N.J.: Chatham House.

———.1995. *The Clinton Presidency: First Appraisals.* Chatham, N.J.: Chatham House.

Campbell, John C. 1979. "The Old People Boom and Japanese Policy Making." *Journal of Japanese Studies* 5 (Summer): 329–350.

Cannon, James. 1994. *Time and Chance: Gerald Ford's Appointment with History.* New York: Harper Collins.

Cannon, Lou. 1982. *Reagan.* New York: G.P. Putnam's.

———.1991. *President Reagan: The Role of a Lifetime.* New York: Simon and Schuster.

Carmines, Edward G., and James A. Stimson. 1981. "Issue Evolution, Population Replacement, and Normal Partisan Change." *American Political Science Review* 75 (March): 107–118.

———.1986. "On the Structure and Sequence of Issue Evolution." *American Political Science Review* 80 (September): 901–920.

————.1989. *Issue Evolution: Race and the Transformation of American Politics.* Princeton: Princeton University Press.

Caro, Robert A. 1982. *The Years of Lyndon Johnson: The Path to Power.* New York: Knopf.

————.1990. *The Years of Lyndon Johnson: Means of Ascent.* New York: Knopf.

Carroll, Richard J. 1995. *An Economic Record of Presidential Performance from Truman to Bush.* Westport, Conn.: Praeger.

Carter, Hodding, III. 1981. "Life Inside the Carter State Department." *Playboy,* 97–98, 212–218.

Carter, Jimmy. 1982. *Keeping Faith: Memoirs of a President.* New York: Bantam.

Cartwright, Dorwin. 1965. "Leadership, Influence, Control." In *Handbook of Organizations,* ed. James G. March. Skokie, Ill.: Rand-McNally.

Cater, Douglass. 1977. "The Struggle for Equality of Educational Opportunity." In *Toward New Human Rights: The Social Policies of the Kennedy and Johnson Administrations,* ed. David C. Warner. Austin, Texas: Lyndon B. Johnson School of Public Affairs.

Chester, Lewis, Godfrey Hodgson, and Bruce Page. 1981. *An American Melodrama: The Presidential Campaign of 1968.* New York: Viking.

Chubb, John E., and Paul E. Peterson. 1985. *The New Direction in American Politics.* Washington, D.C.: Brookings.

Clark, Keith C., and Lawrence J. Legere, eds. 1969. The *President and the Management of National Security.* New York: Praeger.

Clausen, Aage R. 1973. *How Congressmen Decide: A Policy Focus.* New York: St. Martin's.

Clifford, Clark, with Richard C. Holbrooke. 1991. *Counsel to the President: A Memoir.* New York: Random House.

Clines, Francis X. 1996. "Clinton Signs Bill Cutting Welfare." *New York Times,* August 23, A1, A10.

Clymer, Adam. 1998. "Three Issues Stand Out in the Logic of the Committee's Proceeding." *New York Times,* December 14, A21.

Clymer, Adam, Robert Pear, and Robin Toner. 1994. "For Health Care, Time Was a Killer." *New York Times,* August 29, A1, A8–A9.

Cochrane, James L. 1981. "Carter Energy Policy and the Ninety-fifth Congress." In *Energy Policy in Perspective: Today's Problems, Yesterday's Solutions,* ed. Craufurd D. Goodwin. Washington, D.C.: Brookings.

Cohen, Richard E. 1995. *Washington at Work: Back Rooms and Clean Air,* 2d ed. Boston: Allyn and Bacon.

Cole, Richard L., and David A. Caputo. 1979. "Presidential Control of the Senior Civil Service." *American Political Science Review* 73 (June): 399–410.

Collier, Kenneth E. 1997. *Between the Branches: The White House Office of Legislative Affairs.* Pittsburgh: University of Pittsburgh Press.

Cook, Blanche Wiesen. 1981. *The Declassified Eisenhower: A Divided Legacy.* New York: Doubleday.

Cook, Timothy E. 1989. *Making Laws and Making News: Media Strategies in the U.S. House of Representatives.* Washington, D.C.: Brookings.

————.1992. "Staging the News and Covering the News: Media Events, Broadcast Network News, and the First Hundred Days of the Bush Presidency." Paper presented at "Off the (Video) Record" research conference, Purdue University, November 15–17.

Cook, Timothy E., and Lyn Ragsdale. 1998. "The President and the Press: Negotiating Newsworthiness at the White House." In *The Presidency and the Political System,* 5th ed., ed. Michael Nelson. Washington, D.C.: CQ Press.

Cronin, Thomas E. 1970. "'Everyone Believes in Democracy Until He Gets to the White House . . .' : An Examination of White House–Departmental Relations." *Law and Contemporary Problems* 35 (Summer): 573–625.

————.1980. *The State of the Presidency.* 2d ed. Boston: Little, Brown.

Cummings, Milton C., Jr. 1966. "Nominations and Elections for the House of Representatives." In *The National Election of 1964,* ed. Milton C. Cummings Jr. Washington, D.C.: Brookings.

Cutler, Robert. 1956. "The Development of the National Security Council." In *Decisions of the Highest Order: Perspective on the National Security Council,* ed. Karl F. Inderfurth and Loch K. Johnson. 1988. Pacific Grove, Calif.: Brooks/Cole, 55–65.

Davidson, Roger H. 1966. *Coalition-Building for Depressed Areas Bills: 1955–1965.* Indianapolis: Bobbs-Merrill.

Davis, Eric L. 1983. "Congressional Liaison: The People and the Institutions." In *Both Ends of the Avenue: The Presidency, the Executive Branch, and Congress in the 1980s,* ed. Anthony King. Washington, D.C.: American Enterprise Institute.

Dean, Jonathan. 1997. "The NATO Mistake." *Washington Monthly,* July/August, 35–37.

DeParle, Jason. 1994. "Arkansas Pushes Plan to Break Welfare Cycle." *New York Times,* March 14, A10.

Destler, I. M. 1972. "Comment: Multiple Advocacy: Some Limits and Costs." *American Political Science Review* 66 (September): 786–790.

————.1974. *Presidents, Bureaucrats, and Foreign Policy.* Princeton: Princeton University Press.

————.1975. "National Security Advice to Presidents." Paper prepared for the Conference on Presidential Advisors, Princeton University, October 31–November 1.

————.1981. "National Security II: The Rise of the Assistant (1961–1981)." In *The Illusion of Presidential Government,* ed. Hugh Heclo and Lester M. Salamon. Boulder, Colo.: Westview.

————.1988. "Reagan and the World: An 'Awesome Stubbornness.'" In *The Reagan Legacy: Promise and Performance,* ed. Charles O. Jones. Chatham, N.J.: Chatham House.

————.1994. "Foreign Policy Making with the Economy at Center Stage." In *Beyond the Beltway: Engaging the Public in U.S. Foreign Policy,* ed. Daniel Yankelovich and I. M. Destler. New York: Norton.

————.1996. *The National Economic Council: A Work in Progress.* Washington: Institute for International Economics.

Destler, I. M., Leslie H. Gelb, and Anthony Lake. 1984. *Our Own Worst Enemy: The Unmaking of American Foreign Policy.* New York: Simon and Schuster.

Dillin, John. 1976. "Carter: His Record as Governor." *Christian Science Monitor,* July 19, 14–15.

————.1988. "George Bush: Out of Reagan's Shadow, He Emerges as a Political Fighter." *Christian Science Monitor,* October 26, 16–17.

Donovan, Robert J. 1956. *Eisenhower: The Inside Story.* New York: Harper.

Dowd, Maureen. 1990. "Offstage on the Budget: Tug of War Over Bush." *New York Times,* October 12, A-10.

Drew, Elizabeth. 1981. "Early Days." *New Yorker,* March 16.

————.1994. *On the Edge: The Clinton Presidency.* New York: Simon and Schuster.

Duffy, Michael, and Dan Goodgame. 1992. *Marching in Place: The Status Quo Presidency of George Bush.* New York: Simon and Schuster.

Dugger, Ronnie. 1982. *The Politician: The Life and Times of Lyndon Johnson: The Drive for Power, from the Frontier to Master of the Senate.* New York: Norton.

Edelman, Peter. 1997. "The Worst Thing Bill Clinton Has Done." *Atlantic,* March, 43–58.

————.1999. "Clinton's Cosmetic Poverty Tour." *New York Times,* July 9, A25.

Edwards, George C., III. 1980. *Presidential Influence in Congress.* San Francisco: Freeman.

————.1989. *At the Margins: Presidential Leadership of Congress.* New Haven: Yale University Press.

————.1995. "Frustration and Folly: Bill Clinton and the Public Presidency." In *The Clinton Presidency: First Appraisals,* ed. Colin Campbell and Bert A. Rockman. Chatham, N.J.: Chatham House.

Edwards, George C., III, John H. Kessel, and Bert A. Rockman, eds. 1993. *Researching the Presidency: Vital Questions, New Approaches.* Pittsburgh: University of Pittsburgh Press.

Eidenberg, Eugene, and Roy D. Morey. 1969. *An Act of Congress: The Legislative Process and the Making of Educational Policy.* New York: Norton.

Eisenhower, Dwight D. 1948. *Crusade in Europe.* New York: Doubleday.

————.1963. *Mandate for Change: 1953–1956.* New York: Signet.

————.1965. *Waging Peace: 1956–1961.* New York: Doubleday.

————.1967. *At Ease: Stories I Tell to Friends.* New York: Doubleday.

Ellwood, Paul M. 1994. "Too Little Time, Too Much Politics: Views on Health Care Fizzle." *New York Times,* September 27, A11.

Ericsson, K. Anders, and Neil Charness. 1994. "Expert Performance: Its Structure and Acquisition." *American Psychologist* 49 (August): 725–747.

Evans, Katherine Winton. 1982. "A Talk with Dave Gergen." *Washington Journalism Review* 4 (April): 41–45.

Ewald, William Bragg, Jr. 1981. *Eisenhower the President: Crucial Days, 1951–1960.* Englewood Cliffs, N.J.: Prentice Hall.

Fallows, James. 1979. "The Passionless Presidency." *Atlantic,* May, 33–48; June, 75–81.

Fein, Rashi. 1992. "Health Care Reform." *Scientific American,* November, 46–53.

Fenno, Richard F., Jr. 1959. *The President's Cabinet.* New York: Vintage.

————.1966. *The Power of the Purse: Appropriation Politics in Congress.* Boston: Little, Brown.

————.1986. "Observation, Context, and Sequence in the Study of Politics." *American Political Science Review* 80 (March): 3–15.

————.1997. *Learning to Govern: An Institutional View of the 104th Congress.* Washington, D.C.: Brookings.

Ferrell, Robert H. 1981. *The Eisenhower Diaries.* New York: Norton.

————.1983. *The Diary of James C. Hagerty: Eisenhower in Mid-Course, 1954–1955.* Bloomington: Indiana University Press.

Fink, Gary M. 1980. *Prelude to the Presidency: The Political Character and Legislative Leadership Style of Governor Jimmy Carter.* Westport, Conn.: Greenwood.

Fishel, Jeff. 1984. *Presidents and Promises.* Washington, D.C.: CQ Press.

Fiske, Edward B. 1990. "Governors' Group and Bush Envision Stronger Schools." *New York Times,* February 26, 1, 13.

Fiske, Susan T. 1993. "Cognitive Theory and the Presidency." In *Researching the Presidency: Vital Questions, New Approaches,* ed. George C. Edwards III, John H. Kessel, and Bert A. Rockman. Pittsburgh: University of Pittsburgh Press.

Fitzwater, Marlin. 1995. *Call the Briefing! Reagan and Bush, Sam and Helen: A Decade with Presidents and the Press.* Holbrook, Mass.: Adams Media.

Ford, Gerald R. 1980. *A Time to Heal.* New York: Berkley.

Francis, David R. 1997. "Grand Ol' Party-ers." *Christian Science Monitor,* May 14, 8.

Frendreis, John P., and Raymond Tatalovich. 1994. *The Modern Presidency and Economic Policy.* Itasca, Ill.: Peacock.

Friedman, Leon, and William F. Levantrosser, eds. 1991. *Richard M. Nixon: Politician, President, Administrator.* Westport, Conn.: Greenwood.

Friedman, Thomas P. 1997a. "Now a Word from X." *New York Times,* May 2, 23.

————.1997b. "NATOwater." *New York Times,* May 19, 13.

Fritz, Sara. 1982. "Reagan's Honeymoon with the Press Is Over." *Washington Journalism Review* 4 (April): 37–40.

Gardner, Howard. 1985. *Frames of Mind: The Theory of Multiple Intelligences,* paperback ed. New York: Basic Books.

Garelik, Glenn. 1992. "Presidential Candidates: What Makes Them Run?" *American Health* 9 (October): 44–49.

Garthoff, Raymond L. 1989. *Reflections on the Cuban Missile Crisis,* rev. ed. Washington D.C.: Brookings.

Gelb, Leslie H. 1980. "The Stuggle over Foreign Policy." *New York Times,* July 20, 26–27, 32, 34–40.

————.1982. "Getting Ready for a Prime Time News Conference." *New York Times,* October 26, 10.

————.1994. "Getting Clinton's Foreign Policy Act Together." *Washington Post National Weekly Edition,* March 14–20.

Gellman, Barton, and Steven Mufson. 1999. "Raising the Possibility of a New Internationalism." *Washington Post National Weekly Edition,* June 14, 7.

George, Alexander. 1972. "The Case for Multiple Advocacy in Making Foreign Policy." *American Political Science Review* 66 (September): 751–785.

————. 1980. *Presidential Decisionmaking in Foreign Policy: The Effective Use of Information and Advice.* Boulder, Colo.: Westview.

Gerth, Jeff. 1992. "Policies Under Clinton Are a Boon to Industry." *New York Times,* April 2, A12.

Geyelin, Philip. 1966. *Lyndon B. Johnson and the World.* New York: Praeger.

Geyer, Georgie Anne. 1994. "Clinton's Foreign Policy Stems From '60s Naivete." *Columbus Dispatch,* January 20, 9A.

Giglio, James N. 1991. *The Presidency of John F. Kennedy.* Lawrence: University Press of Kansas.

Glad, Betty. 1980. *Jimmy Carter: In Search of the Great White House.* New York: Norton.

Glen, Maxwell. 1986. "Front-Loading the Race." *National Journal,* November 29, 2882–2886.

Goldman, Eric F. 1969. *The Tragedy of Lyndon Johnson.* New York: Knopf.

Goldman, Peter, Thomas M. DeFrank, Mark Miller, Andrew Murr, and Tom Mathews. 1994. *Quest for the Presidency: 1992.* College Station: Texas A&M University Press.

Graff, Henry F. 1970. *The Tuesday Cabinet: Deliberation and Decision on Peace and War under Lyndon B. Johnson.* Englewood Cliffs, N.J.: Prentice Hall.

Graham, Hugh Davis. 1981. "The Transformation of Federal Education Policy." In *Exploring the Johnson Years,* ed. Robert A. Divine. Austin: University of Texas Press.

Grantham, Dewey W. 1983. *Southern Progressivism: The Reconciliation of Progress and Tradition.* Knoxville: University of Tennessee Press.

Greene, John Robert. 1995. *The Presidency of Gerald R. Ford.* Lawrence: University Press of Kansas.

Greenfield, Meg. 1962. "Why Are You Calling Me, Son?" *Reporter,* August 16, 29–31.

Greenhouse, Linda. 1998. "Starr's Aggressive Advocacy." *New York Times,* September 12, 1, 6.

Greenstein, Fred I. 1982. *The Hidden-Hand Presidency: Eisenhower as Leader.* New York: Basic Books.

————, ed. 1983. *The Reagan Presidency: An Early Assessment.* Baltimore: Johns Hopkins University Press.

————.1987. "Precis." Paper prepared for a conference on Leadership in the Modern Presidency, Princeton University, April 3–4.

————, ed. 1988a. *Leadership in the Modern Presidency.* Cambridge: Harvard University Press.

——— .1988b. "Dwight D. Eisenhower: A Leadership Theorist in the White House." In *Leadership in the Modern Presidency,* ed. Fred I. Greenstein. Cambridge: Harvard University Press.

——— .1993. Personal communication.

——— .1994. "The Presidential Leadership Style of Bill Clinton: An Early Appraisal." *Political Science Quarterly* 108 (Winter 1993–94): 589–601.

——— .1998. "There He Goes Again: The Alternating Political Style of Bill Clinton." *PS* 31 (June): 179–181.

——— .2000. *The Presidential Difference: Leadership Style from FDR to Clinton.* New York: Free Press.

Greider, William. 1987. "The Price of Money." *New Yorker,* November 9, 54–112.

Griffith, Robert. 1982. "Dwight D. Eisenhower and the Corporate Commonwealth." *American Historical Review* 87 (April): 87–122.

Grogan, Fred L. 1977. "Candidate Promise and Presidential Performance: 1964–1972." Paper presented at the annual meeting of the Midwest Political Science Association, Chicago, April 21–23.

Grossman, Michael Baruch, and Martha Joynt Kumar. 1981. *Portraying the President: The White House and the News Media.* Baltimore: Johns Hopkins University Press.

Grossman, Michael Baruch, Martha Joynt Kumar, and Francis E. Rourke. 1985. "The Aging of Administrations: The Waning of Power and the Opportunity for Rejuvenation During Second Terms." Paper presented at the annual meeting of the American Political Science Association, New Orleans, August 28–September 1.

Gwertzman, Bernard. 1972. "Strategic Arms Talks: Long Road to Success." *New York Times,* June 18, 1, 16.

Haas, Lawrence J. 1988. "What OMB Hath Wrought." *National Journal,* September 3, 2187–2191.

Hager, George, and Eric Pianin. 1997. *Mirage: Why Neither Democrats nor Republicans Can Balance the Budget, End the Deficit, and Satisfy the Public.* New York: Times Books.

Haldeman, H. R. 1994. *The Haldeman Diaries: Inside the Nixon White House.* New York: Putnam.

Hall, David K. 1988. "The 'Custodian-Manager' of the Policy-Making Process." In *Decisions of the Highest Order: Perspective on the National Security Council,* ed. Karl F. Inderfurth and Loch K. Johnson. Pacific Grove, Calif.: Brooks/Cole, 146–154.

Hammond, Paul Y. 1992. *LBJ and the Presidential Management of Foreign Relations.* Austin: University of Texas Press.

Hansen, Susan B. 1986. "The Politics of Federal Tax Policy." In *The President and Economic Policy,* ed. James P. Pfiffner. Philadelphia: Institute for the Study of Human Issues.

Harden, Blaine. 1999. "Waging War on the Serbs: Old Problem, New Lessons." *New York Times,* June 6, 1, 12–13.

Hargrove, Erwin C. 1988a. "Jimmy Carter: The Politics of Public Goods." In *Leadership in the Modern Presidency,* ed. Fred I. Greenstein. Cambridge: Harvard University Press.

———.1988b. *Jimmy Carter as President: Leadership and the Politics of the Public Good.* Baton Rouge: Louisiana State University Press.

Hargrove, Erwin C., and Samuel A. Morley. 1984. *The President and the Council of Economic Advisers: Interviews with CEA Chairmen.* Boulder, Colo.: Westview.

Harrington, Walt. 1986. "The Privilege of Being George Bush." *Washington Post National Weekly Edition,* October 6, 6–10.

Harris, John F. 1995. "Clinton, Stuck in the 80s, Keeps Swinging." *International Herald Tribune,* August 23, 19.

———.1997a. "The Man Who Squared the Oval Office." *Washington Post National Weekly Edition,* January 13.

———.1997b. "For Bill Clinton, a Chance to Build His Legacy." *Washington Post National Weekly Edition,* May 12, 9–10.

Havemann, Judith. 1999. "Welfare Reform's Positive Report Card." *Washington Post National Weekly Edition,* June 14, 34.

Heclo, Hugh. 1978. "Issue Networks and the Executive Establishment." In *The New American Political System,* ed. Anthony King. Washington, D.C.: American Enterprise Institute.

———.1981. "The Presidential Illusion." *In The Illusion of Presidential Government,* ed. Hugh Heclo and Lester M. Salamon. Boulder, Colo.: Westview.

Heller, Francis H., ed. 1980. *The Truman White House: The Administration of the Presidency 1945–1953.* Lawrence, Kans.: Regents Press.

Heller, Walter W. 1967. *New Dimensions of Political Economy.* New York: Norton.

Henneberger, Melinda. 1999. "How Henry Hyde's Resolve Was Shaped Against Clinton." *New York Times,* January 10, 1, 14.

Herbers, John. 1994. "In Three Decades, Nixon Tasted Crisis and Defeat, Victory, Ruin and Revival." *New York Times,* April 24, 13–17.

Hermann, Charles F. 1969. *Crises in Foreign Policy: A Simulation Analysis.* Indianapolis: Bobbs-Merrill.

Hershey, Marjorie Randon. 1997. "The Congressional Election." In *The Election of 1996,* ed. Gerald M. Pomper. Chatham, N.J.: Chatham House.

Hershey, Robert D., Jr. 1991. "Going Slow on Economy Is Risky, Aides Tell Bush." *New York Times,* December 1, 14.

———.1993. "Bush's 'Courageous' Economic Error." *New York Times,* January 13, C-5.

Hertsgaard, Mark. 1989. *On Bended Knee: The Press and the Reagan Presidency.* New York: Schocken.

Hess, Stephen. 1976. *Organizing the Presidency.* Washington, D.C.: Brookings.

———.1981. *The Washington Reporters.* Washington, D.C.: Brookings.

———.1984. *The Government/Press Connection: Press Officers and Their Offices.* Washington, D.C.: Brookings.

———.1988. *Organizing the Presidency,* 2d ed. Washington, D.C.: Brookings.

Hess, Stephen, and David S. Broder. 1967. *The Republican Establishment: The Present and the Future of the GOP.* New York: Harper and Row.

Hobbs, Edward H. 1954. *Behind the President: A Study of Executive Office Agencies.* Washington, D.C.: Public Affairs Press.

Hochman, Steven H. 1991. Personal communication.

Hoff, Joan. 1988. "Richard M. Nixon: The Corporate Presidency." In *Leadership in the Modern Presidency,* ed. Fred I. Greenstein. Cambridge: Harvard University Press.

Hoffman, David. 1988. "Patrician with a Common Touch." *Washington Post National Weekly Edition,* October 14–20, 6–7.

———.1989a. "One Hundred Days of Solitude." *Washington Post National Weekly Edition,* May 8–14, 13.

———.1989b. "Bush: Making Himself Up As He Goes Along." *Washington Post,* August 13, B1, B4.

———.1989c. "The Politics of Timidity." *Washington Post National Weekly Edition,* October 23–29, 6–7.

———.1990a. "Zip My Lips: George Bush's Penchant for Secret Decisions." *Washington Post National Weekly Edition,* January 15–21, 23–24.

———.1990b. "What Bush Lacks in Style He Makes Up for in Method." *Washington Post National Weekly Edition,* April 2–8, 24.

Holbrooke, Richard. 1998a. "Why Are We in Bosnia?" *New Yorker,* May 18, 39–45.

———.1998b. *To End a War.* New York: Random House.

Holmes, Steven A. 1992. "Race Relations in Arkansas Reflect Gains for Clinton, but Raise Questions." *New York Times,* April 3, A10.

Holsti, Ole R. 1988. "Crisis Decision-Making." Duke University. Mimeo.

———.1997. "Continuity and Change in the Domestic and Foreign Policy Beliefs of American Opinion Leaders." Paper presented at the annual meeting of the American Political Science Association, Washington, August 28–31.

Holsti, Ole R., and James N. Rosenau. 1984. *American Leaderhip in World Affairs.* Boston: Allen and Unwin.

———.1986. "Consensus Lost. Consensus Regained? Foreign Policy Beliefs of American Leaders, 1976–1980." *International Studies Quarterly* 30 (December): 375–409.

———.1988. "The Structure of Foreign Policy Attitudes: American Leaders, 1976–1984." Paper presented at the Mershon Center, Ohio State University, May 14.

———.1993. "The Structure of Foreign Policy Beliefs Among American Opinion Leaders: After the Cold War." *Millennium: Journal of International Studies* 22: 235–278.

———.1997. Personal communication.

Holtzman, Abraham. 1970. *Legislative Liaison: Executive Leadership in Congress.* Chicago: Rand-McNally.

Hult, Karen M., and Charles Walcott. 1988. "Writing for the President: Evolution of an Organizational Function." Paper presented at the annual meeting of the American Political Science Association, Washington, September 1–4.

———. 1989. "To Meet the Press: Tracing the Evolution of White House Press Operations." Paper presented at the annual meeting of the Midwest Political Science Association, Chicago, April 15–17.

Huntington, Samuel P. 1983. "The Defense Policy of the Reagan Administration." In *The Reagan Presidency: An Early Assessment,* ed. Fred I. Greenstein. Baltimore: Johns Hopkins University Press.

Ifill, Gwen. 1993a. "A Campaigner Adjusts to Life as the President." *New York Times,* February 15, C6.

———. 1993b. "Economic Plan Grew Slowly Out of a Marathon of Debate." *New York Times,* February 21, 14.

———. 1994. "Looking for a White Knight to Do the Same Old Thing." *New York Times,* January 7, A10.

Ignatieff, Michael. 1999. "The Virtual Commander." *New Yorker,* August 2, 30–36.

Inderfurth Karl F., and Loch K. Johnson, eds. 1988. *Decisions of the Highest Order: Perspective on the National Security Council.* Pacific Grove, Calif.: Brooks/Cole.

Ingwerson, Marshall. 1990. "Bush Effort to Set Goals for Education Earns Praise." *Christian Science Monitor,* February 6, 1–2.

Ippolito, Dennis S. 1990. *Uncertain Legacies: Federal Budget Policy from Roosevelt through Reagan.* Charlottesville: University Press of Virginia.

Janeway, Michael C. 1960. "Lyndon Johnson and the Rise of Conservatism in Texas." Honors thesis, Harvard College.

Johnson, Haynes, and David S. Broder. 1996. *The System: The American Way of Politics at the Breaking Point.* Boston: Little, Brown.

Johnson, Loch K. 1996. *Secret Agencies: U.S. Intelligence in a Hostile World.* New Haven: Yale University Press.

———. 1997. "Reinventing the CIA: Strategic Intelligence and the End of the Cold War." In *U.S. Foreign Policy After the Cold War,* ed. James M. Lindsay and Randall B. Ripley. Pittsburgh: University of Pittsburgh Press.

Johnson, Lyndon B. 1971. *The Vantage Point: Perspectives on the Presidency 1963–1969.* New York: Popular Library.

Johnston, David. 1988. "Upbeat 'Head Hunter' for a Lame Duck President." *New York Times,* February 16, 28.

Jones, Charles O. 1968. "The Minority Party and Policy-Making in the House of Representatives." *American Political Science Review* 62 (June): 358–367.

———. 1970. *The Minority Party in Congress.* Boston: Little, Brown.

———. 1979. "Congress and the Making of Energy Policy." In *New Dimensions of Energy Policy,* ed. Robert Lawrence. Lexington, Mass.: Lexington Books.

———. 1981. "Congress and the Presidency." In *The New Congress,* ed. Thomas E. Mann and Norman J. Ornstein. Washington, D.C.: American Enterprise Institute.

———. 1983. "Presidential Negotiation with Congress." In *Both Ends of the Avenue,* ed. Anthony King. Washington, D.C.: American Enterprise Institute.

———. 1987. Comments at panel on "Predicting the Reagan Presidency: The

Contributions of Political Science." Annual meeting of the American Political Science Association, September 3–6, 1987.

———.1988a. *The Trusteeship Presidency: Jimmy Carter and the United States Congress.* Baton Rouge: Louisiana State University Press.

———, ed. 1988b. *The Reagan Legacy: Promise and Performance.* Chatham, N.J.: Chatham House.

———.1988c. "Ronald Reagan and the U.S. Congress: Visible-Hand Politics." In *The Reagan Legacy: Promise and Performance,* ed. Charles O. Jones. Chatham, N.J.: Chatham House.

———.1991. "Meeting Low Expectations: Strategy and Prospects for the Bush Presidency." In *The Bush Presidency: First Appraisals,* ed. Colin Campbell and Bert A. Rockman. Chatham, N.J.: Chatham House.

———.1994. *The Presidency in a Separated System.* Washington, D.C.: Brookings.

———.1995. "Campaigning to Govern: The Clinton Style." In *The Clinton Presidency: First Appraisals,* ed. Colin Campbell and Bert A. Rockman. Chatham, N.J.: Chatham House.

Jones, Roger W. 1980. "The Executive Office Agencies." In *The Truman White House: The Administration of the Presidency, 1945–1953,* ed. Francis H. Heller. Lawrence, Kans.: Regents Press.

Jordan, Hamilton. 1982. *Crisis: The Last Year of the Carter Presidency.* New York: Putnam.

Kalb, Marvin, and Bernard Kalb. 1974. *Kissinger.* New York: Dell.

Kearns, Doris. 1976. "Lyndon Johnson's Political Personality." *Political Science Quarterly* 91 (Fall): 385–409.

———.1977. *Lyndon Johnson and the American Dream.* New York: Signet.

Kelley, Stanley, Jr. 1956. *Professional Public Relations and Political Power.* Baltimore: Johns Hopkins University Press.

Kelly, Michael. 1994. "The President's Past." *New York Times Magazine,* July 31, 20–29, 34, 38, 45.

Kennan, George F. 1997. "A Fateful Error." *New York Times,* February 5.

Kernell, Samuel. 1979. "Explaining Presidential Popularity." *American Political Science Review* 72 (June): 506–522.

———.1985. "Campaigning, Governing and the Contemporary Presidency." In *The New Direction in American Politics,* ed. John E. Chubb and Paul E. Peterson. Washington, D.C.: Brookings.

———.1986. *Going Public: New Strategies of Presidential Leadership.* Washington, D.C.: CQ Press. ·

Kernell, Samuel, and Samuel L. Popkin, eds. 1986. *Chief of Staff: Twenty-Five Years of Managing the Presidency.* Berkeley: University of California Press.

Kessel, John H. 1974. "The Parameters of Presidential Politics." *Social Science Quarterly* 55 (June): 8–24.

———.1977. "The Seasons of Presidential Politics." *Social Science Quarterly* 58 (December): 418–435.

———.1984a. "The Structures of the Reagan White House." *American Journal of Political Science* 28 (May): 231–258.

———.1984b. *Presidential Parties.* Homewood, Ill.: Dorsey.

———.1988. *Presidential Campaign Politics: Coalition Strategies and Citizen Response,* 3d ed. Chicago: Dorsey.

———.1992. *Presidential Campaign Politics,* 4th ed. Pacific Grove, Calif.: Brooks/Cole.

Kettl, Donald F. 1986. *Leadership at the Fed.* New Haven: Yale University Press.

———.1987. "The Political Education of Lyndon Johnson: Guns, Butter, and Taxes." In *The Johnson Years,* vol. 2, *Vietnam, the Environment, and Science,* ed. Robert A. Divine. Lawrence: University Press of Kansas.

Kiewiet, D. Roderick, and Douglas Rivers. 1985. "The Economic Basis of Reagan's Appeal." In *The New Direction in American Politics,* ed. John E. Chubb and Paul E. Peterson. Washington, D.C.: Brookings.

Kilborn, Peter T. 1985. "How the Big Six Steer the Economy." *New York Times,* November 17, F1, F8–F9.

Kilborn, Peter T., and Sam Howe Verhovek. 1996. "Clinton's Welfare Shift Reflects New Democrat." *New York Times,* August 2, A1, A8–A9.

King, Anthony, ed. 1978. *The New American Political System.* Washington, D.C.: American Enterprise Institute.

———, ed. 1983. *Both Ends of the Avenue: The Presidency, the Executive Branch, and Congress in the 1980s.* Washington, D.C.: American Enterprise Institute.

King, Gary, and Lyn Ragsdale. 1988. *The Elusive Executive: Discovering Statistical Patterns in the Presidency.* Washington, D.C.: CQ Press.

King, Ronald F. 1985. "The President and Fiscal Policy in 1966: The Year Taxes Were Not Raised." *Polity* 18 (Summer): 684–714.

———.1993. *Money, Time and Politics: Investment Tax Subsidies and American Democracy.* New Haven: Yale University Press.

Kingdon, John W. 1984. *Agendas, Alternatives, and Public Policies.* Boston: Little, Brown.

Kosterlitz, Julie, and W. John Moore. 1988. "Saving the Welfare State." *National Journal,* May 14, 1276–1288.

KPBS. 1990. *The Presidency, the Press, and the People.* A co-production of KPBS-TV and the University of California, San Diego, taped January 5, 1990. Mimeographed transcript.

Krosnick, Jon A., and Laura A. Brannon. 1993. "The Impact of the Gulf War on the Ingredients of Presidential Evaluation: Multidimensional Effects of Political Involvement." *American Political Science Review* 87 (December): 963–975.

Krosnick, Jon A., and Richard E. Petty. 1995. "Attitude Strength: An Overview." In *Attitude Strength: Antecedents and Consequences,* ed. Richard E. Petty and Jon A. Krosnick. Hillsdale, N.J.: Erlbaum.

Krosnick, Jon A., D. S. Boninger, Y. C. Chuang, M. C. Berent, and C. G. Carnot. 1993. "Attitude Strength: One Construct or Many Related Constructs?" *Journal of Personality and Social Psychology* 65: 1132–1151.

Kumar, Martha Joynt. 1994. "The President as Message and Manager: Personal Style and Presidential Communication." Paper presented at the annual meeting of the American Political Science Association, New York, September 1–4.

———— .1995. "The Place of Communications in the Campaign to Mobilize for Change: The Clinton and Reagan Models." Paper presented at the annual meeting of the Midwest Political Science Association, Chicago, April 6–8.

———— .1996. "The White House Beat at the Century Mark: Reporters Establish Position to Cover the 'Elective Kingship.'" Paper presented at the annual meeting of the American Political Science Association, San Francisco, August 29–September 1.

———— .1997a. "The President and the News Media." In *The President, the Public, and the Parties,* 2d ed. Washington, D.C.: CQ Press.

———— .1997b. "The White House Beat at the Century Mark." *Press/Politics* 2 (3):10–30.

Kumar, Martha Joynt, and Terry Sullivan. 1996. "The White House Communications Director: Presidential Fire Walker." Paper presented at the annual meeting of the Midwest Political Science Association, Chicago, April 18–20.

Kurtz, Howard. 1998. *Spin Cycle: Inside the Clinton Propaganda Machine.* New York: Free Press.

Kymlicka, B. B., and Jean V. Matthews, eds. 1988. *The Reagan Revolution?* Chicago: Dorsey.

Lacy, Alex B., Jr. 1967. "The Development of the White House Office, 1939–1967." Paper presented at the annual meeting of the American Political Science Association, Chicago, September 5–9.

Leadership Directories. 2000. *Federal Yellow Book Spring 2000: Who's Who in Federal Departments and Agencies.* Washington, D.C.: Leadership Directories.

Leuchtenberg, William E. 1983. *In the Shadow of FDR: From Harry Truman to Ronald Reagan.* Ithaca, N.Y.: Cornell University Press.

Lieber, Robert J. 1990. "The Middle East." In *Looking Back on the Reagan Presidency,* ed. Larry Berman. Baltimore: Johns Hopkins University Press.

Light, Paul C.1985. *Artful Work: The Politics of Social Security Reform.* New York: Random House.

———— . 1991. *The President's Agenda: Domestic Policy Choice from Kennedy to Reagan,* rev. ed. Baltimore: Johns Hopkins University Press.

———— .1999. *The President's Agenda: Domestic Policy Choice from Kennedy to Clinton,* 3d ed. Baltimore: Johns Hopkins University Press.

Light, Paul C., and Celinda Lake. 1985. "The Election: Candidates, Strategies, and Decisions." In *The Elections of 1984,* ed. Michael Nelson. Washington, D.C.: CQ Press.

Lindsay, James M., and Randall B. Ripley, eds. 1997. *U.S. Foreign Policy after the Cold War.* Pittsburgh: University of Pittsburgh Press.

Lippman, Thomas, and Ann Devroy. 1995. "Matching Policy to Rhetoric." *Washington Post National Weekly Edition,* September 18–24, 6–7.

Mackaye, Milton. 1960. "Ike's Man Friday." *Saturday Evening Post,* May 21, 34–35, 52, 54, 57–58.

MacKenzie, G. Calvin. 1981a. *The Politics of Presidential Appointments.* New York: Free Press.

————.1981b. "Cabinet and Subcabinet Personnel Selection in Reagan's First Year: New Variations on Some Not-So-Old Themes." Paper delivered at the annual meeting of the American Political Science Association, Chicago, September 3–6, 1981.

MacNeil, Neil. 1970. *Dirksen.* New York: World.

Malbin, Michael J. 1983. "Rhetoric and Leadership: A Look Backward at the Carter National Energy Plan." In *Both Ends of the Avenue: The Presidency, the Executive Branch, and Congress in the 1980s,* ed. Anthony King. Washington, D.C.: American Enterprise Institute.

Maltese, John Anthony. 1992. *Spin Control: The White House Office of Communications and the Management of Presidential News.* Chapel Hill: University of North Carolina Press.

————.1994. *Spin Control: The White House Office of Communications and the Management of Presidential News,* 2d ed., rev. Chapel Hill: University of North Carolina Press.

Maraniss, David. 1992a. "Mixed Reviews on Gov. Clinton from His Audience Back Home." *Washington Post National Weekly Edition,* February 10–16, 15–16.

————.1992b. "A Political Life: William Jefferson Clinton" (a series of three articles). *Washington Post,* July 13–15.

————.1992c. "The Place Where Clinton's Coming From." *Washington Post,* September 30, B1, B4.

————.1992d. "What Kind of a President?" *Washington Post,* October 25, A1, A18.

————.1994. "Clinton's Past as Prologue." *Washington Post National Weekly Edition,* December 5–11, 6–7.

————.1995. *First in His Class: The Biography of Bill Clinton.* New York: Simon and Schuster.

————.1998. "Clinton's Personality Patterns." *Washington Post National Weekly Edition,* February 2, 6–8.

Matalin, Mary, and James Carville, with Peter Knobler. 1994. *All's Fair: Love, War, and Running for President.* New York: Random House.

Matthews, Donald R. 1976. "Winnowing: The News Media and the 1976 Presidential Nominations." In *Race for the Presidency: The Media and the Nominating Process,* ed. James David Barber Englewood Cliffs, N.J.: Prentice Hall.

Matuso, Allen J. 1998. *Nixon's Economy: Booms, Busts, Dollars, and Votes.* Lawrence: University Press of Kansas.

May, Ernest R., and Philip D. Zelikow. 1997. *The Kennedy Tapes: Inside the White House during the Cuban Missile Crisis.* Cambridge: Belknap.

Mazo, Earl. 1959. *Richard Nixon: A Personal and Political Portrait.* New York: Harper.

McClelland, David C. 1961. *The Achieving Society.* New York: Free Press.

McConnell, Grant. 1963. *Steel and the Presidency, 1962.* New York: Norton.

McPherson, Harry. 1972. *A Political Education.* Boston: Little, Brown.

Miller, Warren E., and M. Kent Jennings. 1986. *Parties in Transition: A Longitudinal Study of Party Elites and Party Supporters.* New York: Russell Sage Foundation.

Miroff, Bruce. 1976. *Pragmatic Illusions: The Presidential Politics of John F. Kennedy.* New York: McKay.

Monroe, Kristen R. 1984. *Presidential Popularity and the Economy.* New York: Praeger.

Moynihan, Daniel P. 1973. *The Politics of a Guaranteed Income: The Nixon Administration and the Family Assistance Plan.* New York: Vintage.

Mueller, Keith, and Mary Daake. 1994. "Social Policy in the Clinton Administration." Paper presented at the annual meeting of the Midwest Political Science Association, Chicago, April 14–16.

Munger, Frank J., and Richard F. Fenno. 1962. *National Politics and Federal Aid to Education.* Syracuse: Syracuse University Press.

Myers, Steven Lee. 2000. "Russian Resistance a Key to Delay on Missile Shield." *New York Times,* September 3, 1, 10.

*National Journal.* 1988. "Reagan's Legacy: The Paradox of Power." May 14, 1241–1314.

Nelson, Anna Kasten. 1981. "National Security I: Inventing a Process (1945–1960)." In *The Illusion of Presidential Government,* ed. Hugh Heclo and Lester M. Salamon. Boulder, Colo.: Westview.

Nessen, Ron. 1978. *It Sure Looks Different from the Inside.* Chicago: Playboy.

Neustadt, Richard E. 1954. "Presidency and Legislation: The Growth of Central Clearance." *American Political Science Review* 48 (September): 641–671.

———. 1955. "Presidency and Legislation: Planning the President's Program." *American Political Science Review* 49 (December): 980–1021.

———. 1956. "The Presidency at Mid-Century." *Law and Contemporary Problems* 21 (Autumn): 609–645.

———. 1960. *Presidential Power: The Politics of Leadership.* New York: Wiley.

———. 1968. *Presidential Power: The Politics of Leadership with an Afterword on JFK.* New York: Wiley.

———. 1970. *Alliance Politics.* New York: Columbia University Press.

———. 1987. "Does the White House Need a Strong Chief of Staff?" *Presidency Research* 10 (Fall): 7–10.

———. 1980a. *Presidential Power: The Politics of Leadership from FDR to Carter.* New York: Wiley.

———. 1980b. "The White House Staff: Later Period." In *The Truman White House: The Administration of the Presidency, 1945–1953,* ed. Francis H. Heller. Lawrence, Kans.: Regents Press.

———. 1986. "Forward." In *Chief of Staff: Twenty-Five Years of Managing the Presidency,* ed. Samuel Kernell and Samuel L. Popkin. Berkeley: University of California Press.

Neustadt, Richard E., and Ernest R. May. 1986. *Thinking in Time: The Uses of History for Decision Makers.* New York: Free Press.

Newcomb, Theodore N., Ralph H. Turner, and Philip E. Converse. 1965. *Social Psychology: The Study of Human Interaction.* New York: Holt, Rinehart and Winston.

Nivola, Pietro. 1979. "The Natural Gas Policy Act of 1978." Paper presented at the annual meeting of the American Political Science Association, Washington, D.C.

Noonan, Peggy. 1990. *What I Saw at the Revolution: A Political Life in the Reagan Era.* New York: Ballantine.

Nordhaus, William. 1975. "The Political Business Cycle." *Review of Economic Studies* 42 (April): 169–190.

Oberdorfer, Don. 1988. "A Moderate Foreign Policy, Low on Ideology." *Washington Post National Weekly Edition,* November 14–20, 7–8.

———.1991. *The Turn from the Cold War to a New Era: The United States and the Soviet Union, 1983–1990.* New York: Poseidon.

O'Brien, Lawrence F. 1974. *No Final Victories: A Life in Politics—from John F. Kennedy to Watergate.* New York: Doubleday.

Office of Management and Budget. 1994. "Making OMB More Effective in Serving the Presidency: Changes as a Result of the OMB 2000 Review." Office Memorandum No. 94-16, March 1.

Office of the Federal Registrar. 1999. *The United States Government Manual, 1999/2000.* Washington, D.C.: U.S. Government Printing Office.

Olson, Lynne. 1981. "The Reticence of Ronald Reagan." *Washington Journalism Review* 3 (November): 42–44.

O'Neill, Thomas P., with William Novak. 1987. *Man of the House: The Life and Political Memories of Speaker Tip O'Neill.* New York: Random House.

Ornstein, Norman J. 1983. "The Open Congress Meets the President." In *Both Ends of the Avenue: The Presidency, the Executive Branch, and Congress in the 1980s,* ed. Anthony King. Washington, D.C.: American Enterprise Institute.

———.1988. "What Should Sununu Do?" *Washington Post,* December 30, A19.

Ornstein, Norman J., Thomas E. Mann, and Michael J. Malbin. 1987. *Vital Statistics on Congress, 1987–1988.* Washington, D.C.: Congressional Quarterly.

———.1996. *Vital Statistics on Congress, 1995–1996.* Washington, D.C.: Congressional Quarterly.

Ornstein, Norman J., Thomas E. Mann, Michael J. Malbin, Allen Schick, and John F. Bibby. 1984. *Vital Statistics on Congress, 1984–1985.* Washington, D.C.: American Enterprise Institute.

Osborne, John. 1977. *White House Watch: The Ford Years.* Washington, D.C.: New Republic Books.

Pach, Chester J., and Elmo Richardson. 1991. *The Presidency of Dwight D. Eisenhower.* Lawrence: University Press of Kansas.

Page, Benjamin I. 1978. *Choices and Echoes in Presidential Elections: Rational Man and Electoral Democracy.* Chicago: University of Chicago Press.

Palmer, John L., and Isabel V. Sawhill. 1984. *The Reagan Record.* Cambridge: Ballinger.

Parmet, Herbert S. 1972. *Eisenhower and the American Crusades.* New York: Macmillan.

————.1980. *Jack: The Struggles of John F. Kennedy*. New York: Dial.

————.1983. *JFK: The Presidency of John F. Kennedy*. New York: Dial.

————.1997. *George Bush: The Life of a Lone Star Yankee*. New York: Scribner's.

Pastor, Robert A. 1990. "The Centrality of Central America." In *Looking Back on the Reagan Presidency*, ed. Larry Berman. Baltimore: Johns Hopkins University Press.

Patterson, Bradley H., Jr. 1988. *The Ring of Power: The White House Staff and Its Expanding Role in Government*. New York: Basic Books.

Pear, Robert. 1993. "Expert's Grades: A in Security, C in Simplicity, D+ in Savings." *New York Times*, September 24, A10.

————.1994. "Early Doubts on Health, Papers Show." *New York Times*, September 8, A11.

————.1996. "Clinton to Sign Welfare Bill." *New York Times*, August 1, A1, A8.

Pechman, Joseph A. 1975. "Making Economic Policy." In *Handbook of Political Science*, vol. 6, ed. Fred I. Greenstein and Nelson W. Polsby. Reading, Mass.: Addison Wesley.

————.1987. *Federal Tax Policy*, 5th ed. Washington, D.C.: Brookings.

Penner, Rudolph G., and Hugh Heclo. 1983. "Fiscal and Political Strategy in the Reagan Administration." In *The Reagan Presidency: An Early Assessment*, ed. Fred I. Greenstein. Baltimore: Johns Hopkins University Press.

*Pentagon Papers*. 1971. *The Pentagon Papers: The Complete and Unabridged Series as Published in the* New York Times. New York: Bantam.

Peterson, Mark A. 1990. *Legislating Together: The White House and Capitol Hill from Eisenhower to Reagan*. Cambridge: Harvard University Press.

Peterson, Paul E., and Mark Rom. 1988. "Lower Taxes, More Spending, and Budget Deficits." In *The Reagan Legacy: Promise and Performance*, ed. Charles O. Jones. Chatham, N.J.: Chatham House.

Pfiffner, James P., ed. 1986. *The President and Economic Policy*. Philadelphia: Institute for the Study of Human Issues.

Pichirallo, Joe, and Patrick E. Tyler. 1990. "Countdown to an Invasion." *Washington Post National Weekly Edition*, January 22–28, 31–32.

Pierce, Lawrence C. 1971. *The Politics of Fiscal Policy Formation*. Pacific Palisades, Calif.: Goodyear Press.

————.1972. "Politics and Nixon's New Economic Policy." Paper presented at the annual meeting of the American Political Science Association, Washington, D.C., September 5–9.

Pika, Joseph A. 1984. "Changing Players But Not the Game: The Organizational Presidency." Paper presented at the annual meeting of the American Political Science Association, Washington, D.C., August 30–September 2.

Pinker, Steven. 1997. *How the Mind Works*. New York: Norton.

————.1999. "His Brain Measured Up." *New York Times*, June 24, A31.

Pomper, Gerald M. 1997. "The Presidential Election." In *The Election of 1996*, ed. Gerald M. Pomper. Chatham, N.J.: Chatham House.

Pomper, Gerald M., and Susan S. Lederman. 1980. *Elections in America: Control and Influence in Democratic Politics*, 2d ed. New York: Longman.

Porter, Roger B. 1980. *Presidential Decision Making: The Economic Policy Board.* New York: Cambridge University Press.

————.1988. "Gerald R. Ford: A Healing Presidency." In *Leadership in the Modern Presidency,* ed. Fred I. Greenstein. Cambridge: Harvard University Press.

Prados, John. 1991. *Keepers of the Keys: A History of the National Security Council from Truman to Bush.* New York: Morrow.

Price, Raymond. 1977. *With Nixon.* New York: Viking.

Priest, Dana. 1999a. "The War That Never Was." *Washington Post National Weekly Edition,* September 27, 6–9.

————.1999b. "Divided, They Withstood." *Washington Post National Weekly Edition,* October 4, 8–9.

Powell, Jody. 1984. *The Other Side of the Story.* New York: Morrow.

Purdum, Todd S. 1996. "Clinton Recalls His Promise, Considers History, and Signs." *New York Times,* August 1, A1, A8.

Quandt, William B. 1986. *Camp David: Peacemaking and Politics.* Washington, D.C.: Brookings.

————.1994. "Discussion on Middle East Problems and Politics." In *Jimmy Carter: Foreign Policy and Post-Presidential Years,* ed. Herbert D. Rosenbaum and Alexej Ugrinsky. Westport, Conn.: Greenwood, 160–163.

Quirk, Paul J. 1991. "Domestic Policy: Divided Government and Cooperative Presidential Leadership." In *The Bush Presidency: First Appraisals,* ed. Colin Campbell and Bert A. Rockman. Chatham, N.J.: Chatham House.

Quirk, Paul J., and Joseph Hinchliffe. 1996. "Domestic Policy: The Trials of a Centrist Democrat." In *The Clinton Presidency: First Appraisals,* ed. Colin Campbell and Bert A. Rockman. Chatham, N.J.: Chatham House.

Quirk, Paul J., and William Cunion. 1999. "Clinton's Domestic Policy: The Lessons of a 'New Democrat.'" In *The Clinton Legacy,* ed. Colin Campbell and Bert A. Rockman. New York: Chatham House.

Ragsdale, Lyn. 1984. "The Politics of Presidential Speechmaking." *American Political Science Review* 78 (December): 971–984.

————.1996. *Vital Statistics on the Presidency: Washington to Clinton.* Washington, D.C.: CQ Press.

Ragsdale, Lyn, and John J. Theis III. 1997. "The Institutionalization of the American Presidency, 1924–1992." *American Journal of Political Science* 41 (October): 121–139.

Ranney, Austin, ed. 1981. *The American Elections of 1980.* Washington, D.C.: American Enterprise Institute.

————.1985. *The American Elections of 1984.* Durham, N.C.: Duke University Press.

Rattner, Steven. 1980. "Rating Carter on the Economy." *New York Times,* October 8, 21, 23.

Rauch, Jonathan, Lawrence J. Haas, and Bruce Stokes. 1988. "Payment Deferred." *National Journal,* May 14, 1256–1265.

Reeves, Richard. 1993. *President Kennedy: Profile of Power.* New York: Simon and Schuster.

Reichley, A. James. 1981. *Conservatives in an Age of Change: The Nixon and Ford Administrations.* Washington, D.C.: Brookings.

Rice, Condoleezza. 1990. "US-Soviet Relations." In *Looking Back on the Reagan Presidency,* ed. Larry Berman. Baltimore: Johns Hopkins University Press.

Riker, William H., and Donald Niemi. 1962. "Stability of Roll Calls in the House of Representatives." *American Political Science Review* 56 (March): 58–65.

Ripley, Randall B. 1972. *Kennedy and Congress.* Morristown, N.J.: General Learning Press.

———.1988. *Congress: Process and Policy,* 4th ed. New York: Norton.

Rockman, Bert A. 1981. "America's Departments of State: Regular and Irregular Syndromes of Policy Making." *American Political Science Review* 75 (December): 911–927.

———.1991. "The Leadership Style of George Bush." In *The Bush Presidency: First Appraisals,* ed. Colin Campbell and Bert A. Rockman. Chatham, N.J.: Chatham House.

———.1995a. "Leadership in the Post–Cold War World: Clinton Meets Foreign Policy." Paper presented at the annual meeting of the Midwest Political Science Association, Chicago, April 6–8.

———.1995b. "Leadership Style and the Clinton Presidency." In *The Clinton Presidency: First Appraisals,* ed. Colin Campbell and Bert A. Rockman. Chatham, N.J.: Chatham House.

———.1997. "The Presidency and Bureaucratic Change after the Cold War." In *U.S. Foreign Policy after the Cold War,* ed. James M. Lindsay and Randall B. Ripley. Pittsburgh: University of Pittsburgh Press.

Rosenbaum, David E. 1995. "Good Economics Joins with Very Good Politics." *New York Times,* June 15, A-11.

Rowen, Hobart. 1980. "Superb Rhetoric, Terrible Performance." *Washington Post,* October 16, A-19.

Safire, William. 1975. *Before the Fall: An Insider's View of the Pre-Watergate White House.* New York: Doubleday.

Salinger, Pierre. 1966. *With Kennedy.* New York: Doubleday.

Saunders, Harold H. 1988. "Beyond 'Us' and 'Them': Building Mature International Relationships." Washington, D.C.: Brookings. Mimeo.

———.1994. "Discussion on Middle East Problems and Politics." In *Jimmy Carter: Foreign Policy and Post-Presidential Years,* ed. Herbert D. Rosenbaum and Alexej Ugrinsky. Westport, Conn.: Greenwood.

Sciolino, Elaine, and Ethan Bronner. 1999. "How a President, Distracted by Scandal, Entered Balkan War." *New York Times,* April 18, 1, 12–13.

Schlesinger, Arthur M., Jr. 1965. *A Thousand Days: John F. Kennedy in the White House.* Boston: Houghton Mifflin.

Schram, Martin. 1977. *Running for President, 1976: The Carter Campaign.* New York: Stein and Day.

Schultze, Charles L. 1994. "Discussion on Domestic Policies." In *The Presidency and Domestic Policies of Jimmy Carter,* ed. Herbert D. Rosenbaum and Alexej Ugrinsky. Westport, Conn.: Greenwood.

Sears, John. 1980. "President Reagan: An Endorser of Others' Decisions." *Washington Post,* November 9, D1, D4.

Shuman, Howard E. 1992. *Politics and the Budget: The Struggle Between the President and the Congress,* 3d ed. New York: Prentice Hall.

Simendinger, Alexis. 1997 "Horse-Trading at the Finish Line." *National Journal,* November 8, 2254–2255.

Simon, Herbert A. 1959. "Theories of Decision-Making in Economics and Behavioral Science." *American Economic Review* 49 (June): 253–283.

———. 1985. "Human Nature in Politics: The Dialogue of Psychology with Political Science." *American Political Science Review* 79 (June): 293–304.

Simon, Herbert A., Donald W. Smithburg, and Victor A. Thompson. 1950. *Public Administration.* New York: Knopf.

Sinclair, Barbara. 1977. "From Party Voting to Regional Fragmentation: The House of Representatives, 1933–1956." Paper presented at the annual meeting of the American Political Science Association, Chicago, September 1–4.

———. 1980. "House Voting Alignments in the 1970s: The Effects of New Members." Paper presented at the annual meeting of the Midwest Political Science Association, Chicago, April 24–27.

———. 1981. "The Speaker's Task Force in the Post-Reform House of Representatives." *American Political Science Review* 75 (June): 397–410.

———. 1991. "Governing Unheroically (and Sometimes Unappetizingly): George Bush and the 101st Congress." In *The Bush Presidency: First Appraisals,* ed. Colin Campbell and Bert A. Rockman. Chatham, N.J.: Chatham House.

———. 1996. "Trying to Govern Positively in a Negative Era: Clinton and the 103rd Congress." In *The Clinton Presidency: First Appraisals,* ed. Colin Campbell and Bert A. Rockman. Chatham, N.J.: Chatham House.

———. 1998. "The Plot Thickens: Congress and the President." In *Great Theater: The American Congress in the 1990s,* ed. Herbert F. Weisberg and Samuel C. Patterson. New York: Cambridge University Press.

———. 1999. "The President as Legislative Leader." In *The Clinton Legacy,* ed. Colin Campbell and Bert A. Rockman. New York: Chatham House.

Small, Melvin. 1999. *The Presidency of Richard Nixon.* Lawrence: University Press of Kansas.

Smith, Hedrick. 1988. *The Power Game: How Washington Works.* New York: Ballantine Books.

Smith, R. Jeffrey, and Walter Pincus. 1995. "Director of the Central Intelligence Budget." *Washington Post National Weekly Edition,* December 18–24.

Solomon, Bert. 1994. "Despite a Take-Charge Conductor, the Orchestra Is Still Off Key." *National Journal,* October 1, 2298–2299.

Sorensen, Theodore C. 1963. *Decision-Making in the White House.* New York: Columbia University Press.

———. 1966. *Kennedy.* New York: Bantam Books.

Speakes, Larry, with Robert Pack. 1988. *Speaking Out.* New York: Scribner's.

Staats, Elmer B. 1980. "The Executive Office Agencies." In *The Truman White House: The Administration of the Presidency, 1945–1953*, ed. Francis H. Heller. Lawrence, Kans.: Regents Press.

Steel, Ronald. 1980. *Walter Lippmann and the American Century.* Boston: Atlantic/Little, Brown.

Stein, Herbert. 1985. *Presidential Economics: The Making of Economic Policy from Roosevelt to Reagan and Beyond*, rev. ed. New York: Simon and Schuster.

Steinbruner, John D. 1974. *The Cybernetic Theory of Decision.* Princeton: Princeton University Press.

Stephanopoulos, George. 1999. *All Too Human: A Political Education.* Boston: Little, Brown.

Stevens, William K. 1989. "Researchers Find Acid Rain Imperils Forests over Time." *New York Times,* December 31, 1,16.

Stever, H. Guyford. 1980. "Science Advice: Out of and Back Into the White House." In *Science Advice to the President,* ed. William T. Golden. New York: Pergamon Press.

Stockman, David A. 1987. *The Triumph of Politics.* New York: Avon.

Stockton, Paul N. 1997. "When the Bear Leaves the Woods: Department of Defense Reorganization in the Post–Cold War Era." In *U.S. Foreign Policy After the Cold War,* ed. James M. Lindsay and Randall B. Ripley. Pittsburgh: University of Pittsburgh Press.

Stokes, Donald E. 1966. "Some Dynamic Elements of Contests for the Presidency." *American Political Science Review* 60 (March): 19–28.

Sullivan, John L., and Robert E. O'Connor. 1972. "Electoral Choice and Popular Control of Public Policy: The Case of the 1966 House Elections." *American Political Science Review* 66 (December): 1256–1268.

Sullivan, Terry. 1990. "Bargaining with the President: A Simple Game and New Evidence." *American Political Science Review* 84 (December): 1167–1195.

Sundquist, James L. 1968. *Politics and Policy; The Eisenhower, Kennedy, and Johnson Years.* Washington, D.C.: Brookings.

Taylor, Richard. 1962. "Pressure Groups and the Democratic Platform: Kennedy in Control." In *Inside Politics: The National Conventions, 1960,* ed. Paul Tillett. Dobbs Ferry, N.Y.: Oceana Press.

Telhami, Shibley. 1989. "Evaluating Bargaining Performance: The Case of Camp David." Ohio State University. Mimeo.

——— .1990. *Power and Leadership in International Bargaining: The Path to the Camp David Accords.* New York: Columbia University Press.

terHorst, Jerald F. 1974. *Gerald Ford and the Future of the Presidency.* New York: Third Press.

Thomas, Norman C. 1975. "Policy Formulation for Education." In *The Presidency in Contemporary Context,* ed. Norman C. Thomas. New York: Dodd Mead.

——— .1983. "Case Studies." In *Studying the Presidency,* ed. George C. Edwards III and Stephen J. Wayne. Knoxville: University of Tennessee Press.

Thomas, Norman C., and Harold L. Wolman. 1969. "The Presidency and Policy Formulation: The Task Force Device." *Public Administration Review* 29 (September/October): 459–471.

Thompson, Robert J., and Carmine Scavo. 1992. "The Home Front: Domestic Policy in the Bush Years." In *Leadership and the Bush Presidency: Prudence or Drift in an Era of Change?* ed. Ryan J. Barilleaux and Mary E. Study. Westport, Conn.: Praeger.

Thurman, James Skip. 1998. "Mike McCurry: Media 'Piñata' to the President." *Christian Science Monitor,* February 10, 1, 8.

Tobin, James. 1988. "Reaganomics in Retrospect." In *The Reagan Revolution?* ed. B. B. Kymlicka and Jean V. Matthews. Chicago: Dorsey.

Toner, Robin. 1994. "Autopsy on Health Care." *New York Times,* September 27, A1, A10.

Toobin, Jeffrey. 1998. "Circling the Wagons." *New Yorker,* July 6, 28–33.

Tower Commission Report. 1987. *Report of the President's Special Review Board.* New York: Times Books and Bantam Books.

Tufte, Edward. 1978. *Political Control of the Economy.* Princeton: Princeton University Press.

Uchitelle, Louis. 1989. "Alan Greenspan: Caution at the Fed." *New York Times Magazine,* January 15, 18–21, 37, 41–42, 63.

Vance, Cyrus. 1983. *Hard Choices.* New York: Simon and Schuster.

Walcott, Charles, and Karen Hult. 1987a. "Organizing the White House: Structure, Environment and Organizational Governance." *American Journal of Political Science* 31 (February): 109–125.

———.1987b. "Management Science and the Great Engineer: Governing the White House During the Hoover Administration." Paper presented at the annual meeting of the Midwest Political Science Association, Chicago, April 9–11.

———.1989. "The Conundrum of Domestic Policy Organization in the White House: From Hoover to Johnson." Paper presented at the annual meeting of the American Political Science Association, Atlanta, August 31–September 3.

———.1995. *Governing the White House: From Hoover through LBJ.* Lawrence: University Press of Kansas.

Warshaw, Shirley Anne. 1996. *The Domestic Presidency: Policy Making in the White House.* Boston: Allyn and Bacon.

Wayne, Stephen J. 1978. *The Legislative Presidency.* New York: Harper.

Weatherford, M. Stephen. 1986. "The President and the Political Business Cycle." In *The President and Economic Policy,* ed. James P. Pfiffner. Philadelphia: Institute for the Study of Human Issues.

———.1987. "The Interplay of Ideology and Advice in Economic Policy-Making: The Case of Political Business Cycles." *Journal of Politics* 49 (August): 925–952.

———.1988. "The International Economy as a Constraint on U.S. Macroeconomic Policymaking." *International Organization* 42 (Autumn): 605–637.

Weatherford, Stephen J., and Lorraine M. McDonnell. 1990. "Ideology and Economic Policy." In *Looking Back on the Reagan Presidency,* ed. Larry Berman. Baltimore: Johns Hopkins University Press.

————.1995. "Clinton and Economic Policy: Blowing the Story Line." Paper presented at the annual meeting of the Midwest Political Science Association, Chicago, April 6–8.

————.1996a. "The Idea of the Guardian Presidency: Economic Policymaking in the Bush Administration." Paper presented at the annual meeting of the American Political Science Association, San Francisco, August 29–31.

————.1996b. "Clinton and the Economy: The Paradox of Policy Success and Political Mishap." *Political Science Quarterly* 111 (3): 403–436.

————.1997. "Do Presidents Make a Difference in the Economy? (And If So, How?)." Paper presented at the annual meeting of the American Political Science Association, Washington, D.C., August 28–31.

Weaver, R. Kent. 1988. "Social Policy in the Reagan Era." In *The Reagan Revolution?* ed. B. B. Kymlicka and Jean V. Matthews. Chicago: Dorsey.

Weaver, Warren, Jr. 1976. "Political Fever Is Causing Washington Malaise." *New York Times,* August 15.

Weiner, Tim. 1998a. "C.I.A. Bares Own Bungling in '61 Report on Bay of Pigs." *New York Times,* February 22, 1, 6.

————.1998b. "Voluntarily, C.I.A. Director Reveals Intelligence Budget." *New York Times,* March 21, 11.

Weisberg, Herbert F., and Samuel C. Patterson, eds. 1998. *Great Theater: The American Congress in the 1990s.* New York: Cambridge University Press.

Weisberg, Jacob. 1998. "Keeping the Boom from Busting." *New York Times Magazine,* July 19, 24–29, 38, 40, 53–55.

Weisskopf, Michael, and David Maraniss. 1996. "Endgame: The Revolution Stalls" (a series of three articles on the confrontation between congressional Republicans and Clinton over the FY 1996 budget). *Washington Post National Weekly Edition,* January 29–February 4; February 5–11.

Whitaker, John C. 1991. "Comments." In *Richard M. Nixon: Politician, President, Administrator,* ed. Leon Friedman and William F. Levantrosser. Westport, Conn.: Greenwood.

White, Leonard D. 1958. *The Republican Era: 1869–1901.* New York: Macmillan.

White, Theodore H. 1961. *The Making of the President, 1960.* New York: Atheneum.

————.1969. *The Making of the President, 1968.* New York: Atheneum.

————.1973. *The Making of the President, 1972.* New York: Atheneum.

————.1975. *Breach of Faith: The Fall of Richard Nixon.* New York: Atheneum.

White, William S. 1964. *The Professional: Lyndon B. Johnson.* Cambridge: Houghton Mifflin.

Wildavsky, Aaron. 1988a. *The New Politics of the Budgetary Process.* Glenview, Ill.: Scott Foresman/Little, Brown.

————.1988b. "President Reagan as a Political Strategist." In *The Reagan Legacy: Promise and Performance*, ed. Charles O. Jones. Chatham, N.J.: Chatham House.

Witcover, Jules. 1977. *Marathon: The Pursuit of the Presidency, 1972–1976*. New York: Viking.

Witte, John F. 1985. *The Politics and Development of the Federal Income Tax*. Madison: University of Wisconsin Press.

————.1988. "The President vs. Congress on Tax Policy." In *The President and Economic Policy*, ed. James P. Pfiffner. Philadelphia: Institute for the Study of Human Issues.

Wittkopf, Eugene R. 1986. "On the Foreign Policy Beliefs of the American People: A Critique and Some Evidence." *International Studies Quarterly* 30 (December): 425–446.

Wohlforth, William C., ed. 1996. *Witnesses to the End of the Cold War*. Baltimore: Johns Hopkins University Press.

Wood, Robert C. 1970. "When Government Works." *Public Interest* (Winter): 39–51.

Woodward, Bob. 1987. *Veil: The Secret Wars of the CIA, 1981–1987*. New York: Simon and Schuster.

————.1991. *The Commanders*. New York: Pocket Books.

————.1992. "Origin of the Tax Pledge" (a series of four articles about economic policy in the Bush administration). *Washington Post*, October 4–October 7.

————.1994a. *The Agenda: Inside the Clinton White House*. New York: Simon and Schuster.

————.1994b. *The Choice*. New York: Simon and Schuster.

————.1999. *Shadow: Five Presidents and the Legacy of Watergate*. New York: Simon and Schuster.

Wooley, John T. 1986. "The Federal Reserve and the Politics of Monetary Policy." In *The President and Economic Policy*, ed. James P. Pfiffner. Philadelphia: Institute for the Study of Human Issues.

Zisk, Kimberly Marten. 1997. "The Threat of Soviet Decline: The CIA, the Joint Chiefs of Staff, and the End of the Cold War." In *U.S. Foreign Policy After the Cold War: Processes, Structures, and Politics*, ed. James M. Lindsay and Randall B. Ripley. Pittsburgh: University of Pittsburgh Press.

# Index